Dein Englischbuch enthält folgende Teile:

Units 1 2 3	die drei Kapitel des Buches
Getting ready for a test	Hier kannst du dich gezielt auf einen Test vorbereiten.
Extra: English for jobs	Hier kannst du typische Situationen des Berufsalltags üben.
Extra: Exam File	vielfältige Prüfungsaufgaben zur Vorbereitung auf die Abschlussprüfung
Extra: Text File	viele interessante Texte zum Lesen (passend zu den Units)
Skills File (SF)	Beschreibung wichtiger Lern- und Arbeitstechniken
Grammar File (GF)	Zusammenfassung der wichtigsten Grammatikthemen der Bände 1–6; Übersichten über die Zeitformen (*present, past, future*)
Vocabulary	Wörterverzeichnis zum Lernen der neuen Wörter jeder Unit
Dictionary	alphabetisches englisch-deutsches Wörterverzeichnis

Die Units bestehen aus diesen Teilen:

Lead-in	Einstieg in das neue Thema
Part A, B (Unit 1: Part C)	neuer Lernstoff mit vielen Aktivitäten
Practice	Übungen
How am I doing?	Hier kannst du dein Wissen und Können überprüfen.

In den Units findest du diese Überschriften und Symbole:

STUDY SKILLS	Einführung in Lern- und Arbeitstechniken
Dossier	Schöne und wichtige Arbeiten kannst du in einer Mappe sammeln.
EVERYDAY ENGLISH	Hier übst du wichtige Alltagssituationen.
MEDIATION	Hier vermittelst du zwischen zwei Sprachen.
VIEWING	Aufgaben zu Filmausschnitten
Now you	Hier sprichst und schreibst du über dich selbst.
REVISION	Übungen zur Wiederholung
WORDS	Übungen zu Wortfeldern und Wortverbindungen
	Partnerarbeit / Gruppenarbeit
	nur auf CD / auf CD und im Schülerbuch
	Filmausschnitte auf DVD
	Textaufgaben
Extra	zusätzliche Aktivitäten und Übungen
○ ●	leichtere Übungen / schwierigere Übungen
// ○ // ●	parallele Übungen auf zwei Niveaus
more help	Hier findest du zusätzliche Hilfen für das Lösen einer Aufgabe.

Contents

Love life!

The world we live in

Have your say!

Love life!

The world we live in

Have your say!

The characters

an exciting drama series for young people

Toby
He's very confident and very good-looking. Lots of girls fancy him and he knows it. He's a bit arrogant. But he's a good friend. Toby and his girlfriend Elly have been together for eight months.

Minty
(real name Katy Minton) Everybody respects Minty. She's quite serious and a bit bossy. She doesn't care about fashion or how she looks. She's very different from her brother, Toby.

Ed
(real name James Ford) The first things that you notice about Ed are that he's tall and that he has red hair. He's very funny and easy-going. He hasn't got a girlfriend but would really like one. Ed and Peanut are old friends.

Bex
(or Becky) She's Minty's best friend. She's very relaxed and laughs a lot. And you never see Bex without her make-up. Bex fancies Ed, but he hasn't noticed and she hasn't told him – yet.

Peanut
(real name Philip Nutt)
He's thin and wears big glasses. He knows everything about everything, from science to football to music. He's quite shy, but he's popular.

The episodes

Episode 1:
Just be cool

Peanut is excited. He has met a girl and she has said she'll go out with him, but now she isn't answering his calls.

[»]

Episode 2:
Top chat-up lines

Ed wants to ask a girl out. But he doesn't know how. Peanut has some ideas.

[»]

1 Who is it?

Read about the characters. Complete the sentences.

1 ... and ... are best friends.
2 ... and ... are old friends.
3 ... and ... are going out.
4 ... and ... are brother and sister.
5 ... has lots of friends.
6 ... fancies ...

2 Just be cool (Episode 1)

a) *Listen and choose the correct answers.*

1 Peanut asks Toby to give him his phone ...
A because he's lost his own phone.
B because he wants to phone a girl.
2 Toby ...
A gives his phone to Peanut.
B doesn't give his phone to Peanut.
3 Peanut called the girl ...
A twice. B three times.
4 Toby tells Peanut ...
A to text the girl.
B to wait for the girl to call him.

b) *Do you agree with Toby? Why (not)?*

3 Top chat-up lines (Episode 2)

a) *Listen to* ***part 1****. Choose the correct answers.*

1 Ed wants to know how to ...
A be a star. B talk to girls.
2 First Ed talks to ...
A Toby. B Peanut.
3 Toby is ...
A helpful. B not helpful.
4 Peanut's first tip for Ed is to ...
A smile at the girl.
B tell the girl that he likes her.

b) *Listen to* ***part 2****. Which statement sums up best what happens?*

A Ed fancies Bex and decides to ask her out. She says yes, so they go for a pizza together.
B Ed wants to ask a girl out so he asks Bex for some advice. Then Bex asks Ed out.

c) **Extra** *Which character in the* West Street *series do you like best. Why?*

► *SF Listening (p. 132)*

REAL-LIFE RELATIONSHIPS

1

Got a problem? Write to Jake about it.

I don't want to go to Spain

I don't know what to do. My mum died three years ago. My dad now has a new girlfriend and wants to move to Spain. He's found a job in a holiday place and he's found a school for me and my sister. My sister (she's 13, I'm 16) thinks it's a great idea. But I don't want to go. I have a girlfriend and she's really important to me, and I have lots of good friends here. I could stay at home and live with my granny or a friend, but I don't really want to do that. I think it's so unfair. What can I do? *Sam*

Jake says:

You're in a difficult situation, Sam. You should talk to your dad. Maybe he thinks that this is the best thing for your family. If you really don't want to go to Spain, you could stay with your grandmother or a friend and spend the school holidays in Spain. But perhaps it's a good idea to go to Spain for a year and see if you like it. Only you can decide what to do, but you should talk to your dad in a calm way and try to understand his reasons first.

Good luck!

1 *True or false?*
1 *Sam's sister wants to go to Spain.*
2 *Sam doesn't want to leave his granny.*

2 *What is Jake's advice?*
A *Go to Spain.* B *Don't go to Spain.*
C *Talk to your dad and then decide what to do.*

Your comments:

☐ What about going to Spain for the school term? You could come back in the holidays – and see your friends and spend time with your girlfriend then. Could your girlfriend come and visit you in the holidays? *Ally x*

☐ I think your dad is really unfair. He's thinking about himself, not you. *Dani*

☐ If I were you I'd go to Spain – it might be fun! And with the internet and cheap phone calls you can keep in touch with your friends. *JC*

Who do you agree with: Jake, Ally, Dani or JC? What do you think Sam should do? Why? more help ▸ *D p. 102*

2

More problems for Jake

Nikki:

My best friend started going out with this guy about a month ago. Now she spends all her time with her boyfriend and doesn't hang out with her old friends any more. I've talked to her about it but she says I'm just jealous. I think she's stupid. Her relationship with her boyfriend probably won't last, and then she'll need her friends. But I don't know if I'll want to spend time with her after all this.

Mel:

I've been with my girlfriend for 11 months and I really love her. But two weeks ago her best friend told me that she fancies me. This other girl is very attractive. She always stands very close to me and texts me all the time. I don't know what to do. Should I tell my girlfriend or not? They've been friends for 12 years.

Send your comments to jake@r-lifemag.co.uk and we'll print some of them next week with Jake's comments.

1 *Choose a heading for Nikki and Mel's problems.*

1 I fancy my friend
2 My girlfriend's friend is flirting with me
3 My friend hasn't got time for me
4 I don't know how to dump my girlfriend

2 *Write down at least four phrases from pp. 8–9 for giving advice.*

– *you should talk to ...*
– ...

3 Now you

a) *Choose one of the problems above and decide how you would answer it. Make notes.*
more help ▸ D p. 102

b) *Together write a short comment for the problem. Put it up on the wall.*
*Tip: Use your notes from **task 2** above.*

c) *Read your classmates' comments. Vote in class for your favourite comment on each problem.*

d) **Extra** *Work on your own. Write an answer to one of the problems on pp. 8–9.*
Tip: You can use the comments that you have read to give you more ideas.

4 Role play

You and your partner are going to tell each other about a problem and ask for advice.
Go to p. 97.

I've got a problem.
I don't want to ...

Really? Why (not)?

Oh, I see. So ...

I think you should ...

P1 WORDS Describing people: character and appearance

a) *Read the description of the girl. Start to collect adjectives and phrases for describing people. Organize them in a network.*

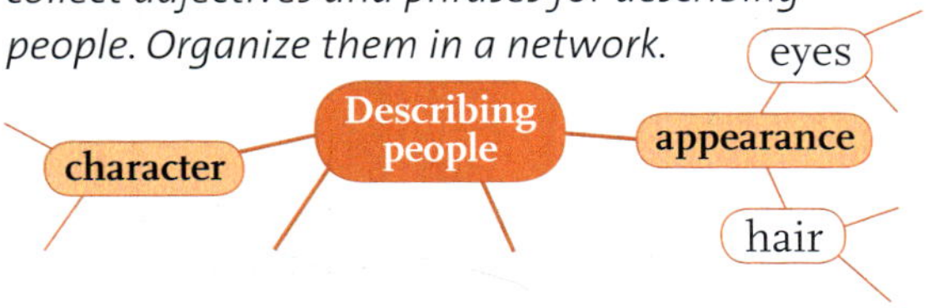

I'm short and a bit fat. I've got grey eyes and black hair. I've got a piercing in my tongue. I'm lazy and I never tidy my room. I'm funny and I'm good at telling jokes, but I'm shy in big groups of people.

b) *Add as many words as you can to your network. You could look at pp. 6–7 for some ideas.*

c) *Write a short description of yourself. Collect all the descriptions. Someone should read them out loud. Can you guess who it is?* more help ▸ D p. 103

P2 //O REVISION Does your family annoy you? (Simple present) ▸ D p. 103

a) *Choose the correct form of the verbs in brackets.*

My brother is really annoying. Every morning he (1) (go/goes) into the bathroom first and he (2) (stay/stays) in there for a long time. He (3) (does/doesn't) get out until it (4) (is/are) nearly time for school. My sister (5) (are/is) completely different. She never (6) (wash/washes)! My brother and sister also (7) (take/takes) my things. They (8) (don't/doesn't) ask me first. They just (9) (come/comes) into my room and (10) (look/looks) around. What about you? (11) (Do/Does) you have problems like this with your family? Actually my parents (12) (doesn't/don't) annoy me too much. They usually (13) (leave/leaves) me alone. What about your parents? (14) (Do/Does) they annoy you?

b) **Extra** *Write a short text about your family.*

▸ GF 3: Talking about the present (p. 152)

P3 //O REVISION A group of friends (Present progressive) ▸ D p. 103

Complete the text with ***is/isn't*** *or* ***are/aren't***.

This is a photo of me and some people I met at summer camp. We (1) ... sitting outside and the sun (2) ... shining. Everyone (3) ... having a good time. I'm in the foreground on the left with my best friend Will (the guy with the black T-shirt). We (4) ... all singing a funny song. Well, Josh and Kate (5) ... singing because they (6) ... kissing. The girl who (7) ... playing the guitar is Rose. Will (8) ... flirting with Rose. This is a bad idea because Rose's boyfriend Seb (9) ... sitting behind him. Seb (10) ... smiling – that's probably because he's jealous. I can't remember the names of the other people in the photo.

▸ GF 3: Talking about the present (p. 152)

P4 SPEAKING Keeping a conversation going

a) *Listen to the conversation between Ed and Nadia. Ed is finding it hard to keep the conversation going. What do you think Ed is doing wrong? What could he do better?* ► *SF Having a conversation (p. 138)*

b) *Copy the dialogue between Ed and another girl, Holly. Complete it with phrases from the box. Then listen to the dialogue and compare.*

Ed Hi, I'm Ed.
Holly Hi.
Ed Er, (1) ...?
Holly I'm Holly. I'm Peanut's cousin.
Ed (2) ...! I didn't know Peanut had a cousin. Er, (3) ... , Holly?
Holly Oh, it's OK. But it's not really my kind of music.
Ed Oh, so (4) ...?
Holly I don't know really, but not this kind.
Ed I see. You're not from around here, are you? (5) ...?
Holly I'm from Fort William in Scotland.
Ed Wow, (6) ...! I've been there on holiday with my family. I remember we went to a nice pizza restaurant in Fort William. Er, (7) ...?

How to keep a conversation going

Make compliments.
- That's a nice/cool T-shirt/tattoo/...
- I like your jacket/mobile phone/...

Try to find out what kind of things the person likes.
- Do you like this music?
- What kind of music/films/... do you like?

Make comments to show you're interested.
- No! I don't believe it!
- Really?
- That's amazing.

Ask questions (who, what, when, where, why, how).
- What's your name?
- Where are you from?
- What's your favourite pizza/ice cream/...?

c) *Imagine you meet someone at a party for the first time and start a conversation. Talk to each other for as long as you can.*

Tip

1. *Write down some useful phrases for starting a conversation.*
2. *Prepare some topics before you start.*
3. *Have a few general questions ready to keep the conversation going.*
4. *Finish the conversation nicely.*

1 Hi, I'm ... • What's your name? • How are you doing? • ...

2
– **Music** (What kind of music ...? • My favourite group is ... Do you like ...?)
– **TV programmes** (What kind of ...?)
– **Sport** (I like ... What about you? • Do you play ...?)
– ...

3 What's your favourite pizza? • What do you think about ...? • ...

4 It was really nice talking to you. • See you later. • ...

RELATIONSHIPS IN FILMS

1 The best films on TV this week

What was the last film you watched on TV? What do you look for in a film?

Twilight ★★★★☆

(Wednesday 8.00 pm, Sky 1)

This is a fantasy film and a thriller at the same time. It's based on the novel by Stephenie Meyer. The film stars Kristen Stewart as Bella and Robert Pattinson as Edward. The film is set in the north-west of the US. Bella has just moved to a small town. At her new school she fancies Edward. But there's a problem: Edward is a vampire! He's worried about what could happen if he and Bella get together. But the problem isn't that she could get pregnant. There's a different danger: he might lose control and bite her! Fans of the book will love this film. The special effects are excellent.

Bend it like Beckham ★★★★★

(Friday 9.00 pm, Virgin 1)

You've probably seen it already, but you can watch this comedy again and again. Football-mad Jess (Parminder Nagra) is 18 and lives in London. She wants to play for a top women's football team. The problem is that her traditional Indian parents want her to find a nice Indian husband, learn how to cook and study law! Although it's a very funny film, it also looks at serious topics (like racism and parent-teenager relationships). The soundtrack is a perfect mix of Indian and British music. This is a film that everybody will enjoy!

a) *Choose the right answer.*

Both films are ... A comedies. B set in America. C about young people.

b) *Read the film reviews again. What does each review mention?*
Copy the chart and tick (✓) the right boxes.

Title	Kind of film	Plot and characters	Actors	Who will like it	Soundtrack	Special effects
Twilight	✓	✓				
Bend it like Beckham						

▸ SF Skimming and scanning (p. 134)

c) *Which of the films would/wouldn't you watch? Say why.*

I like/don't like thrillers/... , so I'd watch/I wouldn't watch ...
I think ... sounds good/boring/... because the review says ...

2 VIEWING A review of *Juno*

a) *Watch the film review and put the pictures in the right order.*

b) *Add the film* Juno *to your chart from p. 12. Then watch the film review again. Tick (✓) the things that the reviewer mentions.*

c) *True or false? The reviewer says the following things:*

1 He's a big fan of romantic films.
2 The acting isn't very good.
3 Juno decides to look for the perfect parents for her baby.
4 Juno talks to her dad about relationships.
5 At the start of the film Paulie Bleaker doesn't seem cool or confident.
6 3 out of 5 is the right score for the film.

d) **Extra** *What do you think of the film review? Does it make you want to watch* Juno*? Why (not)?*

more help ► D p. 104

3 Now you

a) *Imagine your dream partner. Copy the chart and tick (✓) the right boxes.*

My dream partner must …	very important	quite important	not important
be good-looking			
be a relaxed person			
wear trendy clothes			
be very intelligent			
have the same interests			
have the same religion			
like the same music			
…			

► **Text File 1** (pp. 112–113)

b) *Talk to a partner. Compare your charts.*

A: I think it's very/quite/not important that my dream partner is/has/likes/…
B: I disagree. I think that's quite/very/not important. / I agree. I've got the same as you for that.

P1 WORDS Describing films

a) Organize the words and phrases from the box into a chart like this:

Kind of film	Plot	Reviewer's opinion	Film people	What's special about the film

action film • actor • boring • brilliant • cartoon • +costumes • +director • drama • exciting • famous • funny • it has a happy ending • hero • horror film • love story • music • plays • scene • silly • it stars ... • science fiction film • it won an Oscar • ...

b) *Add more words to your chart. Look at the film reviews on p. 12 for some ideas.*

c) *Compare your chart with a partner'. Can you add any more words or phrases?*

d) *Agree on a film. Each of you write two sentences and say what you liked ore didn't like about the film. Then compare your descriptions. Are they very different?*

P2 SPEAKING About a film

a) *Think of a film you like. Prepare a talk about it. Use the ideas below. Make notes on cards.*

b) *Practise your talk. Then give your talk to a group or record it.*

Introduction
- *title of the film*
- *kind of film*
- *names of main actors, the director, ...*

- Today I'm going to talk about the film ...
- It's a romantic film/an adventure film/...
- It stars ...
- The director is ...

Plot
- *where the film is set*
- *what happens*

- Next I want to talk about the plot.
- The film is set in ...
- It's about ... / It tells the story of ...
- At the start/Later/During the film ...

Main characters
- *names, age*
- *what they look like*
- *what they do, how they feel, ...*

- The main/My favourite character is ...
- He/She is funny/.../likes/wants to/...

What's special about it?
- *special effects, soundtrack, ...*

- I think it has a good soundtrack/brilliant special effects/amazing costumes/...
- It won an Oscar.

Your personal opinion
- *reasons why you liked/didn't like the film*
- *say if you would/wouldn't recommend it*

- To sum up, I love this film because ...
- My favourite part in the film is when ...
- Everybody/People who like ... will love this film.
- I'd give it ... stars out of five.
- You must see it!

► *SF Giving a presentation (p. 130)*

P3 MEDIATION Which film?

Partner B: Go to p. 98.

a) *Partner A: You and your friend are looking for an English DVD to watch together. Tell your friend about the film below in German. The questions in the box can help you.*

- Was ist es für ein Film?
- Worum geht es?
- Würdest du den Film anschauen?

b) *Your partner will tell you about another film. Listen carefully.*

c) *Which film would you like to watch? Why?*

What Happens in Vegas

This comedy stars Ashton Kutcher and Cameron Diaz. The film is set in Las Vegas and it's about two people, Jack and Joy, who meet in Las Vegas and have a wild party. Next morning they wake up and find out that they got married the night before. They aren't happy about this! They both want to get divorced, but then Jack wins $3 million on a game machine with money that Joy gave him. So who gets the money? You'll have to watch the film to find out. It's not the best film in the world, but it's quite funny and it's easy to watch. And it's got a great ending.

▸ *SF Mediation (p. 147)*

P4 WRITING A short love story (Creative writing)

a) *Use the pictures below to write a short story.*

more help ▸ *D p. 104*

▸ *SF Writing course (p. 141–142)*

b) *Read your story to your partner. Then listen to your partner's story. Say what you liked/didn't like about it.*

Tip

1. *Think of a plot. Collect words and phrases for each picture.* ▸ *SF Brainstorming (p. 140)*
2. *Think of names for the characters.*
3. *Write full sentences.*
4. *Use the past tenses* (he was late, she was waiting, ...).

Extra The Absolutely True Diary of a Part-time[1] Indian

(Extracts from the novel by Sherman Alexie, adapted and abridged)

Arnold is the main character[2] in this story. From the pictures on pp. 16–18, do you think Arnold is …
1 boring or funny? 2 confident or nervous? 3 rich or poor?

The story so far[3]

Arnold lives and goes to school on the Spokane Indian Reservation in Wellpinit, Washington State. The Indians on the reservation are very poor and Arnold can see that most of them have no hope for the future. He makes a brave decision. He leaves the reservation school and starts at Reardan High School. Reardan High is an all-white school in a town called Reardan, 22 miles outside of the reservation. Arnold is different from everyone else in Reardan: a poor Indian boy in a rich, racist town. But slowly he starts to make friends at his new school. He even starts to go out with the beautiful Penelope.

▸ SF Reading English texts (p. 136)

Me (drawn by me)

Penelope in her dad's old hat (drawn by me)

BIG DREAMS

Everybody is absolutely shocked that Penelope chose me to be her new friend. I am an absolute stranger at the school.

And I am an Indian. And Penelope's father, Earl, is a racist. The first time I met him, he said, "Kid, she's only dating[4] you because she knows it will piss me off[5]. So I won't get pissed. And she'll stop dating you."

Okay, so Penelope was probably dating me ONLY to annoy her father, she was probably dating me ONLY because I was an Indian boy. And, okay, so she wasn't seriously dating me. We held hands sometimes and we kissed once or twice, but that was it.

I don't know how important I was to her. I think she was bored of being the prettiest, smartest and most popular girl in the world. She wanted to do something a little crazy, you know?

And I was sort of crazy. I looked and talked and dreamed and walked differently than everybody else. I was new.

But there were bigger and better reasons why Penelope and I were friends.

"Arnold," she said one day after school, "I hate this little town. It's so small, too small. Everything about it is small. The people here have small ideas. Small dreams. They all want to marry each other and live here forever[6]."

"What do you want to do?" I asked.

"I want to leave as soon as[7] I can. I think I was born with a suitcase."

Yeah, she talked like that. All big and dramatic. I wanted to laugh, but she was so serious.

"Where do you want to go?" I asked.

"Everywhere. I want to walk on the Great Wall of China. I want to walk to the top of pyramids in Egypt. I want to swim in every ocean[8]. I want to climb the highest mountain.

[1] part-time *Teilzeit-* [2] character ['kærəktə] *Person, Figur (in Roman, Film, Theaterstück)* [3] so far *bis jetzt, bis hierher* [4] (to) date sb. [deɪt] *mit jm. (aus)gehen* [5] (to) piss sb. off *(infml, vulgär) jn. wütend machen, jn. ankotzen* [6] forever [fər'evə] *für immer, ewig* [7] as soon as *sobald* [8] ocean ['əʊʃn] *Ozean*

I want to go on an African safari. I want to do everything and see everything."

Her eyes had this strange, dreamy look. I laughed.

"Don't laugh at me," she said

"I'm not laughing at you," I said. "I'm laughing at your eyes."

"That's the problem. Nobody takes me seriously."

"Well, come on, it's hard to take you seriously when you're talking about China and Egypt and stuff. Those are just big, crazy dreams. They're not real."

"They're real to me," she said.

"Why don't you tell me what you really want to do with your life," I said. "Make it simple."

"I want to be an architect.[1]"

"Wow, that's cool," I said. "But why an architect?"

"Because I want to build something beautiful. Because I want to be remembered."

And I couldn't laugh at that dream. It was my dream too. But Indian boys shouldn't dream like that. And white girls from small towns shouldn't dream big either[2]. We should be happy with what we have. But there was no way Penelope and I were going to sit still[3]. No, we both wanted to fly.

This bird is an Australian Arnelope. It is good at flying long distances.

> *Are these sentences true or false?*

1. Arnold lives near Reardan High School.
2. People are surprised that Arnold and Penelope are friends.
3. Penelope's father is happy that his daughter is dating an Indian boy.
4. Penelope likes Arnold because he's different from the other students in the school.
5. Arnold doesn't share Penelope's dream to do something big and important.

PANCAKES[4] OF DOOM[5]

Arnold often hitchhikes[6] between Reardan and home. But he doesn't tell his classmates because he doesn't want them to know how poor he is. One night after a school dance, Arnold plans to wait until everybody has gone, and then hitchhike home in the dark. But Penelope's friend, Roger, has a different idea.

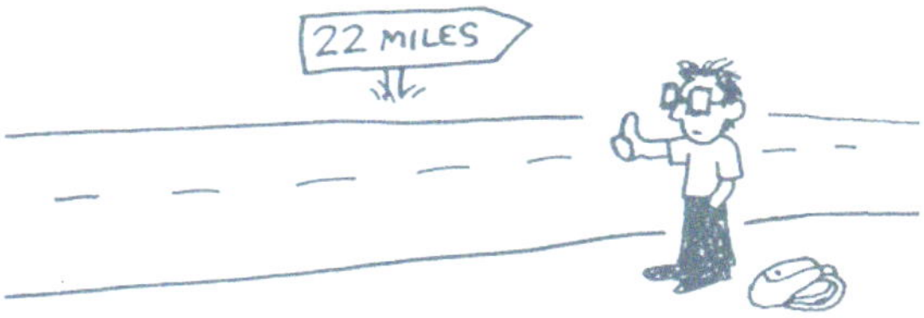

Roger and a few of the other popular guys decided they were going to drive into Spokane and have pancakes at a twenty-four-hour diner[7] and Roger invited us to come along[8].

Penelope was very excited about the idea.

I was so scared that I felt sick.

I had five bucks[9] in my pocket. What could I buy with that? Maybe one plate of pancakes. Maybe.

What a nightmare[10].

"What do you say, Arnie?" Roger asked. "Do you want to come with us?"

"What do you want to do, Penelope?" I asked.

"Oh, I want to go, I want to go," she said.

I was absolutely terrified.

An hour later, about twenty of us were sitting in Denny's in Spokane.

Me being absolutely terrified

---

[1] architect ['a:kɪtekt] [2] not (...) either ['aɪðə, 'i:ðə] *auch nicht* [3] there was no way Penelope and I were going to sit still *auf keinen Fall würden Penelope und ich still sitzen* [4] pancake ['pænkeɪk] *Pfannkuchen* [5] doom [du:m] *Verderben, Verhängnis, Untergang* [6] (to) hitchhike ['hɪtʃhaɪk] *trampen, per Anhalter fahren* [7] diner ['daɪnə] *(bes. AE) einfaches, meist preiswertes Restaurant* [8] (to) come along *mitkommen* [9] buck [bʌk] *(bes. AE, infml) Dollar* [10] nightmare ['naɪtmeə] *Albtraum*

Everybody ordered pancakes.

I ordered pancakes for Penelope and me. I ordered orange juice and coffee and toast and hot chocolate and French fries too, even though[1] I knew I wouldn't be able to pay for any of it.

I decided it was my last meal before my death, and I was going to have a feast[2].

Halfway through our meal, I went to the bathroom[3]. I thought maybe I was going to throw up[4]. Roger came into the bathroom.

"Hey, Arnie," he said. "Are you okay?"

"Yeah," I said, "I'm just tired."

"All right, man," he said. "I'm happy you guys came tonight."

"Hey, listen," I said. I thought about telling him the whole truth[5], but I just couldn't. "The thing is," I said, "I, er, forgot my wallet[6]. I left my money at home, man."

"Dude[7]!" Roger said. "Man, don't worry about it. You should have said something[8] earlier."

He opened his wallet and gave me forty bucks.

I couldn't believe it.

What kind of kid can just give someone forty bucks like that?

"I'll pay you back, man," I said

"Whenever, man. Just have a good time, all right?"

We walked back to the table together, finished our food and Roger drove me back to the school. I told them my dad was going to pick me up there.

"Dude," Roger said, "It's three in the morning."

"It's okay," I said. "My dad works nights. He's coming here from work."

"Are you sure?"

"Yeah, everything is cool."

So Penelope and I got out of Roger's car to say goodbye.

"Roger told me he lent[9] you some money," she said.

"Yeah," I said. "I forgot my wallet."

"Arnold."

"Yeah."

"Can I ask you something big?"

"Yeah. I guess."

"Are you poor?"

I couldn't lie[10] to her any more.

"Yes," I said, "I'm poor."

I thought she was going to march[11] out of my life right then. But she didn't. Instead[12] she kissed me.

"Roger guessed you were poor," she said

"Oh, great now he's going to tell everybody."

"He's not going to tell anybody. Roger likes you. He's a great guy. He's like my big brother. He can be your friend too."

That sounded pretty good to me. I needed friends.

"Is your Dad really coming to pick you up?" she asked.

"Yes," I said.

"Is that true?"

"No," I said.

"How will you get home?" she asked.

"I usually walk home. I hitchhike. Somebody usually picks me up. I've only had to walk the whole way a few times."

She started to cry.

FOR ME!

I didn't know that a girl could look so sexy when she cried.

"Oh, my God, Arnold, you can't do that," she said. "I won't let you do that. Roger will drive you home. He'll be happy to[13] drive you home."

Penelope ran over to Roger's car and told him the truth.

And Roger drove me home that night.

And he drove me home lots of other nights too.

If you let people into your life a little bit, they can be pretty damn[14] amazing.

---

[1] even though ['iːvn ˌðəʊ] *selbst wenn* [2] feast [fiːst] *Festessen, Festmahl* [3] bathroom *hier (AE): Toilette* [4] (to) throw up *sich übergeben* [5] truth [truːθ] *Wahrheit* [6] wallet ['wɒlɪt] *Brieftasche* [7] dude [duːd] *(bes. AE, infml) Mann* [8] you should have said sth. *du hättest etwas sagen sollen* [9] (to) lend sb. sth., lent [lend, lent] *jm. etwas ausleihen* [10] (to) lie [laɪ] *lügen* [11] (to) march [mɑːtʃ] *marschieren* [12] instead [ɪn'sted] *statt dessen* [13] (to) be happy to do sth. *etw. gern tun (für eine andere Person)* [14] damn [dæm] *(adv, infml) verdammt*

Working with the text

1 //○ Tell the story ▸ D p. 105

What happens at the diner? Put the sentences in the correct order.

a Later, Penelope asks Arnold if he is poor.
b Arnold tells Roger that he has forgotten his wallet, so Roger gives him some money.
c Penelope doesn't want him to hitchhike, so Roger drives him home.
d Arnold goes to the bathroom because he feels sick.
e Penelope wants to go, but Arnold is scared because he hasn't got any money.
f Roger asks Penelope and Arnold to go to a diner with him and some friends.
g At the diner Arnold orders lots of food and drinks.

2 What do they mean?

a) *Copy the chart. Read the sentences in column one. Who said it? Write down the name (**Arnold**, **Penelope** or **Roger**) in column two.*

What do they say?	Who says it?	What do they mean?	What are they like?
1. "I was born with a suitcase."	...	I've always wanted ...	crazy, ...
2. "Nobody takes me seriously."			
3. "Man, don't worry about it."			
4. "If you let people into your life a little bit, they can be pretty damn amazing."			

b) *Look at column one again and then read the six sentences below. In column three, write the sentence that means the same as the sentence in the first column.*

1 Hey, no problem!
2 People think it's funny when I talk about important things.
3 I've always wanted to travel and have adventures.
4 If you want to make friends, it's a good idea to invite people to your house.
5 Hey, stop it! You're annoying me.
6 It's good to talk to people about your problems. It's surprising how helpful they can be.

c) *In column four, write suitable adjectives to describe what the characters are like, or how they feel when they say the words in column one. The adjectives in the box can help you.*

annoyed • confident • crazy • easy-going • fed up • helpful • hurt • kind • likeable • relaxed • romantic • serious • surprised • upset • ...

3 ● Penelope's diary

Imagine you are Penelope. In your diary, write about what happened after the school dance.

more help ▸ D p. 105

▸ *SF Brainstorming (p. 140) • SF Writing course (pp. 141–142)*

1 A holiday by the sea is more exciting (Comparison of adjectives)

What do you think? Write complete sentences. Use the words in brackets.

1 a holiday by the sea / a holiday in the mountains (exciting)
I think that a holiday by the sea is more exciting than a holiday in the mountains.
2 travelling by train / travelling by car (comfortable)
3 a sports holiday / a holiday at the beach (cool)
4 beaches in Spain / beaches in Germany (crowded)
5 a camping holiday / staying at a B&B (expensive)
6 visiting a science museum / visiting a zoo (interesting)
7 going on holiday with lots of friends / going with your partner (exciting)

I think that ... / In my opinion ...
- ... is more/less exciting/... than ...
- ... is cooler than ...
- ... is/isn't as exciting/cool/... as ...

► GF 10: Adjectives: comparison (p. 160)

2 SPEAKING Making holiday plans

a) *Sarah and her classmate Dustin are planning a class trip. Put the sentences into the correct order to complete their phone conversation.*

Dustin ___ Hello.
Sarah ___ Hi, Dustin! This is Sarah. I'm phoning about the class trip. Do you have any ideas?

A *Dustin* ___ Good idea. I hope everyone will like our plans. See you tomorrow. 9

B *Dustin* ___ Yes, I have. What do you think about a trip to the country? There's a sports camp in Norfolk ... 1

C *Sarah* ___ Yes, but I'm afraid some of our classmates hate sports. What else can you do there? 4

D *Dustin* ___ Cities? Oh, I don't know, I like holidays in the country much better than holidays in the city. You can play football, hike, ride bikes, go canoeing ... 3

E *Sarah* ___ A sports camp? In the country? Sounds a bit boring. I like cities better. 2

F *Dustin* ___ It's not just sports. Norwich isn't far away. You can go shopping and do some sightseeing there. 5

G *Dustin* ___ No, there are cheap houses for school groups. Oh, and there's an indoor swimming pool. 7

H *Sarah* ___ Oh, Norwich sounds OK, but do we have to sleep in tents? 6

I *Sarah* ___ Now, that sounds good. Let's talk about it in class next week. 8

b) *Act out the conversation with a partner.*

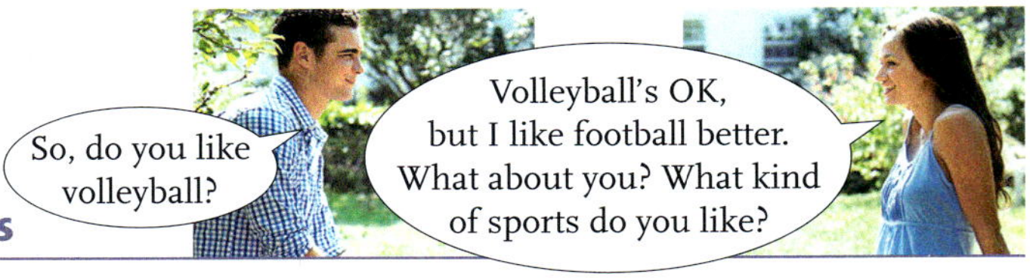

3 SPEAKING Likes and dislikes

Ask your partner about free time activities (sports, holidays, ...). The phrases below will help you.

I like ...	I love ...	I hate ...	I don't mind[1] ...
I quite like ...	I like ... a lot/very much.	I can't stand ...	... is OK/all right.
I like ... better than ...	I like ... the best/most.	I like ... the least.	I don't like ... very much.
... is pretty/quite good.	... is great/fantastic.	... is terrible/awful.	I'm not very interested in ...
I'm looking forward to ...	I can't wait to ...		

[1] I don't mind *Es macht mir nichts aus. / Es ist mir gleichgültig.*

4 WORDS A teenage magazine

a) *Zink! is a teenage magazine with six sections:*

CINEMA & TV | SPORT | HEALTH | MUSIC | BOOKS | COMPUTER

Make a list of words under each heading. First use the words from the box. Then add more words.

Tip
Some words can go under more than one heading.

CINEMA & TV	SPORT	...
cartoon	athletics	...
...	...	

athletics • cable • cartoon • channel • comic • competition • concert • energetic • episode • exercise • fruit • healthy food • (to) install • label • link • menu • novel • pitch • playlist • plot • presenter • prime time • (to) release • repeat • save • scene • sound file • (to) suggest • (to) surf the internet • (to) train • vegetables • whole-grain • writer • ...

b) *You want to tell your friend about some of the things you have read in* Zink!*. Choose the right word for each sentence.*

1. If you want to stay fit, you should eat healthy food and do daily exercise/meal/competition.
2. Don't spend hours in front of the TV or the computer. Go outside with your friends and be more interested/relaxed/energetic.
3. You must read the latest thriller/channel/programme by John Pierson. *Zink!* thinks it's hot.
4. *Zink!* says the new software is cheap and easy to install/join/repair.
5. Don't miss this Sunday's actor/episode/copy of *Park Grove*. *Zink!* loves this soap opera.
6. *Zink!* suggests a concert/playlist/tune of religious music at Bristol Cathedral tomorrow.

▶ *You could now do tasks 1 and 2 in the Practice test on p. 24.*

5 WORDS Talking about religions

a) *For each group, find the word that doesn't fit.*

1. Jewish • English • Hindu • Muslim
2. Catholic • cathedral • Christian • Protestant
3. church • mosque • palace • synagogue
4. bell • funeral • wedding • service
5. believe • bell • cathedral • tower

b) *Complete the sentences with a word from each group in a).*

1. Our friend Murat is Turkish. Like most Turkish people, he's a ...
2. My wife and I are both Christians, but she's a Catholic and I'm a ...
3. Our Jewish friends go to the ... on Saturdays.
4. You can hear the church ... a mile away.
5. Jews, Muslims and Christians all ... in one God.

6 WORDS The world of soap opera

a) *Who's who in this soap opera? Look at the diagram. Then complete sentences 1 to 6 with a word from the box.*

ex-husband • father • granddaughter • lover • uncle • wife

1 Gary is Fay's ...
2 Hanif is Ella's ...
3 Ella is Gary's ...
4 Diana is Chris' ...
5 Hanif is Diana's ...
6 Bill is Layla's ...

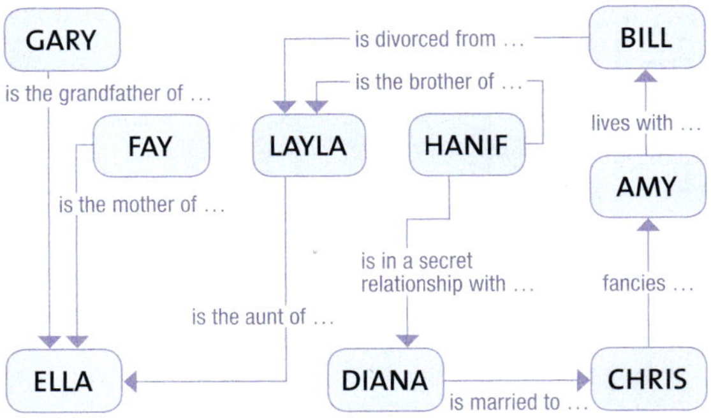

b) *Fay and Layla are at a café. Complete their conversation with words from the box.*

baby • divorced • father • love • relationship • single

Fay Hi, Layla. Guess what! I've just heard that Chris and Diana are getting (1) ...
Layla What? Is that because Chris has fallen in (2) ... with Amy?
Fay I don't know but maybe it's because he's heard about Diana's (3) ... with Hanif.
Layla Actually, I saw her today. I think she's going to have a (4) ...
Fay No! But who's the (5) ...? Her husband or her lover?
Layla Well, let's hope it's Hanif so they can get married quickly. Who wants to be a (6) ... mum? Oh – sorry, Fay!

7 Are you fit and healthy? (Simple present: questions)

a) *Write the questions in the* ***simple present****. Use the verbs in brackets.*

1 ... you ... a healthy life? (live)
Do you live a healthy life?
2 ... you ... any sports in your free time? (play)
3 How often ... you ... every week? (train)
4 ... you ... to school by bike? (go)
5 How many meals ... you ... every day? (have)
6 What ... you usually ... for breakfast? (have)
7 How often ... you ... fruit and vegetables? (eat)
8 ... you ... enough sleep every night? (get)
9 What else ... you ... to stay fit and healthy? (do)

b) *Answer the questions in a) for yourself.*

c) *Ask your partner the questions and take notes about your partner's answers.*

d) **Extra** *Write two or three more questions to find out about somebody's lifestyle.*
Do you like fast food / soft drinks / ...?
How much water / ... do you drink? ...

► GF 2: Making questions (p. 151) • GF 3: Talking about the present (p. 152)

► You could now do tasks 3 and 4 in the Practice test on p. 25.

8 Being a teenage mum is not easy

a) Zink! *chat is an online forum where people can write about their problems and give advice. Read about Rebecca's problem and then read Maria's advice.*

I was 16 when I got pregnant. I had been with my boyfriend for six months and he was the first boy I had sex with. I was on the pill[1] but sometimes I forgot to take it. My parents were really upset, but I wanted to keep the baby.
At first my boyfriend stayed with me but then he left me because he wanted to live his own life. Now I live alone with my son. I love him but being a teenage mum is not easy. You have to grow up quickly. A baby isn't always sweet and it's hard when your baby is screaming at 3 am because he is hungry.
I want to go back and finish school, but I will need help from my parents. I think it will be hard to study and be a mum at the same time. But my parents are still upset and do not believe that I've grown up. What can I do? [Rebecca]

Talk to your parents about your plans for the future. Explain to them what you want to do and tell them that you need their help. When they see how much you have grown up, I'm sure that they will try to help you. Good luck! [Maria]

[1] (to) be on the pill *die (Antibaby-)Pille nehmen*

b) *True or false? Note down 'T' or 'F'. Correct the false statements. Use information from a).*

1 Rebecca got pregnant because she wasn't on the pill.
2 When she told her parents that she was pregnant they were very happy.
3 Rebecca lives alone with her son because she wants to live her own life.
4 Rebecca thinks you shouldn't be a mum at 16 because it's a hard life.
5 In the future, Rebecca wants to go back to school and study.
6 Rebecca wants help from her parents because she wants to go out with her friends at night.
7 Maria thinks Rebecca should talk to her parents.

9 SPEAKING Giving your opinion

a) *Read the dialogue about teenage mums. Swap the phrases in blue for phrases from the boxes and practise the dialogue with your partner.*

A: I feel that young girls shouldn't be mothers. → I think (that) ... • If you ask me ...
B: It's true that it's not an ideal situation, but it's not impossible. → You're right (that) ... • I agree that ...
A: I believe that it isn't good for the baby, and it's hard for the mother too. → In my opinion ... • I think that ...
B: Well, I really believe that you're wrong there. It isn't too bad, especially if the mother gets enough help. → I just don't think that you're right. • I'm sorry, but I can't agree with you there.

b) *Choose one of these topics for discussion. Use phrases from a) to give your opinion.*

Fast food, soft drinks and sweets shouldn't be sold in schools.

Watching a film at home is better than going to the cinema.

▸ SF Having a discussion (p. 139)

1 LISTENING What can we do this weekend?

a) *First read the summaries below. Then listen carefully to the girls talking and decide which summary fits their phone call best.*

A Two girls are planning their weekend together. Tina has lots of interesting ideas, but Helen decides that she wants to plan a surprise for Tina.

B Tina phones Helen because the girls want to spend Saturday evening together. Helen has got some ideas, but Tina does not like them. In the end Helen is fed up with Tina and decides to stay at home alone.

C Two girls are making plans for the weekend. They want to go to their athletics training on Saturday and to visit Manchester on Sunday. After their training they are going to meet at Helen's house. They decide to watch a film on TV and listen to some music together.

b) *Listen again and write down at least three activities that Helen suggests for Saturday evening.*

go to the ..., play ..., ...

2 SPEAKING Holiday plans

a) *With a partner, use the information in the chart below to prepare a dialogue for this situation:*

You want to go on holiday with your friend after the exams[1], but you both have different ideas about what you want to do. You both talk about your ideas and try to agree on a holiday plan.

Partner A: The exams are over at last. Now we can have some fun!
Partner B: Great! Let's talk about holiday plans!
Partner A: OK. Well, what do you think about ...

	Partner A	Partner B
1 Idea	a youth hostel – near the sea	camping – in the mountains
2 What does it cost?	15 euros a night	35 euros a night
3 What can you do there?	swimming, surfing, beach volleyball	hiking, mountain biking, swimming in lakes
4 Location	500 metres from railway station and beach	60 km from nearest town

b) *Act out the dialogue with your partner.*

[1] exams *Prüfung, Examen*

3 LISTENING Living together

You will hear a radio phone-in programme about relationships between people of different religions. Look at the statements below for one minute. Then listen and choose the correct answers A, B, C or D. You will hear the phone-in twice.

1 *All about me* is about ...
- A life 50 years ago.
- B English cities.
- C married people with problems.
- D a successful mixed relationship.

2 Sharon's ...
- A parents are both Muslims.
- B mum is a Muslim.
- C dad is a Muslim.
- A parents have lots of problems.

3 Sean ...
- A has a girlfriend who is a Catholic.
- B has a girlfriend who often goes to church.
- C is a Protestant.
- D tries to go to church every week.

4 Afra ...
- A isn't with her boyfriend now.
- B is a Hindu.
- C has children.
- D says mixed relationships aren't a problem.

5 Bob ...
- A met his girlfriend in England.
- B has an Italian girlfriend.
- C is Irish.
- D is English.

6 Bob says that ...
- A he plays rugby.
- B he's a rugby fan.
- C his girlfriend is a rugby fan.
- D his team always wins.

4 LISTENING Radio adverts

Listen to three radio adverts. You will hear the recordings twice. Are the following statements true or false?

a)	1 Although the woman is on a diet[1], the man has bought her chocolates.
	2 *Her World* sells flowers[2] and special chocolates for women.
b)	3 The second advert is for people who are happily married.
	4 *A lifetime's love* is the title of a book.
c)	5 The third advert is for men.
	6 It says that in three months you can look fit and strong on the beach.

[1] diet *Diät* [2] flower *Blume*

5 SPEAKING Too young to be a mum?

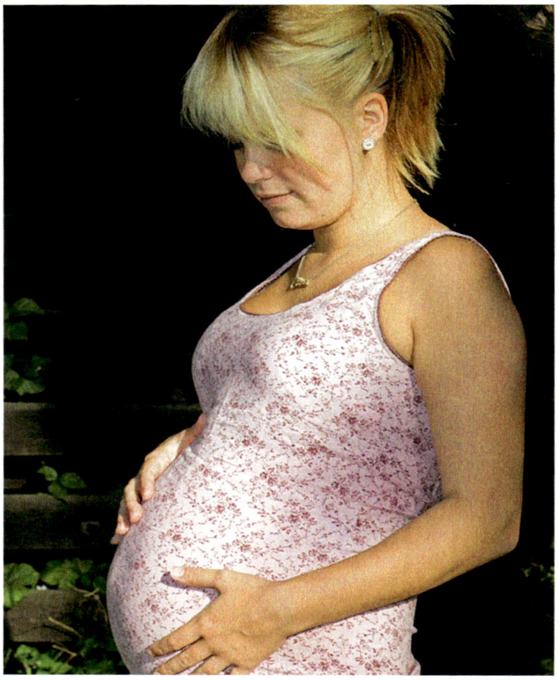

Talk about the pictures. The following questions can help you:

- What can you see in the pictures?
- What do you think the girls are thinking?
- How do you think their parents and friends reacted to the news that they were pregnant?
- How does having a baby change a teenager's life?
- What role should the baby's father play?
- What do you think is the best age to have a baby? Why?

6 PRESENTATION My lifestyle

Tell the class how careful you are (or aren't) about looking after yourself and keeping healthy.

Talk about:

Food: likes/dislikes • healthy/unhealthy food
Exercise: keeping fit • the role of sport
Social life: friends • free-time activities

Prepare your presentation before you talk to the class. Use good, clear notes in English.

How am I doing?

Im Practice test *konntest du einige Aufgaben ausprobieren, die dir in einer zukünftigen Abschlussprüfung begegnen könnten. Wenn Du Probleme bei einzelnen Testaufgaben hattest, können dir die folgenden Fragen helfen herauszufinden, was du üben musst.*

1 Wie leicht oder schwer waren die Aufgaben?
Überprüfe deine Antworten auf S. 207–208 und entscheide, wie leicht/schwer du sie fandest.

	leicht	ging so	ziemlich schwer	sehr schwer
Task 1				
Task 2				
Task 3				

Listening (Task 1, 3, 4)

2 Was war schwer bei den Höraufgaben?
a) Ich habe die Arbeitsanweisungen nicht verstanden.
b) Die Personen sprachen zu schnell.
c) Die Akzente waren schwer zu verstehen.
d) Es gab sehr viele Informationen im Text. Ich konnte nicht die richtigen Antworten herausfinden.
e) Es gab Wörter und Wendungen, die ich einfach nicht verstanden habe.
f) Die Zeit war zu kurz, ich konnte nicht alle Aufgaben beenden.

3 Wie hast du die Höraufgaben gelöst?
a) Ich habe mir die Aufgaben erst nur kurz angesehen und sie dann später gründlich beim Hören gelesen.
b) Zuerst habe ich die Aufgaben gründlich gelesen, damit ich genau wusste, was ich heraushören sollte.
c) (Nr. 3 und 4) Ich habe beim ersten Hören so viele Antworten wie möglich notiert. Beim zweiten Hören habe ich alles überprüft (und fehlende Antworten ergänzt).
d) Es gab so viele Dinge, die ich nicht verstanden habe, dass ich in Panik geraten bin.

► *SF Listening (p. 132)*

▶ *You will find more LISTENING tasks in the Exam File, pp. 86–88.*

Speaking (Task 2, 5, 6)

4 Was war schwer bei den Sprechaufgaben?
a) Ich war sehr nervös.
b) Ich wusste nicht, was ich sagen sollte.
c) Ich wusste nicht genug über das Thema.
d) Mir fielen nicht die passenden Worte ein.

► *SF Speaking course (pp. 138–139)*

▶ *You will find more SPEAKING tasks in the Exam File, pp. 79–81.*

Bitte deine Lehrkraft um eine Kopie des Assessment Sheets *und fülle diese aus.*

Assessment sheet	☹		😐		☺	
Name ...	**1**	**2**	**3**	**4**	**5**	**Comments**
2 SPEAKING Holiday plans						
a) Wir haben einander zugehört und versucht, uns auf einen Urlaubsplan zu einigen.						
b) Unsere Antworten waren lang genug.						
c) Wir haben beide Interesse gezeigt an dem, was unser Partner zu sagen hatte.						
d) Wir waren in der Lage, das Gespräch in Gang zu halten.						
5 SPEAKING Too young to be a mum?						
e) Ich habe die Aussage der Bilder verstanden und meine Ideen gut beschrieben.						
f) Ich habe die Fragen benutzt, um Ideen zu bekommen und meinen Vortrag zu strukturieren.						
g) Ich habe genügend über das Thema zu sagen gehabt.						
h) Ich habe laut und deutlich genug gesprochen.						
6 PRESENTATION My lifestyle						
i) Ich habe laut und deutlich genug gesprochen.						
j) Ich habe alle wichtigen Punkte angesprochen.						
k) Ich habe visuelle Materialien (Folien, Poster, ...) eingesetzt und sie gut erklärt.						
l) Ich habe die meiste Zeit meine Zuhörer angeschaut und nicht nur meine Notizen.						

Unit 2 The world we live in

1 Technology in your life

a) *Look at the picture above. Try to name all the examples of technology. The words in the box can help you.*

> computer • electric toothbrush • games console • hairdryer • microwave • mobile phone • electric razor • …

b) *How often do you use the things in the picture? Make notes.*

I never / always / often / … use a/an …
I use a/an … every day / week / month / …

c) *Make appointments with three students and talk about technology in your life. Use your notes from b).*

d) *Read Tasha's text on the right and write a similar text about yourself. You can put your text in your DOSSIER.*

► *SF Writing course (pp. 141–142)*

2 What is it?

Listen to the CD. Guess what electronic appliances the people are talking about and write them down.

► *SF Listening (p. 132)*

Tasha says:
1 July 2010
at 9.50 pm

I live in a house with lots of electronic appliances – four computers, two games consoles, four TVs, two DVD players … I even use an electric toothbrush! Like most people, we have a dishwasher, a washing machine, a microwave and a fridge. All those machines use a lot of energy.

We often go by car because it's quicker and easier than cycling or going by bus.

But now I've decided to use less energy. I try to cycle to school every day (when it's not raining) and I often go by bus. I usually remember to turn off my computer and other electronic appliances when I'm not using them. If I'm cold, I put on a pullover first, before I turn up the heating. But I think I could do more for the environment.

3 How big is your footprint?

We need a lot of energy for all the machines that we use. Producing this energy sends greenhouse gases like carbon dioxide (CO_2) into the air. Greenhouse gases make the planet warmer: this effect is called global warming. The result is climate change, and this has serious effects on living conditions all over the world. Many animals are in danger because their homes and food are disappearing.
Your carbon footprint tells you how much CO_2 you produce. Every time you turn on the lights, make a cup of tea, watch a TV programme or play a computer game, your carbon footprint gets bigger.

> *Complete these sentences with information from the text.*

1 When we produce energy, greenhouse gases like ... are sent into the air.
2 Greenhouse gases cause ... warming.
3 ... change has serious effects on living conditions all over the world.

Average carbon footprints in tonnes of CO_2 per person per year (2009)

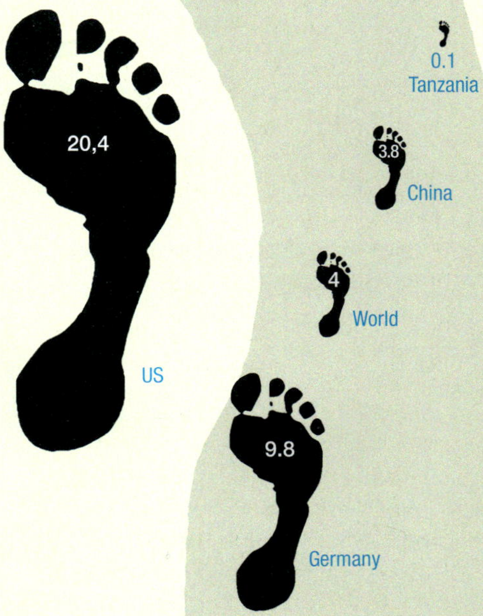

Source: www.carbonfootprint.com

2 World target to stop climate change

a) *Calculate your carbon footprint. Go to www.englishg.de/footprint and use the carbon calculator.*

b) *Compare your carbon footprints to the average carbon footprints on the left. Are your carbon footprints bigger or smaller?*

A: My/Your carbon footprint is smaller/bigger than the footprint for the USA, and it's ...
B: Yes, that's right. But it's bigger/smaller than ...

c) *Look at your footprints. Why are they big or small?*

My carbon footprint is small/big because I/my family always/never/... go by car/...

d) *What could you do to reduce your carbon footprint?*

To reduce my carbon footprint I could ...
– cycle/go by car/have a bath ... more/less often.
– turn off my computer/... when I'm not using it/them.
– ask my parents to use green energy/...

► Text File 2 *(pp. 114–116)*

LIVING WITH TECHNOLOGY

The Daily News, 1st April 2009

Six of the BEST

This week British scientists named some modern inventions that they think changed our world. Here are some of their choices.

1 GPS technology

This technology was developed for the US army in 1978, but GPS (Global Positioning System) is now used in cars, planes, boats, and even mobile phones. Before we had GPS, people used paper maps or asked people for directions.

2 Trainers

Trainers were invented in the US in 1892. At first they were worn only for sports, but they became really popular in the 1970s and since then they have changed fashion. They have also changed our feet: the army says that young people's feet are now too soft to wear traditional army boots.

3 TV dinners

'Ready' meals became popular in the 1970s because they saved a lot of time. They changed the way families ate meals. Since then it has become normal for people to sit in front of the TV to eat. Many people think that we were healthier before TV dinners because there is a lot of unhealthy fat, salt and sugar in them.

4 Social networking sites

Facebook and other social networking sites like MySpace and Twitter have completely changed the way we communicate and who we communicate with. In the past it wasn't so easy to keep in touch.

5 The Sony Walkman®

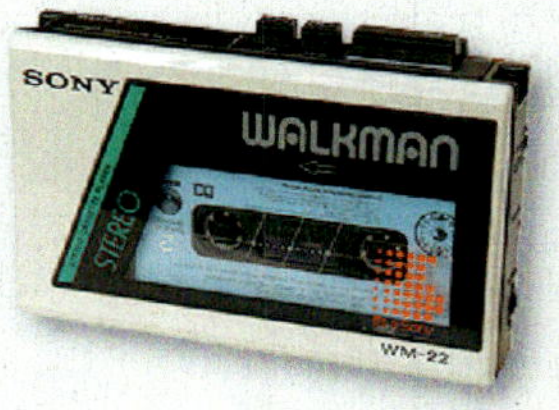

This famous personal stereo changed music forever. For the first time it was possible for people to listen to music on the way to work or during a run in the park. Then, in 2000, the Apple iPod® was invented and people could carry all their music in one pocket.

6 The Language Mediator

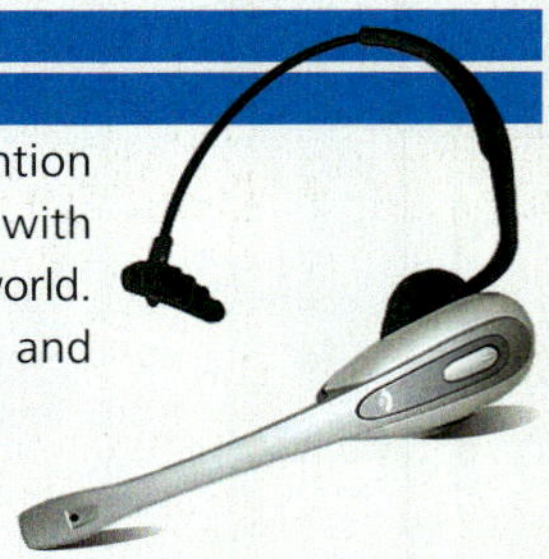

With this amazing invention we can communicate with people anywhere in the world. Put on the headphones and the machine translates what you hear and what you say. Now the British don't have to speak English very s-l-o-w-l-y and LOUDLY to foreign people when they are on holiday!

One of these inventions is a joke! Can you guess which one it is? (The answer is on p. 211)

▸ WB 5–6 (p. 24)

1 Inventions that changed the world

a) *Complete the sentences with the inventions from p. 30.*

1 ... made it easier to stay in contact with friends.
2 ... gave people something to listen to while they were running.
3 ... save time but aren't good for your health.
4 ... made soldiers' feet soft.
5 ... was used only by soldiers. Now it's used by sailors, drivers and lots of other people.
6 ... could be bad news for language teachers.

b) ***Think:*** *Look again at the inventions on p. 30. Which two do you think are the most important? Give reasons.*

Pair: *Compare lists with a partner and agree on your top two inventions.*

Share: *Discuss your choices with another pair. Agree on your top two inventions.*

c) *Present your top two inventions to the class. Explain your choices.*

– We think ... is the most important ...
– This invention changed our lives because ...
– For the first time people could ...
– We can't imagine living without it because ...

2 VIEWING Human Power Station

In the TV programme *Human Power Station*, the Collins family are taking part in an experiment. They are going to live in a special house for a day, but they don't know what the experiment is.

a) *Watch* ***scene 1*** *without the sound. Choose the correct answer:*
When the man turns on the shower, the cyclists ... (relax / work a bit harder / work a lot harder)

b) *Watch* ***scene 1*** *again with the sound. True or false? Correct the mistakes.*
1 In the end, 89 cyclists were needed to produce the electricity for the shower.
2 On average, a shower takes 5 minutes.

c) *The Collins family go for a walk and one of the presenters goes into the house. Watch* ***scene 2*** *and answer these questions:*
1 Which appliances does the presenter find 'on' or 'on standby'? Make a list.
2 What does the presenter want to show us when he burns the 'money'?

d) **Extra** *Do you think you will turn off your appliances more often now? Say why (not).*

P1 //○ REVISION Things are different today (Simple present and simple past) ▸ D p. 106

*Complete the sentences with the correct verb forms – **simple present** or **simple past**.*

1 In the past people *used* (use/used) the sun to find out the time, now there ... (are/were) watches and clocks.

2 Now we ... (send/sent) e-mails, but before the internet people ... (write/wrote) letters.

3 In the old days there ... (aren't/weren't) any planes or cars, so people ... (travel/travelled) by ship or ... (ride/rode) horses. Today we ... (use/used) planes and cars for long journeys.

4 Today there ... (are/were) fridges. But in the old days people ... (keep/kept) their food fresh with salt.

5 In the 1960s TVs ... (don't have/didn't have) remote controls, so people ... (have/had) to get up to change channels. Today we ... (stay/stayed) comfortably on the sofa.

6 Now we ... (have/had) lots of TVs in our homes and children often ... (watch/watched) TV in their rooms. But in the 1970s families ... (sit/sat) together in one room to watch TV. They often ... (argue/argued) about which channel to watch!

▸ *GF 3: Talking about the present (p. 152) • GF 4: Talking about the past (p. 153–154)*

P2 WORDS Technology

a) ○ *Collect words and phrases on the topic of TECHNOLOGY from pp. 28–31.*

b) *Make a mind map with the words and phrases. Use headings like these:*

communication • fashion • fun • in the bathroom • in the kitchen • transport • ...

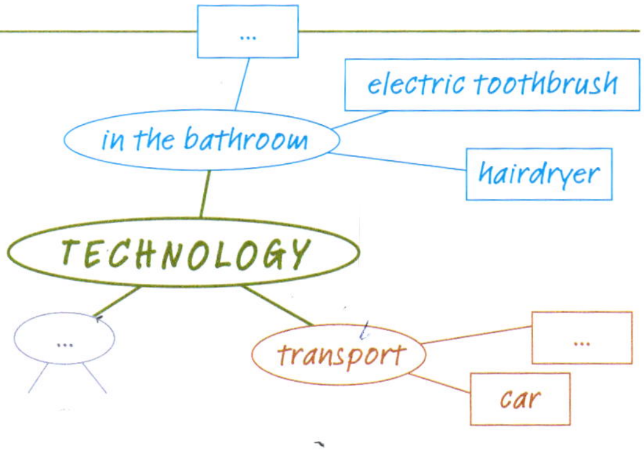

c) *Compare your results with a partner. Add more words and phrases if you can.*

d) *Write a short text about an invention that you use every day and that is very important to you. Think about:*

– what you use it for
– what people did before it was invented.

I use my computer every day. It's very important to me because I need it to send e-mails to friends. I also use it to ... Before they had computers, people ...

P3 Extra ● Research and gallery walk

a) *Do research on another invention that you think is important. Try to answer these questions.*

Why is it important?
Who invented it?
When was it invented?
What interesting facts can you find about it?

b) *Make a poster with your results and put it on the wall. Walk round and look at all the other posters.*

c) *In your class vote for the best poster.*

▸ *SF Internet research (p. 129) • SF Using visual materials with a presentation (p. 130) • WB 7 (p. 24)*

P4 LISTENING A science competition

High school student Jake Martin built a 'gasifier' for a science competition called 'Realize the dream'.

Martin and his gasifier

a) *Look at the picture. What do you think Jake's machine is?*

A A machine that checks if what you say is true.
B An engine for a car that uses gas that was produced by cows.
C A machine that produces gas for a house or a car.
D A machine that burns old clothes to make energy.

b) *Listen to the interview and check if you were right.*

c) *Listen again and answer these questions. Then check with a partner.*

1 How much did Jake win? (700 dollars/7,000 dollars)
2 What does he burn in his machine? (wood/oil)
3 How long does the machine have to run to give a house power for a day? (60 hours/6 hours)
4 What is he going to do with the money that he won? (spend it/save it)

► *SF Listening (p. 132)*

P5 SPEAKING Making compliments

a) *Imagine you're talking to students at a science competition. Which phrases can you use to make compliments about their work?*

A I really like your ...
B What a great/an interesting ...!
C You've done a very good job.
D This ... looks great on you.
E Congratulations.
F Well done.
G That's cool. Where did you buy it?

b) *Listen to the dialogue. Put up your hand when you hear one of the phrases.*

c) *Choose two of these situations. Take turns to make compliments about the people's work.*

P6 MEDIATION A smartphone application

Deine Mutter fragt nach deiner neuen Smartphone-Anwendung. Erkläre ihr auf Deutsch, was man mit dieser Anwendung tun kann.

AllAround**You** is the latest application for your smartphone. It helps you to find all kinds of places near you. Do you want to find the nearest clothes shop, supermarket, railway station or café? Are you looking for a doctor? Just choose your favourite location from the list and **All**Around**You** will show you how far it is from where you are. You can see the location on a map, look at the route and even email the information to a friend. **All**Around**You** is a fast, easy-to-use application for you – wherever you are.

► *SF Mediation (p. 147)* • *WB 8–9 (p. 25)*

SAVING THE PLANET

1 The Carbon Diaries 2015 (From the novel by Saci Lloyd, 2008, adapted and abridged)

It's 2015. The UK government wants to fight against global warming, so it is introducing carbon rationing to reduce the country's carbon footprint. From 8th January 2015 people in the UK will have a carbon allowance of 200 points a month. Everything they do, like driving the car, listening to music, having a shower, will cost them points on their carbon cards. In the text 16-year-old Laura Brown describes what this means for her family.

> *What do you think life with carbon rationing will be like for Laura? Choose one word from each pair of words in the box:*

difficult/easy • comfortable/uncomfortable • warm/cold • boring/exciting

▸ *SF Reading English texts (p. 136)*

Sat, Jan 3rd

Dad sat down with us tonight to go through a stupid government online form and find out what our family CO_2 allowance is. We've got a carbon allowance of 200 Carbon Points per month to spend on travel, heat, food.

The worst thing is, me and Kim have to give up lots of our points for the family carbon allowance. That leaves us almost nothing for travel, college, going out, ...

We're going to use the car much less, all of us can use the PC, TV, stereo for only two hours a day, heating is down to 16 °C in the living room and 1 hour a day for the rest of the house, 5-minute showers, baths only at weekends. We have to choose – hairdryer, toaster, microwave, smartphone, kettle, lights, fridge or cooker and on and on. Flights are a real no-no and shopping and going out not much better. It's all kind of a *choice*.

Mon, Jan 5th

Carbon cards came today ...

They've got these little blocks down the side going from green to red and as you use your year's ration they disappear one by one till you're down to your last red and then you're all alone and you're crying in the dark.

Thurs, Jan 8th

Back to college, and I got in late because I had to go with Mum to the bus stop. Her eyes filled with tears as we walked past the Saab. She whispered, 'It's not for ever,' and softly touched it.

We missed the first bus, so we had to wait 15 minutes in the rain till the next one. When it finally came I jumped on, swiped my carbon card and started running upstairs. Mum was looking through her purse, bag and pockets. She looked up at me.

'Laura, darling, I can't find my card. Can you lend me some ...'

The driver shook his head. 'No carbon card, no ride, love.'

'But, please ...'

A woman out in the rain shouted, 'Get off, you stupid cow! You're holding us up.'

And then Mum started to cry. I went back down and helped her off the bus. 'We'll have to go home and get your card, Mum.'

'I'm so sorry, Laura,' Mum said. 'I know I should be strong, but I feel so responsible for my generation – we're the ones who've messed it all up for you.'

When I finally got to college there was a huge queue because everyone had to swipe their CO_2 cards at the gate, but the machine wasn't working. I don't know what we were swiping for anyway – the building was freezing cold.

'Welcome to the future,' said Adisa, my best mate.

Tues, Jan 13th

My family has disappeared. Dad spends all night on his laptop, Mum is always lost on a bus somewhere and Kim just lives in her room. She's got the TV on 24/7 in her room. I can hear it through the wall.

Weds, Jan 14th

I woke up this morning and it was freezing, freezing cold. I'm only allowed heat on in my room between 7 and 8. Even for our one hour of heat Dad keeps the bedroom temperature at 15 °C. What a joke – it's not even warm enough to melt the ice on the windows.

Thurs, Jan 15th

There's heavy snowstorms all over the south of Europe.

Mon, Jan 19th

The snowstorms in Europe are getting worse – and they're moving north. Italy has just lost all its electricity.

Tues, Jan 20th

We had a power cut in the night. The house is so cold now, it feels like 200 years of cold in my bones. Cuts give me the creeps – you know, when you go to turn on the light and it's dead?

Working with the text

1 Your reaction to the story

a) *Go back to the question at the beginning of the text (p. 34). Were you right? Give examples from the text.*

I thought life for Laura would be ...
I was right/wrong about that because ...
– she has to/can't ...

b) *What do you think of the story?*

I (don't) like the story because ...
– I think it's unrealistic/funny/...
– I (don't) like science fiction/...
– it's a good way to show ...

2 True or false?

1. Points are taken off your carbon card when you go by bus or turn on the heating.
2. Kim and Laura can use their carbon points for anything they like.
3. The family can't have baths.
4. Laura's mum can't find her card when she gets on the bus.
5. Students have to pay for heating in the college with their carbon cards.
6. Laura and her family are spending more time together.

3 What could you give up?

a) *Look at ll. 16–25. Write down two things you could easily give up and two things you couldn't give up.*

b) *Explain your choices to your partner.*

c) *Report your choices to the class.*

4 Now you

a) *Imagine that, like Laura, you have been given a small carbon allowance. Write at least three sentences to explain how you feel about carbon rationing and why.*

I feel angry / worried / happy / ... because ...
– I could / couldn't give up ...
– I like a warm house / going by car / ...
I think carbon rationing ...
– is a good / stupid idea because ...
– will / won't help to solve the problem of climate change because ...

b) *Make appointments with two partners. Discuss how you feel about carbon allowances.*

2 dinge auf die ich verzichten könnte & 2 auf die nicht

P1 You can make a difference

a) Partner B: Go to p. 99.
Partner A: You and your partner have different tips under each heading in the text **Go Green**. *Read your tips and take notes in a chart under these headings:*

b) Ask your partner about his/her tips to go green. Add the tips to your chart.
What's your tip to use less energy/save trees/...?

Use less energy	*Save trees*	*Think about your food*	*Reduce rubbish*
– buy ...	*– ...*	*– ...*	*– ...*

▸ *SF Taking notes (p. 133)*

Go Green!

Here are some simple things that you can do to help to stop global warming.

Use less energy

Producing electricity causes a lot of CO_2. So, to save electricity, buy low-energy appliances. If your family has an old fridge, try to get a new one. New models use much less energy. They'll reduce your family's electricity bill – and your carbon footprint!

Think about your food

To help to fight against climate change, try to eat less meat. Meat has a big carbon footprint because producing it takes a lot of energy. And animals, especially cows, produce methane, which is a greenhouse gas.

Save trees

Why don't you plant a tree? Trees use CO_2 and they produce clean air – clean air that we need! More trees mean less CO_2 in the air.

Reduce rubbish

About 75 % of the things we throw away could be recycled. Recycling is great because it reduces rubbish and saves energy. You can recycle paper, plastic and glass.

c) Which of these tips are easy to follow in your everyday life? Which tips are more difficult to follow? Discuss with your partner.

A: I think it's easy to turn off your computer when you're not using it. What about you?
B: ...

P2 SPEAKING A cartoon (Talking about a cartoon)

a) Describe the cartoon to your partner. Then discuss what you think its message is.

b) Form a group with another pair. Compare your ideas about the cartoon. Then give your opinion of the cartoon and its message.

more help ▸ *D p. 106*

▸ *SF Describing cartoons (p. 126)* • **Text File 3** *(p. 117)*

P3 //O WORDS The environment

► D p. 107

a) Find nouns that go with these verbs. You can use the nouns in the box.

– recycle	glass, ...
– save	energy, ...
– don't buy so much/many	meat, ...
– turn off	appliances, ...
– use	recycled paper, ...

green energy • clothes • energy • appliances • glass • electricity • the environment • lights • local products • meat • recycled paper • rubbish • water • ...

b) What can we do to save the environment? Make at least four sentences.

We can	recycle	rubbish like glass, paper and plastic.
	save	public transport.
	buy	more green energy because it produces less CO_2.
	turn off	lights and electronic appliances to save energy.
	use	...

P4 ● WRITING Can I save the planet? (A written discussion)

Produce a written discussion on the following statement:

Carbon rationing should be introduced in Germany.

a) Collect and organize ideas on the topic.

- *Brainstorm your ideas and make notes.*
- *Organize your ideas into arguments for and against the statement.*

b) Write an outline.

- *Decide on your opinion on the statement: Are you for or against it?*
- *Structure your notes in an outline.*

► *SF From outline to written discussion (p. 146)*

STUDY SKILLS A written discussion

*In a **written discussion** you present arguments for or against a statement. At the end of the discussion you write a **conclusion**, in which you give your own opinion. Before you start writing, structure your ideas in an **outline**:*

Outline
1 Introduction
2 Arguments (for or against)
   2.1. First argument
   2.2. Second argument
   2.3. ...
3 Conclusion

c) Write your text.

Introduction
Say why the topic is important.

- This topic is important because ...
- ... is a big problem in the world today.
- People often say that ...

Your arguments
List your arguments. Give reasons and examples for each argument.

- First ... / Second ... / Finally ...
- For example ... / A good example of this is ...
- ... because ... / So ... / That's why ...

Conclusion
Sum up and give your opinion.

- To sum up, I think ...
- In my opinion ...

d) *Read your texts and correct them. You can put your text in your DOSSIER.*

► *SF Correcting your text (p. 142)*

1 WORDS Travel

a) *Use words from the box to make lists of words under these headings: **air** (5 words), **railway** (4 words), **road** (7 words), **sea** (4 words). Add more words if you can.*

airport • boat • cab • (to) cycle • (to) drive • ferry • flight • gate • harbour • (to) land • motorway[1] • petrol station • plane • platform • ship • traffic jam • train • truck • the Tube • underground • ...

b) *Choose the right verb for each sentence.*

1 Bob and I **drove/went** on a trip to Brighton last year.
Bob and I went on a trip to Brighton last year.
2 At 6 in the morning, I **picked/drove** him up at his house.
3 We had planned to **travel/ask** on the early train.
4 But there was an accident on the line and they **closed/arrived** it for the rest of the day.
5 So I phoned mum and she offered to **drive/travel** us to Brighton.
6 We had to **pick/ask** a policeman for directions and then we were on our way. We had a great day!

2 London's underground (Simple past and present perfect)

*Complete the sentences. Choose the correct tense: **simple past** or **present perfect**.*

London's underground railway is called the Tube. In 1863, when the Tube (1) **opened/has opened**, the railway line (2) **was/has been** only six kilometres long. On the first day, 30,000 people (3) **travelled/have travelled** on the Tube. Since 1863, the Tube (4) **became/has become** more and more popular and now over three million people use it every day. The trains (5) **were/have been** electric since 1890. The famous logo, which you can see in the picture, was designed in 1908. It (6) **was/has been** part of London life for more than 100 years now.

► *GF 4: Talking about the past (pp. 153–154)*

3 Transport in London (Word order)

Read these statements about transport in London. Choose the right place for the words in brackets.

1 Julie: I love buses. I always try ... to sit ... so I can enjoy the view. (at the top)
2 Maria: I was ... in a terrible traffic jam .... (yesterday)
I don't think that I'll go ... into London by car .... (again)
3 Jack: I wanted to reduce my carbon footprint, so I ... my car a long time ago .... (sold)
4 Paul: Will bus drivers give me information about travel times if I ... them ...? (ask)
5 Mike: When I got to the stop, the last bus had ... left .... I was really angry. (early)
6 Sue: I always take ... the Tube ... when I go shopping. (on Saturdays)

▶ *You could now do task 1 in the Practice test on p. 42.*

► *GF 1: Word order (p. 150)*

[1] motorway *Autobahn, Schnellstraße*

4 WORDS After the accident

Complete the dialogue with words from the box.

accident • ambulance • drunk • first aid • headache • healthy • hurts • operations • sick • weak

Doctor Mike, can you hear me? You had an (1) *accident* on your motorbike. Your friend Julie is still unconscious[2]. Both of you have broken arms and legs. You'll both have to have (2) ... But first we have to ask you some questions. Did you drink any alcohol today?
Mike No, I didn't. Julie had one or two glasses of wine, but she wasn't (3) ...
Doctor Have you or Julie had a cold in the last few weeks?
Mike No, we've been really (4) ...
Doctor Good. Do you feel any pain right now?
Mike Yes, I do. My leg (5) ... terribly and I've got quite a bad (6) ... and a stomach ache too.
Doctor Well, you were in shock after the accident.
Mike Yes, I was shaking all the time and my legs felt (7) ...! And I remember feeling (8) ... and cold. Doctor, who called the (9) ...?
Doctor Luckily, there was a paramedic in the car behind you. He gave you (10) ...

▶ *You could now do task 2 in the Practice test on p. 42.*

5 STUDY SKILLS Writing (The 5 Ws and 'how')

a) *Use the phrases in the boxes to complete the report.*

A he was driving at over 80 miles per hour
B when broken glass flew into it
C in the late afternoon rush hour
D one of the worst accidents
E St Pauls and Eastville Park
F 23-year-old truck driver

Young dad loses left eye in accident
Yesterday a (1) ... was badly hurt in (2) ... in the Bristol area this year. The father of two sons wasn't able to stop in time when he saw a traffic jam in front of him because (3) ... where only 60 are allowed. Martin Smith from St Pauls in Bristol lost his left eye (4) ... Luckily doctors were able to save the other eye. The accident happened (5) ... when thousands of people were travelling home from work. The M32 was closed for two hours between (6) ..., and there was traffic chaos in the centre of Bristol. Police said it was lucky that Mr Smith hadn't been killed.

b) *Match the phrases from a) to the 5 Ws and 'how'.*

Who?	*a 23-year-old truck driver*	**Where?**	
What?		**Why?**	
When?		**How?**	

▶ *SF Writing a report (p. 142)*

[2] unconscious *bewusstlos*

6 WORDS For a greener world

a) *For each group, find the word that doesn't fit.*

1 sun • plastic • paper • glass
2 oil • water • wind • sun
3 pollute • recycle • reduce • save
4 climate change • green energy • air pollution • global warming
5 trees • electricity • cars • heating

b) *Match the sentence beginnings (1–6) to the endings (a–f).*

1 Locally grown products ...
2 You need more energy to produce meat ...
3 You can buy cool clothes cheaply ...
4 Buying recycled paper can ...
5 It's much better to recycle glass ...
6 Using plastic shopping bags more than once ...

a than to produce vegetables.
b are usually better for the environment.
c than to throw it into the dustbin.
d at second-hand shops.
e helps to protect the environment.
f help to save trees.

7 Our green holiday (Simple past: questions)

Write Lucy's questions to complete the dialogue.

Lucy So / enjoy / your / did / you / holiday?
So did you enjoy your holiday?
Sharon Yes, I did. I think it was the best holiday I've ever had.
Lucy stay? / Where / you / did
Sharon At a 'green' hotel in the south of France, near Marseille.
Lucy find / you / out / How / about / it? / did
Sharon Our neighbours told us about it. They were there last year.
Lucy was / What / special / hotel? / the / about
Sharon Special? Well, the food was delicious – all locally grown.
Lucy organic food[1]? / And / it / was
Sharon Of course it was organic food. And most of the fruit and vegetables came from the hotel garden.
Lucy do? / did / you / What
Sharon Well, we helped in the hotel garden and we went down to the beach every day.
Lucy hotel / the / it? / was / How / far / from
Sharon It wasn't too far. Just over half a mile.
Lucy nice / Did / have / you / weather?
Sharon Yes, we had fantastic weather. Twenty-five degrees and lots of sun every day!

► *GF 2: Making questions (p. 151)* • *GF 4: Talking about the past (pp. 153–154)*

[1] organic food *biologisch angebaute Lebensmittel; Biokost* / (organic ... *Bio-...*)

8 Ben's blog (Simple past: negative statements)

Ben has started to 'shop green'. Read his blog. Complete the sentences with the simple past form of the verbs in brackets.

Friday
:-) Went shopping in town by bike today. I (1) … (take) the bus because it uses too much energy.
I didn't take the bus because it uses too much energy.
:-(Asked for recycled paper but they (2) … (have) any.
:-) Bought some fruit. The big red apples from Italy looked nice, but I (3) … (choose) them. I chose the small, locally grown ones.
:-) Got some eggs. I (4) … (buy) organic ones, but they came from a local farm, so I think that was OK.

Sunday
:-(Went to town again. I wanted to go to the second-hand shops, but I (5) … (know) they are closed on Sundays.
:-(Bought a T-shirt made in China at a jumble sale. I just (6) … (see) any that were made in this country.

▶ *You could now do tasks 3 and 4 in the Practice test on p. 43.*

► *GF 4: Talking about the past (pp. 153–154)*

9 WRITING An essay

Put these paragraphs in the right order (introduction, first argument (= for), second argument (= against), conclusion).

A But many other people think that there are arguments against buying clothes from developing countries[1], at least if the label has no reliable information about their background. First, fashion isn't everything. Second, conditions in clothes factories can be terrible. For example, one report describes how young children work for no pay, and are beaten if they don't produce enough.

B You often hear people say that there is a problem with clothes from developing countries. Here in Europe, these clothes can be very cheap. But the people who produce them for western markets often have to work very hard for very little. So the question is: should teenagers buy these clothes or not?

► *SF From outline to written discussion (p. 146)*

C After looking at both sides, I think it is safer not to buy clothes from developing countries if you know nothing about conditions in the factories. For me, fashion is very important, but children's rights are even more important.

D Some people believe that it is all right to buy clothes from developing countries. First, most teenagers are interested in fashion, but they do not have much money. So it is an advantage to be able to buy clothes cheaply. Second, you cannot know the background to all the clothes you buy. And buying clothes from developing countries helps people there to make some money.

[1] developing countries *Entwicklungsländer*

1 LANGUAGE Congestion charge

Read the text. Choose the correct word or phrase to complete it.

They said it would never work!

The traffic jams in London were terrible because there were too many cars, so the Mayor[1] of London decided to try and solve the problem. People said his plan would never work, but it did! In 2003, London (1) **became / has become** the first city in the world to introduce a 'congestion charge[2]'. Drivers now have to pay £8 a day to enter the centre of London. At first people said it would cause lots of problems because they thought that the technology would never (2) **work / react**. But it did!

Drivers must (3) **pay / paid** the congestion charge from Monday to Friday from 7 am to 6.30 pm. Since the introduction of the congestion charge, the number of cars per day in the centre of London (4) **has gone down / went down** by[3] 50,000. Another positive effect is that (5) **the rush hour / traffic** has started to move faster. Only the managers of big (6) **stations / department stores** are less happy because they (7) **have had / will have** fewer customers since the congestion charge was introduced. And many people say that it is unfair that only people with lots of money can (8) **drive / cycle** into London, because the congestion charge AND parking are too expensive for most people.

[1] Mayor *Bürgermeister* [2] congestion charge *City-Maut (wörtlich: Verkehrsbelastungsgebühr)* [3] (to) go down by ... *zurückgehen um*

2 WRITING A visit to the doctor's

A dialogue

You are at the doctor's. You fell off your bike yesterday evening. Your left arm hurts terribly and you have a headache and stomach ache. You felt weak and sick after the accident. You were shaking all the time and felt cold. You want to know if your arm is broken.

In your exercise book, complete your part of the dialogue. Write about 60 words.

Doctor Good morning. And how can I help you today?

You (1) ...
I fell off my bike yesterday evening.

Doctor Poor you! Do you feel any pain at the moment?

You (2) ...

Doctor Hmm. And do you have any pain in other parts of your body?

You (3) ...

Doctor Can you remember what happened after the accident?

You (4) ...

Doctor You were probably in shock. OK. So let me have a look at your arm. Does that hurt?

You Yes, it does. (5) ...?

Doctor No, it isn't broken. You were lucky. Your arm will feel better in a few days. Try not to use it too much. And here, take this to the chemist's and they'll give you something for your head and stomach. You should be able to go back to school tomorrow.

You (6) ...

3 WRITING A report

*Choose **one** of the following topics and write a report about it. Remember to answer the 5 Ws and 'how'. Write about 80 words.*

– You saw an accident between a car and somebody on a bike.

OR

– You spent a camping holiday in the country with your parents.

4 WRITING A shopping survey

Read the questions and answers on the form below. Then answer the questions for yourself. Write a short comment for each of your answers.

Question	Y/N	Comment
1 Do you think it's a good idea to buy organic food?	*No*	*Organic food is too expensive.*
2 Do you agree it's better to eat less meat and more vegetables?	*Yes*	*I know that meat has a big carbon footprint, and I really like vegetables. And I love animals – alive, and not on my plate!*
3 Do you think it's a good idea to buy recycled paper?	*No*	*Recycled paper saves trees, but it's more expensive and the quality isn't very good.*
4 Do you use plastic shopping bags more than once?	*Yes*	*... usually. This reduces rubbish and saves energy. But I'm afraid I sometimes forget to take bags with me when I go shopping.*
5 Have you ever bought clothes at second-hand shops?	*No*	*Second-hand stuff is better for the environment, but I like to buy new stuff.*

5 WRITING A letter to a newspaper

Child slaves work for western fashion companies

Children have been found in an Indian factory in Delhi where clothes for European shops are produced.

Some of the children were only eight years old. The children were found by two reporters from a British newspaper.

The reporters told the factory managers that they worked for a large British fashion company and so they were allowed to enter the factory and look around. The reporters said that the conditions inside the factory were unbelievable. 'The children were working in dark and dirty rooms. They looked very tired and very hungry.'

Later the reporters returned to the factory with the police. The children said that they worked for long hours for almost no money. They came from very poor families. One of the reporters, Julian Thomson, said: 'It's really important for people to ask where clothes were made before they buy them.'

Read the newspaper article. Then complete the letter to the newspaper. Think of the following questions:

- How did you feel when you read the article?
- What do you think about children who have to work and why?
- What should people in Germany do?

<your address>

The Daily News
London
E1 8YS

<date>

Dear Sir or Madam

When I read your article about ... in last Saturday's paper I felt ...

I think ...

I think people in Germany should ...

Yours faithfully

<your name>

6 WRITING Opinions

Choose one of the following statements and produce a written discussion about it. Write about 60–80 words. The phrases in the box can help you.

A City centres would be nicer places if there were fewer cars there.
B The most important thing about food is that it is cheap.
C I can't worry about what workers in clothes factories earn. I don't have enough money myself.

Lots of people think ... / You often hear people say ...

First ... • Second ... • ...
Finally ...

To sum up, I think ...

How am I doing?

Im Practice test *konntest du einige Aufgaben ausprobieren, die dir in einer zukünftigen Abschlussprüfung begegnen könnten. Wenn Du Probleme bei einzelnen Testaufgaben hattest, können dir die folgenden Fragen helfen herauszufinden, was du üben musst.*

1 Wie leicht oder schwer waren die Aufgaben?
Überprüfe deine Antworten auf S. 209–210 und entscheide, wie leicht/schwer du die Aufgaben fandest.

	leicht	ging so	ziemlich schwer	sehr schwer
Task 1				
Task 2				
Task 3				

Language (Task 1)

2 Was war schwer bei der LANGUAGE-Aufgabe?

a) Ich habe die Aufgabenstellung nicht verstanden.
b) Ich fand das Format mit der Antwortauswahl im Text schwierig.
c) Ich konnte mich oft nicht entscheiden, welche Antwort richtig war.
d) Ich habe den Text nicht ganz verstanden und Panik bekommen.

Writing (Tasks 2–6)

3 Was war schwer bei den Schreibaufgaben?

a) Ich war sehr nervös.
b) Ich wusste nicht was ich schreiben sollte.
c) Mir fielen nicht die passenden Worte ein.
d) Ich war mir nicht mehr sicher, welche Regeln ich beim Schreiben der unterschiedlichen Texte (z. B. Bericht, Brief, ...) beachten muss.
e) Die Texte, die ich geschrieben habe, waren nicht klar genug.
f) Ich habe viele Schreib- und Grammatikfehler gemacht.
g) Die Zeit war zu kurz, ich konnte nicht alle Aufgaben beenden.

▸ *SF Writing course (pp. 141–142)*

4 Wie hast du die Schreibaufgaben gelöst?
Bitte deine Lehrkraft um eine Kopie des Assessment Sheets *rechts. Benutze es, um die Arbeit deines Partners einzuschätzen.*

Assessment sheet	☹		😐		☺	
Name ...	1	2	3	4	5	Com
2 WRITING A dialogue: Hat dein/e Partner/in ...						
a) alle Fragen der Ärztin beantwortet?						
b) alle Ideen aus der Arbeits–anweisung beachtet und genug geschrieben?						
3 WRITING A report: Hat dein/e Partner/in ...						
c) den Bericht gut strukturiert und einen deutlichen Eindruck von dem, was passiert ist, gegeben?						
d) mit den wichtigsten Informationen begonnen und erst dann notwendige Details ergänzt?						
e) die 5 Ws und 'how' beantwortet?						
f) das *simple past* verwendet?						
4 WRITING A shopping survey: Hat dein/e Partner/						
g) alle Fragen auf dem Umfrage-bogen beantwortet?						
h) Gründe/Erklärungen für jede Antwort geliefert?						
5 WRITING A letter to a newspaper: Hat dein/e Pa						
i) die äußere Gestaltung des Briefes aus dem Muster im Buch korrekt übernommen? (Adresse, Datum, Anrede, Schlussformel, ...)						
j) die eigene Meinung klar erklärt?						
k) Langformen verwendet? (*I am, I would like* statt *I'm, I'd like*)						
6 WRITING Opinions: Hat dein/e Partner/in ...						
l) den Text gut strukturiert? (*introduction – first/second/... argument – conclusion*)						
m) Beispiele für die Argumente gegeben und am Ende die eigene Meinung deutlich geäußert?						
n) längere Sätze mit *linking words* verbunden?						

▶ *You will find more WRITING tasks in the Exam File, pp. 82–85.*

Unit 3 Have your say!

1 What's the issue?

a) *Choose a photo and describe it.*

- It's a photo of ...
- The woman/children/... is/are wearing/carrying/standing near to ...
- She/... looks tired ...
- I think she/... is shy/...
- The background/room/... looks ...

b) *Match the issues from the box to the photos.*

child poverty • discrimination • the environment • fair pay for young people • facilities for young people • the right to vote

2 What we care about

a) *Listen to six young people. They're talking about issues that they care about. Match the speakers 1–6 to the photos A–F.*

b) *Listen again. In a chart, write down key words and phrases for the things the speakers care about.*

► SF Taking notes (p. 133)

Speaker	Key words and phrases
1	environment, pollution, ...

c) *Compare your charts. Can you add more key words?*

3 Now you

Which issue do you care about most? Say why.

QUIZ

How much do you care?

If you think something is unfair, do you care enough to speak out or get involved? Do this quiz to find out.

1 You need a new T-shirt. Do you buy the one with the trendy label or the fair-trade label?

A If the two T-shirts are the same price, I'd probably buy the fair-trade T-shirt.

B I always choose fair-trade products because fair trade means fair pay for the people who make the products.

C The trendy label. It's really important to look good.

2 There's a new student at your school. You try to talk to him, but he doesn't speak your language very well. What do you do?

A I wait until he's learned to speak my language.

B I ask him to play football or another game where language isn't important.

C I smile at him every time I see him.

3 Do you leave your mobile phone on overnight?

A Sometimes. But I feel a bit guilty because I know it uses a lot of electricity.

B Of course. This way my phone is always ready for me to use.

C I would never do that! In the UK we waste £27 million a year this way!

4 Are you interested in the news?

A No – but I sometimes look at the TV pages in the newspaper, and the sports pages too.

B Not really, but I sometimes notice something interesting on the TV news when my parents are watching it.

C Yes, I get information from lots of sources: news programmes, online news sites, blogs, …

5 You have three wishes. What's your first wish?

A Good health for my family and friends.

B World peace.

C To be rich and good-looking.

6 Which statement do you agree with most?

A If you don't vote, you don't have the right to complain if you don't like something.

B Why should I vote? Politicians don't listen anyway.

C Voting is important, but you also have to get up and do something.

7 They want to close your youth club. What do you do?

A I email my local newspaper, go on a demonstration in front of the town hall and start an online campaign. Anything I can do to save my youth club.

B I sign a petition or join an online group.

C Nothing – no one will listen to a group of kids.

4 How much do you care?

a) Do the quiz. Then go to p. 212 to find your result.

b) Find out the results of the people in your group. Are you surprised by the results? Why (not)?

– It says that I/you …
– I'm (not) surprised by that. I think that I/you …
– Really? I think it's true that I/you … but …

5 Extra The story behind the picture

Choose a person in one of the photos on p. 46 and write about him/her.

– Where is he/she?
– What is he/she doing?
– What is he/she feeling?
– What is he/she thinking?
– What was he/she doing before the photo was taken?
– What will happen next?

more help ► D p. 107

► SF Describing pictures (pp. 125–126)

YOUR RIGHT TO BE HEARD

1 What's the right age?

a) *At what age are you allowed to do these things in Germany? Copy the chart. Discuss with your partner and try to complete the chart.*

	United States	Germany
get married	14–17 *	...
drive a car (on your own)	16–18 *	...
vote in a national election	18	...
buy cigarettes	18	...
buy alcohol	21	...
leave home	18	...

* The rules are different in different states.

A: I think that in Germany you have to be 18/... before you can ...
B: I agree. / I disagree. I think that you have to be older / can be younger.
(Look at p. 211 to see if you were right.)

b) **Extra** *Find out about other countries that you know.*

c) *At what age should you be allowed to do these things? Discuss with your partner.*
– I think that 14/ ... is too young/too old/the right age to ... because ...
– I could/couldn't wait until I was 21/... to ...
– It's more/less likely that young people would get divorced/have accidents/alcohol problems/...

▸ *SF Having a discussion (p. 139)*

2

COMMENTS E-MAIL PRINT

WE ARE PEOPLE TOO!

by Oliver Munslow (16) – 23 August 2010

Look at the title of the article and the pictures. What do you think Oliver cares about? Who do you think he's talking to (adults or teenagers)?

So, you think young people are different? Well, it's true! We're younger than you. But if you think that that means we don't have rights, you're wrong.

Did you know that here in Britain every citizen under 18 has important rights? For example, we all have the right to say what we think and adults should listen to us and take us seriously. And we have the right to get together with our friends in public (if we respect the rights of other people and do not break the law).

But British children aren't taken seriously until they're 18. Too many adults think that we have nothing important to say and that we don't deserve equal rights. Here are some examples of discrimination against teenagers from my everyday life.

Every day I see signs on shop doors that say '2 children at a time', 'no school bags', or even 'no children unless they are with an adult'. Children must wait outside and watch adults going in and out of the shop in front of them. Then, when they go into the shop, they must leave their bag outside. It's so unfair. It doesn't matter if they have an expensive computer or tennis racket in the bag. It has to stay outside. If I want to meet my friends, I can't wait for them outside the shops or

the burger restaurant near my house. Why? Because there is that horrible 'mosquito' device.

The mosquito is a machine that makes a terrible noise that only teenagers can hear. It hurts our ears and shop owners use it to keep anti-social teenagers away. But the noise also keeps nice friendly teenagers away, people like me and my friends. In fact, teenage troublemakers are only a very small percentage of the youth population.

But did anyone think about the huge majority of young people who do not cause problems? I apply for a part-time job in a hotel. If I get the part-time job, I will get about £3 an hour because I am 16. But 18 to 21-year-olds get £4.60 an hour and workers who are over 22 get £5.52. So, we do the same jobs, but we earn less money. Is that fair?

This country is a democracy. Every day, MPs and town councillors make decisions that make a big difference to our lives. But, as a 16-year-old, I don't have the right to vote. I can leave home, get married, apply for a job, be a soldier and fight for my country, but I can't vote to change the government. Why should political parties care about our problems? Adults in this country should start to understand that we're old enough to help to improve things and that we have the right to be heard. ▲

a) *Match the sentence halves.*

1 Oliver says teenagers are only different because ...	*a* adults can't hear.
2 He thinks that too many adults think ...	*b* can't vote for a different government.
3 The mosquito makes a noise that ...	*c* they are younger than adults.
4 If Oliver gets a job, he will be paid ...	*d* that teenagers shouldn't have equal rights.
5 If they aren't happy about the situation, 16-year-olds ...	*e* listen to what young people have to say.
6 Oliver wants adults to ...	*f* less money than older workers.

b) *Oliver thinks that teenagers are discriminated against. Find examples for his point of view in the article.*

3 Now you

a) *Discuss with a partner: Have you ever been in a situation when you thought you were discriminated against as a teenager? Say*
– where you were
– what you were doing
– what happened and why
– how you felt and why.

more help ► *D p. 108*

► *SF Having a discussion (p. 139)*

b) *Write to Oliver and comment on his article.*

more help ► *D p. 108*

Hi Oliver
I liked/didn't like your article. You say that ...
I agree/disagree. I think that ...

► *SF Writing course (pp. 141–142)* • **Text File 4** *(pp. 118–121)*

P1 WORDS Have your say

a) //O *Copy this chart and complete the words and phrases from this unit.* ▸ D p. 109

Issues	Sources of information	Action you can take
the env - - - - - - - t	bl - - s	buy fair-t - - - - pro - - - - s
fair p - -	online news s - - - s	start an on - - - e cam - - - - -
dis - - - - - - - - - - n	ta - k to fr - - - - s	go on a dem - - - - - - - - - n

b) *Compare your charts and add more words. Here are some ideas:*

child poverty • email a local newspaper • equal rights • join an online group • make posters • radio • youth clubs • ...

c) *Make appointments with three partners. Tell each partner:*
- what issues you care about most
- what sources of information you use most
- what kinds of action you take.

P2 VIEWING The mosquito: An anti-teenager device!

a) *Before you watch the news report: What is the mosquito device?*

b) *Look at the stills from the news report and try to guess the answers to these questions:*
1 Who will the reporter speak to?
2 What will they say?

c) *Watch the news report. Were your ideas in b) right?*

d) *Watch again and answer the questions in the box below.*

1 Where did the idea for the device come from?
A Canada B Great Britain C the US
2 The mosquito can be heard by ...
A little kids, teenagers and dogs.
B teenagers and dogs.
C teenagers.
3 Which of these comments was not made by the teenagers in the report?
A It's disgusting.
B It's really bad for our ears.
C I can't hear it.
4 Why is Riverside Elementary School using the mosquito?
A To stop teenagers who bully little kids.
B To stop teenagers who hang around outside the school and drink.
C To make sure that students leave school quickly at the end of the day.
5 How does one dad use the mosquito with his daughter?
A To call her on the phone.
B To tell her to come inside.
C To wake her up.

e) **Extra** *After watching this report, what do you think about the mosquito device?*

P3 REVISION Will the mosquito device keep troublemakers away? (*will*-future)

a) //○ *Tom and Jill are thinking about using the mosquito outside their shop. Tom thinks it's a good idea, but Jill thinks it's a bad idea. Complete their arguments with* **will** *and* **won't**. ▸ D p. 109

Tom (for the mosquito)

1 The mosquito ... keep troublemakers away.
2 Our customers ... feel safer.
3 More people ... come and shop here.
4 With the mosquito there ... be big groups of teenagers outside the shop.
5 We ... have to pick up their rubbish outside our shop.

Jill (against the mosquito)

6 The mosquito ... stop troublemakers.
7 They ... just go somewhere else and cause trouble.
8 The noise ... annoy all young people.
9 Teenagers ... shop here any more.
10 Teenagers ... have a safe place to meet parents or friends.

▸ *GF 5: Talking about the future (p. 155)*

b) *Act out the dialogue between Jill and Tom.*
▸ *SF Having a discussion (p. 139)*

c) *What do you think about using the mosquito outside your school?*
I think we should/shouldn't use the mosquito at our school because it will/won't ...

P4 Extra ● SPEAKING Role play: A discussion about video cameras at school

There are problems with smoking, vandalism, graffiti and bullying at school. The head teacher wants to install video cameras outside the school and in the corridors and classrooms. There is a meeting to discuss this question:
Will video cameras make the school a cleaner and safer place?

a) *Decide who takes the role of moderator. The rest of the class makes five groups.*

Moderator

Your job is to make sure that everyone has their say and to keep the discussion going. Don't give your own opinion.
- *Go to p. 100.*
- *Read through your role card and practise the phrases quietly.*

Other students

- *Go to p. 100*
- *Each group, choose a role card and think of arguments (and examples to support them).*
- *Make notes.*
- *Remember phrases you can use in a discussion.*

▸ *SF Having a discussion (p. 139)*

b) *Have the discussion. You could use the fishbowl method.*

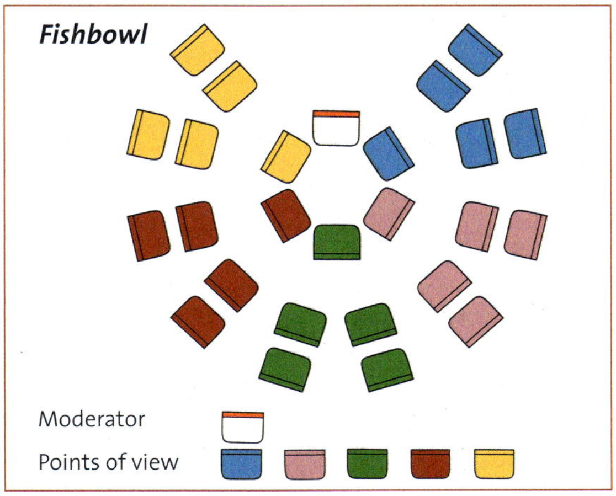

c) *Which side had the better arguments? Vote in class.*

d) *Write a short text: Should there be video cameras at your school? You can put your text in your DOSSIER.*

▸ *SF From outline to written discussion (p. 146)*

SPEAKING OUT

A class debate (Adapted from the novel *Speak* by Laurie Halse Anderson)

Speak is a novel about Melinda, who learns that it is important to speak out. In this text Melinda, the narrator of the story, describes a History class.

> *When you read the story, don't stop for every difficult word. You don't need to understand every word to understand the story. If the word is important, try to guess its meaning. If that doesn't work, use a dictionary.*
> ▸ *SF Working out the meaning of words (p. 134)* • *SF Reading English texts (p. 136)*

Mr Neck storms into class. He is very angry. We sit down quickly and quietly. I'm sure he's going to explode.

IMMIGRATION. He writes it on the board.

Mr Neck: "My family has been in this country for over two hundred years. We built this place, fought in every war, paid taxes, and voted. So tell me why my son can't get a job."

A few hands go up. Mr Neck ignores them. It isn't a real question, it's one he asked so that he could give the answer. I relax.

His son wanted to be a firefighter, but didn't get the job. Mr Neck says we should close our borders so that real Americans can get jobs.

I concentrate on trying to draw a pine tree.

Mr Neck writes on the board again: "DEBATE: America should have closed her borders in 1900." That gets a reaction. I can see kids counting on their fingers, trying to figure out if their grandparents or great-grandparents came to America before or after 1900. When they figure out that they might now be in a country that hates them, or a place with no schools, or a place with no future, they put up their hands. They do not agree with Mr Neck.

I don't know where my family came from. I don't know how long we've been in America. I start drawing an apple tree.

The arguments jump across the room. A few kids quickly figure out which side Mr Neck is on, so they fight to throw out the "foreigners". The kids from families who arrived in America after 1900 talk about how hard their families have worked, what they do for the country and the taxes that they pay. One student tries to say that we are all foreigners and we should give the country back to the Native Americans, but most people disagree loudly with this idea.

Mr Neck enjoys the noise, until one brave kid says: "Maybe your son didn't get that job because he's not good enough. Or he's lazy. Or the other guy was better than him, no matter what his skin color. I think that some white people don't know how to work – they've had it too easy."

The supporters of immigration clap and cheer.

Mr Neck: "Be careful, mister. You are talking about my son. I don't want to hear any more from you. That's enough debate – get your books out."

The Neck is back in control. I concentrate on my tree again. Then David Petrakis stands up. The class stops talking. I put my pencil down.

Mr Neck: "Sit down, Mr Petrakis."

David Petrakis is a smart boy. He's never in trouble. What is he thinking? Has he gone crazy?

David: "If the class is debating, then each student has the right to say what he thinks."

Mr Neck: "I decide who talks in here."

David: "You started a debate. You can't stop it just because it is not going your way."

Mr Neck: "Sit down, Mr Petrakis."

David: "In this country you don't have different classes of citizenship based on how long you've lived here. I am a citizen, with the same rights as your son, or you. As a citizen, and as a student, I say that this lesson is racist, intolerant and xenophobic."

Mr Neck: "Sit your butt in that chair, Petrakis, and watch your mouth! I try to start a debate and you people turn it into a race thing. Sit down or you're going to the principal."

David stares at Mr Neck, looks at the flag for a minute, then picks up his books and walks out of the room. He says a million things without saying a word. I make a note to study David Petrakis.

Working with the text

1 Telling the story with pictures

a) ☐ *Put the pictures in the correct order.*

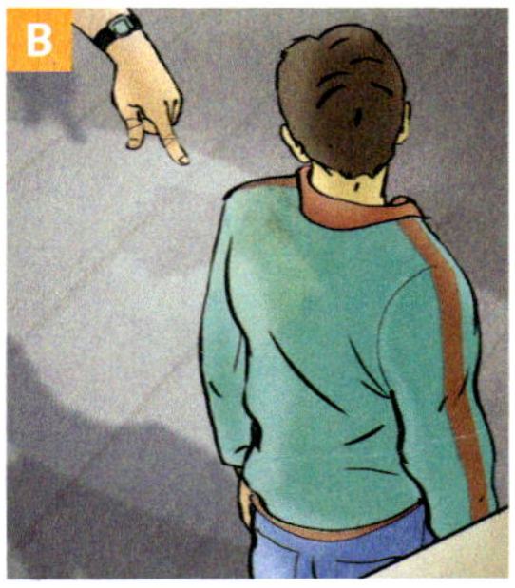

b) *Find lines from the text that match each of the pictures.*

2 // ☐ The summary ▸ D p. (p. 109)

Complete the text with words from the box.

agree • before • debate • firefighter • immigration • racist

At the start, Mr Neck is angry because his son can't get a job as a (1) ... He thinks that (2) ... should stop so that 'real Americans' can get jobs. For him, real Americans are people who came to America (3) ... 1900. He stops the (4) ... when a boy says that maybe his son is too lazy or not good enough for the job. David says that the teacher can't just stop the debate when he doesn't (5) ... with the things others say. David says that the lesson is (6) ..., picks up his books and leaves the room.

3 The characters

a) *Say how you think Mr Neck and David feel when ...*

- Mr Neck comes into the room. (ll. 4–6)
- Mr Neck stops the debate. (ll. 52–55)
- David stands up and speaks. (ll. 57–65)

angry • annoyed • bored • brave • calm • excited • fed up • nervous • proud • sad • scared • shocked • shy • surprised • unhappy • upset • ...

b) ● *Say why you think the characters act or feel that way.*

▸ SF Drawing conclusions (p. 135)

4 Extra VIEWING *Speak*

Watch the film version of the classroom scene. Are the characters as you expected?

▸ Text File 5 (pp. 122–123)

P1 WRITING Should young drivers be banned from driving at night?

a) *Some people want to ban drivers under 25 from driving after 10 pm. What's your first reaction to this idea?*
I think it's an interesting/crazy/... idea.

b) *Listen to the radio programme. Are the callers for or against banning young drivers after 10 pm?*

	for	against
Jon		✓
Jess		
Keira		
Grace		

c) *Listen again and complete these statements.*

1 Young drivers have more ... than other drivers.
2 Too many young people drive fast and do ... things.
3 It's a great idea because it would stop the idiots that ... too much.
4 Banning young drivers would save ... for police and hospitals.
5 Girls are more ... drivers than boys.
6 What about all the people who work at ...? They sometimes need to drive.
7 Some adults are ... drivers too.

d) *Imagine German politicians want to ban drivers under 25 from driving after 10 pm. Email your English friend and say what you think about the idea and why. Write at least 120 words.*

Tip

1 Collect ideas for arguments (for or against). You can use ideas from the radio debate in c).
2 Look up useful words and phrases for giving your opinion.

► *SF From outline to written discussion (p. 146)*

P2 MEDIATION The rules for alcohol

Your family is visiting the US. Your parents want to know about the rules for alcohol there. Read this online article and answer your parents' questions in German.

– Gelten überall in den USA dieselben Regeln?
– Wo kann man Alkohol kaufen?
– Wie sollte man sich verhalten?

In the US the rules for alcohol are decided by the individual states and bars close at different times in different cities. Some parts of the US are still 'dry'. This means that there are some places where you cannot buy alcohol at all. In some states you can only buy alcohol in special shops, called ABC (Alcohol and Beverage Control) stores.
You cannot drink alcohol in public. Taking a beer out of a bar onto the sidewalk is illegal in most states. Walking down the street with a beer will get you into trouble with the police. Since 1984, it has been illegal in all states in the US for people under 21 to buy alcohol or to drink alcohol in public. Even if you are a grey-haired old lady, you often have to show an official document (for example, a driving licence or a passport) that shows your picture and your birth date if you want to buy alcohol.
Many people in the US think the alcohol rules are unfair because young people are seen as adults in most other areas of life. 18- to 20-year-olds can get married, have children, buy cars, homes and guns, but they can't drink a glass of wine in a restaurant, or even a glass of champagne at their own wedding.

► *SF Mediation (p. 147)*

P3 SPEAKING Solving conflicts

a) *Choose boxes with phrases to ...*

1 start a conversation
2 name a problem
3 disagree that there is a problem
4 say that you're sorry
5 end a conflict.

A
– What annoys me is ...
– I don't like the way you ...
– The problem is ...

B
– I don't see what's wrong with ...
– Where's the problem?

C
– Don't worry about it.
– OK. No worries.

D
– Can I have a word with you?
– Excuse me, but ...

E
– I'm sorry, I didn't mean to ...
– I'm sorry, I didn't know ...

b) *Look at these two dialogues between people at a youth hostel. Complete them with phrases from a).*

Fin Mia, (1) ...?
Mia Yes, of course.
Fin Er ... Your perfume – it's very strong!
Mia Great, isn't it? It was from my boyfriend.
Fin Well, (2) ... that it isn't great for me. Can you stop using it please?
Mia Sorry, but (3) ... it. Are you crazy?
Fin I just have problems with perfume. It hurts my eyes and my skin goes red. And we share a room, so I can't sleep.
Mia Oh dear. Of course I'll stop using it. (4) ... it had that effect on you.
Fin (5) ... And thanks.

Ali (1) ... did you use my shampoo?
PJ Oh yeah. I forgot mine, so I used yours.
Ali OK, but (2) ... that you've used it all.
PJ There's still some in the bottle, so (3) ...?
Ali Yeah, there's a bit in the bottle, but not much. And (4) ... you didn't ask me first.
PJ But you weren't there. Anyway, (5) ... use so much. It was an accident.
Ali (6) ... It does come out of the bottle very quickly.
PJ Yes, it does. But I'll buy you some more later, OK?

c) *Listen and check your answers in b).*

d) *Choose one of these situations or use your own ideas. Make a dialogue.*

more help ▸ D p. 110

1 WORDS Getting involved

Choose the right word to complete each sentence.

1 We have decided/described to do something against plans to close our youth club.
2 At a meeting last week, the club leader got up and made a chat/speech about what we should do.
3 Then he opened/talked the discussion.
4 Lots of people had a chance[1] to speak/have their say.
5 Some people thought we should raise/grow money for the club.
6 I had the idea to elect/organize a jumble sale.
7 We also decided to go on a journey/demonstration through the town centre.
8 I'm sure the politicians will listen to us because we'll soon be old enough to spend/vote in elections!

2 Are you going to work in the holidays? (*going to*-future)

a) *Act out this dialogue with a partner.*

Meg Are you going to work this summer?
Con Yes. I'm going to be a waiter.
Meg Oh, really? Where are you going to work?
Con In the big hotel near the station. Next year I'm going to look for an apprenticeship as a cook so I want some experience in a restaurant. What about you?
Meg I want to spend two weeks in Spain with my family. But I'm going to look for a job when I get back.
Con Spain? Fantastic! How long are you going to stay there?
Meg For two weeks. And this year I'm going to be very lazy. I'm not going to go sightseeing. I'm going to sit on the beach and relax.
Con Mm! That sounds great! And what kind of job are you going to look for?
Meg Well, I'm not going to work inside, that's for sure. I'm going to look for a job in the open air.

b) *Talk to your partner about your plans for the holidays. Use the going to-future.*

▸ *GF 5: Talking about the future (p. 155)*

3 EVERYDAY ENGLISH What are we going to do tomorrow?

Joe and Liam are making plans. Put Joe's ideas into the correct order to complete the dialogue.

Liam What are we going to do tomorrow?
Joe *(D) Let's ...*
Liam But what if it rains? I think we should do something inside. Why don't we go to the cinema?
Joe ...
Liam What about that Australian comedy?
Joe ...
Liam It starts at 3.30. We could meet there at 3.
Joe ...
Liam That's fine. I'll see you there. Don't be late!

A Good idea ... Do you know what time it starts?

B That's a bit early for me. Is 3.15 OK?

C Oh yes. Let's do that. But which film are we going to watch?

D Let's go to the park and play football.

[1] chance *Gelegenheit; Möglichkeit*

4 READING Which event? (Drawing conclusions)

a) *Read the information about Lily and then read about the two events. Which event is more suitable for Lily? Give reasons.*
Event ... is suitable for Lily because she ...
Event ... is not suitable for Lily because she ...

About Lily
Lily, 17, wants to get involved in helping animals. As a student she has very little money and spends most of it on her dog.

Tip
In the texts, look for reasons why the event is suitable or not suitable. Then choose an event for Lily.

EVENT 1

RSPCA[1] Christmas Event
Are you a dog owner who would like to help animals in trouble? Why don't you buy a decoration[2] for the RSPCA Christmas tree? We will put your dog's picture in the decoration and hang it from our tree in December. The decorations aren't cheap, but your money will help to pay for vets to look after homeless, sick animals.

EVENT 2

RSPCA Volunteer Information Day
Volunteering with the RSPCA is a great way to meet people who share your love of animals. As a volunteer you'll have the chance to look after animals in trouble. Come to Volunteer Information Day and hear other volunteers talk about their experience. Anyone between the ages of 16 and 70 can be a volunteer.

► *SF Drawing conclusions (p. 135)*

b) *Read the information about Ella and Adam. Then read about the three events. Which event is most suitable for Ella and which is most suitable for Adam? Give reasons.*
Ella should choose event ... because there she can ...
Adam is interested in ... so event ... is the most suitable for him.

About Ella
Ella works in a supermarket, but would love to be a gardener. Hobbies: action films, hiking

About Adam
Adam is a biology student. He's very interested in global warming. Hobbies: singing, acting

EVENT 1

Film and discussion

Earth 2100 is a documentary that explores how our world might look at the start of the next century if we do not start to fight climate change now. The film, based on the latest research, also shows ways of creating[3] a different future.

EVENT 2

Queen's Park project week

Act now to create a greener and more beautiful public space. The Friends of Queen's Park's spring project needs volunteers with green fingers who can help to clean up after the long winter. A chance to practise your garden skills and maybe get a few tips from the experts.

EVENT 3

Westport Lake clean-up

On World Environment Day this year we are going to walk around Westport Lake and collect all the rubbish that we can find. Come and help us … and bring your kids too. Remember: If children never get to know their environment, they'll never learn to love and protect it.

▶ *You could now do tasks 1 and 2 in the Practice test on pp. 59–60.*

[1] RSPCA (= Royal Society for the Prevention of Cruelty to Animals) *britischer Tierschutzverein* [2] (Christmas) decoration *(Christbaum-)Schmuck*
[3] (to) create sth. *etwas entwerfen/gestalten*

5 WORDS Paraphrasing

If you can't think of an English word, you can paraphrase it.

a) *Read the paraphrases below. Then find the matching picture.*

1 It is something that shows that you are allowed to drive a car or a motorbike.

2 It is somebody who interviews guests in a live discussion or a talkshow on TV.

3 It is a place where people can go if they need advice on topics like rights, jobs, immigration, flats ...

A citizens' advice bureau

B driving licence

C (chat-show) host

b) *Match the sentence halves to paraphrase the German words in the box.*

Abgeordnete(r) • Comicfigur • Partei • Untertitel • Ziel

1 A 'Ziel' is something that ...
2 A 'Comicfigur' is a funny drawing of a person (or an animal) that ...
3 'Untertitel' are words at the bottom of a screen that ...
4 An 'Abgeordneter' is somebody who ...

a ... represents you in parliament.
b ... you really want to be able to do in your life.
c ... help you to understand a film in a foreign language.
d ... you can find in magazines, comics or cartoon films.

► *SF Paraphrasing (p. 140)*

6 READING What does it mean? (Working out the meaning of words)

a) *How can you work out the meaning of the* **green** *words in the box? Make a copy of the chart and write down the* **green** *words under the right headings. Sometimes there is more than one way to work out what a word means.*

1 The German word is similar	2 I know part of the word	3 The context helps
opposition ...	...	...

1 If politicians want to improve their **popularity**, maybe they should try to be more interesting.
2 The government party lost the election and went into **opposition**.
3 Parliament doesn't **sit** during the summer.
4 The South-East is the richest **region** in the UK.
5 The youngest candidate for the UKYP election wants free **collections** for any rubbish that can be recycled.

b) *Compare your results with a partner.*

Opposition is the same in German.

► *SF Working out the meaning of words (p. 134)*

1 READING Events

Three teenagers are looking at a youth club notice board for events that would be suitable for them.

Read the teenagers' statements and the descriptions of the events. Then decide which event would be best for each person. Copy the names and write the correct letter next to each name.

Ben: I can't imagine living anywhere else. I love the fresh salt air and the little harbours with their colourful boats. The problem is that lots of day tourists from big cities come here. And many of them make a mess because they don't tidy up after their picnics.

Jill: I live 15 miles from the next town and I'm too young to drive. I can now get home by bus on Saturday nights – thanks to our protests. But public transport is still too expensive.

Megan: I have lots of different rights. But I'm still 'too young' to choose the person who represents me in Parliament. Something has to be done to improve this situation.

A

Beach clean-up weekend
Once again local clubs are being asked to come to the beach (meet at North Bay) on Saturday or Sunday to help to tidy it up after the summer. Please come and join us. Wear gloves[1], bring plastic bags and give a few hours of your time for our most popular place.

B

Teen rights, OK?
Local citizens' advice bureau[2] worker Diane Fry explains what young people can and can't do. Find out about your rights and responsibilities[3] in many areas: voting, working, cheaper travel tickets, drinking, smoking, driving, passports, boyfriends, girlfriends, etc.
Sunday, 10 am

C

Demonstration in front of Town Hall
Young people over 14 pay as much as adults on our local buses – a problem if you need the bus to get out at weekends. It's a £6 bus ride to and from the cinemas and clubs in and around Canterbury.
Join our demonstration in front of the town hall.
Saturday, 2 pm

[1] gloves *Handschuhe* [2] citizens' advice bureau *Bürgerberatungsstelle* [3] responsibilities *Pflichten*

2 MEDIATION An advertisement

Du willst im Sommer in Großbritannien arbeiten und hast die folgende Anzeige online gefunden. Um deine Eltern von deinem Plan zu überzeugen, mach dir Notizen auf Deutsch zu den folgenden Punkten:

– was deine Hauptaufgabe sein wird
– welche Voraussetzungen du unbedingt mitbringen solltest
– wo du wohnen wirst
– was du verdienen wirst.

Torbay International Youth Camp is looking for …

➢ ***Service team volunteers***

Your main job will be to
- organize activities for young people from all over the world

You will also be responsible for
- helping in the dining room during meals

You must be
- between 17 and 20 years old
- able to communicate with 11- to 15-year-olds
- energetic

It will be an advantage if you
- have experience of working with young people
- can speak at least one foreign language
- have a driving licence[1]

We offer you
- a free room in our international village
- breakfast and two hot meals a day
- £25 pocket money per week

Interested? Apply online

3 MEDIATION Helping a visitor to Germany

Your Scottish friend, Maggie, is staying with you. She needs to find out about politics in Germany for a school project. You find an event in the newspaper. Maggie is not at home and you have to leave before she returns. Write a short message in English to Maggie. In your message, tell her

– where the event is
– what you can watch
– what else you can do
– what time it starts.

Hi Maggie
I've found an event at the youth club in Böllstraße that you might be interested in.
You can watch a …

Mit Cartoons in die Politik einsteigen

Wir werden eine DVD zeigen, die die Ziele der im Deutschen Bundestag vertretenen politischen Parteien mit Cartoons illustriert. Comicfiguren und lustige Zeichnungen erklären unterschiedliche Bereiche der Politik wie zum Beispiel Bildung und Gesundheit.
Der Film dauert ca. 45 Minuten und hat englische Untertitel.

Was noch?
- Anschließend werden wir Probleme zum Thema „Bildung und Schule" diskutieren.
  Gastgeber: Tom Meyer
  Gäste: Abgeordnete der fünf großen Parteien
- Danach gibt's Livemusik von Poll Position.

Wann und wo?
Freitag, 19.30, Jugendzentrum, Böllstraße 22

[1] driving licence *Führerschein*

4 READING Notices, short adverts and signs

Read each short text. Then decide if the statements below are true or false.

Need a weekend job?

We're looking for a reliable and friendly student to help out with selling snacks in our sandwich bar on Saturdays and/or Sundays. You must be 16 or older and have a clean and tidy appearance.
You will earn £8 an hour.
For more information, come in and talk to the manager.

They're watching you
There are over 4 million video cameras (CCTV) in Britain. They're watching you in the street, in shops, at railway stations, everywhere. Find out more on Panorama next Monday at 8.30 pm on BBC 1.

How well can you drive?
The RoSPA[1] Young Driver Assessment will tell you how good a driver you are. The assessment is for drivers between 17 and 24, and can be taken six months or more after passing the driving test[2].

Trip to the Houses of Parliament

Newton Youth Forum is organizing a special day trip to London, where our local MP Mike Worth will take us on a two-hour tour of the Houses of Parliament.

Tour starts: May 5th, 8.45 am
Departure from: Newton Station
Cost: £5 per person (Forum members pay only £3)
Return to Newton: 6.30 pm

More information and booking:
www.newtonyouthforum.org.uk

1 The sandwich bar needs someone to tidy up.
2 If you're interested in the job in the sandwich bar, you should go and see the manager.
3 RoSPA helps young people to pass the driving test.
4 Only good drivers can do the RoSPA Young Driver Assessment.
5 The Newton Youth Forum trip to London starts at the Houses of Parliament.
6 If you go on the trip to London, you will return to Newton the same day.
7 Members of Newton Youth Forum have to pay £3 for the trip to London.
8 The BBC TV programme about CCTV cameras is on in the morning.

[1] RoSPA (Royal Society for the Prevention of Accidents) *britische Gesellschaft zur Förderung der Straßensicherheit* [2] (to) pass a test *eine Prüfung bestehen*

5 READING A news report

Read the text and do the tasks below.

Sunderland votes in UKYP election

Over 16,000 young people will be able to vote in the Sunderland region in this year's election to the UK Youth Parliament (UKYP). Voting at 55 schools will take place over 7 days from 26th February.

> UKYP is an organization that allows young people between the ages of 11 and 18 to have their say. There are no parties and no government or opposition. The 600 Members of Youth Parliament (MYPs) from all over the UK come together to debate and to organize campaigns for change. An MYP can sit in the UK Youth Parliament and in regional youth parliaments.

This year, 22 candidates are standing for election in the Sunderland area, more than ever before. On 5th March, the names of the four winners will be published. We spoke with a few of the candidates.

The youngest, 11-year-old Will Black from West Windon Primary School, wants free recycling at all schools. 'At the moment, schools have to pay for the collection of all rubbish. We should have free collections for anything that can be recycled. Then schools would have a reason to recycle as much as possible.'

Barbara McKenzie, 16, from St Ambrose School for Girls, believes public transport for students should be cheaper. 'Young people need to be mobile, but they can't afford to pay the full ticket price for buses and trains while they're at school. We should only have to pay half of what adults pay.'

The oldest candidate in this year's election , 17-year-old Jack Smith, says that there aren't enough places for young people. 'There isn't a suitable place for music concerts in the area. The places we can use are too small, or they aren't free when we need them.'

Jack, from Rosebrook Technology College, said: 'There's so much negative stuff about young people in the media, but many of us are working hard to change the situation.'

a) *True, false or not in the text?*

1 The article is about the results of the Youth Parliament elections.

2 Adults vote in Youth Parliament elections.

3 Members of Youth Parliament are called MYPs.

4 Sunderland is the biggest region in the UK.

b) *Read the tasks (1–4) and decide which answer (A – C) is correct.*

1 How many people from Sunderland will be elected to the UK Youth parliament?
- A 4
- B 22
- C 55

2 Will Black wants schools to pay ...
- A nothing for all rubbish.
- B as much as possible for all rubbish.
- C nothing for rubbish that can be recycled.

3 In Barbara's opinion, who should pay less for public transport?
- A everyone
- B students
- C all young people

4 Jack Smith would like ...
- A cheaper concerts.
- B more places for concerts.
- C more big bands to play concerts in the area.

How am I doing?

Im Practice test *konntest du einige Aufgaben ausprobieren, die dir in einer zukünftigen Abschlussprüfung begegnen könnten. Wenn Du Probleme bei einzelnen Testaufgaben hattest, können dir die folgenden Fragen helfen herauszufinden, was du üben musst.*

1 Wie leicht oder schwer waren die Aufgaben?

	leicht	ging so	ziemlich schwer	sehr schwer
Task 1				
Task 2				
[illegible]				

Reading (Tasks 1, 4, 5)

1 Was war schwer bei den Leseaufgaben?

a) Einige der Texte waren recht lang und/oder kompliziert.
b) Es gab Wörter und Wendungen, die ich einfach nicht verstanden habe.
c) Es gab sehr viele Informationen in den Texten. Ich konnte manchmal nicht die richtigen Antworten finden.
d) Die Aufgabenstellungen waren anders als die, die wir sonst im Unterricht hatten.

2 Probleme mit speziellen Aufgaben:

Task 1
– Ich habe die meisten Texte verstanden, aber es war trotzdem schwer, die Informationen zu finden, die ich brauchte, um Personen und Ereignisse einander zuzuordnen.

Task 4
– Die Mischung unterschiedlicher Textarten (z. B. *notices, ads, signs*) machte es schwer, sich auf den Inhalt zu konzentrieren.
– Ich war nicht immer sicher, welcher der Texte die Information enthielt, die ich zum Lösen der Aufgabe benötigte.

Task 5
– Der Zeitungsartikel war schwer zu lesen.
– Die Mischung der Aufgabentypen *(true/false/not in the text, multiple choice)* machte es schwieriger, die Antworten zu finden.

3 Wie hast du die Aufgaben gelöst?

a) Zuerst habe ich die Aufgaben aufmerksam gelesen, damit ich genau wusste, wonach ich in den Texten suchen sollte.
b) Ich habe zuerst versucht, die Hauptgedanken eines jeden Textes zu verstehen. Das hat mir geholfen, Wörter und Wendungen, über deren Bedeutung ich mir nicht sicher war, zu erschließen.
c) Wenn ich eine ganz bestimmte Information brauchte, habe ich die Texte mithilfe von *Scanning* durchsucht.
e) Wenn ich mir bei einer Aufgabe nicht sicher war, habe ich sie ausgelassen und bin später zu ihr zurückgekommen.
f) Ich habe meine Antworten am Schluss überprüft und alle Fehler, die mir auffielen, korrigiert.

▸ *SF Reading course (pp. 134–135)*

Mediation (Tasks 2, 3)

Bitte deine Lehrkraft um eine Kopie des Assessment Sheets *und fülle diese aus.*

	Assessment sheet	☹		😐		☺	
	Name ...	**1**	**2**	**3**	**4**	**5**	**Comments**
2	a) Es fiel mir leicht, Notizen zum englischen Text auf Deutsch zu machen.						
2	b) In meinen Notizen habe ich mich auf die wichtigsten Informationen beschränkt und nicht Wort für Wort übersetzt.						
2	c) Ich habe Informationen zu allen wichtigen Punkten gefunden und gegeben.						
3	d) Ich fand es leicht, einen deutschen Text als Grundlage für das Schreiben einer englischen Nachricht zu nutzen.						
3	e) In meiner Nachricht habe ich nur die wichtigsten Informationen über die Veranstaltung gegeben (*when, where, what*). Ich habe nicht Wort für Wort übersetzt.						
3	f) Ich habe kurze, einfache Sätze geschrieben.						
3	g) Wenn ich ein wichtiges Wort nicht in Englisch kannte, habe ich versucht, es zu umschreiben oder ein ähnliches Wort/eine ähnliche Wendung zu benutzen.						

▶ *You will find more READING and MEDIATION tasks in the Exam File, pp. 90–96.*

English for jobs

Das Kapitel **English for jobs** bereitet dich auf Situationen in deinem zukünftigen Berufsalltag vor, in denen du Englisch brauchst.

Du verfolgst den beruflichen Werdegang von zwei englischen Jugendlichen von der Bewerbung über den damit verbundenen Schriftverkehr und das Vorstellungsgespräch bis hin zu verschiedenen Situationen am Arbeitsplatz.

Anhand realistischer Situationen wie z. B. dienstliche Telefonate, Kundengespräche oder Präsentationen von Produkten kannst du auf den folgenden Seiten wichtige Wörter und Wendungen für den englischsprachigen Arbeitsalltag auffrischen, ergänzen und anwenden.

EFJ 1 1 Two personal statements

Sarah Dee and Nat Wilde finish school this year.

Read the list of strengths (1–8) below. Listen and write N (for Nat) or S (for Sarah) in your exercise book. Example: 1 S

1 can explain technology
2 loves travelling
3 can speak foreign languages
4 likes working in a team
5 likes music
6 is organized
7 is reliable
8 is good at helping people

2 Company websites

a) *Read the job information below. Look at your answers in 1 and decide which company Sarah and Nat should apply to.*

GHC Health

GHC is a private health care service[1] with 37 old people's homes in the UK. We are looking for care assistants who are able to travel around the country and help out when a colleague[2] is ill or on holiday. A perfect job for those who like to help others.

Send in your CV with a letter of application.

WOW ELECTRONICS

Imagine working for an exciting company with first-class training programmes to support you. The UK's number one electronics store is looking for new sales assistants[3]. You work well in a team? You like good service and contact with customers? You can explain how a camera or an MP3 player works? You're looking for a career? Then send in your CV and a letter of application.

SAYGO CAREERS

Welcome to Saygo's careers website. With 15,000 employees[4] in the UK and abroad[5], we're Britain's big player in the holiday industry. We offer jobs in our UK offices and at our holiday destinations[6] abroad. At Saygo we work to make our customers' dreams come true.
If you'd like to join us, why not send in your CV and a letter of application?

b) *Explain your decision to your partner.*

3 A letter of application

Complete Sarah's letter of application with the phrases from the box below.

A I will finish school in ...
B I would like to apply for a job as a ...
C I am good at working in a ...
D I am interested in ...
E I am writing to you about ...

► SF Writing formal and informal letters (p. 145)

Dear Sir or Madam

... (1) the careers that you offer on your company website. ... (2) sales assistant.

I am 17 years old and ... (3) June this year. I am a helpful person and ... (4) team. ... (5) technology and I like explaining how things work to people.

I look forward to hearing from you.

Yours faithfully

Sarah Dee

[1] health care service *Gesundheitspflegedienst* [2] colleague *Kollege/Kollegin* [3] sales assistant *Fachverkäufer/in* [4] employee *Angestellte/r*
[4] abroad *das/im Ausland* [5] holiday destination *Urlaubsziel*

EFJ 2 1 Accepting[2] an invitation

Sarah has been invited to an interview.

WOW ELECTRONI

Ms Sarah Dee
12 Hallow Road
Redhill RH1 6DF

Dear Ms Dee

Thank you for your letter of application. We would like to invite you to an interview at our office in Brighton in the week 14th–18th June. Please let us know which date works better for you.

Train and bus connections to Brighton are excellent. If you like, we can help you to plan your trip.

We plan to interview ten candidates each day, and there will be a chance for group discussions during lunch in our canteen.

We look forward to hearing from you, if possible by e-mail to the address below.

Yours sincerely

Petra Pym
pym@wow.co.uk

a) *Sarah would like to travel to the interview by car. She doesn't eat meat. Read the letter from WOW Electronics. Which of these questions will she need to ask?*

1 What time will the interview take place?
2 Is it possible to use public transport?
3 Are there car parking facilities?
4 Will there be a meal?
5 Does the canteen serve vegetarian meals?

b) *Put the sentences from Sarah's e-mail to Petra Pym in a suitable order.*

- It will be interesting to meet other candidates during lunch.
- Dear Ms Pym
- I would like to travel to Brighton by car.
- Yours sincerely Sarah Dee
- Can you tell me if your canteen offers vegetarian food?
- Please let me know when I should arrive at your office.
- Thank you for your letter of 25th May.
- Is there a car park near your office?
- I can come for an interview on Wednesday 16th June.
- I look forward to meeting you.

c) *Compare your e-mail with a partner.*

2 Agreeing on details

27th May

Dear Ms Dee

Thank you for your e-mail of 26th May. I saw that you can come for an interview on Wed.16th June. Would you like an interview at 9.30 am or 2.30 pm? If you choose the afternoon interview, please arrive in time for lunch at 12.15 pm.

I am afraid we do not have car parking facilities for candidates. It would probably be easier to come to Brighton by train or bus. If you decide to do this we can book your tickets for you.
I am happy to say that our canteen offers vegetarian dishes too.
I look forward to meeting you.

Yours sincerely
Petra Pym

Read Petra Pym's e-mail. Then complete Sarah's answer with words from the box.

Yours • travel • forward • book • Dear • email • sure • ticket • interview • lunch • train

… Ms Pym

Thank you for your …
I would prefer an … at 2.30 pm and will make … that I arrive by 12.15. I have decided to … Brighton by … I would be very happy if you could … my … as you offered in your e-mail.
I am very glad that you can arrange a vegetarian … for me. Many thanks. I look … to meeting you and the other candidates.

… sincerely
Sarah Dee

[1] (to) make arrangements *Vereinbarungen treffen* [2] (to) accept (an invitation) *(eine Einladung) annehmen*

EFJ 3

1 Giving good answers

***a)** How should Nat answer Ms Wood's questions? Choose A or B.*

Nat has been invited to an interview too. It takes place today ...

Ms Wood Hello, nice to meet you, Nat. My name is Polly Wood.
Nat A Hello Ms Wood. Nice to meet you. B Hi, Polly!
Ms Wood Well, Nat. Thank you for your interest in Saygo. Maybe you can tell me why you'd like to work for us.
Nat A Because travelling is really cool.
B Well, I really enjoy travelling and being in other countries.
Ms Wood Maybe you can say something about your strengths. What are you good at?
Nat A Well, I'm really brilliant at languages. And I'm just so organized and reliable.
B Well, I speak two foreign languages quite well. And I'm very organized and reliable.
Ms Wood If you worked for Saygo, you would have to look after tourists with questions or problems.
Nat A I hope they won't have too many problems!
B Problems are there to be solved. I think I can do that.
Ms Wood Of course, there would also be quite a lot of desk work to do.
Nat A I can imagine that. I'm very happy to do office work. B No worries, Ms Wood!

***b)** Compare your answers with a partner. Discuss (in German) why the other answers weren't so good.*

***c)** Read the rest of the interview. Say why Nat's answers aren't very good. Think of better answers.*

Ms Wood Do you have computer experience?
Nat Sure, I spend lots of time surfing the internet.
Ms Wood How soon would you be able to start if we offered you a job?
Nat I don't know. Maybe next month.
Ms Wood Why should we choose you?
Nat Why not?
Ms Wood Well, that's it. Thank you for coming. We'll call you soon. Goodbye.
Nat See you.

2 Now you: Role play

***a)** Put the sentences into the right order to make a dialogue for an interview.*

A Yes, when will I hear if I have got the job?

B We will contact you next week. Thank you for coming today.

C Hello. It's nice to meet you too.

D Thank you for your interest in this job. First, can you tell me about your strengths?

E Well, I'm a friendly, helpful person and I'm good at serving customers.

F OK. Do you have any questions?

G Hello, nice to meet you.

H Thank you. Goodbye.

I I stay calm and friendly. I tell one that I will be with them soon. Then I serve the other one quickly.

J I see. Now imagine that two customers want something from you at the same time. What do you do?

***b)** Act out the dialogue and then swap roles.*

EFJ 4

1 Leaving a message

a) *Sarah is phoning CX Computers. Put the sentences into the correct order to complete the conversation.*

Tim __ CX Computers. Tim speaking.
Sarah __ Hello, Tim. This is Sarah from WOW Electronics. Can you put me through[1] to Jane Parks, please?
Tim __ ...

S __ Thank you, Tim. Bye.
S __ 01705 – 4912214
T __ OK. That's great. Thanks.
S __ Can I leave a message?
T __ Yes, of course. Can you give me your last name, Sarah?
S __ Could you ask her to phone me when she has a moment?
T __ Yes, hold on[2], please. ... I'm sorry, Sarah, but Jane isn't answering her phone.
S __ Dee. I'll spell it. D double E.
T __ And your phone number?
T __ Sure, I'll get a pen ... OK, your message?

Sarah has started at WOW Electronics. Right now, she's making a phone call.

b) *Listen and check. Then practise the conversation. Use different names and phone numbers.*

2 More telephone phrases

a) *You will hear four short phone conversations. In which conversation do you hear the English phrases for these German ones?*

A Ich verbinde.
B Kann ich etwas ausrichten?
C Bleiben Sie am Apparat.
D Ich gebe Ihre Nachricht weiter.

b) *Listen again. Write down the phrases from a) in English. Compare with a partner.*

c) *Complete these short dialogues with the expressions from b) and practise them with your partner:*

1	Can you ask Mrs Parks to call me back?	- Yes, ... as soon as[3] I see him.
2	Is Adam in the office today, please?	- Yes, I'll ...
3	I'm sorry he's not here at the moment. ...	- Yes, please. Can you tell him that Jade called.
4	Can I speak to Joe Harris, please?	- Yes. ... I'll check if he's in the office.

3 Now you: Guided dialogue[4]

Prepare a dialogue and act it out.

Partner A: You get a call from a customer.
Partner B: You want to order something.

A: Grüße und nenne den Namen deiner Firma. →
B: Stelle dich vor. Sage, dass du Tim sprechen möchtest. ←
A: Sage, dass du B verbindest. →
B: Sage, dass du am Apparat bleibst. ←
A: Entschuldige dich: Tim antwortet nicht. →
B: Frage, ob Tim dich zurückrufen kann. Nenne deine Telefonnummer. ←
A: Wiederhole die Telefonnummer. Bitte B, ihren/seinen Nachnamen zu buchstabieren. →
B: Reagiere.

more help ▸ D p. 110

[1] (to) put sb. through *jn. durchstellen* [2] (to) hold on *am Apparat bleiben* [3] as soon as *sobald* [4] guided dialogue *gelenkter Dialog*

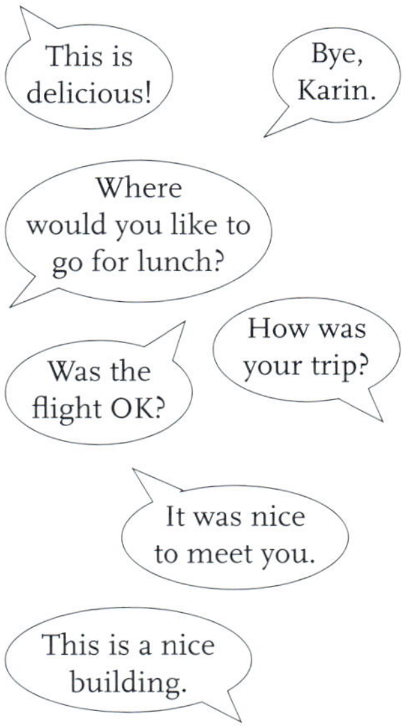

EFJ 5 1 Speaking to a visitor

Nat is working at Saygo's office in Malaga. Last week he had a meeting there with Karin Lang, from Saygo's German office.

This is delicious!

Bye, Karin.

Where would you like to go for lunch?

How was your trip?

Was the flight OK?

It was nice to meet you.

This is a nice building.

a) *Look at the sentences above. When are they used during the meeting? Complete a copy of the chart.*

Start of the meeting	Break for a meal	End of the meeting
Was the flight OK?	Where ...	...

b) *Listen and check. Then compare your chart with a partner.*

c) *Find phrases in the box that you can use when somebody*

1 thanks you
2 says sorry to you
3 says something you agree with.

Don't worry about it. • No problem. • Not at all.[1] • That's fine with me.[2] • That's OK. • That's true. • You're quite right. • You're welcome.

d) *Listen again and check. Then compare your answers with a partner.*

2 Now you: Guided dialogue

Prepare a dialogue and act it out.

Partner A: You work for a German company.	Partner B: You're a guest from abroad.
Grüße und frage, wie die Reise war. →	Beschreibe deine Reise. Sage, dass das Wetter heute sehr angenehm ist.
← Stimme zu. Biete B etwas zu trinken an. →	Bedanke dich.
← Reagiere. Frage, wann B essen möchte. →	Frage, ob 12.30 in Ordnung wäre?
← Reagiere. Schlage vor, dass ihr mit der Arbeit beginnt. →	Stimme zu.

[1] Not at all! *Bitteschön! Nichts zu danken!* [2] That's fine with me. *Von mir aus gerne.*

EFJ 6

1 Reacting to problems

a) *Read the dialogue.*

Today Sarah is working in one of WoW's big stores. She has a customer with a problem. But she didn't sleep very well last night ...

Sarah What do you want?
Customer I bought this mobile last week and it doesn't work very well.
Sarah 'Doesn't work very well.' What does that mean? Listen, mate. Just say exactly what's wrong with it.
Customer Well, the keys[1] are hard to press and it doesn't take good photos.
Sarah What do you expect if you buy a cheap phone?
Customer Maybe you're right. Anyway, I'd like to change it. I have no problem paying more for a better phone.
Sarah Wait there! I'll ask the manager.
Customer Thank you. Could I ask you to be quick? I'm a bit late for a doctor's appointment.
Sarah Well, why didn't you come here earlier? Honestly! Customers!

What's the problem with this dialogue?
- A The customer is not very nice to Sarah.
- B Sarah is not very polite to the customer.
- C The cheap mobile is the only problem.

b) *Find better phrases for Sarah in the box and rewrite her parts of the dialogue.*

Starting a conversation
A Good morning/... How can I help you?
B Can I do anything for you, sir/madam?

Sounding friendly
C I see.
D Of course, sir/madam.
E That's no problem. I'll ...
F Could I ask you to ...

Reacting to problems
G What seems to be the problem?
H Could you be a bit more exact, please?
I I'll see what I can do.
J Of course, there are sometimes problems with less expensive models/older models/...
K I'm sorry, but ...

c) *Act out your new version of the dialogue.*

2 Now you: Role play

Partner B: *Go to p. 98.*
Partner A: Follow the instructions on the role card below. Be as polite and friendly as you can.

You're a sales assistant in a big electronics store. You are talking to a customer who has a problem with a TV that he bought from you last week.
- Start the conversation. (Ask how you can help.)
- Ask for more information about the problem.
- Ask if the customer would like a different TV.
- React to this. (Say that you will see what you can do.)

[1] keys *(pl)* Tasten

EFJ 7 1 Deciding what to say

a) Look at Sarah's list above. Then listen to the conversation. Which points does Sarah decide to drop from her list? Why? Do you agree with her?

Sarah has to present a new mobile to WOW sales assistants. She's discussing her list of points with a colleague[1]. Is it too long?

SAMTO: New mobile
1 How mobile phone technology works
2 Earlier SAMTO models and history of product
3 Country of production
4 What the new SAMTO can do
5 How to use the new SAMTO
6 SAMTO uses 35 per cent less energy.
7 Super ringtones!
8 Price
9 Details about guarantee[2]
10 Dangers of using mobile while driving a car

b) Read Nat's list and agree on five points to drop from Nat's list. Then listen to the start of his presentation. Did he drop the same points as you?

Nat has to present a hotel to his colleagues. He wants to reduce the number of points in his list from 10 to 5.

Beach City Hotel, Malaga
1 Location (city centre)
2 Extra (tennis club near hotel)
3 Rooms (clean and comfortable)
4 Happy hour (in hotel bar until 7 pm)
5 Restaurant (breakfast, lunch and evening meal)
6 Staff[3] (friendly and helpful)
7 New air conditioning[4] (next year)
8 Shuttle service[5] to airport
9 Prices
10 Other hotels in Malaga

2 Structuring a presentation

*a) Make a chart with headings for the different parts of a presentation: **Introduction**, **Main part**, **End**. Match the points on the right to the correct heading.*

b) Go to p. 139. Find phrases that you can use for each point in a). Add them to your chart.

c) Listen to all of Nat's presentation. Which phrases from your chart does he use?

- Go into detail about your main points.
- List the points you plan to make.
- Sum up your main ideas and say what your conclusion is.
- Thank your audience and offer to answer questions.
- Tell your audience what your main topic is.
- Use pictures to illustrate[6] your main points.

3 Now you: Presentation

Choose a product (for example a mobile phone, a soft drink, a food product, a computer game ...) and prepare a short presentation about it.

► *SF Giving a presentation (pp. 130; 139)*

[1] colleague *Kollege/Kollegin* [2] guarantee *Garantie* [3] staff *Personal* [4] air-conditioning *Klimaanlage* [5] shuttle service *Zubringer(bus)*
[6] (to) illustrate *illustrieren, bildlich darstellen*

EFJ 8 1 Giving the figures

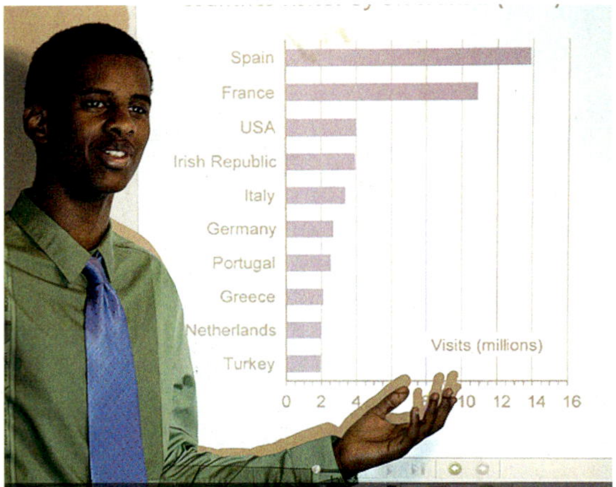

Nat has to present some statistics[1] about holidays abroad[2] by UK citizens. He's already prepared some charts ...

Remember

When you talk about statistics you usually ...

describe The chart here shows ...

explain As you can see, there are ...

evaluate[3] It's very clear that ...

Sometimes you'll also want to ...

draw conclusions This means ...

► *SF Talking about charts (p. 131)*

a) *Look at the chart and write down the missing information.*
b) *Then listen and compare.*

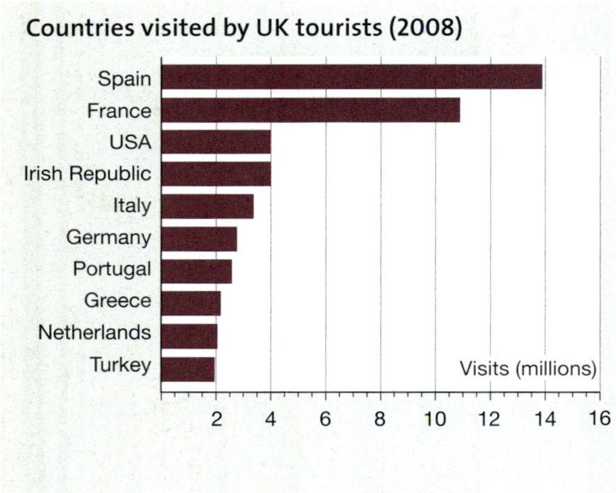

The chart here shows which countries tourists from the UK visited in 2008.
As you can see, there were just under 14 million visits to Spain and about (1) ... million visits to France. (2) ... million people went to the USA and Ireland. Over (3) ... million travelled to Germany, Portugal and Greece. And almost exactly (4) ... million went to the Netherlands and Turkey.
It's very clear that (5) ... and (6) ... are the most popular destinations[4].
This means we'll need to offer lots of holidays in (7) ... and (8) ...

2 Now you

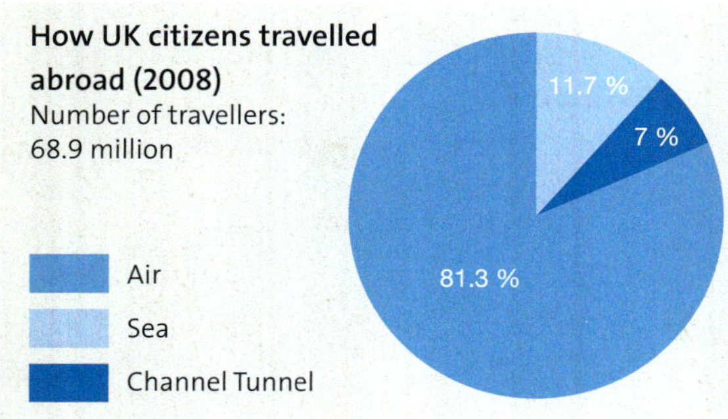

Talk about this chart:
This chart shows ...
81 per cent of journeys were by ... Almost 12 per cent travelled by ... And 7 per cent used the ...
The most popular kind of transport is ...
This means that Nat's company will need to ... air/ferry/channel tunnel tickets.

Source statistics: Office for National Statistics

[1] statistics *(pl) Statistiken* [2] abroad *hier: im Ausland* [3] (to) evaluate *bewerten* [4] destination *Reiseziel*

EFJ 9

1 Explaining a brochure

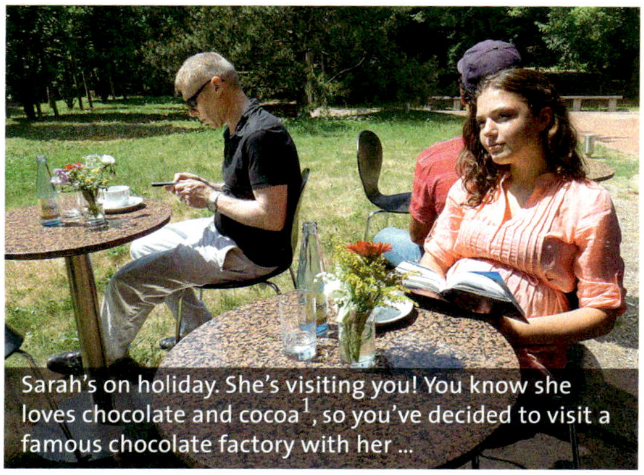

Sarah's on holiday. She's visiting you! You know she loves chocolate and cocoa[1], so you've decided to visit a famous chocolate factory with her ...

a) Read the brochure on the right.
Then answer these questions:

1 What can a visitor do? (Find four things.)
2 When is the factory open?
3 Do you have to pay to get in?

b) Partner A: Use your notes from a) to talk about the factory tour.
Partner B: Listen to your partner. Ask at least one question about the factory tour.

SCHMIDT-SCHOKOLADE

Erleben Sie die Welt der Schokolade in unserer spannenden Ausstellung!

Öffnungszeiten: Mo–Fr 8.00 bis 18.30 Uhr, Sa 9.00 bis 18.00 Uhr.

Der Eintritt ist frei.

Kommen Sie mit uns auf eine Entdeckungsreise mit allen Sinnen: Sehend, hörend, riechend, schmeckend und fühlend erfahren neugierige Schokoladen-Liebhaber alles rund um die „Speise der Götter", den Kakao. Interaktiv und Schritt für Schritt wird der gesamte Prozess von der Kakaobohne bis hin zur fertigen Schokolade erklärt. Ein spannendes Quiz bietet Kindern und auch Erwachsenen viel Spaß – so lässt sich spielerisch die Welt der Schokolade entdecken!

Genießen Sie die ganze Vielfalt der Schokolade in unserem Schoko-Geschäft neben der Ausstellung. Probieren Sie unsere leckeren Schokoladen, bevor Sie sie kaufen, entdecken Sie neue Sorten und versorgen Sie sich mit leckerem Proviant für unterwegs. Außerdem gibt es in unserem Fabrikverkauf immer wieder günstige Angebote und ein umfangreiches, wechselndes Sortiment. Lassen Sie sich überraschen!

Nach Voranmeldung bieten wir auch Rundgänge durch unsere Fabrik an.

2 Explaining what someone says

You're with Sarah in the factory. She doesn't understand everything the guide says.
Listen and answer her questions.

What was that about?

– He's going to tell us ...
– We can take the caps off when ...
– We mustn't touch ... But we can ...
– The staff might do something wrong if ...
– We ... the machines because ...
– There are toilets ...

3 Passing on questions[2]

Sarah wants you to ask the guide some questions.
What do you say to him in German?

1 Can you buy Schmidt chocolate in England?
2 How many kilos of chocolate are produced every day?
3 Which sort of chocolate is the most popular?
4 Who invents the new sorts of chocolate?
5 Does the company make organic[3] chocolate too?

[1] cocoa (bean) *Kakao(bohne)* [2] (to) pass on questions *Fragen weitergeben* [3] organic *Bio-...*

Inhalt

Im **Exam File** findest du ein breites Angebot an Prüfungsaufgaben, die dich auf deine zentrale Abschlussprüfung vorbereiten. Natürlich können hier nicht alle denkbaren Aufgabentypen geübt werden, aber die verschiedenen Übungen helfen dir bei einer gelungenen Prüfungsvorbereitung in allen Kompetenzbereichen: *Speaking, Writing, Listening, Reading* und *Mediation*.

Mit der Material- und Aufgabensammlung des **Exam File** kannst du
- den „Ernstfall" der Prüfungssituation üben
- dich gezielt in verschiedenen Kompetenzen und wichtigen Aufgabenformaten testen
- dich selbstständig oder gemeinsam in der Klasse auf die Prüfung vorbereiten
- das Trainingsangebot der *Getting ready for a test*-Seiten abrunden.

► Wenn du eine Listening-Aufgabe zu Hause machen willst, geh zu www.englishg.de. Wähle die B-Ausgabe und gibt dort den Web-Code ein, der bei deiner Listening-Aufgabe steht. Die Lösungen zu allen Exam File-Aufgaben findest du unter www.englishg.de/examfile.

Die Kompetenzbereiche und Übungsthemen im **Exam File** im Überblick:

Dein Weg zum Prüfungserfolg

In einer Prüfung kannst du zeigen, was du gelernt hast. Du brauchst keine Angst davor zu haben, denn alles, was in der Prüfung drankommt, kennst du schon aus dem Unterricht.

Während des Schuljahres

1 Bereite dich langfristig vor, nicht erst am Abend vor der Prüfung.
2 Überlege, welche Bereiche du wiederholen solltest. Besprich das auch mit deinem Lehrer/deiner Lehrerin. Mach dir einen Plan, wie du deine Vorbereitung am besten einteilst.
3 Denk daran: Dein *Skills File* enthält viele nützliche Tipps und Hilfen.
4 Mach dich mit verschiedenen Prüfungsformaten vertraut. Hierzu gibt es im **Prüfungswegweiser** auf den Seiten 76 bis 78 hilfreiche Hinweise.

Im **Prüfungswegweiser** findest du
- eine Beschreibung typischer Prüfungsformate
- Verweise auf Beispiele für die verschiedenen Formate
- eine Übersicht typischer Arbeitsanweisungen
- Tipps und Verweise auf das *Skills File*.

Am Abend vor der Prüfung

1 Entspanne dich. Du kannst lesen, dich in die Badewanne legen, Musik hören, fernsehen, ...
2 Geh zur gewohnten Zeit ins Bett.

Am Tag der Prüfung

1 Stehe rechtzeitig auf, damit du nicht hetzen musst.
2 Nimm dir Zeit für ein entspanntes Frühstück.
3 Lies etwas „zum Aufwärmen", aber schau nicht mehr in dein Schülerbuch.
4 Denk daran, du hast dich gut vorbereitet. Es gibt keinen Grund, nervös zu sein.

Während des Prüfung

1 Konzentriere dich auf den Test, lass dich nicht ablenken.
2 Lies dir die Aufgaben genau durch.

Bevor du die Aufgaben bearbeitest, überlege was du tun sollst. Lies die Aufgabenstellung langsam und gründlich durch. Sollst du z. B. ganze Sätze schreiben oder dir nur Notizen machen? Du kannst besonders wichtige Dinge in der Aufgabenstellung unterstreichen und die Aufgabe, wenn nötig, für dich in einzelne Schritte unterteilen.

3 Löse zuerst die Aufgaben, die dir einfach scheinen. Beginne dann mit den schwereren Aufgaben.
4 Aufgaben, die du bearbeitet hast, hakst du ab. So siehst du, wie du vorankommst, und behältst den Überblick.
5 Schau ab und zu auf die Uhr. Du solltest dir für den Schluss noch Zeit einplanen, um deine Antworten noch einmal durchzulesen und zu korrigieren.

Good luck!

VIEWING ***Mr Bean – The Exam***

Watch the video. What tipps would you give Mr Bean?

Prüfungswegweiser

Typische Aufgaben ► *Beispiele im* Exam File	**Typische Arbeitsanweisungen** ► Skills File
SPEAKING	
Talking about photos, cartoons, etc. ► *S. 79, Aufgaben 1, 2, 3* Über Fotos, Cartoons usw. sprechen (allein oder in Partnerarbeit)	• *Talk about the photo/cartoon (to a partner).* • *Look at the photo/cartoon and describe what's happening /…* • *What is the message of the photo/cartoon?* • *Show your photo/cartoon to your partner and describe …* • *Discuss …* ► *SF Describing pictures (pp. 125–126)* ► *SF Describing cartoons (p. 126)*
Simulated situations ► *S. 80, Aufgaben 4, 5* Simulierte Situationen im Dialog bewältigen (z. B. Vorhaben, Auswahl, … diskutieren oder erklären)	• *Choose … and make a list. Then talk to your partner. Explain your choice. Finally, try to agree on …* • *Look at the list/chart and think about/talk about … Decide together on …* ► *SF Having a discussion (p. 139)*
Guided dialogue ► *S. 81, Aufgabe 6* Einen gelenkten Dialog führen	• *Prepare a dialogue. Act it out.* • *Act out the conversation in English.* ► *SF Having a conversation (p. 138)*
Role play ► *S. 81, Aufgabe 7* Rollenspiel zu einer Situation, die auf einer Rollenkarte beschrieben wird	• *Look at the role card and act out the conversation with your partner.* • *Look at the picture/role card. Discuss the situation with your partner.* ► *SF Having a conversation (p. 138)* ► *SF Having a discussion (p. 139)*

In der mündlichen Prüfung kann es sein, dass zwei oder mehr Kandidat(inn)en gleichzeitig getestet werden. In diesem Fall können folgende Redemittel nützlich sein:

Einen Einstieg finden

- Would you like to begin?
- I'll start if you like.
- You first, please.
- Is it my turn or yours?

An den Partner/die Partnerin übergeben

- That's your special field.
- Maybe you can answer that question.
- Have you got any views on this?

Deinem Partner/deiner Partnerin zustimmen/widersprechen

- I agree. / I think so too.
- You're quite right.
- I don't agree. / I don't think so.
- I don't think you're right there.

Wenn du deinen Partner nicht verstehst

- Could you say that again, please?
- Could you repeat that, please?
- I'm not sure if I understand what you mean.
- Can you explain what you mean, please?

Typische Aufgaben ▸ *Beispiele im* **Exam File**	**Typische Arbeitsanweisungen** **Tipps** ▸ **Skills File**

WRITING

Questionnaire/Form ▸ *S. 82, Aufgabe 1* Fragebogen/Formulare ausfüllen	• *Fill in the questionnaire/form.* • *Complete the survey.* • *Answer the questions ...* **Tipp** Oft musst du keine ganzen Sätze schreiben. Achte genau auf die Arbeitsanweisung.
Story ▸ *S. 82, Aufgabe 2; S. 83, Aufgabe 3* Geschichten zu Bild- oder Textimpulsen schreiben	• *Look at the pictures. Then write a story (of about ... words).* • *Tell the story behind the picture. Use your imagination.* ▸ *SF Writing course (pp. 141–142)*
E-mail/Letter/Postcard/Letter of application ▸ *S. 83, Aufgabe 4; S. 84, Aufgabe 5c)* E-Mails, Briefe, Bewerbungsschreiben usw. verfassen	• *Write an e-mail/a letter/a postcard/a letter of application to...* • *Answer (Jack's) e-mail/letter.* • *Write for more information.* ▸ *SF Writing formal and informal letters (p. 145)*
Working with texts ▸ *S. 84, Aufgabe 5; S. 85, Aufgabe 6* Schreibaufgaben, die sich auf einen längeren Sach- oder Literaturtext beziehen.	• *First read the text. Then do the tasks below.* **Tipp** Hier helfen auch die Lesetechniken, die du gelernt hast. ▸ *SF Reading course (pp. 134–135)* ▸ *SF Writing course (pp. 141–142)*
Summary ▸ *S. 84, Aufgabe 5 a* Texte (Literatur, Sachtext, ...) oder einzelne Fakten zu einem Thema zusammenfassen	• *Sum up the story/article/main points ...* • *Give a short summary of ...* • *Write a summary of (100) words.* • *Say what happened (in the story/...)* ▸ *SF Summarizing texts (p. 143)*
Description/Creative writing ▸ *S. 84, Aufgabe 5 b; S. 85, Aufgabe 6 c* Beschreibung, Charakterisierung, kreatives Schreiben	• *What does the text say about ...?* • *Describe ...* • *Continue the story.* • *What happens next/when ...?* **Tipp** Wenn du nach Ideen suchst, helfen dir die Brainstorming-Techniken, die du gelernt hast. ▸ *SF Brainstorming (p. 140)*
Article/Report ▸ *S. 84, Aufgabe 5 d* Artikel/Bericht für ein Print- oder Onlinemagazin verfassen	• *Write an article for your school mag/...* • *Write a report on/about ...* ▸ *SF Writing a report (p. 142)*
Giving your opinion ▸ *S. 85, Aufgabe 6 b.2* Eigene Meinung zu einem Thema formulieren	• *What do you think about ...? Give reasons for your opinion.* • *Write/give your opinion.* • *What would you do or say if ...?* • *Should/Would ...?* ▸ *SF From outline to written discussion (p. 146)*

Typische Aufgaben ▸ *Beispiele im* Exam File	Typische Arbeitsanweisungen	Tipps ▸ Skills File
LISTENING		
True/False ▸ *S. 86, Aufgabe 1; S. 88, Aufgabe 5* Entscheiden, ob Aussagen zum Hörtext richtig oder falsch sind	• *Decide if the statements are true or false (right or wrong).* • *Tick the correct answer.*	*1* Du wirst **verschiedene Textsorten** (Dialoge, Bekanntmachungen ...) und **verschiedene Akzente** hören. Manchmal sollst du zeigen, dass du Details verstanden hast, z. B. einen Preis, Abfahrtszeiten o. Ä. Bei anderen Aufgaben geht es um die **Kernaussage**, z. B. ob jemand mit seinen Eltern klar kommt oder sich optimistisch oder pessimistisch gibt. ▸ *SF Listening (p. 132)*
Multiple choice ▸ *S. 86, Aufgabe 2* Aus mehreren Antworten die richtige auswählen	• *Choose/Write down the correct answer for each task.* • *Tick the right statement.*	
Missing information ▸ *S. 87, Aufgaben 3, 4* Lücken in Sätzen/Tabellen ergänzen	• *Complete the text with the missing information.* • *Fill in the missing information.*	
Matching ▸ *S. 88, Aufgabe 6* Zuordnungsaufgaben	• *Choose the right statement.* • *Match the sentence parts.*	
READING		
Matching ▸ *S. 89, Aufgabe 1* Einen Text einem Bild oder einem anderen Text zuordnen	• *Match the tips to the photos.* • *Which statement/ ... goes with which picture/description/...*	*1* In der Prüfung kann es **verschiedene Textsorten** geben: Listen, Poster, Blogs, Sachtexte, Kurzgeschichten ... *2* Manchmal geht es um die **Hauptaussage** des Textes, manchmal um **Details**, und manchmal sollst du **Schlussfolgerungen** ziehen. *3* Bei der Bewältigung Unterschiedlicher Aufgaben helfen dir die verschiedenen **Lesetechniken**, die du gelernt hast. ▸ *SF Reading course (pp. 134–135)*
Completing a chart ▸ *S. 90, Aufgabe 2b* Textinhalte tabellarisch wiedergeben	• *Complete the chart/table/grid ....* • *Fill in the chart/timeline/...*	
True/false ▸ *S. 92, Aufgabe 3b* Entscheiden, ob Aussagen zum Text richtig oder falsch sind	• *Are these statements true or false?* • *Tick the right answers and correct the wrong statements.*	
Multiple choice ▸ *S. 92, Aufgabe 3c; S. 93, Aufgabe 4b* Die richtige Antworten auswählen	• *Decide which answer is correct.* • *Tick the right/correct/best answer.* • *Mark the correct statement.*	
Finish sentences ▸ *S. 92, Aufgabe 3d* Sätze über den Text vervollständigen	• *Complete/Finish these sentences (using information from the text).*	
Questions on the text ▸ *S. 93, Aufgabe 4b* Fragen zum Textinhalt beantworten	• *Answer these questions.* • *Answer the questions in complete sentences.*	
MEDIATION		
English ▸ German ▸ *S. 94, Aufgaben 1, 2; S. 95, Aufgabe 4, S. 96, Aufgabe 5* Sprachmittlung Englisch ▸ Deutsch	*Typische Arbeitsanweisungen* • *beschreiben die Situation (**Du bist mit deiner Familie in Urlaub in England** o. Ä.).* • *nennen häufig die Punkte, die du in der Zielsprache wiedergeben sollst.*	Hier kommen **mehrere Sprachkompetenzen** zum Einsatz – z. B. liest du einen Text, um dann Fakten mündlich oder schriftlich weiterzugeben. *4* Nennt die Arbeitsanweisung nicht die Punkte, die du vermitteln sollst, gib nur die **Kerninformationen** weiter. ▸ *SF Mediation (p. 147)*
German ▸ English ▸ *S. 95, Aufgabe 3* Sprachmittlung Deutsch ▸ Englisch		
German ▸ English ▸ German ▸ *S. 96, Aufgabe 6* Sprachmittlung zwischen 2 Personen		

SPEAKING

1 Talking about a photo

Describe the photo. The questions below can help you.
- Why do you think the girl is standing at the side of the road?
- Where do you think she wants to go?
- What could she have in her bag and suitcase?
- If you could travel somewhere now, where would you go?
- What would you take with you?

2 Talking about a cartoon

Look at the cartoon and describe what's happening:
- How does the father feel about his daughter's answer? Why do you think so?
- What does the cartoon tell us about modern life?
- Some people think that teenagers spend too much time in front of the computer. Do you agree? Why (not)?

(to) write a blog • communicate • different generations (parents – children) • modern technology • (to) read a newspaper/blog

3 Discussing photos

Work with a partner. Partner B: *Go to p. 101*

a) *Partner A: Show Partner B your photo and describe what you can see in it. Then Partner B will talk about his/her photo.*
Discuss the different things that dogs can do for people. Say how you feel about dogs and why.

b) *Partner A: Show Partner B your photo and describe what you can see in it. Then Partner B will talk about his/her photo.*
Discuss different ways that people can spend their holidays. Say what kind of holiday you like best and why.

4 Choosing a present

Work with a partner. You're both going to stay with a family in London and you want to take a present for the son, Daniel (16).

a) *Choose one of the presents below.*

b) *Then talk to your partner: Say which present you think you should choose and why. Listen to your partner's ideas.*

c) *Try to agree on one present.*

5 Deciding on a day trip to a theme park[1]

You and your friend are in Ontario, Canada. You want to go on a day trip together to visit a Canadian theme park. You find out about two trips that you can do today.

a) *Look at the information about the two trips and decide which trip you think is better for you and why.*

b) *Work with a partner. Talk about the two trips. Say what you like/don't like about them. Decide together on the best day trip.*

Trip	Theme park	What does the theme park offer?	What is included?	Price / person
1	Marineland (Niagara Falls)	Lots of sea animals. Exciting water shows with dolphins[2] and whales[3]. Also many rides[4] and roller coasters[5].	Bus ride, all tickets.	$89.00
2	Canada's Wonderland (near Toronto)	Over 200 attractions. 15 roller coasters! Big water park. Live shows.	Bus ride, tickets, lunch in café.	$55.00

[1] theme park *Freizeitpark* [2] dolphin *Delfin* [3] whale *Wal* [4] ride *Fahrgeschäft* [5] roller coaster *Achterbahn*

6 Talking about holiday jobs

Two friends, Joe and Lucy, meet in the street. They're talking about holiday jobs. Prepare a dialogue with your partner. Act it out.

Partner A (Joe)

Begrüße Lucy und frage sie, wie es ihr geht.

Partner B (Lucy)

Grüß zurück und sage, dass es dir gut geht, und dass du gerade einen Ferienjob angefangen hast.

Partner A (Joe)

Frage Lucy, was für einen Job sie macht.

Partner B (Lucy)

Erzähle, dass du Zeitungen austrägst.

Partner A (Joe)

Frage, ob das Zeitungsaustragen ein guter Ferienjob ist.

Partner B (Lucy)

Antworte, dass es bei gutem Wetter richtig Spaß macht, und frage Joe, ob er einen Ferienjob hat.

Partner A (Joe)

Antworte, dass du in einer Fabrik arbeitest.

Partner B (Lucy)

Frage, um was für eine Fabrik es sich handelt.

Partner A (Joe)

Antworte, dass in der Fabrik Maschinen hergestellt werden, du aber nur am Computer sitzt.

Partner B (Lucy)

Frage, ob Joe diese Arbeit gefällt.

Partner A (Joe)

Antworte ja, aber es fällt dir schwer, immer so früh aufzustehen.

Partner B (Lucy)

Sage, du wettest, Joe steht nicht so früh auf wie du.

7 Role plays: Solving problems abroad[1]

Partner B: Go to p. 101.

a) *Partner A: Look at the role card and act out the conversation with your partner.*

You're on holiday abroad with your family. You want to find a cheap hotel so you go to an internet café. You find a hotel on the internet, but you aren't sure how far away it is. You speak to the person at the next PC.

- Ask if he/she lives in this town. (▸ *Do you live ...*)
- Give the name of the hotel you've found. (▸ *The Sun Hotel*) Ask if your partner knows it.
- Give the address of the hotel. (▸ *John Street*) Ask how far it is from the café.
- Ask if your partner knows something nearer the centre of town.
- React positively to this information. Ask for directions.
- React.

b) *Partner A: Look at the role card and act out the conversation with your partner.*

Your holiday in Spain is over. All European airports have been closed for a week for safety reasons. You can't fly back home. You are at a travel agent's[2]. You want to find an alternative to flying.

- Explain why you can't fly.
- Say where you want to go and ask if you can buy a train ticket.
- Ask about your arrival time.
- Ask how long the journey takes.
- React and say if you want to buy the ticket.

[1] abroad *im Ausland* [2] travel agent's *Reisebüro*

WRITING

1 Guided writing: A questionnaire[1]

A class from a school in the UK wants information about life in Germany. Answer the questions below. You must fill in each item. You may use your imagination[2]. You needn't write complete sentences.*

Hi from St Mary's school! We would like your help with our European project. We're sorry we don't know much German, so we hope you can understand English.
What is life like in Germany?
Please fill in the the questionnaire and give it back to your teacher.

Country:	Town/City:	Age: ....
Questions:		**Answers:**
1. What do you have for breakfast?		
2. What time do you have to be at school?		
3. How long is a typical school day?		
4. What do you have for lunch?		
5. How much homework do you get?		
6. When do you do your homework?		
7. What do you have for your evening meal?		
8. What do you do in the evening on school days?		

* Write in your exercise book or ask your teacher for a copy of the form.

2 Picture story: A parcel for Darkwood

Look at the pictures. Then write a story (about 80 words). You can use the key words in your sentences. Use your imagination to explain what happened after Joe pressed the bell. What made him run away?

A Joe Lee – Whizz Parcel Service

B parcel for Dr Bones, The Old House, Darkwood

C long drive – big, old house – tall trees

D big door – bell

E hear noise – scared

F end of day – back at Whizz – explain what happened

[1] questionnaire *Fragebogen* [2] imagination *Fantasie*

3 The story behind the picture

Tell the story behind the picture. Use your imagination[1]. The questions below can help you:

- Who are the people?
- Who or what are they looking at?
- How do they feel? (Why?)
- What do you think they did that day? *(Use the **simple past**.)*
- What will they do next?
- What is their life like?

4 A summer job

a) *Read the job advertisement.*

b) *You're interested in the job. Write an e-mail for more information. Use the ideas below.*
Before you write, decide the best order for the different points.

- where the school is
- how you can get there
- exact dates
- why you want to be in the soap
- where you can sleep
- three important facts about yourself
- how much you'll earn

c) *Imagine you got a part in the TV soap. What happened on the first day of filming? Write a report.*

TV Europe: Summer jobs for students

We are filming an episode for a new European TV soap. This summer we are filming in a German school while the students are on holiday. Would you like to be one of the students in the film (non-speaking role)? We are looking for reliable young people (14–19) who are able to understand simple instructions in English.

Write an e-mail today to:
j.gubbins@tv-europe.de

[1] imagination *Fantasie*

5 Text-based writing: A teen mag article

First read the text. Then do the tasks below.

SURVIVAL TRIP

Last summer four teachers and a national park ranger took a group of 20 students from Riverside High School in Launceston, the second largest city on the island of Tasmania, Australia, to Mt Cameron National Park.

They were away from 'civilization' (houses, shops, restaurants, roads, cinemas, ...) for three days. The trip was to teach the students to look after themselves in a difficult situation. Each student was only allowed to take one bag with them for all their things – and they had to make the bags themselves! Joseph Shrimpton, 17, told us he had made his bag from an old potato sack. Later, in the middle of the bush, the bag broke ... It was difficult for him to carry all his things after that!

When they got to the National Park, the students travelled into the bush in special minibuses. They had to wear blindfolds[1] so that they couldn't see where they were going. When the buses stopped, the blindfolds were taken off and the students were on their own! They had to use a map to hike to a place where the park ranger had left some things so that they could make 'tents' for the night. They hiked for three days, 20 kilometres per day, with two nights in the bush. As they hiked they had to find the answers to questions that their teachers had given them.

They also had to discover where food had been hidden. There was food powder[2] (not very nice!) and a few cans[3] of chilli con carne, which were for the students who had answered the most questions correctly during the hike each day. They were allowed to put the chilli con carne on the camp fire and eat it out of the can. Each of the others had to take turns[4] at preparing their food powder with some water in the empty chilli con carne can, because they had no cooking things or plates with them. One evening the park ranger brought some insects[5], and he cooked them on the camp fire. Some students were brave (or hungry!) enough to eat the insects.

After three long days in the bush the buses picked the students up and took them back to Launceston. The teens were tired and dirty, but happy. They had survived! Carla McBeath said, 'Although it was hard, I learned to look after myself. But the insects were really awful!' ■

a) *Sum up the article. Say what happened before and during the trip.*

b) *What does the text say about food? Describe what the students ate and how they felt about it.*

c) *Choose task 1 or 2. Write about 80–100 words.*

1 Write a letter to a friend about a hike that you did.

2 Tasmania National Parks are looking for young people to help with survival camps in the summer. Write a letter of application to Phil Wilson, GPO Box 1751, HOBART, TAS 7001.

d) *Write an article for your school mag. Write about 80–100 words. Choose topic 1 or 2.*

1 My most exciting holiday

2 My best class trip

[1] blindfold *Augenbinde* [2] food powder *Lebensmittelpulver* [3] can *Büchse, Dose* [4] (to) take turns *sich abwechseln*
[5] insect *Insekt*

6 Text-based writing: A short story

a) *First read the text.*

Back home

Jody Miller from Chicago sat on the train, looking out of the window. She was getting nearer by the minute to high school. Her year in Germany was over. She was back home, in the Midwest of the USA. She was looking forward to the football season – Jody wondered if her cheerleader's costume would still fit her after all that German food – and it would soon be time for the baseball World Series. And then there was football's Super Bowl in the winter.

But she also couldn't stop thinking about her time as an exchange student for a whole year at a Realschule in Freiburg. Freiburg was a beautiful town in the south-west of Germany. It was a great place, full of students, sun, restaurants and cafes. As her train arrived at the station and she realized[1] it was time to get off, she thought about the wonderful trips she had made from Freiburg, up into the Black Forest for picnics, hiking and, in the long winter, cross-country skiing.

She got off the train and walked the last few minutes to the high school. She couldn't see any of her friends. She felt alone. Where were they all? 'Come on,' she said to herself. 'The place isn't that bad. And you couldn't have stayed in Germany. Well, maybe for one more year. But this is your home. This is where you'll get a job one day.'

She couldn't stop thinking about Benny, a student at the German school. He had helped her with homework, explained all those difficult German words to her and been her partner at the end-of-year school dance. She couldn't forget him, his blue eyes, his long blond hair, the way he spoke English and the way he had looked at her. He would have been a reason for staying in Germany for the rest of her life. But what had he said to her at that dance, holding her in his arms? 'I'm sorry, Jody. I already have a girlfriend. She's in California as an exchange student at the moment.' He already had a girlfriend! Why hadn't he told her earlier? And what if she had stayed, would that have made a difference? What if ...? Stop it!

She opened the door of the classroom and twenty happy faces were looking at her – her best friends Mel and Davina, Rosie, Helen and, in the corner, Dave. He had changed a lot in the time she had been away. 'Welcome back, Jody!' Everybody was clapping. Jody smiled. She was back home, and it felt good!

b) *Now do these tasks.*

1 Write down 5 things that we learn about Jody in the text.

2 What are the advantages and disadvantages of being away from home for a year? Support[2] your opinion with examples from the text. (Write about 80–100 words)

c) *Choose task 1 or 2. Write about 60–80 words.*

1 Imagine you are Jody. Write a letter to Benny in Germany and tell him how you feel now that you're back home.

2 How does the story go on? Imagine Jody goes back to Freiburg in her next holiday. What happens? You could start like this: *When Jody got off the train, ...*

---

[1] (to) realize *erkennen, begreifen* [2] (to) support *belegen, unterstützen*

LISTENING

1 Report: Belinda's Britain

Web-Code: EG21-D6-GA-086-1

a) *First read the statements (1–6).*

1 Belinda reports from Britain for a TV station in San Francisco.
2 The British use public transport more than cars.
3 Travelling by train is more expensive than travelling by bus.
4 A lot of travelling within Britain is by air.
5 People in Britain often walk when they don't have far to go.
6 In London, if you park your car where it is not allowed, the police will take it away.

b) *Now listen to the report and decide if the statements (1–6) are true or false. Write your answers down.*

c) *Listen again and check your answers.*

2 Announcements

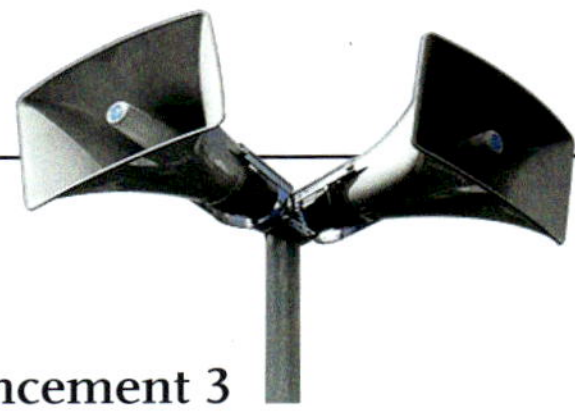

Web-Code: EG21-D6-GA-086-2

You are going to hear four announcements.

a) *First read the tasks (1–10).*

Announcement 1

1 The non-stop train to York will leave today from platform
A 3. B 4. C 5.
2 The non-stop train to York will be ...
A 5 minutes late.
B 10 minutes late.
C 30 minutes late.
3 The train that stops in Peterborough will leave at ...
A 5.53. B 6.03. C 6.30.

Announcement 2

4 You can buy a pair of Janglers jeans for
A £10. B £49. C £59.
5 The café is on the
A first floor.
B second floor.
C fifth floor.

Announcement 3

6 There are refreshment stations[1]
A every 2 kilometres.
B every 5 kilometres.
C every 42 kilometres.
7 The disco starts at
A 5 pm. B 8 pm.
C 10 pm.
8 The marathon finishes at
A Milson's Point.
B Harbour Bridge.
C Sydney Opera House.

Announcement 4

9 At 10.30 BBC 1 will show ...
A Jim in Germany.
B Red Roses.
C East Enders.
10 You can watch the news on BBC 1 at
A 9.30 pm. B 10 pm. C 10.30 pm.

b) *Now listen to the announcements. Write down the correct letter (a, b or c) for each task (1–10) while you are listening. Choose only one letter for each task.*

c) *Listen to the announcements again and check your answers.*

[1] refreshment (station) *Erfrischung(sstation)*

3 Dialogue: Shopping

Web-Code: EG21-D6-GA-087-3

***a)** First read the statements (1–10).*

1 Diana ordered ... tops from an online shop.
2 Only ... of the tops have arrived.
3 Diana has paid ... for the tops.
4 The service number of the online shop is ...
5 Prices at *Just Jeans* are reduced by ...
6 *HK Fashion* is ... *Just Jeans*.
7 Pete asks Diana to go ... with him.
8 Diana says the shops will be closed in ...
9 Pete wants to look at the ... in the VG Comp store.
10 Diana tells Pete to try the VG Comp ...

***b)** Now listen to the dialogue. Write down the missing words to complete the statements (1–10) while you are listening.*

***c)** Listen to the dialogue again and check your answers.*

4 Dialogue: Practising for an interview

Web-Code: EG21-D6-GA-087-4

Dayamayee has a job interview at a call centre in Delhi tomorrow. In the dialogue she is practising with her friend Harita, who plays the interviewer.

Name	Dayamayee
Personal qualities	good at ... enjoys ...
Computer skills	can use ...
Attitude to modern technology	has got ...
Experience with English	always got good ... speaks ... listens ...
Knowledge of Britain	has visited her ... reads ...
Work experience	part-time: ... weekend job: ...
Weaknesses	forgets ...

***a)** Listen to the dialogue and complete the candidate profile for Dayamayee.*

***b)** Listen to the dialogue again. Add any missing information.*

Web-Code: EG21-D6-GA-088-5

5 Radio advertisement

a) *Listen to the advertisement. Then decide if the statements (1–6) are true or false. Write your answers down.*

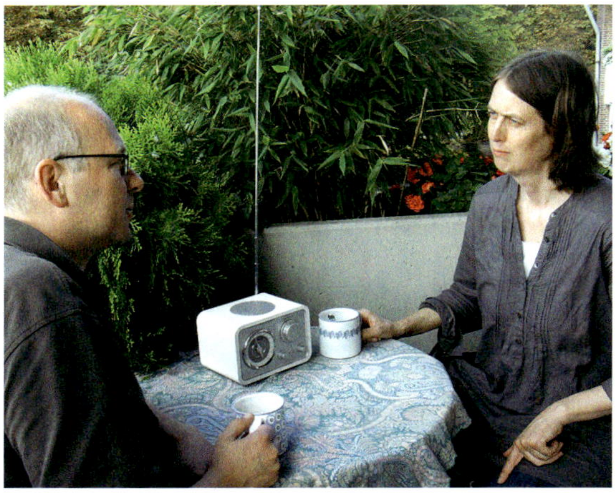

1 In the advertisement, Tom is making a phone call from Bristol.
2 Tom phones his parents because he needs money.
3 BBB offers full and dirty rooms for young people.
4 To book a room, all you need is a credit card number.
5 The advertisement speaks to parents and promises to take away all the worry.
6 In the second message, Tom says that the best thing about his hotel is that the rooms are nice.

b) *Listen again and check your answers.*

Web-Code: EG21-D6-GA-088-6

6 Personal statements: My future

a) *First read statements A–E below.*

b) *Next listen to the speakers. Choose the right statement for each speaker.*
*While you listen, write the correct letter (A–E) next to the speaker's name.**

c) *Listen again and check.*

Statements

A My parents are trying to plan my future for me, but I'm not sure what I want to do yet.
B I still have some time before I need to make a decision about my career.
C My parents didn't understand how much I needed a break.
D I plan to travel around to visit people or work in lots of different countries before I start in my parents' business.
E My parents want me to help them with their business but I think it's easier to earn money somewhere else.

Speaker	Statement
1 Pia	
2 Mikael	
3 Frans	
4 Marietta	
5 Sally	

* *Copy the chart into your exercise book.*

READING

1 A list of tips: What to do when you're down

a) *First read the text.*

Ten top tips when you're down

TIP 1 Talk to a friend. Good friends will want to help. You could call one of your mates and tell them about your problem.

TIP 2 Talk to your parents. Listen to their advice. Try to understand them. Remember: they were young once too and had similar problems.

TIP 3 Sometimes it can help if you express[1] what you feel in a creative way. Write a story or poem, draw or paint something or maybe write some music.

TIP 4 Physical activity can make you feel happier. Go swimming or running, or do some other sport. Be active.

TIP 5 Light makes us feel better. On a grey winter's day, try using a sun lamp. But nothing can beat real sunlight. So go out in the sun if you can.

TIP 6 The beauty of nature can make us feel more relaxed. Go for a walk outdoors and enjoy the fresh air.

TIP 7 Be kind to your body. Fill a bath and lie back in the hot, soapy water. Maybe try a massage or do yoga.

TIP 8 A great therapy if you're feeling down is simply to laugh or smile. You could try watching a comedy on TV or reading a funny book.

TIP 9 Helping others can make you feel better about yourself. You could volunteer to work with children or to help people who can't look after themselves.

TIP 10 Do something nice for yourself. Buy something that you really want – maybe the latest computer game or some trendy clothes.

b) *Now match each tip (1–10) to one of the pictures below (A–L). There are two more pictures than you need.*

[1] (to) express *ausdrücken, äußern*

2 A short biography: Jérôme Boateng, footballer

a) *Read the text first. Then do the tasks below.*

Jérôme Boateng (born 3 September, 1988 in Berlin; 1.92 metres tall) is a German footballer who plays for the English Premier League team, Manchester City. Boateng is a defender[1].

Boateng has both German and Ghanaian nationality. His mother is German, his father Ghanaian. His two half-brothers, Kevin-Prince and George are also footballers. Kevin-Prince plays for Ghana's national team. Football is a bit of a tradition in the Boateng family. Jérôme's uncle also played for Ghana.

Boateng is a strongly built sportsman who can play any full-back position[2]. His career began in 1994 with the youth team of Tennis Borussia Berlin. Then in July 2002, when he was 13 years old, he joined Hertha BSC Berlin. In January 2007, at only 18, he became a Hertha first team member. He played his first match against Hannover 96 in the 2006–07 Bundesliga season.

Boateng was offered a five-year contract[3] with Hertha, but decided against staying on with the Berlin team. Instead, he moved to Hamburger SV in August 2007 for a fee of €1.1 million. There, he became one of the key players in Hamburg's defence. Other clubs were soon interested in him, including VfL Wolfsburg, Arsenal and Manchester City. In June 2010, it was announced that Boateng was moving to Manchester – this time for a fee of over £10 million. The move was a big step in his career and he felt very excited about it. 'I'm looking forward to the challenge[4],' he said. Boateng's contract with City runs for five years.

Boateng also has an impressive international career. He played for the German U-16, U-17 and U-19 teams several times. He is also a former[5] German U-21 international player and won the 2009 UEFA European Under-21 Football Championship with the German team.

In October 2009, Boateng played his first match with the (adult) German national team against Russia, but was sent off in the second half after receiving two yellow cards[6]. This was not typical of Boateng. People who have seen him play describe him as calm and disciplined. Because he had always played with a minimum of fouls, he himself was annoyed by his behaviour on the field. But German national coach, Joachim Löw, was sure that Boateng would learn the right lessons from his mistake.

In the summer of 2010, Boateng was a member of the German team in the FIFA World Cup in South Africa. In Germany's match against Ghana, he played against his own half-brother. This was the first time that brothers played against each other in the World Cup. Germany beat Ghana 1 – 0.

b) *Copy and complete the chart with the information from the text.*

Name	Jérôme ...
Place/Date of birth	
Nationality	
Family	
Clubs (dates)	Tennis Borussia (1994 – ...), ...
International experience	

c) *"People are often annoyed by Jérôme Boateng's unfair behaviour during matches." This statement is true/false, because in the text it says ...*

d) *"The Boatengs are a football family." This statement is true/false, because in the text it says ...*

[1] defender *Abwehrspieler/in* [2] full-back position *Abwehrposition* [3] contract *Vertrag* [4] challenge *Herausforderung*
[5] former *ehemalige/r* [6] two yellow cards *(die) gelb-rote Karte*

3 A short story: Money isn't everything

a) First read the text.

Tim and Lisa had been going out together for six weeks now and it was time for Lisa to meet Tim's parents. She had been invited for tea at Tim's house on Sunday.

Lisa was very nervous. She had met Tim at the local youth club, but he lived on the other side of town. He only went to the same youth club because his grandma lived near there and he liked to visit her once a week between leaving school and going to the youth club.

Tim's parents had a lot of money, not like Lisa's parents. Her mum was a single parent and worked at a supermarket. Her dad had disappeared, to New Zealand her mum thought, when Lisa was only two. But Lisa wasn't unhappy. She had great fun with her mum and her younger brother. Money wasn't everything. And her home? Well, living in a caravan was all right. Although, when Tim asked Lisa where she lived, she just said the name of the village outside the town where the youth club was.

'OK, this is our house,' said Tim, as they walked up to the front door.
'House?' said Lisa. 'It's a palace! I knew your parents were rich, but I never expected a huge place like this. Bye, Tim. I'm going home.'
'Lisa, please,' said Tim. 'Don't be so nervous. They're only my parents.'
He squeezed her hand.
Lisa smiled. 'OK, I'll stay. But I'm not looking forward to this.'

They walked into the big, square hall.
'I'll introduce you to my parents,' Tim said.
'Mum! Dad!' he called. But nobody came.
'That's funny,' said Tim. 'I told Mum we were coming, so why aren't they here?'
'Are you sure they want to meet me?' Lisa asked.
Tim took Lisa's hand again. 'Of course they want to meet you! They can't wait. Come on. Let's go into the living room. I'm sure they'll be here in a few moments.'

Lisa followed Tim across the hall into the living room. She looked around and saw beautiful furniture[1], expensive lamps, a plasma TV and a Danish stereo system. Modern paintings hung on the walls.
Lisa wanted to be polite. 'It's a very nice room,' she said to Tim.
'Do you really like it?' asked Tim.
Lisa didn't. 'It doesn't feel as if people live here,' she thought. 'It's so cold and impersonal.'

They waited for a few minutes, but there was still no sign of Tim's parents.
'Maybe they're in the garden,' Tim said. 'I'll go and look.'
He went outside while Lisa stayed in the living room. After some minutes she heard the sound of voices, loud and angry.
'Somebody's having an argument,' she thought. 'Maybe Tim and his parents are arguing about me.'
She walked out to the hall to be able to listen better.

Standing in the hall, Lisa could hear that the voices were coming from upstairs. There were two people, a man and a woman.
'I don't understand you,' the man said. 'We've got everything money can buy, but still you aren't happy.'
Then the woman: 'Money isn't everything. You're my husband, but you're never at home. We have a beautiful house, but you spend all

[1] furniture *Möbel*

your time at the office. What kind of life is this?'

Lisa shivered[1]. 'Tim's parents can't be very happy,' she thought.

'What do you mean?' the man asked. 'I'm at home today. I'm not at the office. It's Sunday.'

'Yes,' the woman answered. 'Sunday. A day for the family, but we can't enjoy our house together. No, we have to go downstairs and talk to that girl Tim met at that awful youth club.'

'Why don't you want to meet our son's girlfriend?' the man asked. 'I don't see a problem.'

'You don't see a problem?' the woman shouted. 'That girl comes from the worst part of town. Why your mother still lives there I don't know. But I do know that I'd like someone better for my son. ... No! Don't say anything! Let's just go downstairs and be nice to her, if we have to.'

At that moment Tim came into the hall. 'What's the matter, Lisa?' he asked.

b) *Decide if these statements (1–5) are true, false or not in the text. Write your answers down.*

1 Lisa has often been invited to Tim's house.
2 Lisa and Tim have different family backgrounds.
3 Lisa's father works at a supermarket in New Zealand.
4 Lisa thinks you can be happy without a lot of money.
5 When Lisa met Tim, she told him that she lived in a caravan.

c) *Read the tasks (1–3) and decide which answer (A – D) is correct. Choose only one letter for each task.*

1 When Lisa sees Tim's house, she
- A is surprised at how small it is.
- B turns around and goes home.
- C feels more relaxed about meeting his parents.
- D feels more nervous about meeting his parents.

2 When Tim and Lisa enter the house,
- A Tim is surprised that his parents aren't there.
- B Tim's parents are there to welcome them.
- C only Tim's mum is there to welcome them.
- D Tim's parents are waiting in the living room.

3 When Lisa sees the living room in Tim's house, she
- A really likes it.
- B makes a polite comment about it.
- C tells Tim what she thinks about it.
- D wonders why nobody is there.

d) *Complete these sentences (1–4).*

1 Tim went into the garden because ...
2 Lisa went into the hall because ...
3 Lisa thinks Tim's parents can't be happy because ...
4 Tim's mother doesn't want to meet Lisa because ...

e) *Which character in the story might think the following? Write down their names. Careful – you will have to read between the lines!*

1 I hope they will like her.
2 I don't want to go inside.
3 Where are they? I said this day was important.
4 Why does she always grumble?
5 This isn't the life that I expected when I got married.
6 I'm so tired of her stupid prejudices.
7 I don't want to talk to her.
8 How awful! What should I do now?

[1] (to) shiver *erschauern, zittern*

4 A holiday blog: One island, two countries

a) *First read the text.*

Hi. This is Wendy. Tim and I are just back from Ireland. Here are a few notes.

▪ **Thursday 25th August:** Drove to Stranraer in Scotland and took the ferry. Flying is cheaper, but we wanted to use our car for the trip. Less than two hours at sea (ferry was really fast) and we were in Belfast, still in the UK. Northern Ireland is the part of Ireland that is still British.

▪ **Friday 26th August:** The conflict between Catholics and Protestants in Northern Ireland killed so many people. But now – thankfully – it's over, and tourists go there to shop and enjoy the night life. Other attractions in Belfast (the capital): the shipyards[1] where the *Titanic* was built (great!) and the wall paintings done by Protestants and Catholics in their areas of the city.

▪ **Sunday 28th August:** Crossed the border into the Irish Republic today. We didn't need passports and, like in the UK, you drive on the left. But distances[2] are in kilometres, not miles. And we had to change money – they use euros, not pounds. Dublin, the Republic's capital, is full of history – and full of people, with so many shops, cafés and pubs. In the past, the Republic was quite poor. But joining the EU was good for Ireland. The economy[3] improved and the Republic became the 'Celtic Tiger'. OK, so Ireland has had some economic problems recently[4]. But I'm still writing on a laptop that was 'Made in Ireland' and there's a one in four chance that your computer was made there too.

▪ **Tuesday 30th August:** But enough about industry. South-west of Dublin there's an absolute 'must' for tourists – the Rock of Cashel, a great collection of medieval architecture[5] and Celtic art. We loved walking around the historical buildings.

▪ **Wednesday 31st August**: Another highlight was the Ring of Kerry, a 170 km narrow road around the Iveragh Peninsula. As we drove along, we stopped again and again to look at the mountains and the amazing views out to sea. At times we wished[6] there were fewer other tourists. Later, there was a big Irish welcome at a great little bed and breakfast. We were sorry we couldn't stay longer.

b) *Now read the tasks (1–6) and decide which answer is correct:* A, B *or* C.

1 Wendy and Tim went to Northern Ireland by ferry because they
- A wanted to save time.
- B wanted to save money.
- C wanted to take their car with them.

2 Wendy says tourists in Northern Ireland
- A can get killed in the religious conflict.
- B can enjoy the shopping and nightlife.
- C can paint walls in Belfast.

3 In the Irish Republic Wendy noticed that
- A cars drove on the right.
- B distances were in miles.
- C distances were in kilometres.

4 Wendy thinks that joining the EU has
- A made Ireland richer.
- B made Ireland poorer.
- C caused a lot of problems recently.

5 She loves the Rock of Cashel because
- A there is enough industry there.
- B she met lots of tourists there.
- C it has interesting historical buildings.

6 Wendy says that on the Ring of Kerry, she
- A drove over 170 km.
- B spoke to lots of people.
- C enjoyed the countryside.

c) *What did Wendy like about her holiday in Ireland? Name at least four things.*

[1] shipyard *Werft* [2] distance *Entfernung* [3] economy *Wirtschaft* [4] recently *in letzter Zeit, kürzlich*
[5] medieval architecture *mittelalterliche Architektur* [6] (to) wish *sich wünschen*

MEDIATION

1 Signs

Du machst mit deiner Familie Urlaub in England. Deine Eltern verstehen nicht viel Englisch und wollen wissen, was diese Schilder bedeuten. Erkläre es ihnen kurz auf Deutsch.

2 A poster

Du bist mit deiner Familie im Urlaub in Nova Scotia in Kanada. Dein kleiner Bruder fragt, was die auf dem Poster beschriebene Walbeobachtungstour bietet. Erkläre ihm kurz auf Deutsch:

- was man auf der Tour alles sehen kann
- wie man sich mit dem Kapitän verständigen kann
- wie lange die Tour dauert
- wie man sich an Bord verpflegt.

3 What's on TV this evening?

Imagine you have got an American guest. You are trying to decide what to watch on TV tonight. Read this page from a TV magazine and tell your guest what's on. Say:

- what kind of programme it is
- when and what channel it is on
- what it is about.

FERNSEHEN Tagestipps ab 17 Uhr

19:40 | RTL | SOAP

Gute Zeiten schlechte Zeiten

Pia wird furchtbar wütend, als sie John mit einem anderen Mädchen flirten sieht. Als John bemerkt, dass sie eifersüchtig ist, stellt er sie zur Rede.

20:15 | ARD | KRIMI

Tatort: „Tempelräuber"

In Münster ist ein Priester getötet worden. Kommissar Thiel soll den Fall aufklären. Sein Partner Boerne befindet sich diesmal in der Rolle des Zeugen.

20:15 | Pro 7 | SHOW

Schlag den Raab

Wer tritt heute gegen Moderator Stefan Raab an? Den Kandidaten und die Zuschauer erwarten Spiel, Sport, Quiz und vieles mehr.

21:15 | RTL | DOKUSOAP

Bauer sucht Frau

Bauer Heinrich gibt die Hoffnung nicht auf und sucht noch immer nach einer liebevollen Partnerin. Heute startet er einen neuen Versuch.

4 A school brochure

Du möchtest ein Schuljahr in England verbringen. Im Internet hast du folgende Informationen gefunden:

✶ ✶ ✶ THE ROYAL BLUE COATS SCHOOL ✶ ✶ ✶

The Royal Blue Coats School, founded by Charles II in 1666, is a day school for boys and girls aged 12 to 18. Location: in Hexham in the northeast of England in a quiet corner of the old town.

We offer 26 subjects including music, drama, art and design. Students can also choose between many different extra-curricular activities and clubs.

✶ Sports: There are the traditional sports – rugby, cricket and hockey – and many other choices, for example basketball, tennis and swimming (in our own swimming pool).

✶ Fees: £3,502 per term. This includes tuition[1] and books. (The school year, starting in September, has 3 terms.)

✶ Scholarships[2]: There are free places for a small number of students. For information, contact the school office.

✶ School lunches: The cost is £167 per term in Years 7 to 9 and £180 per term in Years 10 to 13. We also offer breakfast and snacks during mid-morning break.

[1] tuition *Unterricht* [2] scholarship *Stipendium*

Berichte deinen Eltern in Stichworten auf Deutsch:

- was es für eine Schule ist
- wo sich die Schule befindet
- was zum regulären Unterricht und zu weiteren Angeboten gesagt wird
- welche Sportarten angeboten werden
- wie hoch das Schulgeld ist
- wie die Kosten reduziert werden können
- was über die Verpflegung gesagt wird.

5 A flyer

Du hast mit deiner Familie eine Reise nach Arizona zum Grand Canyon gewonnen. Deine Mutter will Dein Englisch testen und lässt dich diesen Flyer erklären. Sage auf Deutsch etwas zu den Punkten rechts:

- warum der Abstieg in den Canyon (und auch der Aufstieg) gefährlich sein kann
- welche Übernachtungsmöglichkeiten es gibt
- was man unbedingt mitnehmen sollte.

Beautiful, but ...

Every year thousands of visitors go to the Grand Canyon and look down to the Colorado River one mile below. The view is absolutely fantastic, and some people decide to hike down to the river. This can be quite difficult, because the paths into the canyon are steep[1]. So you need a good pair of strong shoes. And climbing back up the path is even tougher! It can take a very long time, especially in the summer when it can get really hot (40 degrees Celsius). That's why it's important to bring lots of water. The National Parks Service does NOT recommend[2] doing the hike there and back in one day. It is better to get a backcountry permit[3] and spend the night on a campsite. Or there is a small number of beds at the Phantom Ranch in the canyon.

The Grand Canyon is a beautiful place, but it can be dangerous too. Plan your trip well and be careful. Many people have gone down into the canyon and not come out again – at least, not alive ...

6 Passing on[4] questions and answers

During your stay in Arizona, you and your family talk to Susan Diefenbacker, a ranger at the Grand Canyon National Park. Your parents' English is not very good, so you must help them.

Mutter Frag mal bitte, ob man heute in den Canyon hinabwandern kann.
You ...
Susan I wouldn't recommend it in this heat. And it's really too late in the day now.
You ...
Vater Schade. Ich würde gerne zum Fluss hinunter. Frag, wie es morgen wäre.
You ...
Susan If you leave very early in the morning, it should be OK.
You ...
Mutter Und wie ist es, wenn wir im Canyon übernachten wollen? Muss man im Voraus reservieren?
You ...
Susan Yes, but that shouldn't be a problem. Just come into the visitor's centre and we'll book a room at the Phantom Ranch for you.
You ...
Mutter Frag bitte, wann das Center öffnet.
You ...
Susan At 8 o'clock in the morning.
You ...
Vater Gibt es etwas Besonderes, was wir auf die Wanderung mitnehmen sollten?
You ...
Susan Lots of water! Four liters per person per day. Food and snacks – and lots of time! Good luck to you all! Be safe and enjoy your visit!
You ...
Mutter Bedanke dich bitte und sage ihr, dass wir morgen ins Besucherzentrum kommen.
You ...

[1] steep *steil* [2] recommend *empfehlen* [3] backcountry permit *Erlaubnisschein für Übernachtung in der Wildnis*
[4] (to) pass on *weitergeben, übermitteln*

Unit 1 Part A

4 Role play

▸ Unit 1, Part A (p. 9)

You and your partner are going to tell each other about a problem and ask for advice.

a) *Partner A: Read your role card. Then tell your partner about your problem. Ask for advice. Partner B: Listen to your partner and try to give advice.*

ROLE CARD Partner A:
Your results in your last tests weren't very good and your parents want you to do the year again. They say you spend too much time with your friends and not enough time on your school work. You don't want to change class.

Say you've got a problem.
I've got a problem.

Show interest.
Really? Why (not)?
Oh I see, so ...

Say what the main problem is.
I don't want to ...
My parents want me to ...
I'm worried because my friend ...

Ask for more details if you need to.
So, what/who/where ...?

Give some more details.
Well, ...

Say something nice.
Really? That's terrible/difficult.
Poor you.

Ask for advice.
So what should I do?

Give some advice.
I think you should ...
What about ...?
Could you ...?

b) *Partner B: Read your role card. Then tell your partner about your problem. Ask for advice. Partner A: Listen to your partner and try to give advice.*

ROLE CARD Partner B:
You're worried about a friend. She is missing a lot of school and is getting bad marks. She doesn't hang out with you and her other friends any more. You think you saw her take drugs at a party last Saturday. You think she's unhappy. You want to help her, but you don't know what to do.

Unit 1 **Part B**

P3 MEDIATION Which film? ► Unit 1, Part B (p. 15)

a) *Partner B: You and your friend are looking for an English DVD to watch together. Your friend will tell you about a film in German. Listen carefully.*

b) *Tell your partner about the film* Slumdog Millionaire *in German. The questions in the box can help you.*

- Was ist es für ein Film?
- Worum geht es?
- Würdest du den Film anschauen?

c) *Which film would you like to watch? Why?*

Slumdog Millionaire

This Oscar-winning drama, made by British director Danny Boyle, is based on a novel by Vikas Swarup. The film tells the story of Jamal (played by Dev Patel), a poor street kid in Mumbai. When we first see Jamal, he is on a TV quiz show, the Indian version of 'Who Wants to Be a Millionaire?'. With each answer he gives, we learn something about his amazing life. We also learn why Jamal is on the TV show: he's hoping to find his childhood love Latika (played by Freida Pinto). It's not always an easy film to watch – some of the scenes of life in the slums of Mumbai are shocking – but it's an exciting story that is full of action and surprises. This is a film that everyone will enjoy.

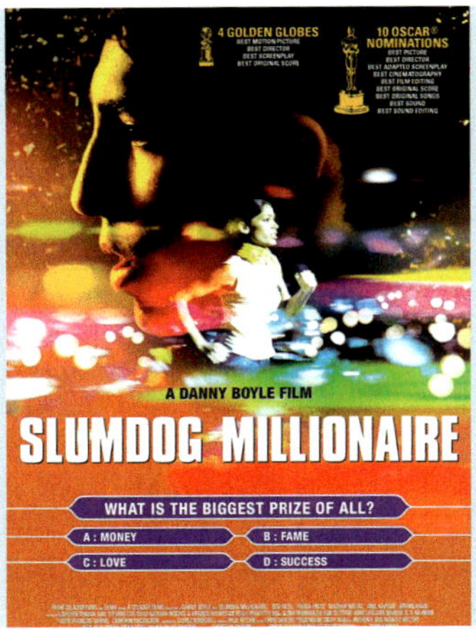

► SF Mediation (p. 147)

English for jobs

2 Now you: Role play ► p. 70

Partner B: Follow the instructions on the role card below. Be as polite and friendly as you can.

Last week you bought a new TV from an electronics store, but there is something wrong with it. Now you're going back to the store to ask if you can change it.

- Your partner will start the conversation.
- Say there's a problem with your TV.
- Give more information about the problem. (The sound/picture/... quality is bad/...)
- Say that you would like a different TV. Explain that you have no problem paying for a better/more expensive/... model.
- Thank A.

Unit 2 **Part B**

P1 You can make a difference

► Unit 2, Part B (p. 36)

a) *Partner B: You and your partner have different tips under each heading in the text* Go Green. *Read your tips and take notes in a chart under these headings:*

Use less energy	*Save trees*	*Think about your food*	*Reduce rubbish*
– turn off …	*– …*	*– …*	*– …*

► *SF Taking notes (p. 133)*

b) *Ask your partner about his/her tips to go green. Add the tips to your chart.*
What's your tip to use less energy/save trees/…?

Go Green!

Here are some simple things that you can do to help to stop global warming.

Use less energy

Producing electricity causes a lot of CO_2. So, to save energy, always turn off the lights when you leave a room. And when you're not using your computer, TV or stereo, turn them off completely.

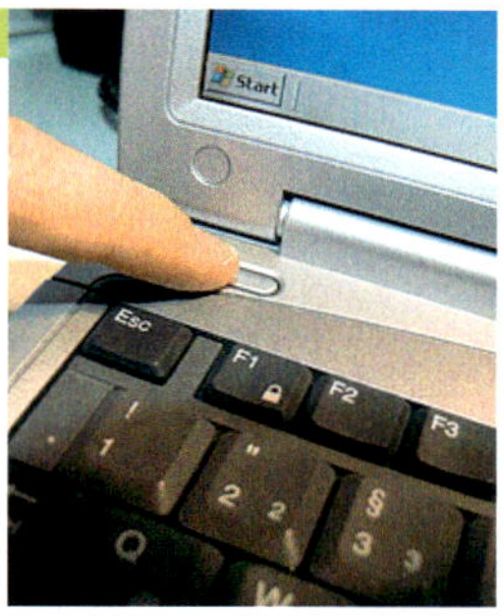

Think about your food

To help to fight against climate change, try to eat more local food. Local food has a small carbon footprint because it doesn't have to travel a long way to your local shop.

Save trees

Every day forests are cut down to make new paper. But we need trees to reduce CO_2 in the air. Think about the paper that you use. Is your printer paper 100% recycled? And what about your toilet paper?

Reduce rubbish

Everyone loves new stuff, but when we throw away our old stuff we produce a lot of rubbish and it takes a lot of energy to recycle it. So why don't you buy second-hand stuff? Clothes, books, mobile phones – anything! Buying second hand will also save you a lot of money!

Unit 3 Part A

P 4 Extra SPEAKING Role play: A discussion about video cameras at school

Role cards

▸ Unit 3, Part A (p. 51)

Moderator

You can use these phrases to ...

▸ ***start the discussion***

– Hello everyone. Thanks for coming to the meeting today.
– Our question/topic is ...
– So, who would like to start the discussion?

▸ ***ask questions***

– What's your opinion?
– Do you agree with that point?
– Can you explain that? / What do you mean?
– How? / Why?

▸ ***end the discussion***

– Time is up*, I'm afraid.
– Thank you all for taking part in the discussion.
– Let's vote now: Who is for/against ...?
– The result is that most people in this class ...

* time is up *die Zeit ist zu Ende*

Teacher AGAINST video cameras

– You think it's <u>your</u> job to make sure that students don't cause trouble.
– You don't want to be watched by cameras.
– The school should use the money for other things (computers, books, ...).
– You think that students will be afraid to speak openly.
– ...

Student 1 FOR video cameras

– With cameras, you would feel safer.
– Your cousin's school uses cameras and now there's less bullying.
– Nice students don't need to worry about the cameras, only the troublemakers.
– Cameras should also be in toilets because there's a lot of bullying and vandalism there too.
– ...

Head teacher FOR video cameras

– You watched a news report on TV about a school in London with cameras: the school is cleaner, safer and students' grades are better.
– There were a lot of problems at your school last year: computers were stolen, students were bullied, graffiti was written on the walls.
– It's expensive to buy new computers, to clean the graffiti, and to repair things in the school.
– ...

Parent FOR video cameras

– Troublemakers will be caught more easily.
– If the school doesn't have to spend so much money on repairing things, there will be more money for school trips, ...
– If teachers don't have to look after troublemakers all the time, they'll have more time for teaching.
– The school will be a nicer, cleaner place for everyone.
– ...

Student 2 AGAINST video cameras

– Bullying won't stop, it will take place outside school.
– Troublemakers shouldn't be watched by cameras, they should be watched by real people.
– There are cameras at your friend's school. Your friend says that it feels like a prison.
– You can't talk openly when you know that there are cameras and microphones.
– ...

▸ SF Having a discussion (p. 139)

Exam File

3 Discussing photos ► p. 79

a) Partner B: Listen to Partner A talking about his/her photo. Then show Partner A your photo and describe what you can see in it.
Discuss the different things that dogs can do for people. Say how you feel about dogs and why.

b) Partner B: Listen to Partner A talking about his/her photo. Then show Partner A your photo and describe what you can see in it.
Discuss different ways that people can spend their holidays. Say what kind of holiday you like best and why.

Exam File

7 Role plays: Solving problems abroad[1] ► p. 81

a) Partner B: Look at the role card and act out the conversation with your partner.

You're in an internet café in your town. The person at the PC next to you asks you some questions.
- Say how long you've lived in the town (► *two years*).
- You don't know the hotel your partner asks about. Ask the name of the street.
- Say how far it is (► *6 miles*).
- Say that there's a good, cheap hostel close to the internet café.
- Offer to show Partner A the way to the hostel.

b) Partner B: Look at the role card and act out the conversation with your partner.

You work at a travel agent's[2] in Spain. All European airports have been closed for a week for safety reasons. You have a lot of customers looking for an alternative way home. Many of them are very stressed. Your next customer comes to your desk and describes his/her situation.
- You know all about the situation. Describe the reactions of some of your customers.
- All trains are booked out for the next few days. Say the earliest date your customer could travel (► *Wednesday*).
- Journeys to German cities take between 25 and 30 hours.
- Say that a ticket costs €190.–
- React.

[1] abroad *im Ausland* [2] travel agent's *Reisebüro*

Unit 1 Part A

1 Hey Jake! ▸ Unit 1, Part A (p. 8)

> more help *Who do you agree with: Jake, Ally, Dani or JC?*
- I agree with …
- I don't agree with any of them.

What do you think Sam should do? Why?
- I think Sam should go to Spain/stay at home because …
- It's hard for Sam because he is older than his sister/has lost his mum/has a girlfriend/…
- It's hard for Sam's dad because he wants to start a new life/…
- Sam/Sam's dad is only thinking of himself.
- Sam should try it before he decides. He could always go back home/go to live in Spain.
- It's easy/difficult/exciting/… to make new friends/to have a girlfriend in a different country/ to start at a new school …
- Sometimes it's good to try new things. It's what makes life interesting.
- Friends are/Family is really important.
- I think it isn't a problem, it's a new experience. You should always be positive.

Unit 1 Part A

3 Now you ▸ Unit 1, Part A (p. 9)

a) more help *Choose one of the problems and decide how you would answer it. Make notes. You can answer the problems in lots of different ways. Here are some ideas:*

Be cool! Don't worry so much.

If you like this girl, you should …

I think you are / your friend / the girl / the boy is wrong / right to …
– feel / talk to you like that.
– worry about / think that …

When you are in a relationship it's OK / it's not OK / it's normal to …
– think that someone else is attractive.
– spend a lot of time with your girlfriend / boyfriend.

Only you can decide.

When people start a new relationship they often …

Maybe you / your girlfriend should …
– talk to her friend and find out what he / she thinks / feels.
– find a new girlfriend / (best) friend.

Don't do / say anything. Just see what happens.
If you wait a few weeks, things might be different.

Unit 1 **Part A**

P1 WORDS Describing people: appearance and character

▸ Unit 1, Part A (p. 10)

c) more help *Write a short description of yourself. Collect all the descriptions. Someone should read them out loud. Can you guess who it is? Here are some ideas:*

- I'm tall / short / thin / ...
- My hair is long / short / black / ...
- My eyes are brown / ...
- I've got a piercing in my nose / ...

- I think I'm (a bit) bossy / shy / ...
- I like / don't like ...
- I love ... / I don't care about ...
- People say I'm easy-going / friendly / ...
- I'm (not so) good at ...

Unit 1 **Part A**

P2 // ● REVISION Does your family annoy you? (Simple present)

▸ Unit 1, Part A (p. 10)

a) *Complete the text with the correct forms of the verbs in brackets. Use the* ***simple present****.*

My brother is really annoying. Every morning he (1) ... (go) into the bathroom first and he (2) ... (stay) in there for a long time. He (3) ... (get out) until it (4) ... (be) nearly time for school. My sister (5) ... (be) completely different. She never (6) ... (wash)! My brother and sister also (7) ... (take) my things. They (8) ... (ask) me first. They just (9) ... (come) into my room and (10) ... (look) around. What about you? (11) ... you ... (have) problems like this with your family? Actually my parents (12) ... (annoy) me too much. They usually (13) ... (leave) me alone. What about your parents? (14) ... they ... (annoy) you?

▸ GF 3: Talking about the present (p. 152)

Unit 1 **Part A**

P3 // ● REVISION A group of friends (Present progressive)

▸ Unit 1, Part A (p. 10)

Complete the description of the photo with the correct forms of the verbs in brackets. Use the ***present progressive****.*

This is a photo of me and some people I met at summer camp in the US. We (1) *are sitting* (sit) outside and the sun (2) ... (shine). Everyone (3) ... (have) a good time. I'm in the foreground on the left with my best friend Will (the guy with the black T-shirt). We (4) ... all ... (sing) a funny song. (4) Well, Josh and Kate (5) ... (sing) because they (6) ... (kiss). The girl who (7) ... (play) the guitar is Rose. Will (8) ... (flirt) with Rose. This is a bad idea because Rose's boyfriend Seb (9) ... (sit) behind him. Seb (10) ... (smile) – that's probably because he's jealous. I can't remember the names of the other people in the photo.

▸ GF 3: Talking about the present (p. 152)

Unit 1 **Part B**

2 VIEWING A review of *Juno*

d) **Extra** more help ▸ *Unit 1, Part B (p. 13)*

What do you think of the film review? Does it make you want to watch Juno*? Why (not)?*
You can use the ideas in the boxes below.

What do you think of the film review?
I think the review was interesting/boring/good/... because ...
- it was easy/difficult to understand.
- it was too long/short.
- it was/wasn't funny.
- the reviewer gave too many/not enough details.
- I found out/didn't find out a lot about the film/plot.

Does it make you want to watch Juno?
I would/wouldn't like to watch Juno because ...
- I like/don't like the main characters/the plot/the soundtrack/...
- I like/don't like this kind of film.
- I have seen *Juno* and I liked/didn't like it because ...

Unit 1 **Part B**

P 4 WRITING A short love story (Creative writing)

a) more help ▸ *Unit 1, Part B (p. 15)*

Use the pictures below to write a short story. The words and phrases in the boxes can help you.
▸ *SF Writing course (pp. 141–142)*

Tip
1. *Think of a plot. Collect words and phrases for each picture.* ▸ *SF Brainstorming (p. 140)*
2. *Think of names for the characters.*
3. *Write full sentences.*
4. *Use the past tenses* (he was late, she was waiting, ...).

were standing in front of the cinema • were waiting for a friend • looked at her/his watch • were annoyed/... • friends didn't come • ...

noticed that somebody else was waiting too • started to talk • liked each other • asked her out for a pizza • ...

went to a restaurant • spent a nice evening • talked for hours about music/... • fell in love • ...

Unit 1 Part C

1 // ● Tell the story ▸ Unit 1, Part C (p. 19)

Match the sentence halves.

1 Roger asks Penelope and Arnold to …	a orders lots of food and drinks.
2 Penelope wants to go, but Arnold is scared because …	b so Roger gives him some money.
3 At the diner Arnold …	c if he is poor.
4 Arnold goes to the bathroom …	d go to a diner with him and some friends.
5 Arnold tells Roger that he has forgotten his wallet, …	e so Roger drives him home.
6 Later, Penelope asks Arnold …	f he hasn't got any money.
7 Penelope doesn't want him to hitchhike, …	g because he feels sick.

Unit 1 Part C

3 ● more help Penelope's diary ▸ Unit 1, Part C (p. 19)

Imagine you are Penelope. In your diary, write about what happened at the diner.

***Step 1**: Decide what are the main facts of the story from Penelope's point of view. Make notes.*

I wanted to go to the diner. / Arnold looked scared. / At the diner he looked a bit sick. / He went to the bathroom. / I was worried …

***Step 2**: Make your text more interesting: connect your sentences with linking words. For example:*

after that • a few minutes later • and then • next • but • so … that • and • because • …

At the diner Arnold looked a bit sick and then he went to the bathroom.
Roger went to see if he was OK because I was worried. …

***Step 3**: Give a personal view at the end of your text.*

I don't care what Daddy says. / I like Arnold. / I think he's sweet / funny / …
I want Arnold to know that he doesn't have to lie to me / he's got friends / …

▸ SF Writing course (pp. 141–142)

Unit 2 **Part A**

P1 //● REVISION Things are different today (Simple present and simple past)

► Unit 2, Part A (p. 32)

Complete the sentences with the correct forms of the verbs in brackets: ***Simple present*** *or* ***simple past****.*

1. In the past people *used* (use) the sun to find out the time, now there ... (be) watches and clocks.
2. Now we ... (send) e-mails, but before the internet people ... (write) letters.
3. In the old days there ... (~~be~~) any planes or cars, so people ... (travel) by ship or ... (ride) horses. Today we ... (use) planes and cars for long journeys.

4. Today there ... (be) fridges. But in the old days people ... (keep) their food fresh with salt.
5. In the 1960s TVs ... (~~have~~) remote controls, so people ... (have) to get up to change channels. Today we ... (stay) comfortably on the sofa.
6. Now we ... (have) lots of TVs in our homes and children often ... (watch) TV in their rooms. But in the 1970s families ... (sit) together in one room to watch TV. They often ... (argue) about which channel to watch!

► GF 3: Talking about the present (p. 152) • GF 4: Talking about the past (p. 153)

Unit 2 **Part B**

P2 more help SPEAKING A cartoon (Talking about a cartoon)

► Unit 2, Part B (p. 36)

Step 1: Describe the cartoon.
- *What can you see in the picture?*
- *What is happening?*

> – I can see ... / There is/are ...
> – The car is eating/trying to eat ...
> – The car has ..., so it looks dangerous/...
> – The earth is/looks ... There's a piece missing because ...
> – ...

Step 2: Say what the message is.
- *What issue do you think the cartoon is about?*
- *What do you think the artist wants to say?*

> – The cartoon is about ...
> – I think the cartoon shows us that ... / the artist wants to say that ...
> – ...

Step 3: Give your opinion.
- *Do you like the cartoon?*
- *Do you agree with its message?*

> – I like/don't like the cartoon because ...
> – I think the artist is right/wrong because ...
> – ...

► SF Describing cartoons (p. 126)

Unit 2 Part B

P3 // ● WORDS The environment ▸ Unit 2, Part B (p. 37)

a) *Find more nouns that go with these verbs.*

– recycle	glass, ...
– save	energy, ...
– don't buy so much/many	meat, ...
– turn off	appliances, ...
– use	recycled paper, ...

b) *What can we do to save the environment? Find suitable verbs and make as many sentences as you can.*

We can	...	rubbish like glass, paper and plastic. public transport. more green energy because it produces less CO_2. lights and electronic appliances to save energy. ...

Unit 3 Lead-in

5 Extra more help The story behind the picture ▸ Unit 3, Lead-in (p. 47)

Choose a person in one of the photos on p. 46 and write about him/her. Answer these questions:

Where is he/she?
I think the man/woman/girl/... is in a kitchen/forest/youth club/...
He/she ... is standing/sitting/... on/in front of/next to ...
In the background there is/are ...
Maybe he/she is on holiday/...

What is he/she doing?
He/She is wearing/holding/making/...
Maybe he/she is waiting for/looking at/talking to/voting for/...

What is he/she feeling?
He/she looks relaxed/tired/...
He/she is probably excited/worried/sad/... because ...
I think she is happy/... because ...

What is he/she thinking?
Maybe he/she is thinking about ...
Perhaps he/she wants to ...

What was he/she doing before the picture was taken?
Maybe he/she was playing football/...

What will happen next?
I think he/she will go home/...
Maybe he/she will tell his/her friends that ...

▸ *SF Describing pictures (pp. 125–126)*

Unit 3 Part A

3 Now you ▸ Unit 3, Part A (p. 49)

a) more help *Discuss with a partner:*
Have you ever been in a situation when you thought you were discriminated against as a teenager?

Say where you were and what you were doing.

I was ...	
– on the bus/at the skate park/in the cinema/at the bus stop/in a shop/ in a café/...	– hanging out with friends/not doing anything wrong/looking at clothes/talking to friends/...

Say what happened and why.

A man/woman/shop owner/shop detective/ policeman/policewoman/...	I think he/she did that because he/she thought that I ...
– shouted at me/was rude to me/served other customers first/laughed at me/was watching me all the time/didn't stop/...	– was a troublemaker/was making too much noise/might steal something/wasn't important/...

Say how you felt and why.

I felt ...	because ...
– angry/annoyed/disappointed/sad/upset/...	– it was so unfair/they were wrong/they wouldn't say that to an adult/...

▸ *SF Having a discussion (p. 139)*

b) more help *Write to Oliver and comment on his article.*
First decide if you agree or disagree with Oliver. Use some of the ideas in the box to make your comment more interesting.

You agree with Oliver:	You disagree with Oliver:
It's unfair that young people can't go into shops/meet outside/... because the mosquito device/shop owners ...	Some teenagers do bad things/steal from shops/aren't interested in politics/...
Adults always think that all teenagers are troublemakers/take drugs/steal things/...	We should respect older people/follow the rules like everyone else/...
Older people should remember that ... we're not all bad/they were young too/we have rights/there aren't enough places for us to go/ we're bored sometimes/...	Big groups of teenagers look scary. / Shop owners have the right to ... / ...

▸ *SF Writing course (pp. 141–142)*

Unit 3 **Part A**

P1 WORDS Have your say ▸ Unit 3, Part A (p. 50)

a) // ● *Copy this chart. Collect words and phrases from the unit so far.*

Issues	Sources of information	Action you can take
the environment …	blogs …	buy fair-trade products …

Unit 3 **Part A**

▸ Unit 3, Part A (p. 51)

P3 REVISION Will the mosquito device keep troublemakers away? (*will*-future)

a) // ● *Tom and Jill are thinking about using the mosquito outside their shop. Tom thinks it's a good idea, but Jill thinks it's a bad idea. Write down their arguments. Use* **will** *and* **won't**.

Tom (for the mosquito)

1. mosquito – keep troublemakers away
2. our customers – feel safer
3. more people – come and shop here
4. with mosquito – there – not be big groups of teenagers outside shop
5. we – not have to pick up their rubbish

Jill (against the mosquito)

1. mosquito – not stop troublemakers
2. they – just go somewhere else and cause trouble
3. noise – annoy all young people
4. teenagers – not shop here any more
5. teenagers – not have safe place to meet parents or friends

▸ GF 5: Talking about the future (p. 155)

Unit 3 **Part B**

2 // ● The summary ▸ Unit 3, Part B (p. 53)

Complete the text.

At the start, Mr Neck is angry because his son can't get a job as a (1) … He thinks that (2) … should stop so that 'real Americans' can get jobs. For him, real Americans are people came to America (3) … 1900. He stops the (4) … when a boy says that maybe his son is too lazy or not good enough for the job. David says that the teacher can't just stop the debate when he doesn't (5) … with the things others say. David says that the lesson is (6) …, picks up his books and leaves the room.

Unit 3 Part B

P 3 SPEAKING Solving conflicts

▸ Unit 3, Part B (p. 55)

d) more help *Choose one of the situations in the pictures below. Decide who you are in the picture. Make a dialogue.*

Partner A: Explain your problem and ask your partner to do something about it. Be polite.

– The problem is ... – What annoys me is ...	– that you didn't ask if ... – that I can't/don't want to ... – that I'm trying to ... – ...
– Could you ...? – Maybe you could ...	– go somewhere else to talk on the phone? – change your socks? – play something else? – ...

Partner B: React to your partner. Think of a way to solve the conflict. Be polite.

I'm sorry ...	– I didn't mean to annoy you. – I didn't know that they smelt so bad. / you didn't like my music. / I was on the phone for so long. /... – I thought that they smelt OK. / everyone liked that music. / I was talking quietly. / ...
Of course I can/I'll ...	– play/do something else. – go somewhere else to play my music. / go outside to talk on the phone. /... – find some clean ones. / listen to another band. / ...

▸ *SF Writing course (pp. 141–142)*

English for jobs

3 Now you: Guided dialogue

▸ *p. 68*

Prepare a dialogue and act it out.

Partner A: You get a call from a customer.	Partner B: You want to order something.
Hello, ... (company name) ... (your name) speaking. →	Hello, this is ... (your name). Can I ...?
Yes, I'll ... →	OK, I'll ...
I'm sorry, but ... isn't ... →	Could you ask him to ...? My phone number is ... (your number)
That's ... Please, can you ...? →	Yes, ...

TF 1 My love is like ...

1 Love songs and poems

a) *Have you noticed that most songs and poems seem to be about love? What's your favourite love song or poem at the moment? What do its lyrics say about love?*

b) *Listen to and read songs A and B. For both songs, say*

– what the song is about.

losing someone • saying how wonderful someone is • wanting someone to be your girlfriend • boyfriend • ...

– how the singer feels.

angry • sad • romantic • ...

– what the singer's message is.

He wants us/his girlfriend to know that ...

A Love is all around

I feel it in my fingers, I feel it in my toes.
Well love is all around me, and so the feeling[1] grows.
It's written on the wind, it's everywhere I go.
So if you really love me, come on and let it show.
You know I love you, I always will.
My mind's made up[2] by the way that I feel.
There's no beginning, there'll be no end
'Cause on my love you can depend[3].
I see your face before me as I lay on my bed.
I kinda get to thinking of all the things you said.
You gave your promise to me and I gave mine to you.
I need someone beside[4] me in everything I do.

Reg Presley (born 1943)

B Bye bye love

Chorus
Bye bye love
Bye bye happiness
Hello loneliness
I think I'm gonna cry
Bye bye love
Bye bye sweet caress[5]
Hello emptiness
I feel like I could die
Bye bye my love, goodbye

There goes my baby
With someone new
She sure looks happy
I sure am blue[6]
She was my baby
Till he stepped in[7]
Goodbye to romance
That might have been[8]
Chorus
I'm through with[9] romance[10]
I'm through with love
I'm through with counting
The stars above
And here's the reason
That I'm so free
My loving baby
Is through with me
Chorus

Felice Bryant (1925–2003) Boudleaux Bryant (1920–1987)

[1] feeling ['fi:lɪŋ] *Gefühl* [2] (to) make up one's mind *sich entscheiden* [3] (to) depend on sth. [dɪ'pend] *sich auf etwas verlassen können* [4] beside [bɪ'saɪd] *neben* [5] caress [kə'res] *Zärtlichkeit, Streicheln* [6] blue *hier: traurig, deprimiert* [7] (to) step in *hier: dazwischenkommen* [8] that might have been *der/die/das hätte sein können* [9] (to) be through with sth. *mit etwas fertig sein* [10] romance [rəʊ'mæns] *Romantik*

2 Taking a closer look

Writers write poems and songs because they want us to feel, see, understand or imagine something about the world or life. They use special techniques to help to communicate their ideas. Read the study skills box and then answer these questions.

a) *Listen again to song A. Notice the slow rhythm. How does it make you feel?*

b) *Match the examples (1–3) to the statements (a–c) about song A.*

1 'toes-grows, you-do, bed-said'
2 'written in the wind'
3 'I feel it in my fingers, I feel it in my toes'
a The song uses this image to show that love is all around us.
b This phrase is repeated to show that how the singer feels is important in the song.
c The rhymes at the end of the lines connect the lines of the song together.

STUDY SKILLS Poem and song techniques

Rhymes[1] (e. g. sadness – madness, die – cry, new – blue): Writers don't always use rhymes, but they can help to make a poem (or song) sound good. They also help to structure a poem (or song) because they connect the lines together.
Rhythm[2]: The rhythm of a poem or song can change the way you feel. For example, a slow rhythm can make you feel thoughtful[3], relaxed or calm. A fast rhythm can make you feel energetic, excited or happy.

Repetition[4] (e. g. 'I'm through with romance, I'm through with love, ...'): If a sound, a word or a phrase is repeated, this shows us that the idea is important. It can also connect the lines together.
Images[5] (e. g. 'She fights like a tiger.', 'He is a rock.'): Images are used to make a picture with words or to show us an interesting, new way of looking at something.

► *SF Reading literature (pp. 136–137)*

3 A telephone conversation

Look at song B again and think about the singer's feelings. Write and act out a telephone conversation between the singer and a friend. You can use the example below to start your conversation.

A: Hi! Are you coming to my party tonight? You can bring your girlfriend.
B: Well ... we're not together any more.
A: Oh? What happened? Did you fight?
B: ...

4 What do you think?

Which is the best love song – the one you chose in 1a or one of the songs on page 112? Give reasons. (the music, rhythm, words, message, ...)

I think ... is the best song because ...
- it makes me feel happy/sad/calm/...
- it makes me (want to) dance/laugh/ sing along/...
- the music/words/rhythm/... is/are sad/ thoughtful/relaxed/happy/exciting/ ...
- the message is interesting/good/...

[1] rhyme [raɪm] *Reim* [2] rhythm ['rɪðəm] *Rhythmus, Takt* [3] thoughtful ['θɔːtfl] *hier: nachdenklich* [4] repetition [ˌrepə'tɪʃn] *Wiederholung* [5] image ['ɪmɪdʒ] hier: *Bild*

TF 2 Uniting Europe

1 AIRBUS – a European dream?

In 1969, a group of European aircraft[1] companies from France, Germany, Spain and the UK decided that they were too small to compete[2] with big American companies like Boeing. So they got together and founded Airbus.

Today, Airbus produces aircraft parts at 15 factories in France, Germany, Spain and the UK. The parts are then transported by ship, by road and by huge aircraft called Belugas to Toulouse (France), Hamburg (Germany) or, since 2009, to Tianjin (China) where they are finally put together.

The Airbus A380 is the world's largest passenger[3] aircraft. It is so big that you could park 70 cars on its wings. Airbus say it is greener than any other aircraft because it is quieter, produces less pollution and can take more passengers.

When things go well, Airbus seems to be a model of European cooperation[4]. But the company has had problems and has not always delivered[5] its aircraft to customers on time. One problem was caused when factories in different countries used different software. Since 2007, Airbus has lost money, cut jobs[6] and sold factories. When decisions are made about which countries will lose jobs, Airbus countries start arguing and national interests become more important than European cooperation.

The A380 can carry up to 525 passengers.

The A380 transport system

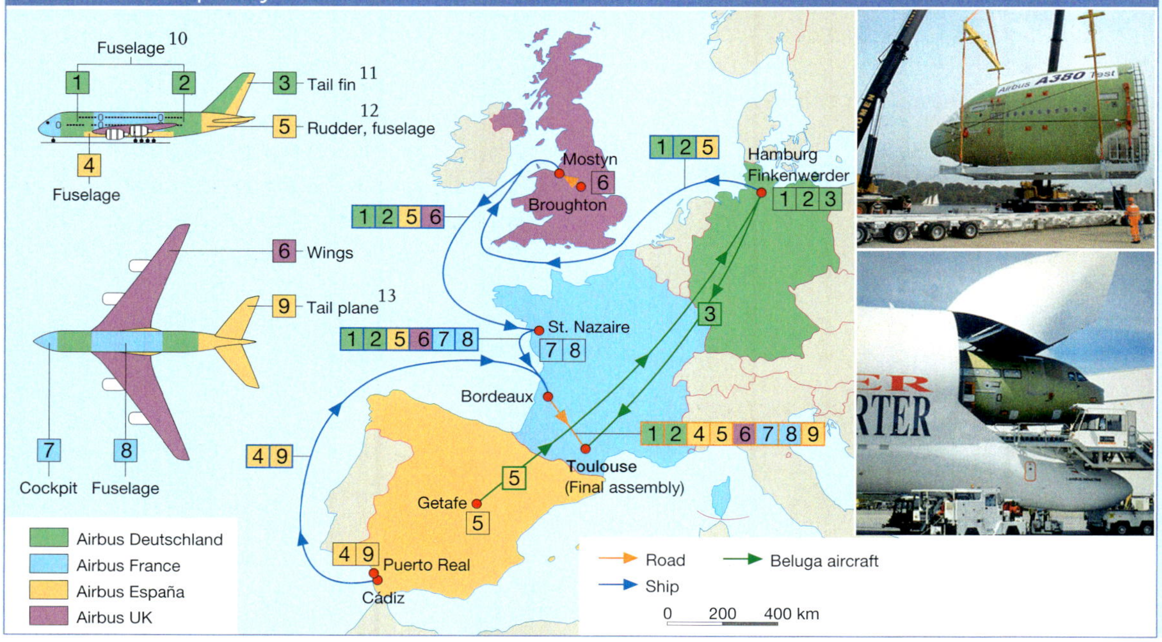

[1] truly ['tru:li] *wahrhaft* [2] aircraft ['eəkrɑ:ft] *Flugzeug* [3] site *Standort* [4] assembly line [ə'sembli laɪn] *Montagestraße* [5] (to) develop [dɪ'veləp] *entwickeln; aufbauen* [6] cargo plane ['kɑ:gəʊ pleɪn] *Frachtflugzeug* [7] (to) run *betreiben* [8] range [reɪndʒ] *Sortiment, Reihe* [9] seat [si:t] *Sitz(platz)* [10] fuselage ['fju:zəlɑ:ʒ] *Flugzeugrumpf* [11] tail fin ['teɪlfɪn] *Heckruder* [12] rudder ['rʌdə] *Seitenruder* [13] tail plane ['teɪlpleɪn] *Leitwerk*

Sam – Apprentice[1]

"I joined Airbus after secondary school and during my apprenticeship I have worked with people from France, Germany and Britain. It has been a very good experience and I have made lots of great friends from all three countries. I feel very lucky to have this apprenticeship. I would like to continue along the Airbus career path as far as I can."

a) *Read about Airbus and then answer these questions.*

1 Why did the European countries come together to build aircraft?
2 When does European cooperation become difficult for Airbus?
3 What does Sam like about his apprenticeship with Airbus?

b) *Look at the map on p. 114 and with the help of the skills and language boxes answer these questions:*

1 What does the map show?
2 Which parts of the Airbus A380 are made in Germany?
3 Where are the wings produced and how do they get to Toulouse?
4 How does the rudder get from Getafe to Toulouse?

c) *Do you agree or disagree with the following?*
It would be better if Airbus planes were all made in one place.

Make notes on your reasons and use them to discuss the question in class. You could think about:

European cooperation • transport problems • the environment • jobs in your country • competition with American companies • ...

GEOGRAPHY SKILLS Talking about maps

When you talk about maps,
– look at the title and the key[2] and make sure you understand what the map is about.
– start with a general statement about the map, then talk about the details.

Activate your English
– The map shows ...
– Broughton/... is situated in/near/ ...
– ... is about ... km away from ...
– ... is between ... and ...
– The wings/... are produced/made in ...
– They are carried/taken/transported/shipped/flown from ... to ...
– They are transported by road/ship/air/cargo plane/...
– The aircraft parts are put together in ...

[1] apprentice [ə'prentɪs] *Auszubildende/r* [2] key [ki:] *Legende*

2 Young people and the European Union

a) *What does the EU mean to you personally? Think about the question for a minute and write down your ideas. Then collect all the answers in class and write down the three most popular ideas.*

b) *Now describe the chart below. The skills box on the right will help. Say*
- what the chart is about
- what the source and date are
- what you have learnt from the chart.

GEOGRAPHY SKILLS Talking about charts

When you talk about charts,
- look at the title and the key and make sure you understand what the chart is about.
- check what the numbers on the chart mean. They might be age, population in millions, kilometres, per cent of people, ...
- start with a general statement about the chart and then talk about the details.

▸ *SF Talking about charts (p. 131)*

c) *Compare your ideas in a) with the chart.*

YOUNG PEOPLE AND EUROPE
What the European Union means for Europeans aged 15–30

I can travel, study and work anywhere.	90%
My rights are protected.	72%
It's good for the economy[1].	71%
It's good that there's a European government.	56%
Too many complicated rules. / It's a waste of time[2] and money.	40%
Cultures mix too much.	35%

Source: The Gallup Organization / The European Commission (February 2007)

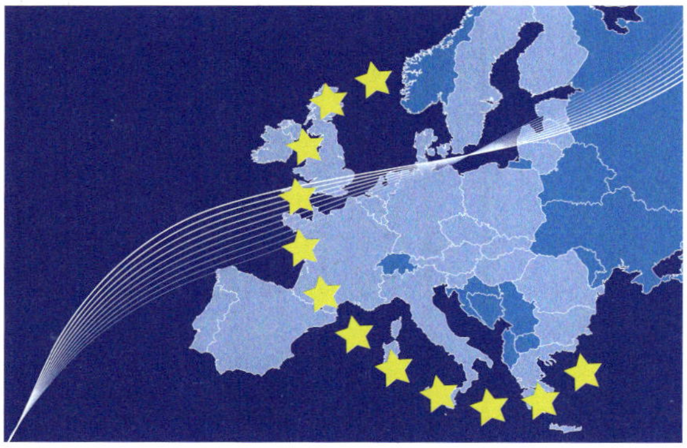

Activate your English
- Their results are similar/completely different to ours.
- The most important issue[3] for us/them is ...
- The second/third/... most important issue is ...
- Everyone/no one/not many people in our group said that ...
- I find their results very interesting/strange/hard to believe/...

[1] economy [ɪ'kɒnəmi] *Wirtschaft* [2] waste of time [weɪst əv taɪm] *Zeitverschwendung* [3] issue ['ʃuː] *Thema, Problem*

TF 3 The Meatrix

1 The Matrix

Read the summary of the plot[1] *of* The Matrix. *Make notes under the headings in the box.*

Characters • Pills • Dream world • Real world

Neo feels that something's wrong with the world. Morpheus offers Neo two pills. With the red pill he will find out the truth[2]. With the blue pill his life will continue[3] as before. Neo takes the red pill and he realizes[4] that he is living in a dream world called the Matrix. The Matrix was created[5] by intelligent machines to control humans and keep them happy. The humans think that their lives are continuing as normal, but this is an illusion[6]. In the real world they are prisoners on large farms where the machines use them to produce energy.

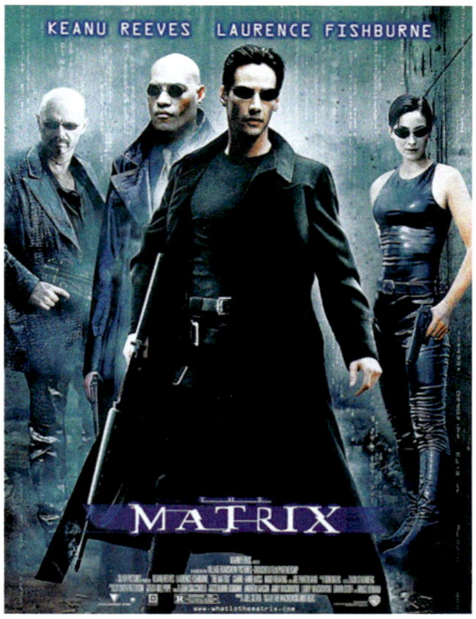

2 The Meatrix

a) *Compare the* Meatrix *poster with the* Matrix *poster. What do you think the cartoon* The Meatrix *is about?*

b) *Partner A: Watch the cartoon, but cover your ears so that you can't hear the sound. Partner B: Listen, but don't look at the screen. When the cartoon ends, discuss these questions: Who are the two main characters? Where is the story set at first? Where is it set later?*

c) *Which of these statements are wrong? Correct them.*

1. At first Leo thinks he is living on a family farm.
2. Leo tells Moopheus about the Meatrix.
3. The Meatrix is the story that we tell ourselves about the family farms that produce our food.
4. Leo doesn't want to find out the truth about the Meatrix.
5. Now he realizes he's living on a factory farm.
6. Moopheus describes what is bad about factory farming.
7. Moopheus, Leo and their friends can stop the Meatrix on their own.

d) *Watch the film again (with pictures and sound) and check your answers to c).*

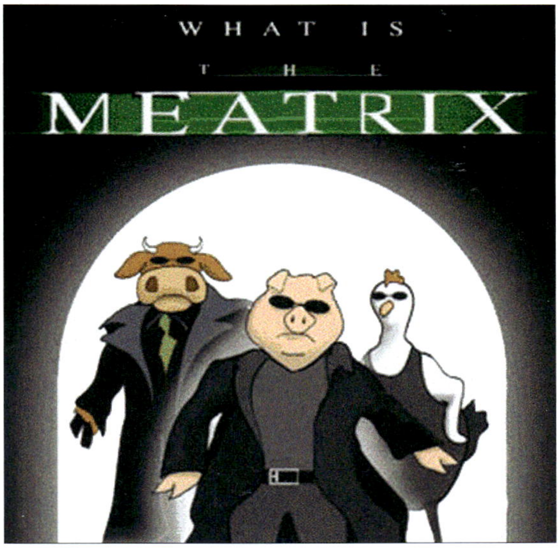

3 The Meatrix – just a cartoon?

a) *What is the message of the cartoon?*

b) *How does* The Meatrix *use* The Matrix *to do this? (Think about the titles, the plots and the characters.)*

– The Meatrix uses a similar ...
– In both films the characters ...

c) *What do you think of the cartoon?*

It made me/didn't make me want to eat no/more/less ...

---

[1] plot *Handlung* [2] truth [tru:θ] *Wahrheit* [3] (to) continue [kən'tɪnju:] *hier: weitergehen* [4] realize ['ri:əlaɪz] *erkennen* [5] (to) create [kri'eɪt] *hier: erschaffen* [6] illusion [ɪ'lu:ʒn]

TF 4 If only Papa hadn't danced (by Patricia McCormick, abridged and adapted)

Before you read the story, look at the picture below. Describe what is going on. Who do you think the people are? What do you think their relationship to each other is? Where do you think they are? What do you think will happen next? Make some notes and then discuss your ideas in a group.

BUT who could blame him? When they saw the results of the presidential election[1], a lot of people danced and sang in the streets. Finally the Old Man had lost. The man who stole from the poor to make himself rich was finished.

But not everyone in the village danced that night. Some men stood in the shadows[2] and watched. They were the men who had become rich and fat, thanks to the Old Man.

The next day, Papa and his friends listened to the radio. They heard that the election results were a mistake. The votes must be counted again. Papa spat in the dust[3] and said it was a lie.

Two weeks later, the Old Man was still in his big house in the capital. Papa and his friends grumbled to each other, but not loud enough for anyone else to hear.

Then one night we awoke to the hot breath[4] of fire. Our corn field was on fire[5]. We jumped from our beds and ran to the field. But we were too late. Our entire[6] crop[7] was gone.

The police came and looked at our field with eyes of stone and told us to take all our things from our house.

'Take what you can,' one of the policemen said. 'They will be back tonight. This time they will burn your house.' 'They?' I asked Papa when the policemen had gone. 'Who are they?' Papa sighed and shook his head. 'Our neighbours,' he said. 'People we have known all our lives. People with full stomachs thanks to the Old Man.'

Mama was angry with Papa. 'Everyone saw you dancing,' she said. 'They know you voted against the Old Man and now we will pay for it.' She looked at the fields of the men who had danced with Papa. Their fields were all burned

---

[1] presidential election *Präsidentschaftswahl* [2] shadow *Schatten* [3] (to) spit in the dust *in den Staub spucken* [4] breath *Atem*
[5] (to) be on fire *brennen* [6] entire *ganz, komplett* [7] crop *Ernte*

too. The other fields were as green as they'd been the day before.

And so we packed our things, took one last look at our home, then turned to face our future[1].

'Where will we go?' I asked Papa.

'We will walk until we find a friendly place where we can stay,' he said. 'When it is safe, when the real president is in power, then we will return home.'

As we came to the centre of the village, we met up with other families like ours. 'Why?' the children asked. 'Why must we leave home?' But the parents did not dare[2] to answer – in case[3] 'they' were listening.

The world outside the village was new and strange. We walked at night, and slept under trees in the day. We walked and walked and walked.

At last we came to a village. We thought that it was our safe place, the place where we would rest[4] until we could go home. But as we came near, we saw that the village looked just like ours. One house burned, the one next door untouched.

And so we walked on and on, each village the same. We heard news as we walked. 'The Old Man is still in power[5],' people said.

Then we came to a big river. I knew from my school lessons that we had come to the end of our country. On the other side of the river was a free country, a place where the people had voted[6] for a president who had spent years in jail fighting for justice[7].

Mama washed her face in the river, but I knew that she was trying to hide her tears. 'This is our homeland,' she said. 'No one wants us over there.'

Then I saw the long metal fence, like a snake,
on the other side of the river. I saw a man in an orange jumpsuit[8] with a pistol in his belt. He was mending[9] a hole at the bottom of the fence – someone must have escaped the night before.

Papa said that I was needed. There was a sign, he said, that he needed me to read. The sign said: beware of[10] crocodiles. That night, we hid until it was dark. We wanted to cross the river at midnight, when the man in the orange jumpsuit had gone home and when the crocodiles, we hoped, were asleep.

When it was time to go, Papa said 'Wait here,' And then he lifted[11] Mama up and carried her across[12] the river in the darkness[13]. When he returned he lifted me onto his shoulders and walked into the water. Every stick I saw was a crocodile. When we reached the other side, I jumped from his shoulders and kissed the sand.

I watched Papa disappear into the dark again and thought how much I loved his strong back; how it carried all our worries, and all our hopes. Finally Papa came out of the darkness carrying all our bags on his head.

Then we looked for a place to dig[14]. But the ground was hard and the fence was strong. Soon it would be light and we'd be caught between the crocodiles and the man with the pistol in his belt.

Papa found a place where the ground was not so hard and said we would have to dig here quickly.

And so all three of us dug – Mama in the middle and Papa and I on either side. Soon I'd dug a hole just big enough for a man's foot. I looked for Papa to show him my work – and saw the man in the orange jumpsuit walking towards us.

The man put his hand on the belt that held his pistol. 'Take me,' Papa said. 'Let the woman and the girl go free.' The man took out a huge cutting tool[15]. With one big snap[16] he cut a hole in the fence and held it open. 'Hurry,' he said. We weren't sure what he was saying, but we didn't wait.

'You go first,' Papa said to me. 'I want you to be the first in our family to feel freedom[17].' I climbed through the fence, stood next to the man in the orange jumpsuit and looked back at our homeland[18].

---

[1] (to) face the future *der Zukunft ins Auge sehen* [2] (to) dare *wagen* [3] in case *falls* [4] (to) rest *ausruhen* [5] (to) be in power *an der Macht sein* [6] (to) vote *wählen* [7] justice *Gerechtigkeit* [8] jumpsuit *Overall* [9] (to) mend *reparieren* [10] beware of *Vorsicht vor* [11] (to) lift sb. up *jn. hochheben* [12] across *durch* [13] darkness *Dunkelheit* [14] (to) dig *graben* [15] cutting tool *Schneidewerkzeug* [16] snap *Schnappen* [17] freedom *Freiheit* [18] homeland *Heimat*

'You will miss it for a long time,' the man said to me. 'I ran from the Old Man a long time ago and I still miss it.'

'Quickly now,' he said, when Mama and Papa had come through the fence. 'Walk, as fast as you can, until you see a house with white flowers in the garden. The people there are from our country. They will feed you and hide you until night. Then they will send you to the next safe house, which will send you to the next, and the next – until finally you are in the city and you can hide in the crowds of people there.'

We found the house with the white flowers. A woman there brought us inside, gave us water and meat and showed us where we could rest. I fell asleep immediately[1] When I woke up I went outside. The sun was setting[2], and I could see Papa's silhouette against the sky. He put up his arms and started to hum[3]. And then I saw Papa dance.

Working with the text

1 Your impressions[4]

Think back to your group discussion about the picture on p. 118. Were any of your ideas correct? How close were your ideas to what happened in the story.

2 The setting and plot[5]

a) *What can you say about the setting of the story?*

– The story is set in ...
– The setting might be ...

b) *Put the boxes into the right order to complete the plot of the story* If only Papa hadn't danced.

STUDY SKILLS Reading fiction[6] (1)

Setting[7] and plot

The **setting** of a story is the place and time it happens. The setting might be:

– an American city after an earthquake
– the Australian outback in the 1950s
– a fantasy world in the future
– ...

The **plot** is the action and events that take place in a story. These events often happen because one event causes another. Stories also often use flashbacks[8] in their plots.

▸ *SF Reading literature (pp. 136–137)*

A They walk across the country and find that the same thing has happened in other villages.

B They cross the river and then they try to dig a hole under the fence, but the man finds them.

C One night, the fields of the people who voted against the Old Man burn.

D The police say that the family's house will burn too, so they leave the village.

E Papa dances because the Old Man loses the election. The next day the radio says that the election result was wrong.

F They come to a river and they decide to cross it to get to the free country on the other side.

G He sends them to a safe house and that evening the girl sees her father dance again.

H But it isn't easy: There is a big fence, a man with a pistol and there are crocodiles in the river.

I They are surprised when the man cuts the fence and helps them to get into the other country.

[1] immediately *sofort* [2] the sun was setting *die Sonne ging unter* [3] (to) hum (-mm-) *summen* [4] impression [ɪm'preʃn] *Eindruck* [5] plot *Handlung* [6] fiction ['fɪkʃn] *Erzählliteratur, Belletristik* [7] setting ['setɪŋ] *Schauplatz, Handlungsrahmen* [8] flashback ['flæʃbæk] *Rückblende*

3 The characters

a) *Make a network with the character's names: Old Man, narrator*[1]*, Papa, Mama, man in jumpsuit. Add notes to show the links between them (e.g. father of, same homeland as, ...).*

b) *Find at least three examples in the story that tell us something about the father's character. Make notes like this:*

Old Man	*– steals from the poor to make himself rich (ll. 4–5)*	*– bad person*
Papa	*–*	

STUDY SKILLS Reading fiction (2)

Characters

We learn what a character is like from the things the writer or the other characters say about them and from their words, actions, feelings, thoughts, and connections to other characters.

► *SF Reading literature (pp. 136–137)*

c) *Discuss your ideas with a partner.*

4 The atmosphere[2]

a) *Without reading the story again, finish this sentence:*

The atmosphere in the story is ...

b) *Examine the following examples from the story. Explain what kind of atmosphere the writer creates*[3] *with them.*

- 'Then one night we awoke to the hot breath of fire.' (image[4], ll. 19–20)
- 'The police came and looked at our field with eyes of stone ...' (image, ll. 23–24)
- 'We walked, and walked and walked.' (repetition, ll. 56–57)

STUDY SKILLS Reading fiction (3)

Atmosphere

The atmosphere of a story is the feeling you get when you read the story. The atmosphere might be:

- bright and happy
- dangerous and scary
- warm and romantic
- sad and lonely
- ...

To create atmosphere, a writer can use adjectives, images and repetition.

► *SF Reading literature (pp. 136–137)*

5 What do you think?

a) *Which of the following adjectives best describe the story?*

boring • depressing • exciting • interesting • moving[5] • romantic • sad • sentimental • unbelievable • well-written • ...

b) *Why did the narrator's father decide to leave the country with his family?*

c) *Why do people leave their home country?*

---

[1] narrator [nəˈreɪtə] *Erzähler/in* [2] atmosphere [ˈætməsfɪə] *Atmosphäre* [3] (to) create [kriˈeɪt] *erzeugen, erschaffen* [4] image [ˈɪmɪdʒ] *Bild*
[5] moving *bewegend*

TF 5 Two presidents

1 The US president

***a)** What do you think? Are these statements right or wrong?*

1 The US president can tell important people in the government what to do.
2 He only makes speeches.
3 He can stop the parliament (Congress[1]) when they want to make an important law.
4 The president is the leader of the US military.
5 He has got two planes.
6 Even a person born in Germany could become US president.

Did you know?

- If you want to become president, you must have been born in the US (and you must be at least 35 years old).
- The president has two planes. The name 'Air Force One' is used when the president is in one of them.
- Barack Obama is the first black US president.
- There hasn't been a female president in the US yet.
- The US is the most powerful country in the world: it has got the largest military and the largest economy[2].

***b)** Now check your answers with the help of the texts on this page.*

Running the government

The president is the head of the government. He chooses the members of the Cabinet[3] and tells them what to do.

Signing/vetoing laws

The president can make it hard or impossible for Congress to make a law. If he doesn't sign[4] a bill[5] from Congress and vetoes[6] it, they have to discuss and try again. If he signs it, it becomes law.

Commanding the military

The US president is the 'Commander-in-chief'. He directs the military[7] and tells his generals what to do. (But he can't declare war.)

Representing the country

The president is also the head of state[8]. He represents the country and talks to leaders of other countries. On important days, he makes speeches.

***c)** Why is the US president called 'the most powerful person in the world'? Find reasons and use the phrases from the language box.*

– I think he is called the most powerful person in the world because he is ...
– He can ...

Activate your English

The US president ...
– is the head of state.
– runs the government.
– represents the country.
– chooses the members of the Cabinet.
– signs/vetoes laws.
– makes speeches.
– meets leaders from other countries.
– commands the military.

[1] Congress ['kɒŋgres] *US-Parlament, besteht aus Senat und Repräsentantenhaus; vergleichbar mit deutschem Bundestag und Bundesrat*
[2] economy [ɪ'kɒnəmi] *Wirtschaft* [3] Cabinet ['kæbɪnət] *Mitglieder des Kabinetts beraten den Präsidenten* [4] (to) sign [saɪn] *unterzeichnen*
[5] bill *Gesetzesentwurf* [6] (to) veto sth. ['viːtəʊ] *gegen etwas Einspruch erheben* [7] military ['mɪlətri] *Armee* [8] head of state *Staatsoberhaupt*

2 The German president

a) *Name the current[1] German president. Say what you know about him.*

b) *Who does what? Read the e-mail about the German president. Then use the phrases in the language box on p. 122 to complete the chart.*

What does the US president do?

US president	German president
He runs the government. …	He is the head of state. …

Mike is an American exchange student in Germany. One of his friends in the US, Janet, has to give a presentation on the German president, so Mike gives her the most important facts in this e-mail:

Dear Janet
The role of the German president is very different from that of our president. Here in Germany, all the really important things (like running the government, going to important international meetings) are done by the 'chancellor[2]' and NOT by the president!
The German president is the head of state, but he mainly makes speeches. Sometimes he meets leaders of other countries, but he can't make important decisions or tell people what to do (like command[3] the military). He only represents the country.

Good luck with your presentation!

CU Mike

3 Presidents as heroes

Hollywood has made a lot of movies with a US president as the hero. Why are there no German movies with a German president as the hero? What do you think?

[1] current ['kʌrənt] *aktuell, derzeitig* [2] chancellor ['tʃɑ:nsələr] *Kanzler/in* [3] (to) command [kə'mɑ:nd] *befehligen*

Skills File – Inhalt

Das **Skills File** dieses Bandes fasst alle Arbeits- und Lerntechniken zusammen, die du in den Bänden 1 bis 6 kennengelernt hast.

Die Themen, die in Band 6 neu sind, sind mit **NEW** gekennzeichnet:
- **NEW Describing cartoons**, Seite 126
- **NEW Reading literature**, Seite 136.

Die Hinweise im **Skills File** helfen dir bei der Arbeit mit Hör- und Lesetexten, beim Sprechen, beim Schreiben von eigenen Texten, bei der Sprachmittlung und beim Lernen von Methoden.

STUDY AND LANGUAGE SKILLS

SF Learning words

Worauf solltest du beim Lernen und Wiederholen von Vokabeln achten?

- Lerne immer 7–10 Vokabeln auf einmal.
- Lerne neue und wiederhole alte Vokabeln regelmäßig – am besten jeden Tag 5–10 Minuten.
- Lerne mit jemandem zusammen. Fragt euch gegenseitig ab.
- Schreib die neuen Wörter immer auch auf und überprüfe die Schreibweise mithilfe des *Dictionary (pp. 173–203)* oder *Vocabulary (pp. 163–172)*.

Wie kannst du Wörter besser behalten?

Wörter kannst du besser behalten, wenn du sie in Wortgruppen sammelst und ordnest:

- **Gegensatzpaare** sammeln, z. B. **alive ◄► dead**, **majority ◄► minority**, **(to) forget ◄► (to) remember**
- Wörter mit **gleicher oder ähnlicher Bedeutung** sammeln, z. B. **(to) train** – **(to) practise**
- Wörter in **Wortfamilien** sammeln, z. B. **(to) dance**, **dance**, **dancer**, **dancing lessons**; **friend**, **boyfriend**, **girlfriend**, **friendly**, **unfriendly, ...**
- Wörter in **Wortnetzen** *(networks)* sammeln und ordnen.

SF REVISION Describing pictures

Wie kann ich Bilder beschreiben?

- Um zu sagen, wo genau etwas abgebildet ist, benutze:
  at the top/bottom • **in the foreground/background** • **in the middle** • **on the left/right**
- Diese Präpositionen sind auch hilfreich:
  behind • **between** • **in front of** • **next to** • **under**
- Um zu beschreiben, was die Personen auf dem Bild tun, benutze das **present progressive**.
  The girl is standing next to a woman.

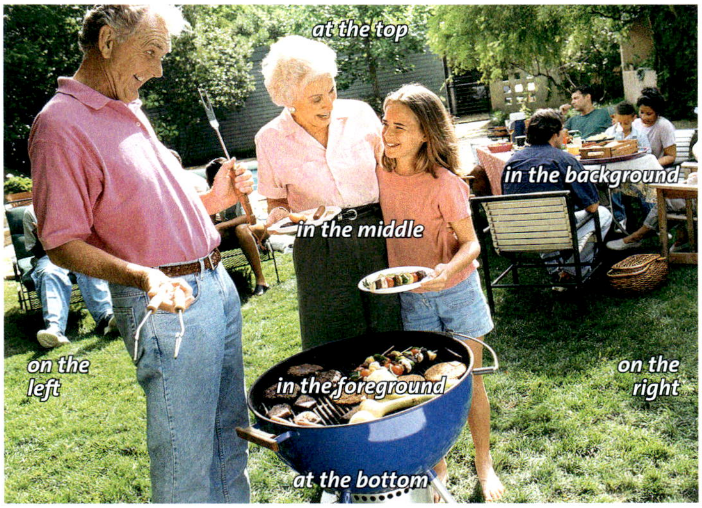

Wie kann ich beschreiben, was die Personen fühlen?

Oft sollst du dich in eine Person auf einem Foto hineinversetzen und beschreiben, was sie fühlt oder denkt. Schau dir das Foto genau an und nimm dir Zeit, dir die Situation vorzustellen. Beim Formulieren helfen dir *phrases* wie:
Maybe the woman/man in the photo feels ... /is thinking about ... •
I think he/she feels/wants to/...

Manchmal sollst du dir vorstellen, was die Person getan hat, bevor das Foto gemacht wurde. Achte auf Details im Foto (Hat die Person einen Gegenstand in der Hand? Wie sieht sie aus? Was tut sie?) und überlege dir, wie es zu der im Foto gezeigten Situation gekommen sein könnte (Warum ist die Person traurig, fröhlich etc.?). Verwende die **past tenses**:
Maybe he found out that ... • Perhaps he was looking for a place to relax/...

Wenn du beschreiben sollst, was wohl als Nächstes geschehen wird bzw. was die Person danach tun wird, verwendest du die **future tenses**:
He looks as if he's going to cry/... • Maybe he'll decide to ...

SF NEW Describing cartoons ▸ *Unit 2, Part B (p. 36)*

Cartoons sind humorvolle Zeichnungen, die häufig ein aktuelles Thema aufgreifen.

Wie beschreibe ich einen Cartoon?

Bei der Beschreibung eines Cartoons gehst du zunächst vor wie bei der Beschreibung von Fotos oder anderen Zeichnungen.

1. Beschreibe die Personen oder Dinge: Was tun sie gerade? Wo befinden sie sich? usw.
   The cartoon shows ... • In the foreground/ background/... there is/are ...

2. Achte darauf, ob der Cartoon eine Bildunterschrift (*caption*), Sprechblasen oder Gedankenblasen (*speech bubbles, thought bubbles*) hat.
   In the caption it says that ...

GLOBAL WARNING

Wie analysiere ich die Aussage eines Cartoons?

1. Sag, worum es in dem Cartoon geht, welches Thema er behandelt:
   The cartoon is about ...

2. Wenn du analysierst, welche Botschaft (*message*) der Cartoon-Zeichner vermitteln möchte, solltest du alle Elemente des Cartoons noch einmal zusammen betrachten: die Zeichnung sowie die Bildunterschrift und Sprech- oder Gedankenblasen. Achte darauf, ob die Personen oder Dinge positiv oder negativ dargestellt werden. Bedenke, dass ein Cartoon auch ernste Themen humorvoll darstellt und oft stark übertreibt!
   I think the cartoon shows us that ... • The artist wants to say that ...

3. Manchmal sollst du Stellung zur Botschaft des Cartoons nehmen und deine eigene Meinung sagen:
   I like/don't like the cartoon because ... • I think the artist is right/wrong because ...

SF Check yourself

How am I doing?

Damit du weißt, wie gut du die Kompetenzbereiche (**Listening**, **Speaking**, **Reading**, **Writing**, **Mediation**) beherrschst und wo du noch Schwächen hast, solltest du dich immer wieder selbst überprüfen. Das kannst du auf unterschiedlichen Wegen tun. Eine Reihe von Tipps kennst du vermutlich schon. Du kannst dich auch nach jedem *Getting ready for a test* mithilfe der *How am I doing*-Seiten selbst überprüfen. Dabei gehst du wie folgt vor:

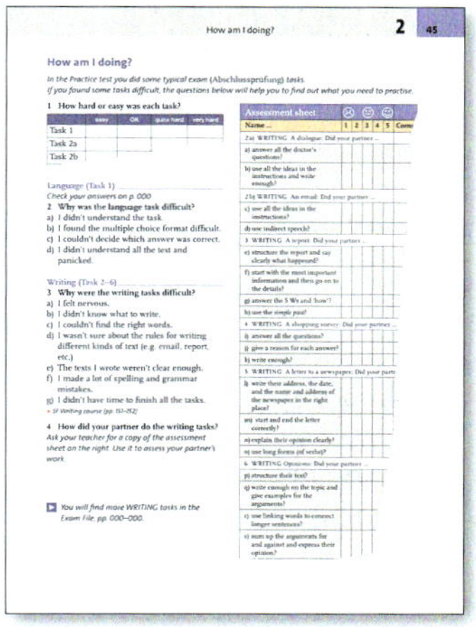

1. Du bearbeitest die Aufgaben und überprüfst deine Ergebnisse.
2. Dann schaust du dir die Bereiche, in denen du Fehler gemacht hast, noch einmal an. Die Verweise zeigen dir, auf welchen Seiten im Schülerbuch du Tipps oder Übungen zu diesen Bereichen findest.
3. Nun solltest du gezielt diese Bereiche üben. Dies kannst du z. B. mithilfe des *Exam File* oder des *Workbook* tun. Frag auch deinen Lehrer oder deine Lehrerin, wo du noch weitere Übungen finden kannst.

Die Arbeit mit einer persönlichen Fehlerliste

Führe eine Liste der Fehler, die du oft machst, und nutze sie beim Schreiben von Texten als persönliche Checkliste. Hefte diese Listen in deinem Englischordner ab oder lege dir dafür ein extra Heft an (z. B. in DIN-A5).
Das Heft kannst du z. B. nach folgenden Schwerpunkten unterteilen:

1. Drittel: *Words* 2. Drittel: *Grammar* 3. Drittel: *Spelling*

Dann untersuchst du deine Klassenarbeiten und andere schriftliche Arbeiten auf deine Fehlerquellen hin. Dein/e Englischlehrer/in zeigt durch Abkürzungen am Rand, was für eine Art Fehler du gemacht hast.

WORDS

Wrong	Correct	REMEMBER
He goes to school ~~with the~~ bus.	He goes to school by bus.	mit dem Bus fahren – go by bus
We've got a ~~strong~~ teacher.	We've got a strict teacher.	Nicht verwechseln! streng – strict / strong – stark
I climbed ~~on~~ a tree.	I climbed a tree.	auf einen Baum klettern – climb a tree

Tipp

- Ergänze das Heft jedes Mal, wenn du eine Klassenarbeit oder einen Text von deinem Lehrer/deiner Lehrerin zurückbekommen hast.
- Überprüfe, ob du bestimmte Fehler immer wieder machst. Wenn ja, such dafür Übungen in deinem Englischbuch, deinem *Workbook*, deinem *e-Workbook* oder frag deinen Lehrer/deine Lehrerin nach Übungen.
- Schau dir vor jeder Klassenarbeit die Fehler an, die du oft machst.
- Mach dir mithilfe des Grammatikteils die Regeln, die dir besonders schwerfallen, noch einmal bewusst.

SF Using a bilingual dictionary

Wann brauche ich ein zweisprachiges Wörterbuch?

Du verstehst einen Text nicht, weil er zu viele Wörter enthält, die dir unbekannt sind, und die Worterschließungstechniken (▸ *SF Working out the meaning of words, p. 134*) helfen dir nicht weiter?
Du sollst einen Text auf Englisch schreiben und dir fehlt das eine oder andere Wort, um deine Ideen auszudrücken? Du willst z. B. sagen, die Handlung in *Twilight* dreht sich um die schwierige Beziehung zwischen Bella und Edward, aber du kennst das englische Wort für „drehen" nicht?
In jedem Fall hilft dir ein zweisprachiges Wörterbuch.

Wie benutze ich ein zweisprachiges Wörterbuch?

- Die **Leitwörter** oben auf der Seite helfen dir, schneller zu finden, was du suchst. Auf der linken Seite steht das erste Stichwort, auf der rechten Seite das letzte Stichwort der Doppelseite.
- „**drehen**" ist das **Stichwort**. Alle Stichwörter sind alphabetisch geordnet: **d** vor **e**, **da** vor **de** und **dre** vor **dri** usw.
- Die **kursiv gedruckten** Hinweise helfen dir, die für deinen Text passende Bedeutung zu finden.
- Die **Ziffern** 1, 2 usw. zeigen, dass ein Stichwort mehrere ganz verschiedene Bedeutungen hat.
- **Beispielsätze** und **Redewendungen** sind dem Stichwort zugeordnet. In den Beispielsätzen und Redewendungen ersetzt eine **Tilde** (~) das Stichwort.
- Im englisch-deutschen Teil der meisten Wörterbücher findest du außerdem Hinweise auf **unregelmäßige Verbformen**, auf die **Steigerungsformen der Adjektive** und Ähnliches.
- Die **Lautschrift** gibt Auskunft darüber, wie das Wort ausgesprochen und betont wird.

Dr.

Dr. (*Abk. für* ***Doktor***) Dr., Doctor
Drache dragon
Drachen *Papierdrachen* kite; *Fluggerät* hang glider

Drehbuch screenplay, script
drehen 1 *Verb mit Obj* turn; *Film* shoot*; *Zigarette* roll **2:** ***sich ~*** turn; *schnell* spin*; ***sich ~ um*** *übertragen* be* about
Drehkreuz turnstile; **Drehorgel** barrel organ [ˈɔːgən]; **Drehort** location; **Drehstuhl** swivel chair; **Drehtür** revolving door
Drehung turn; *um eine Achse* rotation
Drehzahl (number of) revolutions *Pl od.* revs *Pl*
Drehzahlmesser rev counter
drei three
Drei three; *Note etwa* C; ***ich habe eine ~ geschrieben*** I got a C
dreidimensional 1 *Adj* three-dimensional **2** *Adv:* ***etwas ~ darstellen*** depict sth. three-dimensionally; **Dreieck** triangle [ˈtraɪæŋgl]; **dreieckig** triangular [traɪˈæŋgjʊlə]

Bei kniffligen Wörtern gibt es in vielen Wörterbüchern **Info-Boxes**, in denen dir mehr Hilfen und Hinweise gegeben werden, hier z. B. für das deutsche Wort „bringen".

bringen

bring (**herbringen; mitbringen**) wird nur verwendet, wenn jemand oder etwas zum Ort des Sprechers oder Hörers gebracht wird:

Schön, dass du zu meiner Party …	I'm glad you can come to my party. Can …

take (**weg-, hinbringen; mitnehmen**) wird verwendet, wenn jemand oder etwas woanders hingebracht oder mitgenommen wird:

Kannst du morgen deinen Bruder zur Schule bringen?	Can you take your brother to school tomorrow?

Tipp

Nimm nicht einfach die erste Übersetzung, die dir angeboten wird! Lies den Wörterbucheintrag bis du die richtige Übersetzung gefunden hast.

SF Internet research

Wie kann ich das Internet zur Recherche nutzen?

Find some information about the carbon footprint – so oder so ähnlich lauten Aufgaben, die dir oft als Hausaufgabe gestellt werden. Wenn du nach Informationen suchst, dann ist das Internet ist eine wichtige Quelle. Aber manchmal findest du dort so viele Informationen, dass du schnell den Überblick verlierst. Diese Tipps sollen dir helfen, damit du nicht im *world wide web* verloren gehst.

- Bevor du ins Internet gehst, mach dir eine Liste mit Schlüsselwörtern (**key words**) zu deinem Thema: *carbon footprint, CO_2, ...*
- Überlege, welches Schlüsselwort oder welche Kombination von Schlüsselwörtern am besten sein könnte:
  „carbon footprint" oder **carbon+footprint**
- Wenn du dir zunächst einen Überblick verschaffen willst, kannst du auch ein Nachschlagewerk im Internet anklicken:
  www.infoplease.com www.en.wikipedia.org
  Manchmal gibt es dort auch Links, die dir weiterhelfen können.
- Suchmaschinen (wie z.B. *Google, Altavista* oder *Yahoo*) helfen dir, Websites zu deinem Thema zu finden. Verwende eine Suchmaschine und gib deine Schlüsselwörter in das Suchfenster ein.
- Wenn die angezeigten Websites dir nicht helfen oder zu umfangreich sind, versuch es noch einmal, indem du deine Schlüsselwörter präzisierst.

Tipp

- Beachte: Nicht alles, was im Internet steht, ist richtig! Daher solltest du immer mehr als eine Website anschauen, um sicherzugehen, dass die Informationen stimmen.
- Suche Antworten auf die **5 Ws** (**who**, **what**, **where**, **when**, **why**).
- Bei englischen Quellen musst du nicht jedes Wort auf einer Website verstehen. Konzentriere dich auf das Wesentliche. Scanne den Text gezielt nach Informationen (**key words**), die du brauchst. ► *SF Reading course (pp. 134–135)*
- Schreib die Quellen nicht wortwörtlich ab, sondern mach dir Notizen.

Wo kann ich noch Informationen finden?

Neben dem Internet gibt es natürlich weitere Quellen, wo du Informationen zu deinem Thema findest, z.B. in einem Lexikon, Atlas, Wörterbuch, Schulbuch oder auch in Zeitschriften oder Zeitungen. Auch CDs und DVDs sind mögliche Quellen. Benutze möglichst englische Quellen, das kann dir beim Ausformulieren deines englischen Textes helfen.

- Internet/Lexikon: alle Wissensgebiete, wichtige Personen und Ereignisse
- Atlas: geografische und politische Übersichten, Städte, Flüsse
- Wörterbücher: Rechtschreibung und Bedeutung von Wörtern
- Schulbücher: verschiedene Wissensgebiete
- Zeitungen/Zeitschriften: aktuelle Informationen zu allen Themenbereichen

SF Giving a presentation

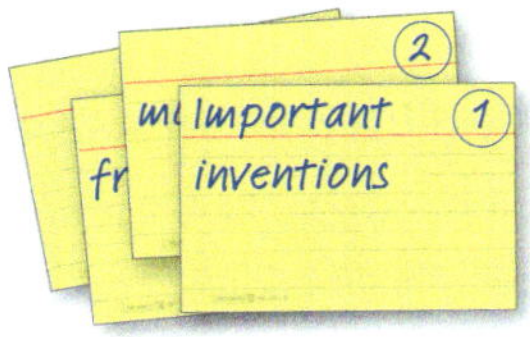

Wie mache ich eine gute Präsentation?

Vorbereitung
- Schreib die wichtigsten Gedanken in Stichworten auf, z. B. auf nummerierte Karteikarten oder in einer Mindmap.
- Übe deine Präsentation zu Hause vor einem Spiegel. Sprich laut, deutlich und langsam und mach Pausen an geeigneten Stellen.

Folien oder Poster
- Folien (für Overhead-Projektoren oder Computerpräsentationen) oder Poster sind gut, um
  - zu zeigen, wie dein Vortrag aufgebaut ist
  - Tabellen, Diagramme usw. für alle lesbar zu präsentieren
  - die wichtigsten Punkte zusammenzufassen.
- Schreib groß und für alle gut lesbar.

Durchführung
- Bevor du beginnst, sortiere deine Vortragskarten.
- Häng das Poster auf oder leg deine Folie auf den ausgeschalteten Projektor bzw. bereite den Beamer vor.
- Warte, bis es ruhig ist. Schau die Zuhörenden an.
- Erkläre zu Anfang, worüber du sprechen wirst.
- Lies nicht von deinen Karten ab, sondern sprich frei.

My presentation is about ... First, I'd like to talk about ... Second, ...

This picture/photo/ ... shows ...

Schluss
- Beende deine Präsentation mit einem abschließenden Satz.
- Frag die Zuhörenden, ob sie Fragen haben. Bedanke dich fürs Zuhören.

That's the end of my presentation. Have you got any questions?

Ausführlichere sprachliche Hilfen für Präsentationen findest du unter:
▸ *SF Giving a presentation – useful phrases (p. 139)*

SF Using visual materials with a presentation

Wofür sind visuelle Materialien gut?

Deine Zuhörer/innen werden deinem Vortrag mit mehr Aufmerksamkeit folgen. Sie können sich viel mehr merken, wenn du nicht nur sprichst, sondern ihnen auch etwas zum Anschauen bietest (Visualisierungen). Das können z. B. Fotos, Cartoons, Landkarten, Zeitleisten, Diagramme, Poster oder Filmausschnitte sein.

Was muss ich bei visuellen Materialien beachten?

Vorbereitung
- Das Gerüst deines Vortrags sollte stehen, bevor du anfängst, dir darüber Gedanken zu machen, welche Visualisierungen gut passen könnten.
- Diagramme und Tabellen sind gut, um Zahlen zu verdeutlichen. Zeitleisten sind gut, um eine Entwicklung zu zeigen. Mit Fotos und Cartoons kannst du deinen Vortrag auflockern.

Durchführung
- Bezieh deine visuellen Materialien in deinen Vortrag ein, um etwas zu veranschaulichen, aber lies nicht einfach von der Folie etc. ab.

Tipp

Denk daran, dass Schriften und Bilder so groß sein sollten, dass alle im Klassenraum sie gut lesen und sehen können.

SF Talking about charts

Welche Informationen kann ich Diagrammen (charts) entnehmen?

Diagramme stellen statistische Vergleiche zwischen mindestens zwei Dingen dar. Es werden entweder absolute Zahlen oder Prozentsätze miteinander verglichen.

Welche unterschiedlichen Formen von Diagrammen gibt es?

Zwei sehr häufige Formen von Diagrammen sind die Säulendiagramme und die Kreis- oder Tortendiagramme.

- **Säulendiagramme (bar charts)** beschreiben häufig die Anzahl oder Größe von zwei oder mehr Dingen:
- **Kreis- oder Tortendiagramme (pie charts)** geben einen schnellen Überblick über die prozentuale Verteilung.

Countries visited by UK tourists (2008)

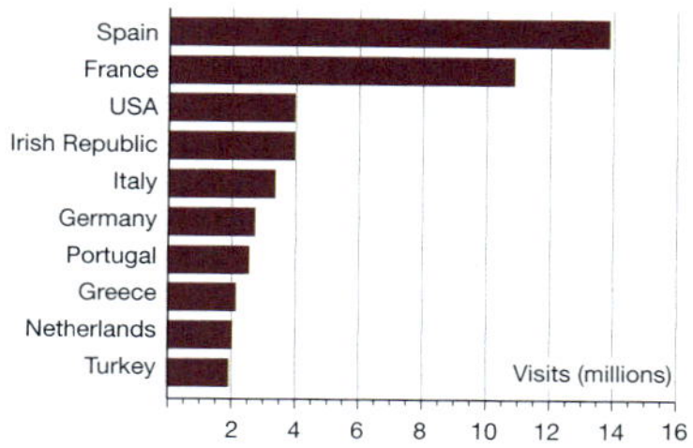

Wie kann ich beschreiben, was die Diagramme darstellen?

Um ein Diagramm zu beschreiben, solltest du folgende Fragen beantworten:

- **What is the chart about?**
  This chart is about ...
- **What does the chart compare or show?**
  The chart compares the size/number of ... •
  It shows the different ...
- **What does the chart tell you? What information does it give you?**
  ... has the largest/second largest •
  ... is (much) bigger/smaller than ... •
  ... are almost/nearly the same ... •
  The chart tells us ... • So ...

Wenn vorhanden, solltest du Aussagen über den Zeitraum der Statistik ergänzen:
The chart is about the years ...

How UK citizens travelled abroad (2008)
Number of travellers:
68.9 million

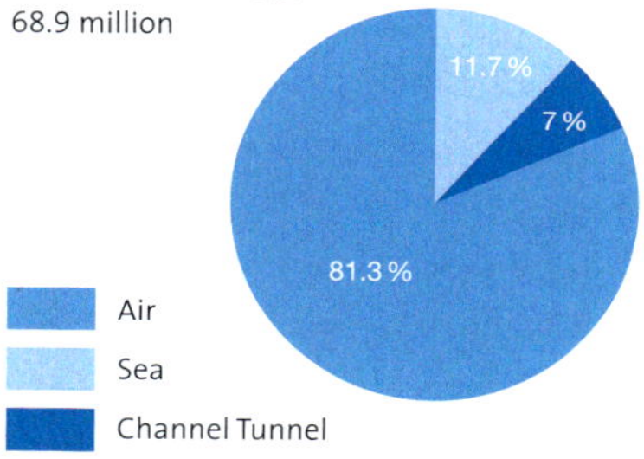

Tipp

Benutze das **simple past**, wenn du dich auf einen Zeitpunkt in der Vergangenheit beziehst: Almost 14 million tourists from the UK visited Spain in 2008.

Benutze das **simple present**, wenn du deine Schlussfolgerungen wiedergibst:
Spain is one of the most popular countries with tourists from the UK.

Benutze das **present perfect**, wenn du dich auf einen Zeitraum beziehst, der von der Vergangenheit bis heute reicht: How many people have visited Spain sicnc 2008?

LISTENING AND READING SKILLS

SF Listening

Was muss ich beim *listening* beachten?

Vor dem Hören:
- Überlege, worum es in dem Hörtext gehen wird. Frag dich, was du schon über das Thema weißt.
- Lies die Aufgaben gut durch, damit du weißt, worauf du achten sollst:
  - auf die **Hauptgedanken** oder die **Kernaussage** des Textes, z. B. wenn du sagen sollst, um welches Thema es geht, oder welche Meinung der Sprecher zu dem Thema hat.
  - auf bestimmte **Details**, z. B. wenn du Namen, Uhrzeiten, Jahreszahlen heraushören sollst.
- Bereite dich darauf vor, Notizen zu machen. Leg z. B. eine Tabelle oder Liste an.

Beim Hören:
- Keine Panik! Du musst nicht alles verstehen. Konzentriere dich auf das Wesentliche. Oft werden wichtige Informationen wiederholt.
- Achte auf Geräusche und unterschiedliche Stimmen. Was ein Sprecher/eine Sprecherin besonders betont, das ist wichtig!
- Wenn du gezielt nach Informationen suchst, denk an die Aufgabe und lass dich von anderen Einzelheiten nicht ablenken. Aufgepasst: die Informationen, die du suchst, kommen vielleicht in einer anderen Reihenfolge vor, als du sie erwartest.

- Manche Signalwörter machen es dir leichter, den Hörtext zu verstehen:
  - Aufzählung: **and**, **another**, **too**
  - Gegensatz: **although**, **but**
  - Grund, Folge: **because, so**, **so that**
  - Vergleich: **larger/older/... than**, **more**, **most**
  - Reihenfolge: **before**, **after**, **then**, **next**, **later**, **when**, **at last**, **at the same time**
- Mache kurze Notizen, z. B. Anfangsbuchstaben, Symbole oder Stichworte.

Nach dem Hören:
- Vervollständige deine Notizen sofort.
- Konzentriere dich beim zweiten Hören auf das, was du beim ersten Mal nicht gut verstanden hast.

Worauf sollte ich bei automatischen Telefonansagen achten?

Wenn du eine telefonische Auskunft einholen willst, hörst du manchmal eine automatische Telefonansage.
- Keine Panik! Du kannst eine automatische Telefonansage mehrmals hören.
- Achte besonders auf Zahlen! Meist wirst du aufgefordert, bestimmte Tasten auf deinem Telefon zu drücken, um die gewünschte Information zu erhalten. Oft werden diese Zahlen wiederholt.
- Überlege dir vorher, welche Informationen du suchst und auf welche Schlüsselwörter du dafür achten solltest. Schreib sie auf.
- Höre besonders genau zu, wenn deine Schlüsselwörter genannt werden, und mach dir Notizen zu ihnen.

SF Taking notes

Worum geht es beim Notizen machen?

Wenn du beim Lesen oder Zuhören Notizen machst, kannst du dich später besser an das Gehörte oder Gelesene erinnern, wenn du etwas vortragen, nacherzählen oder einen Bericht schreiben sollst.

Wie mache ich Notizen?

In Texten oder Gesprächen gibt es immer wichtige und unwichtige Wörter. Die wichtigen Wörter werden Schlüsselwörter (**key words**) genannt und nur diese solltest du notieren. Meist sind das Substantive und Verben, manchmal auch Adjektive oder Zahlen.

Tipp

- Verwende Ziffern (z. B. „7" statt „seven").
- Verwende Symbole und Abkürzungen, z. B. ✔ (für „ja") und + (für „und") oder US für United States, C. für Caitlin.
  Du kannst auch eigene Symbole erfinden.
- Verwende not oder ✗ statt „doesn't" oder „don't".

SF Marking up a text

Wann sollte ich einen Text markieren?

Du hast einen Text mit vielen Fakten vor dir liegen und sollst später über bestimmte Dinge berichten. Dann wird es dir helfen, die für die Aufgabenstellung wichtigen Informationen im Text zu markieren.

Wie gehe ich am besten vor?

Lies den Text und markiere nur die für dein Thema wichtigen Informationen. Nicht jeder Satz enthält für deine Aufgabe wichtige Wörter, und oft reicht es aus, nur ein oder zwei Wörter in einem Satz zu markieren.

- Du kannst wichtige Wörter einkreisen.
- Du kannst sie unterstreichen.
- Du kannst sie mit einem Textmarker hervorheben.

ABER:
Markiere nur auf Fotokopien von Texten oder in Büchern, die dir gehören, oder nutze eine Folie und einen wasserlöslichen Folienstift.

Sydney Opera House
The Sydney Opera House is one of the most famous buildings in the world. It houses the large Concert Hall (2,678 seats), the Opera Theatre (1,507 seats), other smaller theatres and a place for open-air events.

Sydney Opera House
The Sydney Opera House is <u>one of the most famous buildings in the world</u>. It houses the large Concert Hall (2,678 seats), the Opera Theatre (1,507 seats), other smaller theatres and a place for open-air events.

Sydney Opera House
The Sydney Opera House is one of the most famous buildings in the world. It houses the large Concert Hall (2,678 seats), the Opera Theatre (1,507 seats), other smaller theatres and a place for open-air events.

READING COURSE

Working out the meaning of words

Das Nachschlagen unbekannter Wörter im Wörterbuch kostet Zeit und nimmt auf Dauer den Spaß am Lesen. Oft geht es auch ohne Wörterbuch!

Was hilft dir, unbekannte Wörter zu verstehen?

1. **Bilder** zeigen oft die Dinge, die du im Text nicht verstehst. Wenn es Bilder zum Text gibt, dann schau sie dir vor dem Lesen genau an.
2. Oft hilft dir der **Textzusammenhang *(context)***, z. B. *When we* ***reached*** *the station, Judy went to the ticket machine to buy our tickets.*
3. Manche englischen Wörter werden **ähnlich wie im Deutschen** geschrieben oder ausgesprochen, z. B. **excellent**, **millionaire**, **nation**, **reality**.
4. Manchmal stecken in unbekannten Wörtern **bekannte Teile**, z. B. **friendliness**, **helpless**, **understandable**, **gardener**, **tea bag**, **waiting room**.

Skimming and scanning

Skimming: Lesen, um sich einen Überblick zu verschaffen

Beim **Skimming** überfliegst du einen Text schnell, um dir einen ersten **Überblick** zu verschaffen, worum es geht. Du willst z. B. herausfinden, ob ein Text (im Internet oder in einem Buch) überhaupt nützliche Informationen zu deinem Thema (z. B. für ein Referat) enthält. Achte beim Skimming auf:
- die **Überschrift**
- die **Zwischenüberschriften** und **hervorgehobene** Wörter oder Sätze
- die **Bilder** und **Bildunterschriften**
- den **ersten** und **letzten Satz** jedes Absatzes
- **Grafiken**, **Statistiken** und die **Quelle** des Textes.

Scanning: Lesen, um nach bestimmten Informationen zu suchen

Beim **Scanning** suchst du in einem Text nach **bestimmten Informationen**, die z. B. für ein Referat wichtig sind. Dazu brauchst du nicht den gesamten Text zu lesen, sondern du suchst nach Schlüsselwörtern (**key words**) und liest nur dort genauer, wo du sie findest. Geh dabei so vor:

Schritt 1: Denk an das Schlüsselwort, nach dem du suchst, oder schreib es auf.

Schritt 2: Geh mit den Augen und dem Finger schnell durch den Text, in breiten Schlingen wie bei einem „S" oder „Z" oder von oben nach unten wie bei einem „U". Dabei hast du das Schriftbild oder das Bild des Wortes, nach dem du suchst, vor Augen. Das gesuchte Wort wird dir sofort „ins Auge springen". Lies nur dort weiter, um Näheres zu erfahren.

Schritt 3: Wenn das Schlüsselwort, nach dem du suchst, im Text nicht vorkommt, überleg dir, welche anderen Wörter mit den benötigten Informationen zu tun haben, und such nach diesen.

Finding the main ideas of a text

Wenn du Texte wie Zeitungsartikel, Berichte oder Kommentare richtig verstehen willst, ist es gut, wenn du ihre Hauptaussagen erkennst und nachvollziehst, wie sie zusammenhängen. Dabei hilft dir ein Blick auf die Struktur dieser Texte.

Wie finde ich die Hauptaussagen eines Textes?

① Jeder Text dreht sich um ein Thema oder hat eine Hauptaussage. Diese findest du oft im ersten Absatz. Lies ihn deshalb besonders gründlich durch.

② Die Hauptaussage wird in der Regel durch weitere Aussagen bzw. Gedanken unterstützt. Du findest sie oft im ersten oder letzten Satz der nachfolgenden Absätze.

③ Diese weiteren Aussagen bzw. Gedanken werden meist durch Beispiele und Begründungen ergänzt.

We are people too!

By Oliver Munslow (16) – 23 August 2010

① So, you think young people are different? Well, it's true! We're younger than you. But if you think that means that we don't have rights, you're wrong.

Did you know that here in Britain every citizen under 18 has important rights? For example, we all have the right to say what we think and adults should listen to us and take us seriously. And we have the right to get together with our friends in public (if we respect the rights of other people and do not break the law).

② But British children aren't taken seriously until they're 18. Too many adults think that we have nothing important to say and that we don't deserve equal rights. Here are some examples of discrimination against teenagers from my everyday life.

③ Every day I see signs on shop doors that say '2 children at a time', 'no school bags', or even 'no children unless they are with an adult'. [...]

Tipp

Die folgenden Wörter oder Wendungen werden oft im Zusammenhang mit Begründungen oder Beispielen verwendet:
and so • because • e.g. / for example • etc. • for lots of reasons • this shows that • that's why • ...

Drawing conclusions

Wenn du Fragen zu einem Text beantworten sollst oder bei einer Recherche Informationen zu einer bestimmten Frage suchst, kann es sein, dass du an mehreren Stellen schauen musst oder dass die Antwort nicht 1:1 im Text steht.

Wie funktioniert schlussfolgerndes Lesen?

1. Die einfachste Form des schlussfolgernden Lesens besteht darin, die Informationen aus verschiedenen Textstellen zusammenzuführen. Bei dem Text *The Carbon Diaries 2015* (S. 35) sollst du sagen, wie *carbon rationing* Lauras Alltag verändert. Dazu musst du dir mehrere Stellen ansehen.

2. Manchmal steht die Antwort auf eine Frage nicht direkt im Text. Dann musst du sie dir erschließen. Du fragst dich z. B., ob Laura Brown und ihre Familie durch die Ausnahmesituation mehr gemeinsam unternehmen. Dafür musst du Aussagen im Text finden, die etwas mit der Frage zu tun haben:

Lines 68–71: *My family has disappeared. Dad spends all night on his laptop, Mum is always lost on a bus somewhere and Kim just lives in her room. (...)*

Conclusion: *The family don't spend more time together because of carbon rationing. In fact, they spend less time together.*

SF Reading English texts

Was ist das Besondere beim Lesen von längeren literarischen Texten auf Englisch?

Geschichten lesen macht Spaß! Wenn du eine Geschichte (*story*) oder einen Roman (*novel*) liest, tauchst du in eine andere Welt ein. Dabei ist es nicht so wichtig, dass du beim Lesen jedes Wort verstehst. Lass dich einfach von der Handlung durch die Geschichte tragen.

Hier sind ein paar Tipps, die es dir erleichtern, längere literarische Texte auf Englisch zu lesen.

Vor dem Lesen:

1. Lies die **Einführung** und die **Überschrift(en)** und sieh dir die **Bilder** zum Text an. Sie geben dir erste Informationen über das, was dich erwartet. Stell dir vor, worum es in der Geschichte gehen könnte.
2. Bei Lektüren oder Romanen gibt es hinten auf dem Buchumschlag meist einen kurzen **Klappentext** mit einer Zusammenfassung der Handlung – natürlich ohne, dass das Ende verraten wird.

Während des Lesens:

1. Tauche in die Geschichte ein. Lies zügig! Kümmere dich nicht um einzelne Wörter, die du nicht verstehst. Lies einfach weiter. Das Wichtigste ist, dass du im Großen und Ganzen die Handlung verstehst.
   Wenn du merkst, dass du der Handlung nicht mehr folgen kannst, weil du zu viele Wörter nicht verstehst, dann nutze alle dir bekannten Techniken, um die Bedeutung zu erschließen:
   – Sieh dir noch einmal die Bilder an.
   – Beachte den Textzusammenhang *(context)*.
   – Kennst du ähnliche englische oder deutsche Wörter?
   – Vielleicht kennst du Teile der unbekannten Wörter?
   ▸ *SF Working out the meaning of words (p. 134)*
2. Wenn das alles nicht hilft, dann schlage das unbekannte Wort im Wörterbuch nach. ▸ *SF Using a bilingual dictionary (p. 128)*

> **Tipp**
> Beim Lesen von englischen Lektüren oder Büchern kann dir eine Lesetagebuch (**reading log**), wie du es sicher aus dem Deutschunterricht kennst, das Verstehen und Behalten erleichtern.

SF NEW Reading literature ▸ *TF 1, TF 4 (pp. 112–113, pp. 118–121)*

Was ist das Besondere an literarischen Texten?

Alles, was du bereits über das Lesen von Texten im Allgemeinen gelernt hast (▸ *Reading course, pp. 134–135; SF Reading English texts, p. 136*), wird dir auch beim Lesen von Literatur helfen.

Literarische Gattungen und ihre Merkmale

Grundsätzlich unterscheidet man drei Arten von literarischen Texten: Gedichte (*poetry*), Erzähltexte (*fiction: stories, novels, etc.*) und Dramen (*plays*). Das sind die Besonderheiten der drei Arten von literarischen Texten:

Erzähltexte (z.B. Kurzgeschichten, Romane) bestehen aus einem fortlaufenden Text, der manchmal durch Kapitel untergliedert ist. Um die Figuren (*characters*)

▸▸▸

der Geschichte herum wird eine Handlung (*plot*) entwickelt, die in einen bestimmten Handlungsrahmen eingebettet ist: ein bestimmter Ort, eine Zeitspanne und ein näher beschriebener Schauplatz (*setting*).

Die Charakterisierung der Figuren kann direkt erfolgen, indem sie mit bestimmten Adjektiven (*cruel, sentimental, ...*) beschrieben werden (*direct characterization*). Bei der indirekten Charakterisierung (*indirect characterization*) wird beschrieben, was die Figuren sagen, tun oder fühlen.

Durch besondere sprachliche Mittel (s. Gedichte, unten) schafft der Autor eine bestimmte Atmosphäre (*atmosphere*). Diese kann z.B. bedrohlich oder humorvoll sein. Die Ereignisse werden von dem Erzähler (*narrator*) der Geschichte aus einer bestimmten Erzählperspektive (*point of view*) beschrieben.

Gedichte bestehen meist aus gebundener Sprache, d.h. aus Verszeilen (*verses*) und Strophen (*stanzas*). Die Sprache von Gedichten unterscheidet sich von der Alltagssprache oft durch die Verwendung von Reimen (*rhyme*), Rhythmus (*rhythm*) und Wiederholungen (*repetition*) sowie einer bildhaften Sprache (Bilder: *images*).

I feel it in my fingers, **I feel it in**
my **toes**.
Well, love is all around me, and
so the feeling **grows**.
It´s **written on the wind**, it´s
everywhere I **go**.
So if you really love me, come on
and let it **show**. [...]

(aus dem Lied *Love is all around*, S. 113)

Dramen bestehen in der Regel aus Monologen und Dialogen in direkter Rede. Meist geben Bühnenanweisungen (*stage directions*) Handlungsanweisungen für die Darsteller, sie sind aber auch für den Leser nützlich, da er sich so den Schauplatz (*setting*) besser vorstellen kann.

Über literarische Texte sprechen und schreiben

Wenn du über literarische Texte sprechen oder schreiben sollst, sind folgende Formulierungen hilfreich:

Setting and plot

The story/novel/play is about ...
The story/novel/play is set in ...
The action takes place during/in ...

Point of view

The story is told from the main character's/... point of view.
... is the narrator of the story.

Characters and characterization

The main character(s) is/are ...
He/she seems to be a strong/weak/brave/... person.

Poems

The poem describes/imagines ...
The poem has a slow/lively/... rhythm.
In line(s) ... you can find an image ...

Language

The language in the text creates an exciting/thrilling/... atmosphere.
I think ... is an image for ...
The word/phrase ... is repeated in line ...

Your reaction

The text made me feel happy/sad/angry/...
I liked it/didn't like it when ...
I found the ending/story/characters interesting/funny/...

SPEAKING AND WRITING SKILLS

SPEAKING COURSE

Having a conversation

Ein Gespräch beginnen

Es gibt immer mehrere Möglichkeiten:
- **wenn du etwas erfragen willst** (z. B. den Weg oder die Uhrzeit)
  Excuse me, do you know ... • Excuse me, can you tell me ...
- **wenn du jemanden begrüßen möchtest oder kennenlernst**
  Hi. • Hello. • Good morning/evening.
  Oft kann man das Gespräch dann mit einer allgemeinen Bemerkung weiterführen: Great day today! • That's a great ...
- **wenn du jemanden wiedertriffst**
  Hi, how are you doing? • Hi, ..., how are things? • Hi, ... Good to see/meet you.

Ein Gespräch führen

Für den weiteren Verlauf des Gesprächs sind diese Wendungen nützlich:
- **sich vorstellen:** By the way, my name's ... • I'm ... • Nice to meet you.
- **Smalltalk machen:** Have you ... before? • Have you ever ...? • Where are you from? • Do you like ...? • I like ... What about you?
- **sich bedanken:** That's great. • Thanks. / Thank you very much.
- **sich verabschieden:** See you tomorrow/next week. • Bye!

Und wenn du etwas nicht verstanden hast, kannst du immer nachfragen:
Sorry, I didn't get that. • Sorry, could you say that again, please?

Tipp

Oft hört man zur Begrüßung auch How are you? Es wird nicht erwartet, dass du darauf eine ausführliche Antwort gibst. Am besten sagst du einfach Fine, thanks. How about you?

Taking part in a job interview

Sich vorbereiten

Auf ein Vorstellungsgespräch musst du dich unbedingt vorbereiten. Du solltest Fragen zu den folgenden Bereichen beantworten können:
- deine Eigenschaften (**personal qualities**), Stärken (**strengths**) und Schwächen (**weaknesses**)
- deine Interessen (**interests**) und Arbeitserfahrungen (**work experience**)
- was dich an dem Jobangebot reizt (**why you're interested in the job**).

Überleg dir auch eigene Fragen, zum Beispiel zu deinem Tätigkeitsbereich (**What kind of work would I have to do?**) oder zum Tätigkeitsbeginn (**When would I have to begin?**).

Im Vorstellungsgespräch

Im Vorstellungsgespräch ist es wichtig, dass du freundlich bist und dich als positiver und interessierter Mensch präsentierst.
- **bei der Begrüßung:** Hello, nice to meet you. • Good morning.
- **warum du dich bewirbst:** I'm really interested in ... • I'm good at ..., so I think ...
- **wenn es um deine Joberfahrungen geht:** I really enjoyed working with ...
- **bei der Verabschiedung:** Goodbye and thank you very much.

Tipp

- Hör gut zu, wenn du etwas gefragt wirst.
- Sprich nicht zu viel, aber auch nicht zu wenig.
- Sprich nicht zu schnell.

Having a discussion

Seine Meinung zum Ausdruck bringen und erklären

1. **Expressing an opinion:** In einer Diskussion ist es gut, wenn du möglichst klar und deutlich sagst, was du zu einer bestimmten Frage denkst:
   I think ... • In my opinion ...
2. **Giving reasons and examples:** Genauso wichtig ist es, dass du Beispiele und Argumente nennst, die deine Meinung unterstützen – schließlich willst du deine Gesprächspartner von deinem Standpunkt überzeugen!
   because ... • First ... / Second ... / And finally ... • For example ... • Let me explain ... • That's why ...

Auf andere in einer Diskussion reagieren

1. **Asking for clarification:** Manchmal ist es notwendig nachzuhaken, weil man ein Argument nicht verstanden hat:
   Could you say that again? • Sorry, but I don't understand what you mean.
2. **Agreeing with someone:** Wenn du die Meinung eines anderen unterstützen willst, kannst du das so zum Ausdruck bringen:
   I agree (with you/...). • That's a good point. • You're right.
3. **Disagreeing with someone:** Oft widerspricht man nicht direkt, sondern leitet seine Reaktion mit Sorry, ... oder I don't think ... ein. Zeig immer Respekt für die Meinung des oder der anderen.
   I don't think you can say ... • I see what you mean, but ... •
   Sorry, but that's not right. • Sorry, I don't agree with you • Yes, but ...

Giving a presentation – useful phrases

Einleitung

Nenne zu Beginn deines Vortrags dein Thema und gib einen kurzen Überblick darüber, worum es in deinem Vortrag geht:
The topic of my talk today is ... • I'm going to divide this talk into four sections. • First, I'll give you some general facts about ... • Next I'll look at ... • Finally, I'll ...

Während der Präsentation

Mach deutlich, wenn du einen neuen Abschnitt in deinem Vortrag beginnst:
Now please have a look at ... • On the next slide ... • Now I'd like to draw your attention to ... • As you can see in ...

Schluss

Fasse am Ende deines Vortrags die wichtigsten Punkte zusammen. Frag deine Zuhörer, ob sie etwas nachfragen oder kommentieren möchten.
To sum up my talk I ... • Please feel free to ask questions or comment on anything I've said.
Ausführlichere Hinweise zur Vorbereitung und Durchführung einer Präsentation findest du unter: ► *SF Giving a presentation (p. 130)*

SF Paraphrasing

Worum geht es beim *paraphrasing*?

Paraphrasing bedeutet, etwas mit anderen Worten zu erklären. Das ist hilfreich, wenn dir ein bestimmtes Wort nicht einfällt oder wenn dein Gegenüber dich nicht verstanden hat (siehe auch ▸ *SF Mediation, p. 147*).

Wie gehe ich beim *paraphrasing* vor?

- Man kann mit einem Wort umschreiben, das dieselbe Bedeutung hat:
  to train is the same as to practise
  Oder man sagt das Gegenteil: **alive is the opposite of dead**
- Manchmal braucht man mehrere Wörter, z. B. wenn man etwas beschreibt oder erklärt. Dabei benutzt man ein allgemeines Wort (**general word**) und nennt weitere Eigenschaften.
  A racing car is a very fast car.
- Oder du umschreibst das Wort mit **... is/are like ...**:
  A chef is like a cook, he or she is the main cook in a restaurant.
- Du kannst auch einen Relativsatz (**relative clause**) verwenden:
  A garage is a place where cars are checked and repaired.

SF Brainstorming

Wofür ist Brainstorming gut?

Bei vielen Aufgaben ist es nützlich, wenn du im ersten Schritt möglichst viele Ideen zum Thema sammelst. Dabei hilft dir das Brainstorming.

Wie gehe ich beim Brainstorming vor?

Schritt 1:
Schreib alle Ideen so auf, wie sie dir einfallen. Es ist zunächst völlig egal, ob sie gut sind oder nicht. Du kannst die Ideen durcheinander auf einen Zettel schreiben oder schon etwas geordnet, z. B. für jede eine neue Zeile.

Schritt 2:
Lies alle deine Ideen durch und wähle die besten aus. Dann sortiere sie und fasse sie sinnvoll zusammen. Dabei kannst du folgende **Techniken** anwenden:

1. Leg eine **Mindmap** an. Schreib das Thema in die Mitte eines Blattes Papier. Überlege, welche Oberbegriffe zu deiner Sammlung von Ideen passen. Verwende unterschiedliche Farben. Ergänze jede Idee, die zu einem Oberbegriff passt, auf einem Nebenast. Nimm dafür nur wichtige Schlüsselwörter. Du kannst statt Wörtern auch Symbole verwenden und Bilder ergänzen.
2. **The 5 Ws**: Schreib die **5 W-Fragen** **Who? What? Where? When? Why?** in eine Tabelle. Die Ideen, die dir zu jeder Frage kommen, schreibst du darunter.

WRITING COURSE

The steps of writing

1. Brainstorming – Ideen sammeln, dann sortieren. ▸ *SF Brainstorming*
2. Schreiben. Dabei achte darauf,
   - deine Sätze zu verbinden und auszubauen ▸ *Writing better sentences*
   - deinen Text gut zu strukturieren ▸ *Using paragraphs*
   - bei einem Bericht die 5 Ws abzudecken ▸ *Writing a report*
3. Deinen Text inhaltlich und sprachlich überprüfen ▸ *Correcting your text*

Writing better sentences

Linking words

Eine Geschichte klingt interessanter, wenn du die Sätze mit **linking words** miteinander verbindest. Dabei gibt es mehrere Möglichkeiten:
- **Time phrases** wie at 7 o'clock, every morning, a few minutes later, then, next
- **Konjunktionen** wie although, because, but, so ... that, that, when, while
- **Relativpronomen** wie that und who

Adjektive und Adverbien

- Mit Adjektiven kannst du Personen, Orte oder Erlebnisse genauer und interessanter beschreiben. Vergleiche: The man looked into the room.
  ▸ The young man looked into the empty room.
- Mit Adverbien kannst du beschreiben, **wie** jemand etwas macht:
  The young man looked nervously into the empty room.

Using paragraphs

Structuring a text

Bei guten Texten lassen sich drei Hauptabschnitte erkennen:
- eine **Einleitung**, die in das Thema einführt
- ein **Hauptteil**, der meist aus mehreren Absätzen besteht
- ein **Schluss**, der den Text mit einer Zusammenfassung oder etwas Persönlichem zu einem interessanten Ende bringt.

Topic sentences

Am Anfang eines Absatzes sind kurze, einleitende Sätze (**topic sentences**) gut, weil sie den Lesern sofort sagen, worum es geht, z.B.
1. Orte: My trip to ... was fantastic. • ... is famous for ... • ... is a great place.
2. Personen: ... is great/funny/interesting/clever ...
3. Aktivitäten: ... is great fun. • Lots of people ... every day.

Wie kann ich meine Absätze interessant gestalten?

- Beginne mit einem interessanten Einstiegssatz:
  You'll never guess what happened to me today! • Did I tell you that ...?
- Fange für jeden neuen Aspekt einen neuen Absatz an.
- Beende deinen Text mit einer Zusammenfassung oder etwas Persönlichem.

Writing a report – collecting and organizing ideas

Worauf kommt es bei einem Bericht an?

- Gib dem Leser **eine schnelle Orientierung**, was passiert ist.
- Beginne mit **wichtigen Informationen** und gib erst dann Detailinformationen.
- Ein Bericht gibt immer Antworten auf die **5 Ws**:
  Who? What? When? Where? Why? und manchmal auch auf **How?**
- Verwende das **simple past**.

Correcting your text

Ein Text ist noch nicht „fertig“, wenn du ihn zu Ende geschrieben hast. Du solltest ihn immer mehr als einmal durchlesen:
- einmal, um zu sehen, ob er vollständig und gut verständlich ist
- noch einmal, um ihn auf Fehler zu überprüfen, z. B. **Rechtschreibfehler *(spelling mistakes)*** oder **Grammatikfehler *(grammar mistakes)***.

tomato [tə'mɑːtəʊ], *pl* **tomatoes** Tomate

wife [waɪf], *pl* **wives** [waɪvz] Ehefrau

drop (-**pp**-) [drɒp] fallen lassen

forget (-**tt**-) [fə'get] vergessen

Spelling mistakes

Lies deinen Text langsam, Wort für Wort, Buchstabe für Buchstabe. Wenn du unsicher bist, hilft dir ein Wörterbuch. Beachte folgende Regeln:

Tipp

- Manche Wörter haben Buchstaben, die man nicht spricht, aber schreibt, z. B. **knife**, **climb**.
- Manchmal ändert sich die Schreibweise, wenn ein Wort eine Endung erhält,
  z. B. **take** → **taking**, **terrible** → **terribly**, **lucky** → **luckily**,
  try → **tries** (**aber** **stay** → **stays**), **run** → **running**, **drop** → **dropped**.
- Beim Plural tritt manchmal noch ein **-e** zum **-s**, z. B. **church** → **churches**.

Grammar mistakes

Diese Tipps helfen dir, typische Fehler zu vermeiden:

Tipp

- Im **simple present** wird in der 3. Person Singular **-s** angehängt: **she knows**
- **Unregelmäßige Verben:** Manche Verben bilden die Formen des *simple past* und des Partizip Perfekt *(past participle)* unregelmäßig. Die unregelmäßigen Formen musst du lernen. Die Liste steht auf S. 215–216.
  go – went – gone; buy – bought – bought
- **Verneinung bei Vollverben:** Im *simple present* mit ***don't/doesn't***, im *simple past* mit **didn't**, z. B. **He doesn't speak French, he didn't learn it at school**.
- **Satzstellung**: Im Englischen gilt immer (auch im Nebensatz):
  a) subject – verb – object (S-V-O) **... when I saw my brother.**
  ... als ich meinen Bruder sah.
  b) Orts- vor Zeitangabe **I bought a nice book in town yesterday.**
  Ich habe gestern in der Stadt ein schönes Buch gekauft.

SF Summarizing texts

Wenn du einen Text zusammenfasst, gibst du die wichtigten Informationen oder Ereignisse in kürzerer Form wieder. Eine schriftliche Zusammenfassung nennt man im Englischen *summary*.

Wie gehe ich beim *summarizing* vor?

1. Lies den Text mindestens einmal genau durch, damit du verstehst, worum es geht. Mach dir noch keine Notizen.

2. Lies den Text erneut, Satz für Satz, durch. Am besten arbeitest du mit einer Kopie, damit du Passagen im Text markieren kannst. Markiere die Textstellen, die dir Antworten auf die 5 Ws geben.
Wenn du keine Kopie hast, mache dir in Stichpunkten Notizen zu den **5 Ws**:
Who? Who is the text about?
What? What happens? / What does he/she do?
Where? Where does it happen?
When? When does it happen?
Why? Why does it happen? / Why does he/she do this?

3. Schreibe eine Zusammenfassung des Texts in deinen eigenen Worten. Verwende das **simple present** (auch wenn du eine Geschichte zusammenfasst, die in der Vergangenheit spielt).
In der **Einleitung** erklärst du in ein oder zwei Sätzen, worum es in dem Text geht:
The story is about ... • The text describes ... • The article shows ... • In the story we get to know ...
Im **Hauptteil** gibst du die wichtigsten Ereignisse (z. B. einer Geschichte) oder die Hauptpunkte eines Textes (z. B. eines Zeitungsartikels) wieder. Bringe die Informationen in eine logische Reihenfolge. Verwende dafür deine Notizen zu den **5 Ws**. Schreibe den Text nicht einfach ab, sondern benutze deine eigenen Worte.

4. Überprüfe deinen Entwurf. Enthält dein Text wirklich die wichtigsten Gedanken oder Ereignisse aus dem Original? Achte auch auf sprachliche Fehler und darauf, dass deine Sätze durch *linking words* verbunden sind, wie z. B. **and • that's why • but • because • ...**

5. Bei einer schriftlichen Zusammenfassung (*summary*) musst du den korrigierten Entwurf zum Schluss in eine Reinschrift bringen.

SF Writing a CV

Was ist ein CV?

„CV“ bedeutet „Lebenslauf“. Ein Lebenslauf ist eine Zusammenfassung deiner bisherigen Ausbildung, deiner Fähigkeiten und deiner Interessen. Du brauchst einen Lebenslauf, wenn du dich um eine berufliche Anstellung bewirbst. Amerikaner benutzen statt *CV* das Wort *resumé*.

CURRICULUM VITAE
Oliver Schäfer

Tulpenweg 34 32051 Herford, Germany
Telephone: 00 49 5221 978036
Email: oliver.schaefer@email-hf.de

Education
2005-2010 Gutenberg-Realschule (secondary school), Herford, Germany
2001-2005 Regenbogen Grundschule (primary school), Herford, Germany

Qualifications
Studying for *Hauptschulabschluss* (equivalent of GCSEs)
Languages: English (6 years)
Driving licence

Work experience
Work experience at a garage (3 weeks)

Hobbies and interests
My hobbies are cycling, doing workouts, repairing all kinds of machines. I am very interested in technical things and computers.

References
Available on request

Geburtsdatum und -ort werden in einem CV oder resumé **oft nicht** genannt. In der Regel fügst du auch **kein Foto** von dir bei.

Gib bei deiner Telefonnummer auch die **internationale Vorwahl** mit an.

Fettgedruckte Überschriften und eine **klare Gliederung** erleichtern das Lesen.

GCSEs gibt es nur in Großbritannien, in den USA entspricht das dem **US high school diploma**.

An dieser Stelle kann auch eine **konkrete Person** als **Referenz** genannt werden. Selbstverständlich musst du ihn oder sie vorher fragen!

Du kannst auch den Abschnitt **Personal statement** hinzufügen, in dem du deine persönlichen Stärken hervorhebst, z.B. *I am a hard-working, reliable student and I like working in a team. I am looking forward to getting more experience in the work place.*

Tipp

Bevor du deinen Lebenslauf losschickst, geh folgende Checkliste durch:
- Habe ich weißes A4-Papier benutzt? Ist das Blatt sauber und ordentlich?
- Habe ich den Lebenslauf mit einem Computer geschrieben?
- Ist die Seite klar gegliedert und gut lesbar?
- Habe ich alle zentralen Bereiche abgedeckt: meine Erfahrungen, meine Interessen, meine Fähigeiten und persönlichen Eigenschaften?
- Habe ich auch wirklich keine sprachlichen Fehler in meinem Schreiben?

SF Writing formal and informal letters

Beim Schreiben von Briefen und E-Mails musst du unterschiedliche Regeln beachten, je nachdem, ob du einen förmlichen Brief (*formal letter*) an unbekannte Personen, Behörden, Zeitungen, Zeitschriften, usw. schreibst oder einen persönlichen, informellen Brief (*informal letter*) an Freunde oder Verwandte.

Worauf kommt es bei förmlichen Briefen an? (formal letters)

1. Schreibe deine Adresse (ohne Namen) und das Datum in die rechte obere Ecke. Verwende keine typisch deutschen Buchstaben wie z. B. ß, ä, ö, oder ü.
2. Die Anschrift steht links.
3. Die Anrede lautet *Dear Sir or Madam*. Bei einem Leserbrief an eine Zeitung oder Zeitschrift kannst du auch *Dear Editor* schreiben. Wenn du den Namen des Adressaten kennst, beginne deinen Brief mit *Dear Mr/Mrs/Ms ...*
4. Verwende Langformen. (*I am, I would like* statt *I'm, I'd like* etc.)
5. Nenne zu Beginn den Grund deines Briefes.
6. Bedanke dich bei Bitten und Anfragen im Voraus. (*I look forward to hearing from you. Thank you.*)
7. Beende den Brief mit *Yours faithfully*, wenn du den Adressaten nicht kennst. Hast du den Adressaten am Anfang des Briefes mit Namen angeredet, dann schreibe *Yours sincerely*.
8. Unterschreibe den Brief und tippe zusätzlich deinen Namen.

Tipp

Beachte, was du zum Schreiben von Texten gelernt hast:
- Vor dem Schreiben: Ideen sammeln, dann sortieren.
- Während des Schreibens: Sätze verbinden und ausbauen; strukturieren.
- Nach dem Schreiben: Überprüfe deinen Brief inhaltlich und sprachlich. ► *SF Writing course, pp. 141–142*

Example for a letter of application

(1) Schillerstr. 17
37067 Goettingen
Germany

(2) Jane Hall
Meadows Home Farm Shop
Harston
Cambridge CB22 4BE
Great Britain

4 May 2010

(3) Dear Ms Hall

(4) (5) I am writing to you about the advertisement in the Cambridge Weekly News of April 21st. I would love (4) to work for you at Meadows Home Farm this summer.

I am 16 years old and I have a good level of English but would like to improve my speaking skills. I am hard-working, friendly and a fast learner. At home I look after two horses so farm work is not new to me. I have also worked in a sports shop so I have experience in serving people and working in a team. My hobbies are horse riding, playing volleyball and hiking. Please find my CV enclosed with this letter.

Thank you for your time. I look forward to hearing (6) from you.

(7) Yours sincerely

(8) *Tamara Wille*
Tamara Wille

Was muss ich bei einem Bewerbungsschreiben beachten?

Eine schrifliche Bewerbung besteht aus einem Lebenslauf (► *SF Writing a CV, p. 144*) und einem Anschreiben (*letter of application/motivation*). Wenn du dich auf eine Arbeitsstelle oder einen Praktikumsplatz bewirbst, musst du alle Regeln eines förmlichen Briefes beachten.

– Sage, auf welche Stellenanzeige du dich beziehst, oder woher du das Unternehmen kennst.
  I am writing about your advertisement in ...
  I learned about your company at our school's career information day/...
– Nenne deine Stärken. Zeige auch, dass du dich über das Unternehmen informiert hast.
  I have good computer skills/... • I am good at ...
  On your website I learned that your company ...

►►►

Tipp

- Dein Anschreiben sollte nicht länger als eine DIN- A4-Seite sein.
- Gib keine Informationen zu deiner Familie.
- Frage beim ersten Kontakt nicht nach der Bezahlung.
- Beachte auch bei einer Bewerbung per E-Mail alle Regeln eines förmlichen Schreibens. Verwende keine unseriös klingende E-Mail-Adresse wie z. B. sexgod88@mail.de!

– Danke dem Adressaten für seine Aufmerksamkeit. Sage, dass du dich auf eine Antwort freust. Du kannst auch ankündigen, dass du dich wieder melden wirst.
  Thank you very much for your time.
  I look forward to hearing from you. / I will contact you in two weeks to see if you need more information.

Was ist bei persönlichen Briefen anders? (informal letters)

Hier sind die Regeln nicht ganz so streng. Aber beachte Folgendes:
– Schreibe deine Adresse (ohne Namen) und das Datum in die rechte obere Ecke.
– Verwende keine typisch deutschen Buchstaben wie z. B. ß, ä, ö, oder ü.
– Du benötigst keine Anschrift.
– Du kannst deinen Brief mit *Dear/Hello/Hi* ... beginnen.
– Nenne zu Beginn den Grund deines Briefes, stelle auch Fragen.
– Beende den Brief mit einem freundlichen Gruß/Ausblick/Erwartungen/...
– Schließe deinen Brief mit *Yours/Best wishes/Love/*... ab.

SF NEW From outline to written discussion ▸ *Unit 2, Part B (p. 37)*

Oft sollst du zu strittigen Fragen schriftlich Stellung nehmen, z. B. **Carbon rationing should be introduced in Germany**. Dabei sollst du deine Position überzeugend darlegen. Eine **Gliederung** (*outline*) hilft dir, deine Argumente vor dem Schreiben zu gliedern:

1. Entscheide dich, ob du **für oder gegen** die geäußerte Meinung bist. Dann sammle Argumente und Beispiele, die deine Meinung stützen.
(▸ *SF Brainstorming, p. 140*)

2. Ordne deine Argumente und Beispiele in einer Gliederung (z. B. sollte das wichtigste Argument zum Schluss kommen) und schreibe sie gemäß dem Schema rechts stichwortartig auf.

1 Introduction
2 Arguments FOR or AGAINST
  2.1. First argument
  2.2. Second argument
  2.3. ...
3 Conclusion

Wie mache ich aus der Gliederung eine Erörterung?

1. Einleitung: Stelle das Thema vor und erläutere, worum es geht. Dabei kannst du von einer persönlichen Erfahrung oder einer allgemeinen Aussage ausgehen.
Lots of people think ... • I once ... • So the question is: Can we ...?

Deine Argumente: Präsentiere deine Argumente dafür oder dagegen.
Nenne jeweils das Argument, begründe deine Meinung und nenne Beispiele (z. B. aus deiner eigenen Erfahrung).
First ...; second ... • People think that ... because ... • For example, ... • Finally ... • That's why ...

2. Schluss: Erläutere deine persönliche Schlussfolgerung, die du aus den genannten Argumenten ziehst. Nenne keine neuen Argumente mehr.
To sum up, I would say that ... • After looking at all the arguments I think ...

MEDIATION SKILLS

SF Mediation

Wann muss ich zwischen zwei Sprachen vermitteln?

Manchmal musst du zwischen zwei Sprachen vermitteln. Das nennt man *mediation*.

1. Du gibst englische Informationen auf Deutsch weiter:
   Du fährst z. B. mit deiner Familie in die USA und deine Eltern oder Geschwister wollen wissen, was jemand in einem Café gesagt hat oder was an einer Informationstafel steht.
2. Du gibst deutsche Informationen auf Englisch weiter:
   Vielleicht ist bei dir zu Hause eine Austauschschülerin aus den USA oder Dänemark zu Gast, die kein Deutsch spricht und Hilfe braucht.
3. In schriftlichen Prüfungen musst du manchmal in einem englischen Text gezielt nach Informationen suchen und diese auf Deutsch wiedergeben. Oder du sollst Informationen aus einem deutschen Text auf Englisch wiedergeben.

Worauf muss ich bei *mediation* achten?

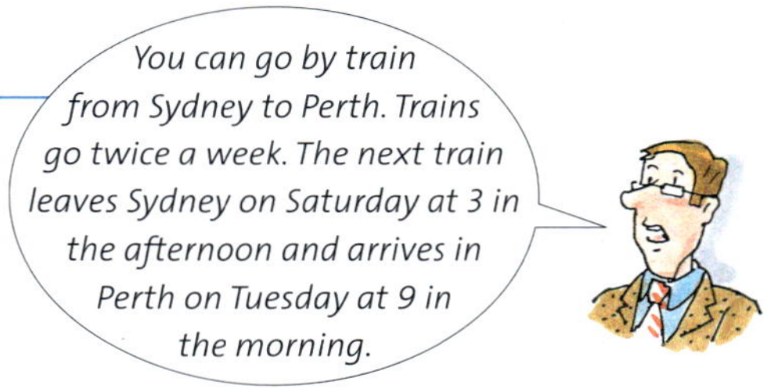

- Übersetze nicht alles wörtlich.
- Gib nur das Wesentliche weiter. Oft gibt dir die Fragestellung Hinweise, worauf es ankommt.
- Verwende kurze und einfache Sätze.
- Wenn du ein Wort nicht kennst, umschreibe es oder ersetze es durch ein anderes Wort.

Was kann ich tun, wenn ich ein wichtiges Wort nicht kenne?

Vielleicht findest du es manchmal schwer, mündliche Aussagen oder schriftliche Textvorlagen in die andere Sprache zu übertragen, z. B. weil
- dein Wortschatz nicht ausreicht
- dir bekannte Wörter im Augenblick nicht einfallen
- spezielle Fachbegriffe auftauchen.

Manche Wörter kannst du umschreiben, z. B. mithilfe von Relativsätzen wie:

It's somebody/a person who ...
It's something that you use to ...
It's an animal that ...
It's a place where ...

▸ *SF Paraphrasing, p. 140*

Grammar File – Inhalt

Im **Grammar File** (S. 148–162) werden wesentliche grammatische Themen aus den Klassen 5 bis 9 noch einmal zusammengefasst.

In der **linken Spalte** stehen Beispielsätze und Übersichten.

In der **rechten Spalte** stehen Erklärungen und Hinweise.

3.1 The simple present

Dave Wilson **usually** gets the bus to school.
On Mondays his mother takes him in the car.
He **never** cycles to school because it's too far.

Dave and his family live in Manchester.
He plays hockey and collects models of old cars.
His dad works for a building company.

Das ***simple present*** wird verwendet,

◄ um über Handlungen und Ereignisse zu sprechen, die **wiederholt, regelmäßig, immer** oder **nie** geschehen (oft mit Zeitangaben wie *always, never, usually, sometimes, often, every week, on Mondays* usw.).

◄ um über **Dauerzustände**, **Hobbys** und **Berufe** zu sprechen.

! ***He, she, it* – das „s" muss mit.**

Verneinte Sätze	I don't cycle to school.	Dave doesn't walk to school.
Fragen	Do you go to school by bus? **Where** do the Wilsons live?	Does your mother take you in the car? **When** does Dave's mother take him in the car?

3.2 The present progressive

What's Dave doing? –
Just now he's cleaning his bike.

Dave (on the phone) I can't talk right now, Jack.

Das ***present progressive*** wird verwendet,

◄ um über Handlungen und Ereignisse zu sprechen, die **jetzt gerade im Gange** sind (oft mit Angaben wie *at the moment, now, just*).

! Die Handlung, um die es geht, kann für einen Augen-

Additional information

The simple present (future meaning)

The next train to Bath **goes** in ten minutes.
The next drawing class **starts** on 2 September.

„Additional information"-Abschnitte enthalten Grammatik, die du nicht selbst zu verwenden brauchst. Du solltest aber verstehen, was dort erklärt wird, damit du keine Schwierigkeiten mit Texten hast, in denen diese Grammatik vorkommt.

GF 1 Word order Wortstellung

1.1 S – V – O

S – V – O

Subject – Verb – Object

		Subject	Verb	Object	
1		Rob	likes	ice cream.	
		The Clarks	have bought	a house	in Bath.
2		Ella	didn't like	the film.	
		Ava	can't speak	German	very well.
3	Can	Jamie	speak	German?	
	Did	you	like	the film?	

Die wichtigste Wortstellungsregel ist **Subject – Verb – Object** (Subjekt – Prädikat – Objekt). Sie gilt in bejahten und verneinten Aussagesätzen (1, 2) und in Fragen (3).

▸ *Fragebildung: 2 (p. 151)*

! Beachte die Unterschiede zum Deutschen:

1 We're going to have **a big party**.
Wir werden **eine große Party** veranstalten.

1 Die Teile des Prädikats (*are going to have*) dürfen nicht durch das Objekt (*a big party*) getrennt werden.

2 We **often** have fish **on Fridays**.
Wir essen **freitags oft** Fisch.

2 Prädikat und Objekt (*have fish*) dürfen nicht durch Adverbien (*often*) oder Zeitangaben (*on Fridays*) getrennt werden.

3 Yesterday **I** got my new computer.
Gestern bekam **ich** meinen neuen Computer.

When I arrived, **the film** had already begun.
Als ich ankam, hatte **der Film** schon begonnen.

3 Die Wortstellung ist auch dann S – V – ..., wenn der Satz mit einer Zeitangabe (*yesterday*) oder einem Nebensatz (*When I arrived*) beginnt.

4 He'll go out with you if you ask **him**.
..., wenn du **ihn** fragst.

Elisabeth told me that she loves **Jeremy**.
..., dass sie **Jeremy** liebt.

4 Die Wortstellung S – V – O gilt auch in Nebensätzen (*if you ask him; that she loves Jeremy*).

1.2 Adverbs and phrases of place and time

Adverbien und Orts- und Zeitangaben

1 Luckily she was able to stop the car.
At first we couldn't see anything.

1 **Satzadverbien** wie *perhaps, maybe, suddenly, luckily, finally, of course, at first* stehen in der Regel <u>am Satzanfang</u>.

2 We don't often get up before 10 on Sundays.
I usually make breakfast for everybody.
We had never been to Spain before.

2 **Adverbien der unbestimmten Zeit oder Häufigkeit** wie *already, always, ever, just, never, often, sometimes, usually* stehen gewöhnlich <u>vor</u> dem Vollverb.

3 Try to speak clearly, then you'll do well.
The guide answered the questions politely.
They went outside and played in the garden.
We're flying to Spain tomorrow.

3 <u>Nach</u> dem Vollverb (+ Objekt) stehen gewöhnlich
– **Adverbien der Art und Weise** (*clearly, politely, well*)
– **Ortsangaben** (*outside, in the garden, on the roof*)
– **Zeitangaben** (*tomorrow, a year ago, in 2008*).

We were in Italy last summer.

Wir waren letzten Sommer in Italien.

! Wenn ein Satz mit einer Orts- <u>und</u> einer Zeitangabe endet, dann gilt die Regel **Ort vor Zeit** – wie im Alphabet: **O vor Z**.

GF 2 Making questions Fragebildung

Word order in questions (except in subject questions)

Wortstellung in Fragen (außer in Fragen nach dem Subjekt)

1 Are you from Scotland?
Do you like pizza?
Have you got a pet?

2 Where are you from?
What is your favourite food?
Why did they move to Wales?

1 **Entscheidungsfragen *(Yes/No questions)*** können nur mit „Ja" oder „Nein" beantwortet werden.

2 **Fragen mit Fragewörtern *(Questions with questions words)*** erfragen weitere Informationen („Wer?" „Was?" „Wann?" „Wo?" „Warum?" „Wie?").

Auxiliary	Subject	Main verb	
Can	you	**drive** a moped?	
Is	Jake	**cleaning** his bike?	
Have	you	**seen** 'Twilight' yet?	
Will	they	**travel** by bus?	
Do	you	**like** pizza?	Magst du ...?
Does	she	**live** in Bristol?	Wohnt sie ...?
Did	they	**move** to Wales?	
Don't	they	**live** here any more?	

◄ **Entscheidungsfragen** beginnen immer mit einem **Hilfsverb *(auxiliary verb)***:
Can ...? Is ...? Have ...? Will ...? ...

Die Wortstellung ist also:
Auxiliary – S – V – ...

In *simple present*- und *simple past*-Fragen braucht man eine Form des Hilfsverbs ***do***:
Do ...? Does ...? Did ...?

Question word	Auxiliary	Subject	Main verb
When	can	you	come to Bath?
What	have	they	bought?
Where	will	you	stay?
How	do	you	know?
Why	does	Ella	want to move?
Who	did	you	meet in London?

◄ Auch in **Fragen**, die mit einem **Fragewort** beginnen, steht ein **Hilfsverb** vor dem Subjekt:
When can ...? What have ...? Where will ...? ...

Die Wortstellung ist also:
Question word – Auxiliary – S – V – ...

Bei Fragewort-Fragen im *simple present* und im *simple past* braucht man wieder eine Form des Hilfsverbs ***do***:
How do ...? Why does ...? Who did ...?

2.2 Word order in subject questions

Wortstellung in Fragen nach dem Subjekt

Question word (= Subject)	Verb	
Who	can drive	a moped?
Who	likes	ice cream?
What	makes	you laugh?
Whose sister	moved	to Bristol?
Which bus	goes	to Bath?

◄ Fragen nach dem Subjekt sind **„Wer oder was?"**-Fragen. In solchen Fragen tritt das Fragewort an die Stelle des Subjekts. Vergleiche:

***Jenny** likes ice cream.*	*Jenny mag Eis.*
***Who** likes ice cream?*	*Wer mag Eis?*

Statement	Subject question	Object question
Liz likes Jake. Liz mag Jake.	Who likes Jake? **Wer** mag Jake?	Who does Liz like? **Wen** mag Liz?
Noise causes headaches.	What causes headaches?	What does noise cause?

! Mit *who, what, whose* ... und *which* ... kann man nach dem Subjekt oder nach dem Objekt fragen. Fragen nach dem Subjekt werden **ohne *do/does/did*** gebildet.

GF 3 Talking about the present — Über die Gegenwart sprechen

Du möchtest ausdrücken,

– dass etwas **regelmäßig** geschieht ▸ *The simple present: GF 3.1*	→	Hanna **gets up** at 7 o'clock every morning. Hanna steht jeden Morgen um 7 Uhr auf.
– dass etwas **gerade jetzt** geschieht ▸ *The present progressive: GF 3.2*	→	It's 7 o'clock. Hanna **is getting up**. Es ist 7 Uhr. Hanna steht (gerade) auf.

3.1 The simple present

Das ***simple present*** wird verwendet,

Dave Wilson **usually** gets the bus to school.
On Mondays his mother takes him in the car.
He **never** cycles to school because it's too far.

◂ um über Handlungen und Ereignisse zu sprechen, die **wiederholt, regelmäßig, immer** oder **nie** geschehen (oft mit Zeitangaben wie *always, never, usually, sometimes, often, every week, on Mondays* usw.).

Dave and his family live in Manchester.
He plays hockey and collects models of old cars.
His dad works for a building company.

◂ um über **Dauerzustände**, **Hobbys** und **Berufe** zu sprechen.

! ***He, she, it* – das „s" muss mit.**

Verneinte Sätze	I don't cycle to school.	Dave doesn't walk to school.
Fragen	Do you go to school by bus? **Where** do the Wilsons live?	Does your mother take you in the car? **When** does Dave's mother take him in the car?

3.2 The present progressive

Das ***present progressive*** wird verwendet,

What's Dave doing? –
Just now he's cleaning his bike.

◂ um über Handlungen und Ereignisse zu sprechen, die **jetzt gerade im Gange** sind (oft mit Angaben wie *at the moment, now, just*).

Dave (on the phone) I can't talk right now, Jack. I'm cleaning my bike.

! Die Handlung, um die es geht, kann für einen Augenblick unterbrochen sein, z. B. durch ein Telefonat. Wichtig ist, dass sie noch nicht abgeschlossen ist.

This week Dave's grandma is staying at the Wilsons' because Dave's mum is ill.

◂ um über **vorübergehende Zustände** zu sprechen (begrenzter Zeitraum: *this week*).

Verneinte Sätze	The Wilsons aren't working.	Dave isn't watching TV.
Fragen	Are you watching TV? **What** are you doing?	Is Dave cleaning his bike? **Who** is Dave talking to?

Dave's dad works for a building company.
Look, he's working at his desk at the moment.

GF 4 Talking about the past Über die Vergangenheit sprechen

Du möchtest ausdrücken,

– dass etwas in der Vergangenheit **geschah**; das Geschehen ist **abgeschlossen** und **vorbei** ▸ *The simple past: GF 4.1*	→ Emma **left** school in 2007. Emma ging im Jahr 2007 von der Schule ab.
– dass etwas in der Vergangenheit **gerade im Gange (noch nicht abgeschlossen) war** ▸ *The past progressive: GF 4.2*	→ We **were leaving** the building when we heard the explosion. Wir waren gerade dabei, das Gebäude zu verlassen, ...
– dass etwas **vor etwas anderem** in der Vergangenheit stattgefunden hatte ▸ *The past perfect: GF 4.3*	→ Connor **had** already **left** when we arrived. Connor war schon gegangen, als wir ankamen.
– dass etwas **irgendwann** geschehen ist, oft mit **Auswirkungen auf die Gegenwart**	→ Jane **has left** her purse at home, so she can't pay for her bus ticket. Jane hat ihre Geldbörse zu Hause gelassen, ...
– dass ein Zustand **in der Vergangenheit begonnen** hat und **noch andauert** ▸ *The present perfect: GF 4.4*	→ We**'ve had** our dog for three years now – since 2008. Wir haben unseren Hund jetzt seit drei Jahren ...

4.1 The simple past

Last Friday Katie's family flew to Spain.
Letzten Freitag ist Katies Familie nach Spanien geflogen / flog Katies Familie nach Spanien.
Two years ago the Websters moved to Bath.
Vor zwei Jahren sind die Websters nach Bath gezogen.

Wenn man über Vergangenes berichtet – zum Beispiel, wenn man etwas erzählt –, benutzt man überwiegend das ***simple past***. Man beschreibt damit Handlungen, Ereignisse und Zustände, die zu einer bestimmten Zeit in der Vergangenheit *(yesterday, last Friday, two years ago, in 2003, between 2005 and 2008, ...)* stattfanden.

! Im Deutschen wird in diesen Fällen oft das Perfekt verwendet, im Englischen jedoch nicht.

Verneinte Sätze	They didn't fly to France.	Katie didn't want to go at first.
Fragen	Did you go on holiday last year? **Where** did you go?	Did Katie like it? **When** did the Websters move to Bath?

4.2 The past progressive

What were you doing yesterday at 3.30? –
I was waiting for my sister at the school doors.
She was still talking to our Maths teacher.

Angela was just crossing the road when she saw her boyfriend.
Angela war gerade dabei, die Straße zu überqueren, ...

Das ***past progressive*** wird verwendet,

◂ um über Handlungen und Ereignisse zu sprechen, die zu einer bestimmten Zeit in der Vergangenheit noch im Gange, also noch nicht abgeschlossen waren.

◂ wenn man beschreiben will, was gerade vor sich ging *(she was just crossing the road)*, als etwas anderes passierte *(she saw her boyfriend)*.

Verneinte Sätze	You weren't listening.	It wasn't snowing when we left the house.
Fragen	Were you watching TV? **What** were they doing?	Was she crossing the road when it happened? **What** was she doing?

▸▸▸

4.3 The past perfect

When Emma arrived home, her parents **had** already **eaten**.
Als Emma zu Hause eintraf, hatten ihre Eltern bereits gegessen.

Wenn man sagen will, dass etwas noch <u>vor etwas anderem</u> in der Vergangenheit stattgefunden hatte, dann benutzt man das ***past perfect***.

Verneinte Sätze	They hadn't gone to bed.	Emma hadn't eaten anything all day.
Fragen	Had you seen that film before? **What** had they done?	Had Emma eaten when she came home? **Where** had she been all day?

4.4 The present perfect

! Das ***present perfect*** hat mit der **Vergangenheit <u>und</u> mit der Gegenwart** zu tun. Es wird verwendet,

Will Smith is great. I've seen most of his films.
Luke has **already** done his Maths homework, but he has**n't** started his French **yet**.
Have you **ever** been to Paris?
– No, I haven't. But I've **always** wanted to go.

Mel has lost her mobile. Her dad is very angry.

◂ wenn man sagen will, **dass** jemand etwas getan hat oder **dass** etwas geschehen ist. Dabei ist nicht wichtig, wann es geschehen ist – ein genauer Zeitpunkt wird nicht genannt. Das *present perfect* steht oft mit Adverbien der <u>unbestimmten</u> Zeit wie *already, just, never, ever, not ... yet*.
Oft hat die Handlung Auswirkungen auf die Gegenwart (Mels Vater ist wütend, weil sie ihr Handy verloren hat).

We've lived in Berlin **since April**.
Wir wohnen <u>seit April</u> in Berlin.

since + Zeitpunkt

We've lived in Berlin **for three months**.
Wir wohnen <u>seit drei Monaten</u> in Berlin.

for + Zeitraum

◂ für **Zustände**, die in der Vergangenheit begonnen haben und jetzt noch andauern (oft mit ***since*** bzw. ***for***).

! Im Deutschen steht in diesen Fällen meist das Präsens, im Englischen <u>muss</u> das *present perfect* stehen.

Verneinte Sätze	I haven't been to Paris yet.	Luke hasn't done his French homework.
Fragen	Have you been to Paris? **What** have you done?	Has Mel found her mobile yet? **Which** of these films have you seen already?

GF 5 Talking about the future Über die Zukunft sprechen

Du möchtest ausdrücken,

- dass etwas für die Zukunft **geplant** ist → **I'm going to watch** the new Bond film tonight.
  Ich sehe mir heute Abend den neuen Bond-Film an.
  ► *The going to-future: GF 5.1*
- wie etwas in der Zukunft **sein wird** (**Vorhersagen, Vermutungen**) → It **will be** warm and sunny in Spain. I'm sure you**'ll like** it there.
  Es wird warm und sonnig sein in Spanien. Ich bin sicher, dass es dir dort gefallen wird.
  ► *The will-future: GF 5.2*
- dass etwas für die Zukunft **fest verabredet** ist (es steht schon im Kalender) → We**'re having** a party on Saturday. Would you like to come?
  Wir geben nächsten Samstag eine Party. ...
  ► *The present progressive: GF 5.3*

5.1 The *going to*-future

My boyfriend says he's going to be an engineer.
Mein Freund sagt, er will Ingenieur werden.

Look at those clouds. There's going to be a storm.
... Es wird ein Gewitter geben.

Das **Futur mit *going to*** wird verwendet,

◄ wenn man über **Vorhaben, Pläne, Absichten** für die Zukunft sprechen will.

◄ um auszudrücken, dass etwas **wahrscheinlich gleich geschehen wird** – es gibt bereits deutliche **Anzeichen** dafür (*hier:* die Wolken am Himmel).

5.2 The *will*-future

It will be cold and windy, and we will get some rain in the afternoon.
I'll be 15 next October.

I expect Ella will be late again as usual.
Ich nehme an, Ella kommt wie üblich wieder zu spät.

Just a moment. I'll open the door for you.
Moment. Ich mache Ihnen die Tür auf.
I won't tell anyone what's happened. I promise.
Ich sage niemandem, was passiert ist. ...

Das **Futur mit *will*** wird verwendet,

◄ um **Vorhersagen** über die Zukunft zu äußern. Oft geht es dabei um Dinge, die man nicht beeinflussen kann, z.B. das Wetter.

◄ um eine **Vermutung** auszudrücken (oft eingeleitet mit *I think, I'm sure, I expect, maybe*).

◄ wenn man sich **spontan** – also ohne es im Voraus geplant zu haben – zu etwas **entschließt**. Oft geht es dabei um **Hilfsangebote** oder **Versprechen**.

5.3 The present progressive (future meaning)

We're driving to Scotland next Friday to visit my grandparents.
I'm meeting a friend in town tonight.

Das ***present progressive*** wird verwendet, wenn etwas **für die Zukunft fest geplant** oder **fest verabredet** ist (manchmal spricht man vom *diary future*). Durch eine Zeitangabe wie *tonight* oder aus dem Zusammenhang muss klar sein, dass es um etwas Zukünftiges geht.

Additional information

5.4 The simple present (future meaning)

The next train to Bath **goes** in ten minutes.
The next drawing class **starts** on 2 September.

Das ***simple present*** wird verwendet, wenn ein **zukünftiges Geschehen** durch einen **Fahrplan**, ein **Programm** oder Ähnliches festgelegt ist (manchmal spricht man vom *timetable future*). Verben wie *arrive, leave, go, open, close, start, stop* werden häufig so verwendet.

GF 6 The passive Das Passiv

6.1 Active and passive

Active: **Alexander Fleming** discovered penicillin in 1928.
Alexander Fleming entdeckte 1928 das Penicillin.

Passive: **Penicillin** was discovered in 1928.
Penicillin wurde 1928 entdeckt.

Aktiv und Passiv

◄ Beide Sätze beschreiben denselben Sachverhalt, betrachten ihn aber aus unterschiedlichen Blickwinkeln:

- Der **Aktivsatz** handelt von Fleming und informiert uns über eine Entdeckung, die er 1928 machte.
- Der **Passivsatz** handelt von Penicillin und informiert uns über den Zeitpunkt seiner Entdeckung.

6.2 Use

1 A new sports centre has been opened in Paddington. ... ist eröffnet worden ...
2 The first goal was scored in the seventh minute. ... wurde erzielt ...
3 Breakfast is served from 7 to 10.30 am. ... wird serviert ...
4 The bank robbers have been sent to prison. ... sind ins Gefängnis gesteckt worden ...

This picture was painted by **a 12-year-old girl.**
... wurde von einem 12-jährigen Mädchen gemalt.

Two cars have been vandalized by **a gang of youths.**
... wurden von einer Bande Jugendlicher zerstört.

Gebrauch

In **Passivsätzen** steht nicht, wer die Handlung ausführt. Oft ist das unwichtig oder nicht bekannt (Sätze 1 und 2), manchmal ist es auch offensichtlich und daher nicht erwähnenswert (Sätze 3 und 4).

Das Passiv findet man oft in Nachrichten, in Zeitungsartikeln (z.B. über Unfälle, Sportereignisse, Verbrechen), in offiziellen Texten, in technischen Beschreibungen und auf Schildern.

! Wenn in Passivsätzen „Täter" oder „Verursacher" doch genannt werden sollen, dann verwendet man die Präposition ***by ...*** („von", „durch").

6.3 Form

Form

Das Passiv bildet man mit einer **Form von *be*** und der 3. Form des Verbs (Partizip Perfekt, *past participle*).

Simple present	I am often invited to parties.	... werde oft eingeladen
Simple past	The bridge was built in the 1950s.	... wurde gebaut
Present perfect	All the sandwiches have been eaten.	... sind gegessen worden
***will*-future**	Our new CD will be released next week.	... wird veröffentlicht werden
Modals	Mobile phones must be turned off now. Concert tickets can be bought online.	... müssen ausgeschaltet werden ... können gekauft werden

GF 7 Modals and their substitutes
Modale Hilfsverben und ihre Ersatzverben

7.1 Modals – what do they express? / Modale Hilfsverben – was drücken sie aus?

Fähigkeit

I can speak French and a little German.	Ich **kann** Französisch und ein bisschen Deutsch.
My sister could read when she was only four.	Meine Schwester **konnte** lesen, als sie erst vier war.

Bitte / Aufforderung

Can I borrow this CD?	**Kann** ich diese CD ausleihen?
Can you be quiet, please?	**Kannst** du bitte leise sein?
Could you show me how to start the DVD?	**Könntest** du mir zeigen, wie man die DVD startet?
Would you help me to lay the table?	**Würdest** du mir helfen, den Tisch zu decken?

Erlaubnis / Verbot

You can use my ruler.	Du **kannst** mein Lineal benutzen.
May I use your phone, please?	**Darf** ich mal dein Telefon benutzen, bitte?
You can't take photos in the museum.	Du **darfst** im Museum **nicht** fotografieren.
In 1968, children could leave school at 15.	... **konnten/durften** Kinder mit 15 die Schule verlassen.
But they couldn't vote till they were 21.	Aber sie **konnten/durften** erst mit 21 wählen.
You mustn't tell Mel about the concert. It's a surprise.	Du **darfst** Mel **nichts** von dem Konzert erzählen. ...

Vorschlag / Ratschlag

Can/Can't we go on a bike trip?	**Können** wir **(nicht)** eine Radtour machen?
You could talk to your teacher.	Du **könntest (doch)** mit deiner Lehrerin sprechen.
You should tell her what happened in Bristol.	Du **solltest** ihr sagen, was in Bristol passiert ist.

Angebot

Can/May I help you with your bags?	**Kann/Darf** ich Ihnen mit Ihren Taschen helfen?
Would you like to stay for dinner?	**Möchtest** du (**nicht**) zum Essen bleiben?

Notwendigkeit, Verpflichtung

You've got a cold. You must stay at home.	Du hast eine Erkältung. Du **musst** zuhause bleiben.
You needn't tell Mel about the concert. She already knows.	Du **brauchst** Mel **nicht** von dem Konzert zu erzählen. ...
Bicycles should be left outside.	Fahrräder **sollten** draußen abgestellt werden.

Möglichkeit, Wahrscheinlichkeit

That must be Luke.	Das **muss** Luke sein.
– No, it can't be Luke. Luke is in Spain.	– Nein, das **kann nicht** Luke sein. Luke ist in Spanien.
Where's Dad? – He could be at Grandma's.	... – Er **könnte** bei Oma sein.
Sarah may still be at her friend's.	Sarah ist **vielleicht** noch bei ihrer Freundin.
John might come today if he's in town.	John kommt **vielleicht** heute vorbei, ...
Kathy should be here by now.	Kathy **sollte** jetzt (eigentlich) hier sein.
There's someone at the door. It will be Janet.	Es ist jemand an der Tür. Das **wird** Janet sein.

7.2 Substitutes

Ersatzverben

Modale Hilfsverben *(can, may, must, ...)* können **nicht alle Zeitformen** bilden. Daher gibt es zu bestimmten modalen Hilfsverben **Ersatzverben**.

„können“: *can – (to) be able to*

My little brother can/is able to swim.
Mein kleiner Bruder kann schwimmen.

I'm taking driving lessons. Next year I'll be able to drive.
... Nächstes Jahr werde ich Auto fahren können.

I could smell fire, but I couldn't see any smoke.
Ich konnte Feuer riechen, aber ich konnte keinen Rauch sehen.

◄ *can* hat auch eine Vergangenheitsform: *could*. *could* steht vor allem in verneinten Sätzen und Fragen sowie mit Verben der Wahrnehmung wie *smell, see, hear*.

„dürfen“: *can, may – (to) be allowed to*

Can/May I have a sleepover on Friday?
Kann/Darf ich ... eine Schlafparty veranstalten?

We weren't allowed to watch the late film last night.
Wir durften den Spätfilm gestern Abend nicht sehen.

I've always been allowed to have pets.
Ich habe schon immer Haustiere haben dürfen.

Jeans must not be worn at this school.
At my school we're not allowed to wear jeans.

! Für ausdrückliche **Verbote** wird *must not (mustn't)* oder *be not allowed to* verwendet.

„müssen“: *must – (to) have to*

Teacher You must work harder, Noah.
Du musst härter arbeiten, Noah.

His teacher says Noah has to work harder.
Seine Lehrerin sagt, dass Noah härter arbeiten muss.

! *have/has to* ist häufiger als *must*.

I needn't get up at 6 tomorrow. /
I don't have to get up at 6 tomorrow.
Ich muss morgen nicht um 6 aufstehen.

! **Verneinung (Gegenwart):** *needn't* oder *don't/doesn't have to*

I had to rewrite my essay.
Ich musste meinen Aufsatz neu schreiben.

We didn't have to wait long.
Wir mussten nicht lange warten.

! **Verneinung (Vergangenheit):** *didn't have to*

GF 8 Conditional sentences Bedingungssätze

8.1 Type 1

If you run, you'll catch the bus.
Wenn du rennst, kriegst du den Bus noch.

If you miss the bus, you can take / should take / must take a taxi.
Wenn du den Bus verpasst, kannst/sollst/musst du ein Taxi nehmen.

Typ 1

◄ **„Was <u>ist</u>, wenn …"**
Diese Bedingungssätze drücken aus, was unter bestimmten Bedingungen **geschieht** oder **geschehen kann/soll** usw.
Sie beziehen sich auf die **Gegenwart** oder die **Zukunft**.

***if*-Satz (Bedingung)**	**Hauptsatz (Folge)**
If *you run,*	*you'll catch the bus.*
If *you miss the bus,*	*you can take a taxi.*
simple present	**– *will-future* – *can/should/must* + Infinitiv**

8.2 Type 2

If you ran, you would catch the bus.
Wenn du rennen würdest, würdest du den Bus noch kriegen.

If you caught the bus, you could be home in time for dinner.
Wenn du den Bus kriegen würdest, könntest du rechtzeitig zum Abendessen daheim sein.

Typ 2

◄ **„Was <u>wäre</u>, wenn …"**
Diese Bedingungssätze drücken aus, was unter bestimmten Bedingungen **geschehen würde** oder **könnte**.
Sie beziehen sich auch auf die **Gegenwart** oder die **Zukunft**.

***if*-Satz (Bedingung)**	**Hauptsatz (Folge)**
If *you ran,*	*you would catch/could catch/ might catch the bus.*
simple past	***would/could/might* + Infinitiv**

GF 9 Relative clauses Relativsätze

There's **the girl** who I met at the party.
Da ist das Mädchen, das ich auf der Party kennengelernt habe.

Relativsätze beziehen sich auf ein **Nomen** – hier: ***the girl.***

Relativsätze bestimmen das Nomen genauer:
Erst durch den Relativsatz weiß man, welches Mädchen genau gemeint ist.

Relativsätze beginnen mit einem **Relativpronomen**:

1 Isn't that **the boy** who/that stole your mobile?
… der Junge, der dein Handy gestohlen hat?

1 Für **Personen** verwendet man ***who*** oder ***that***.

2 That's **the shop** that/which sells cheap CDs.
… der Laden, der billige CDs verkauft.

2 Für **Dinge** verwendet man ***that*** oder ***which***.

GF 10 Adjectives: comparison Adjektive: Steigerung

10.1 Forms

Formen

	Komparativ (Comparative)	Superlativ (Superlative)
clean	cleaner	cleanest
big	bigger	biggest
happy	happier	happiest
useful	more useful	most useful
famous	more famous	most famous
expensive	more expensive	most expensive
difficult	more difficult	most difficult
good	better	best
bad	worse	worst
much/many	more	most
(a) little	less	least

Steigerungsformen werden verwendet, um Personen oder Dinge miteinander zu vergleichen.

◄ **Steigerung** mit *-er/-est*:
- **einsilbige** Adjektive
- **zweisilbige** Adjektive, die auf ***-y*** enden

◄ **Steigerung** mit *more/most*:
- die meisten **zweisilbigen** Adjektive, die nicht auf ***-y*** enden
- Adjektive mit **mehr als zwei Silben**

◄ **unregelmäßige Steigerung**:
- ***good, bad***
- ***much/many, (a) little***

Additional information

She's cleverer / more clever than her sister.
Sie ist cleverer als ihre Schwester.

That's the stupidest / most stupid thing I've ever heard.
Das ist das Dümmste, was ich je gehört habe.

Manche zweisilbigen Adjektive können mit *-er/-est* oder mit *more/most* gesteigert werden; Beispiele: *clever, simple, stupid*.
Wenn du dir nicht sicher bist, musst du die Steigerungsformen in einem Wörterbuch nachschlagen.

10.2 The adjective in comparisons

Das Adjektiv in Vergleichen

Ella is as **old** as John. — ◄ *as … as* „so … wie"

She's not as **old** as Lucy. — ◄ *not as … as* „nicht so … wie"

Lucy is **old**er than her.
(*nicht:* … older than ~~she~~)

◄ **Komparativ + *than*:**
older than „älter als"
more expensive than „teurer … als"

Lucy is the **old**est.

◄ ***the* + Superlativ:**
the oldest „der/die älteste, am ältesten"

Grammatical terms (Grammatische Fachbegriffe)

active ['æktɪv]	Aktiv	*Beckham* ***scored*** *the final goal.*
adjective ['ædʒɪktɪv]	Adjektiv	*good, red, new, boring*
adverb ['ædvɜ:b]	Adverb	*always, badly, here, really, today*
adverb of frequency ['fri:kwənsi]	Häufigkeitsadverb	*always, often, never*
adverb of indefinite time [ɪn,defɪnət 'taɪm]	Adverb der unbestimmten Zeit	*already, ever, just, never*
adverb of manner ['mænə]	Adverb der Art und Weise	*badly, happily, quietly, well*
article ['ɑ:tɪkl]	Artikel	*the, a/an*
auxiliary [ɔ:g'zɪliəri]	Hilfsverb	*be, have, do; will, can, must*
comparison [kəm'pærɪsn]	Steigerung	*old – older – oldest*
conditional sentence [kən,dɪʃənl 'sentəns]	Bedingungssatz	*I'd call him if I knew his number.*
conjunction [kən'dʒʌŋkʃn]	Konjunktion	*and, or, but; because, before*
countable noun ['kaʊntəbl]	zählbares Nomen	*girl – girls, pound – pounds*
definite article ['defɪnət]	bestimmter Artikel	*the*
future ['fju:tʃə]	Zukunft, Futur	
gerund ['dʒerənd]	Gerundium	*I like* ***dancing****.* ***Dancing*** *is fun.*
***going to*-future**	Futur mit *going to*	***I'm going to watch*** *TV tonight.*
***if*-clause** ['ɪf klɔ:z]	*if*-Satz, Nebensatz mit *if*	***If I see Jack****, I'll tell him.*
imperative [ɪm'perətɪv]	Imperativ (Befehlsform)	*Open your books. Don't talk.*
infinitive [ɪn'fɪnətɪv]	Infinitiv (Grundform des Verbs)	*(to) open, (to) see, (to) read*
irregular verb [ɪ,regjələ 'vɜ:b]	unregelmäßiges Verb	*(to) go – went – gone*
main clause	Hauptsatz	***I like Scruffy*** *because I like dogs.*
modal ['məʊdl]	modales Hilfsverb, Modalverb	*can, could, may, must*
negative statement [,negətɪv 'steɪtmənt]	verneinter Aussagesatz	*I don't like bananas.*
noun [naʊn]	Nomen, Substantiv	*Sophie, girl, brother, time*
object ['ɒbdʒɪkt]	Objekt	*My sister is writing* ***a letter****.*
object form ['ɒbdʒɪkt fɔ:m]	Objektform (der Personalpronomen)	*me, you, him, her, it, us, them*
object question ['ɒbdʒɪkt ,kwestʃən]	Frage nach dem Objekt	*Who does Jake love?*
passive ['pæsɪv]	Passiv	*The goal* ***was scored*** *by Beckham.*
past [pɑ:st]	Vergangenheit	
past participle [,pɑ:st 'pɑ:tɪsɪpl]	Partizip Perfekt	*cleaned, planned, gone, taken*
past perfect [,pɑ:st 'pɜ:fɪkt]	Plusquamperfekt, Vorvergangenheit	*He cried – he* ***had hurt*** *his knee.*
past progressive [,pɑ:st prə'gresɪv]	Verlaufsform der Vergangenheit	*At 7.30 I* ***was having*** *dinner.*
personal pronoun [,pɜ:sənl 'prəʊnaʊn]	Personalpronomen (persönliches Fürwort)	*I, you, he, she, it, we, they; me, you, him, her, it, us, them*
plural ['plʊərəl]	Plural, Mehrzahl	
positive statement [,pɒzətɪv 'steɪtmənt]	bejahter Aussagesatz	*I like oranges.*
possessive determiner [pə,zesɪv dɪ'tɜ:mɪnə]	Possessivbegleiter (besitzanzeigender Begleiter)	*my, your, his, her, its, our, their*
possessive form [pə,zesɪv fɔ:m]	*s*-Genitiv	*Jo's brother; my sister's room*
possessive pronoun [pə,zesɪv 'prəʊnaʊn]	Possessivpronomen	*mine, yours, his, hers, ours, theirs*
preposition [,prepə'zɪʃn]	Präposition	*after, at, in, next to, under*
present ['preznt]	Gegenwart	
present participle [,preznt 'pɑ:tɪsɪpl]	Partizip Präsens	*cleaning, planning, going, taking*
present perfect [,preznt 'pɜ:fɪkt]	*present perfect*	*We****'ve made*** *a cake for you.*
present progressive [,preznt prə'gresɪv]	Verlaufsform der Gegenwart	*The Hansons* ***are having*** *lunch.*
progressive form [prə'gresɪv fɔ:m]	Verlaufsform	
pronoun ['prəʊnaʊn]	Pronomen, Fürwort	
quantifier ['kwɒntɪfaɪə]	Mengenangabe	*some, a lot of, many, much*
question word ['kwestʃən wɜ:d]	Fragewort	*what?, when?, where?, how?*
reflexive pronoun [rɪ,fleksɪv 'prəʊnaʊn]	Reflexivpronomen	*myself, yourself, themselves*

regular verb [ˌregjələ 'vɜːb]	regelmäßiges Verb	*(to) help – helped – helped*
relative clause [ˌrelətɪv 'klɔːz]	Relativsatz	*There's the girl **who helped me**.*
relative pronoun [ˌrelətɪv 'prəʊnaʊn]	Relativpronomen	*who, that, which, whose*
short answer [ˌʃɔːt‿'ɑːnsə]	Kurzantwort	*Yes, I am. / No, I don't.*
simple form ['sɪmpl fɔːm]	einfache Form	
simple past [ˌsɪmpl 'pɑːst]	einfache Form der Vergangenheit	*Jo **wrote** two letters yesterday.*
simple present [ˌsɪmpl 'preznt]	einfache Form der Gegenwart	*I always **go** to school by bike.*
singular ['sɪŋgjələ]	Singular, Einzahl	
statement ['steɪtmənt]	Aussagesatz	
subject ['sʌbdʒɪkt]	Subjekt	***My sister** is writing a letter.*
subject form ['sʌbdʒɪkt fɔːm]	Subjektform (der Personalpronomen)	*I, you, he, she, it, we, they*
subject question ['sʌbdʒɪkt ˌkwestʃən]	*Frage nach dem Subjekt*	*Who loves Jake?*
subordinate clause [səˌbɔːdɪnət 'klɔːz]	Nebensatz	*I like Scruffy **because I like dogs**.*
substitute ['sʌbstɪtjuːt]	Ersatzverb (eines modalen Hilfverbs)	*be able to, be allowed to, have to*
tense [tens]	Zeitform	
uncountable noun [ʌn'kaʊntəbl]	nicht zählbares Nomen	*bread, milk, money, news, work*
verb [vɜːb]	Verb	*hear, open, help, go*
***will*-future**	Futur mit *will*	*I think it **will be** cold tonight.*
word order ['wɜːd‿ˌɔːdə]	Wortstellung	
yes/no question	Entscheidungsfrage	*Are you 13? Do you like comics?*

Das **Vocabulary** (S. 163–172) enthält alle neuen Wörter und Wendungen aus Band 6, die du lernen musst. Sie stehen in der Reihenfolge, in der sie in den Units vorkommen.

Das **Dictionary** (S. 173–203) enthält den Wortschatz der Bände 1 bis 6 in alphabetischer Reihenfolge. Dort kannst du nachschlagen, was ein Wort bedeutet, wie man es ausspricht oder wie es genau geschrieben wird.

So ist das Vocabulary aufgebaut:

- Hier siehst du, wo die Wörter vorkommen.
  p. 9/2 = Seite 9, Abschnitt 2
  p. 10/P 1 = Seite 10, Übung 1
- Die Lautschrift zeigt dir, wie ein Wort ausgesprochen und betont wird.
- Eingerückte Wörter lernst du am besten zusammen mit dem vorausgehenden Wort, weil die beiden zusammengehören.
- Die blauen Kästen solltest du dir besonders gut ansehen.

p. 9/2	**attractive** [ə'træktɪv]	attraktiv *(Person)*; reizvoll, verlockend *(Idee, Preis)*	! Betonung: **attractive** [ə'tr **attractive** ◄► **unattracti**
p. 10/P 1	**tongue** [tʌŋ]	Zunge	! Aussprache: **tongue** [tʌŋ]
	chat-up line *(infml)*	Anmachspruch	I can never think of a g ~-~ **line** when I meet so
	(to) **chat** sb. **up** (-tt-) *(infml)*	jn. anquatschen, anbaggern	If you fancy the team c: him **up**?

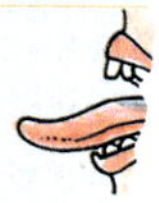

Relationships: going out, asking sb. out

(to) **go out**	Olivia and Jacob would like to **go out**. Ella and Grace **went out** for a pizza last Friday.	**1.** ausgehen, w
	There's Jake. He **went out** with my sister last year.	**2.** miteinand
(to) **ask sb. out**	Why don't you **ask him out** if you fancy him? Colin **asked me out** for a pizza yesterday.	jn. ein

Tipps zum Wörterlernen findest du im Skills File auf Seite 125.

Abkürzungen:

n	= *noun*	*v*	= *verb*
adj	= *adjective*	*adv*	= *adverb*
prep	= *preposition*	*conj*	= *conjunction*
pl	= *plural*	*no pl*	= *no plural*
p.	= page	pp.	= pages
sb.	= somebody	sth.	= something
jn.	= jemanden	jm.	= jemandem
AE	= *American English*	*BE*	= *British English*
infml	= *informal* (umgangssprachlich, informell)		

Symbole:

! Hier stehen Hinweise auf Besonderheiten, bei denen man leicht Fehler machen kann.

◄► ist das „Gegenteil"-Zeichen: **attractive** ◄► **unattractive**

~ Die **Tilde** in den Beispielsätzen steht für das neue Wort. Beispiel: (to) **fancy** sb. – If I ~ a boy, I just give him a phone call.

Unit 1: Love life!

p. 6	**good-looking** [ˌgʊd'lʊkɪŋ]	gut aussehend	
	(to) **fancy** sb. ['fænsi] *(infml)*	auf jn. stehen	If I ~ a boy, I just give him a phone call.
	arrogant ['ærəgənt]	arrogant, überheblich	! Betonung: **arrogant** ['ærəgənt]
	bossy ['bɒsi]	herrisch	
	(to) **care about** sth. [keə]	etwas wichtig nehmen	! • I **care about** what I eat. (= What I eat is important to me.) • Many people **don't care** if their food is healthy. (= Healthy food is not important to them.)
	(to) **notice** ['nəʊtɪs]	bemerken, merken	Lilly was at the party too, but I didn't ~ her. When she wanted to pay, she **~d** that she had lost her purse.

	peanut ['pi:nʌt]	Erdnuss	some **peanuts** 
p.7	**thin** [θɪn]	dünn	! German: **dünn** ◄► **dick** English: **1. thin** ◄► **fat** *(people, animals)* **2. thin** ◄► **thick** *(books, ice, soup, ...)*
	episode ['epɪsəʊd]	Folge *(einer Fernsehserie)*	! Betonung: **episode** ['epɪsəʊd]

Relationships: going out, asking sb. out

(to) **go out**	Olivia and Jacob would like to **go out**. Ella and Grace **went out** for a pizza last Friday.	**1.** ausgehen, weggehen, sich verabreden
	There's Jake. He **went out** with my sister last year.	**2.** miteinander gehen, zusammen sein
(to) **ask sb. out**	Why don't you **ask him out** if you fancy him? Colin **asked me out** for a pizza yesterday.	jn. einladen, zusammen auszugehen

	chat-up line *(infml)*	Anmachspruch	I can never think of a good **~-~ line** when I meet someone I fancy.
	(to) **chat** sb. **up (-tt-)** *(infml)*	jn. anquatschen, anbaggern	If you fancy the team captain, why don't you ~ him **up**?

PART A Real-life relationships

p.8/1	**situation** [ˌsɪtʃu'eɪʃn]	Situation, Lage	! Betonung: **situation** [ˌsɪtʃu'eɪʃn]
	in a friendly/strange/ different **way**	auf freundliche/seltsame/ andere Art und Weise	He looked at her **in a strange ~** and suddenly she felt very scared. When you paraphrase something you try to say it **in a different ~**.
p.9/2	(to) **last** [lɑ:st]	halten *(fortdauern, von Bestand sein)*	I don't think his relationship with Tina will ~. I wouldn't buy cheap shoes. They won't ~ very long.
	attractive [ə'træktɪv]	attraktiv *(Person)*; reizvoll, verlockend *(Idee, Preis)*	! Betonung: **attractive** [ə'træktɪv] **attractive** ◄► **unattractive**
	(to) **flirt** [flɜ:t]	flirten	
p.10/P 1	**appearance** [ə'pɪərəns]	Aussehen, (äußere) Erscheinung	He dresses terribly. He just doesn't care about his ~.
	tongue [tʌŋ]	Zunge	! Aussprache: **tongue** [tʌŋ] 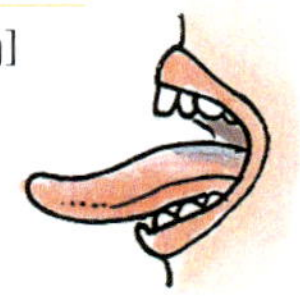
p.10/P 2	(to) **annoy** sb. [ə'nɔɪ]	jn. (ver)ärgern, stören; jm. auf die Nerven gehen	It **~s** me when people don't say 'hello'.
p.11/P 4	(to) **keep** sth. **going**	etwas in Gang halten, etwas aufrechterhalten	(to) **keep** a conversation / a relationship / a party / a fire **going**
	around here	hier in/aus der Gegend	Do you live **around ~**? / Are you from **around ~**?

PART B Relationships in films

p.12/1	**at the same time**	gleichzeitig	It's illegal to drive and use a mobile phone **at the same ~**.
	(to) **be based on** [beɪst]	basieren auf	The film **is ~ on** a book by Stephenie Meyer.
	novel ['nɒvl]	Roman	
	the film **stars** ... [stɑːz]	der Film hat ... in der Hauptrolle / in den Hauptrollen	The film ~ Johnny Depp and Keira Knightley.
	the film/novel **is set in** ...	der Film/Roman spielt in ...	The film **is ~ in** London.
	pregnant ['pregnənt]	schwanger	! She's **six months pregnant**. = ... **im sechsten Monat schwanger**.
	control (of/over) [kən'trəʊl]	Kontrolle (über)	Keep calm and don't lose ~. (= ... verlier nicht die Beherrschung.)
	although [ɔːl'ðəʊ]	obwohl	I went to bed early ~ I wasn't really tired.
	racism ['reɪsɪzəm]	Rassismus	
	plot [plɒt]	Handlung *(eines Romans, Films)*	
	review [rɪ'vjuː]	*(Buch-, Film-)*Kritik, Besprechung, Rezension	
	reviewer [rɪ'vjuːə]	Rezensent/in, Kritiker/in *(von Büchern, Filmen usw.)*	
p.13/2	**couple** ['kʌpl]	Paar, Pärchen	
	romantic [rəʊ'mæntɪk]	romantisch; Liebes-	

	3 **out of** 5	3 von 5	19 ~ **of** 28 students in our form are girls.
p.13/3	(to) **disagree (with** sb.**)** [ˌdɪsə'griː]	nicht übereinstimmen (mit jm.); anderer Meinung sein (als jd.)	I thought it was a good idea, but the others **~d**. (to) **disagree** ◄► (to) **agree**
	intelligent [ɪn'telɪdʒənt]	intelligent, klug	! Betonung: **in<u>tel</u>ligent** [ɪn'telɪdʒənt]
	religion [rɪ'lɪdʒn]	Religion	! Betonung: **re<u>li</u>gion** [rɪ'lɪdʒn]

Religions

Person	Adjective	Building
Christian ['krɪstʃən]	**Christian**	**church, cathedral**
Catholic ['kæθlɪk]	**Catholic**	
Protestant ['prɒtɪstənt]	**Protestant**	
Hindu ['hɪnduː]	**Hindu**	**temple** ['templ] *Tempel*
Jew [dʒuː]	**Jewish** ['dʒuːɪʃ]	**synagogue** ['sɪnəgɒg] *Synagoge*
Muslim ['mʊzlɪm]	**Muslim**	**mosque** [mɒsk] *Moschee*

Other 'religion words':

religious [rɪ'lɪdʒəs] *religiös; gläubig*

service ['sɜːvɪs] *Gottesdienst*

mass [mæs] *Messe*

p.14/P1	**What's special about ...?**	Was ist das Besondere an ...?	**What's ~ about** this place? – It's the oldest pub in Bristol.

costume ['kɒstjuːm]	(Bühnen-)Kostüm	❗ Betonung: <u>co</u>**stume** ['kɒstjuːm]

a **costume**

❗ a **suit** [suːt]

director [də'rektə]	Regisseur/in	

Unit 2: The world we live in

games console

electric toothbrush

hairdryer

microwave

electric razor

p. 28 **toothbrush** ['tuːθbrʌʃ]	Zahnbürste	
console ['kɒnsəʊl]	Konsole, Steuerpult	
hairdryer ['heədraɪə]	Föhn, Haartrockner	
microwave ['maɪkrəweɪv]	Mikrowelle	
razor ['reɪzə]	Rasierapparat, Rasierer	
appliance [ə'plaɪəns]	Gerät *(meist elektrisch)*	Most homes have **~s** like microwaves, dish-washers and washing machines.
(to) **remember** sth.	an etwas denken, sich etwas merken	Please ~ to close the window when you leave. **Remember**: The simple past of 'keep' is 'kept'.
heating ['hiːtɪŋ]	Heizung	It was really cold in our classroom today. The ~ wasn't working.
heat [hiːt]	Hitze, Wärme	It's so hot in here. I can't sleep in this ~. **heat ◄► cold**
(to) **heat** [hiːt]	heizen, erhitzen	We use oil to ~ our flat in winter.
environment [ɪn'vaɪrənmənt]	Umwelt; Umgebung	Lots of kids worry about the pollution of the ~.

greenhouse

footprints

p. 29 **footprint** ['fʊtprɪnt]	Fußabdruck	
greenhouse ['griːnhaʊs]	Gewächshaus, Treibhaus	
gas [gæs]	Gas	
carbon dioxide (CO_2) [ˌkɑːbən daɪ'ɒksaɪd], [ˌsiː‿əʊ 'tuː]	Kohlendioxid (CO_2)	❗ Betonung: **di<u>ox</u>ide** [daɪ'ɒksaɪd] ❗ Oft wird nur das Wort **carbon** („Kohlenstoff") verwendet, wenn eigentlich **carbon dioxide** („Kohlendioxid") gemeint ist.
effect (on) [ɪ'fekt]	(Aus-)Wirkung (auf), Effekt	The cold weather had a bad **~ on** all the plants.
global warming [ˌgləʊbl 'wɔːmɪŋ]	Erwärmung der Erdatmosphäre, globaler Temperaturanstieg	

Tipps zum Wörterlernen → S. 125 · Dictionary (English – German) → S. 173–203

climate ['klaɪmət]	Klima	! Aussprache: **climate** ['klaɪmət]
conditions *(pl)* [kən'dɪʃnz]	Bedingungen, Verhältnisse	**living ~** („Lebensbedingungen"), **weather ~** („Wetterverhältnisse, -bedingungen")
tonne [tʌn]	Tonne *(Gewichtseinheit)*	1000 kilos ! Aussprache: **tonne** [tʌn]
target ['tɑ:gɪt]	Ziel; Zielscheibe	What's your personal ~ for the coming year? Houses with open windows are easy **~s** for thieves.
(to) **reduce** [rɪ'dju:s]	verringern, vermindern, reduzieren	Look, they've **~d** the price from £ 25 to £ 15.

PART A Living with technology

p.30/1 **scientist** ['saɪəntɪst]	(Natur-)Wissenschaftler/in	
invention [ɪn'venʃn]	Erfindung	

Verbs and nouns

(to) **act** **action** ['ækʃn]	handeln, sich verhalten Tat, Handlung; Handeln	(to) **pollute** [pə'lu:t] **pollution**	verschmutzen, verunreinigen Verschmutzung
(to) **inform** [ɪn'fɔ:m] **information** [,ɪnfə'meɪʃn]	informieren Information(en)	(to) **present** [prɪ'zent] **presentation** [,prezn'teɪʃn]	präsentieren, vorstellen Präsentation
(to) **invent** [ɪn'vent] **invention**	erfinden Erfindung	(to) **pronounce** [prə'naʊns] **pronunciation** [prə,nʌnsi'eɪʃn]	aussprechen Aussprache

choice [tʃɔɪs]	Wahl, Auswahl	verb: (to) **choose** – noun: **choice**
(to) **develop (into)** [dɪ'veləp]	entwickeln; sich entwickeln (zu)	We are trying to ~ a new kind of computer. After a boring start, our trip **~ed into** a real adventure.
army ['ɑ:mi]	Armee, Heer	! Betonung: **army** ['ɑ:mi]
in the 1970s	in den 70er-Jahren *(des 20. Jahrhunderts)*	
since then	seitdem	He broke his leg last week. He's been in hospital **~ then**.
fat [fæt]	Fett	
forever (*BE auch:* **for ever**) [fər'evə]	für immer	
for the first time	zum ersten Mal	Today I'm going to play tennis **for the first ~** in my life. (I've never played tennis before.)
foreign ['fɒrən]	ausländisch, fremd	That car must be ~. Look at the number plate. (to) learn ~ languages (Fremdsprachen lernen)
p.31/2 **human** ['hju:mən]	Menschen-, menschlich	When did ~ life on earth begin? Do you know?
power ['paʊə]	Kraft, Energie, Strom	

	power station ['paʊə steɪʃn]	Kraftwerk, Elektrizitätswerk	
	(to) **take part (in)**	teilnehmen (an)	(to) join other people in an activity: 12 students **took ~ in** the school play.
	experiment [ɪk'sperɪmənt]	Experiment	! Betonung: **experiment** [ɪk'sperɪmənt]
	cyclist ['saɪklɪst]	Radfahrer/in	
	(to) **burn** [bɜːn]	brennen; verbrennen	The light in the bedroom was still **~ing** at 4 am. Don't ~ those newspapers! Recycle them!
p.32/P 1	**fresh** [freʃ]	frisch	
p.33/P 5	**compliment** ['kɒmplɪmənt]	Kompliment	! Betonung: **compliment** ['kɒmplɪmənt]
	What a great idea.	Was für eine tolle Idee!	! English: **What a** great idea. / **What a** joke. German: **Was für eine** tolle Idee! / **Was für ein** Witz!
	Congratulations. [kənˌgrætʃu'leɪʃnz]	Herzlichen Glückwunsch!	! Wenn man zum Geburtstag gratuliert, sagt man **Happy birthday**.
p.33/P 6	**application** [ˌæplɪ'keɪʃn] *(kurz auch:* **app***)*	Anwendung, Anwendungsprogramm, -software; App	It's a useful little ~ that you can download from the internet.

PART B Saving the planet

p.34/1	**almost** ['ɔːlməʊst]	fast, beinahe	It's ~ six.
	kettle ['ketl]	(Wasser-)Kessel, Wasserkocher	an electric **kettle** 
	(to) **be a no-no** ['nəʊ nəʊ] *(infml)*	tabu sein, nicht in Frage kommen	Bullying smaller kids **is a** big **~-~** at our school.
	one by one	einer nach dem anderen	She opened her presents **~ by ~**.
	tear [tɪə]	Träne	**tears** 
	(to) **lend** sb. sth. [lend], **lent, lent** [lent]	jm. etwas leihen, etwas an jn. verleihen	Can you ~ me £10 until tomorrow? – Sorry, I never ~ money.
	(to) **borrow** sth. **(from)** ['bɒrəʊ]	(sich) etwas (aus)leihen, borgen (von)	Can I ~ your dictionary? You'll get it back in a minute.

(to) lend – (to) borrow

(to) **lend** = (to) give to

(to) **borrow** = (to) take from

	off [ɒf]	von ... herunter	(to) fall ~ a tree; (to) jump ~ a wall; (to) help someone ~ a bus
	responsible [rɪ'spɒnsəbl]	verantwortlich; verantwortungsbewusst	The team captain is ~ for organizing matches. We need a reliable and ~ person to look after the house while we're away.
	(to) **mess** sth. **up** [ˌmes_'ʌp] *(infml)*	etwas vermasseln, versauen	I **~ed up** my drawing so I had to start again.
p.35/1	**freezing** ['friːzɪŋ]	eisig; eiskalt	It's ~ (cold) outside. There's even ice on the windows.
	24/7 (twenty-four seven)	rund um die Uhr, sieben Tage die Woche	= twenty-four hours, seven days a week
	not even	(noch) nicht einmal	I won't tell anybody, **not** ~ my best friend. The pizza was**n't** ~ hot, it was just warm.
	(to) **melt** [melt]	schmelzen	The sun came out, and the snow began to ~. The sun **~ed** the ice on the windows.
	power cut ['paʊə kʌt]	Stromabschaltung, Stromausfall	
	bone [bəʊn]	Knochen	 **bones**
p.35/2	**reaction (to)** [ri'ækʃn]	Reaktion (auf)	! Betonung: **re<u>ac</u>tion** [ri'ækʃn]
	(to) **react (to)** [ri'ækt]	reagieren (auf)	How did you ~ **to** the story? Did it make you feel sad? Or angry? Or happy?
p.36/P1	(to) **make a difference**	etwas bewirken, etwas bewegen	Help to save the planet! Reduce your carbon footprint! You can **make a ~**!
	low [ləʊ]	niedrig	**low** ◄► **high**
p.37/P4	**outline** ['aʊtlaɪn]	Gliederung	

Unit 3: Have your say!

p.46	**Have your say!**	*etwa:* Übe dein Mitspracherecht aus! / Rede mit!	Adults shouldn't decide everything. Young people should **have their ~** too.
	issue ['ɪʃuː]	Thema, (Streit-)Frage	Global warming is one of the big **~s** of our time.
	poverty ['pɒvəti]	Armut	adjective: **poor** [pɔː, pʊə] – noun: **poverty** ['pɒvəti]
	discrimination (against) [dɪˌskrɪmɪ'neɪʃn]	Diskriminierung (von), Benachteiligung (von)	Men often get more money than women for the same job. That's ~ **against** women.
	(to) **discriminate against** sb. [dɪ'skrɪmɪneɪt]	jn. diskriminieren, jn. benachteiligen	I think it's wrong to ~ **against** minorities. ! **jn.** diskriminieren = (to) discriminate **against sb.**
	facilities *(pl)* [fə'sɪlətiz]	Einrichtungen, Anlagen	We need more sports ~ for kids in this area.
	(to) **vote** [vəʊt]	wählen *(zur Wahl gehen)*; abstimmen	He's only 15, he's too young to ~. Pizza or pasta? Let's ~ on it.
	(to) **vote for/against** sb./sth.	für/gegen jn./etwas stimmen	We all **~d against** building the new airport.

(to) **care about** sth. [keə]	etwas wichtig nehmen	

(to) care

Which issues do you **care about** most?	Welche Themen liegen dir besonders am Herzen? / Welche Themen sind dir am wichtigsten?
I **care about** health and the environment.	Mir sind Gesundheit und Umwelt wichtig.
Do you **care** enough to stand up and have your say?	Ist es dir wichtig genug, dass du aufstehst und deine Meinung sagst?
A lot of people just **don't care**.	Vielen Menschen ist es einfach egal.
Who cares about fashion? I don't!	Wen interessiert schon Mode? Mich nicht!

p.47	(to) **speak out** [ˌspiːk_ˈaʊt]	seine Meinung (offen) sagen	If nobody **speaks ~**, people won't see that there's a problem.
	(to) **get involved (in)** [ɪnˈvɒlvd]	sich engagieren (für, bei); sich beteiligen (an)	Would you like to **get ~** in community work? Then phone 498932.
	trade [treɪd]	Handel	the activity of buying and selling
	(to) **waste** sth. **(on)** [weɪst]	etwas verschwenden, etwas vergeuden (für)	My brother **~s** all his money **on** computer games.
	source [sɔːs]	Quelle *(von Informationen, Energie usw.)*	The internet is a good ~ of information.
	wish [wɪʃ]	Wunsch	
	peace [piːs]	Friede(n)	
	war [wɔː]	Krieg	
	(to) **complain (to** sb. **about** sth.**)** [kəmˈpleɪn]	sich beschweren, sich beklagen (bei jm. über etwas)	If the food isn't hot enough, you should ~ **to** the waiter.
	politician [ˌpɒləˈtɪʃn]	Politiker/in	
	politics [ˈpɒlətɪks]	Politik	
	political [pəˈlɪtɪkl]	politisch	
	demonstration [ˌdemənˈstreɪʃn]	Demonstration	
	town hall [ˌtaʊn ˈhɔːl]	Rathaus	
	campaign [kæmˈpeɪn]	Kampagne, (Werbe-)Feldzug	
	(to) **sign** [saɪn]	unterschreiben, unterzeichnen	
	petition [pəˈtɪʃn]	Unterschriftensammlung, Petition	

PART A Your right to be heard

p.48/1	**on my/your/... own** [əʊn]	allein, selbstständig	Your room looks great. Did you paint it **on your ~**? Or did your parents help you?
	cigarette [ˌsɪgəˈret]	Zigarette	
	alcohol [ˈælkəhɒl]	Alkohol	
	likely [ˈlaɪkli]	wahrscheinlich	Everyone is angry, so it's ~ that lots of people will join the demonstration.

p. 48/2	**citizen** ['sɪtɪzn]	Staatsbürger/in	
	citizenship ['sɪtɪzənʃɪp]	Staatsbürgerschaft	
	(to) **take** sb./sth. **seriously**	jn./etwas ernst nehmen	My older sister doesn't **~ me seriously**.
	(to) **break** [breɪk], **broke** [brəʊk], **broken** ['brəʊkən]	brechen; zerbrechen; kaputt gehen	She **broke** the school rules and was sent home. Please be careful with my MP3 player. Don't **~** it. All the plates fell to the floor and **broke**.
	(to) **deserve** [dɪ'zɜːv]	verdienen *(zu Recht bekommen)*	We've worked very hard, so I think we ~ a break.
	equal ['iːkwəl]	gleich *(Rechte, Bezahlung usw.)*	Do women and men always have **~** rights? Divide £ 1 into five **~** parts. – Easy. 20 p.
	two at a time	zwei auf einmal *(zur selben Zeit)*	! **one at a time** = **einzeln**: Please come in separately, **one at a time**.
	unless [ən'les]	es sei denn; wenn ... nicht	You'll get into trouble with your parents **~** you work harder. (= ... if you don't work harder)
	It doesn't matter.	Es spielt keine Rolle. / Es macht nichts (aus).	Sorry, I forgot the potatoes. – **It doesn't ~**. We can have rice instead.
p. 49/2	**mosquito** [mə'skiːtəʊ]	Moskito, Stechmücke	
	device [dɪ'vaɪs]	Vorrichtung, Gerät	My bike has a little **~** that counts the miles I've cycled.
	owner ['əʊnə]	Besitzer/in	
	in fact [ɪn 'fækt]	tatsächlich; in Wirklichkeit; um genau zu sein	It looks difficult, but **in ~** it's quite easy. Yes, I know her. **In ~**, we were in the same class.
	percentage [pə'sentɪdʒ]	Prozentsatz, prozentualer Anteil	A pretty high **~** of people go to work by bike.
	part-time job	Teilzeitbeschäftigung	**part-time job** ◄► **full-time job** Teilzeitbeschäftigung Ganztagsbeschäftigung
	democracy [dɪ'mɒkrəsi]	Demokratie	
	MP (member of parliament) ['membər_əv 'pɑːləmənt]	Parlamentsmitglied, Abgeord-nete(r)	
	town councillor ['kaʊnsələ]	Stadtrat/Stadträtin	
	party ['pɑːti]	Partei	
	(to) **improve** [ɪm'pruːv]	(sich) verbessern	(to) become better, (to) make better
p. 50/P 1	(to) **take action** ['ækʃn]	handeln; etwas unternehmen	We can't just wait and do nothing. We'll have to **~ action**.
p. 50/P 2	**disgusting** [dɪs'gʌstɪŋ]	widerlich, ekelhaft	The food was **~**. I felt sick after eating it.
	(to) **make sure that ...**	dafür sorgen, dass ...	Please **~ sure that** the windows are closed when you leave the house.

PART B Speaking out

p. 52	**debate** [dɪ'beɪt]	Debatte, Diskussion	
	(to) **debate**	debattieren, erörtern, diskutieren	
	narrator [nə'reɪtə]	Erzähler/in	
	immigration (to) [ˌɪmɪ'greɪʃn]	Einwanderung, Immigration (in, nach)	

	tax [tæks]	*(die)* Steuer	The ~ on petrol is about 70 % of the price.
	so that	sodass; damit	I'm saving money ~ ~ I can buy a new computer.
	(to) **figure** sth. **out** ['fɪgə]	etwas ausrechnen; etwas herausfinden, herauskriegen	I can't ~ **out** how this machine works.
	foreigner ['fɒrənə]	Ausländer/in	
p.53	(to) **stare (at** sb.**)** [steə]	(jn. an)starren	You mustn't ~ **at** people. It's rude.
	character ['kærəktə]	Person, Figur *(in Roman, Film)*	! Betonung: **character** ['kærəktə]
p.54/P 1	**idiot** ['ɪdiət]	Idiot/in	**idiot** ['ɪdiət]
p.55/P 3	**conflict** ['kɒnflɪkt]	Konflikt	**conflict** ['kɒnflɪkt]
	No worries. ['wʌriz] *(infml)*	Kein Problem! / Ist schon in Ordnung!	Sorry, I'm late. – **No ~**, we still have lots of time.
	Can I have a word with you?	Kann ich mal kurz mit dir reden?	
	I didn't mean to ...	Ich wollte nicht ...; Es war nicht meine Absicht, zu ...	I'm sorry, **I didn't ~ to** be rude. **I didn't ~ to** hurt you. Can you forgive me?

Das **Dictionary** enthält den Wortschatz der Bände 1 bis 6 von *English G 21.*
Wenn du wissen möchtest, was ein Wort bedeutet, wie man es ausspricht oder wie es geschrieben wird, kannst du hier nachschlagen.

Im **Dictionary** werden folgende **Abkürzungen und Symbole** verwendet:

jm. = jemandem
jn. = jemanden
sb. = somebody
sth. = something
pl = *plural*
no pl = *no plural*
AE = *American English*
infml = *informal*

- ° Mit diesem Kringel sind Wörter markiert, die nicht zum Lernwortschatz gehören.
- ► Der Pfeil verweist auf Kästchen im **Vocabulary** (S. 163–172), in denen du weitere Informationen zu diesem Wort findest.

Die **Fundstellenangaben** zeigen, wo ein Wort zum ersten Mal vorkommt.
Die Ziffern in Klammern bezeichnen Seitenzahlen:

I, II, III usw. = Band 1, 2, 3 usw.
VI 1 (13) = Band 6, Unit 1, Seite 13
VI 1 (13/165) = Band 6, Unit 1, Seite 165 (im Vocabulary, zu Seite 13)

Tipps zur Arbeit mit einem Wörterbuch findest du im Skills File auf Seite 127.

Tipp

Auf der **Audio-CD im Workbook** findest du sowohl dieses englisch-deutsche Wörterverzeichnis als auch ein deutsch-englisches Wörterverzeichnis mit dem Lernwortschatz der Bände 1–6.

A

a [ə]
1. ein, eine I
2. once/twice a week einmal/zweimal pro Woche III • **a bit** ein bisschen, etwas II • **a few** ein paar, einige II • **a little** ein wenig/ein bisschen IV • **a lot (of)** eine Menge, viel, viele II • **He likes her a lot.** Er mag sie sehr. I
able ['eɪbl]**: be able to do sth.** etwas tun können; fähig sein / in der Lage sein, etwas zu tun III
Aboriginal [ˌæbə'rɪdʒənl] *(bezüglich der Ureinwohner Australiens)* Aborigine- V
Aborigine [ˌæbə'rɪdʒəni] Ureinwohner/in Australiens V
about [ə'baʊt]
1. über I
2. ungefähr II
ask about sth. nach etwas fragen I • **How about ...?** Wie wär's mit ...? III • **This is about Mr Green.** Es geht um Mr Green. I
What about ...? 1. Was ist mit ...? / Und ...? I; **2.** Wie wär's mit ...? I
What are you talking about? Wovon redest du? I • **What was the best thing about ...?** Was war das Beste an ...? II
above [ə'bʌv] oben; über, oberhalb (von) IV
°**abridged** [ə'brɪdʒd] gekürzt *(Buch)*
accent ['æksənt] Akzent II
accident ['æksɪdənt] Unfall II
across [ə'krɒs] (quer) über III
act [ækt]
1. handeln VI 2 (30/167)
2. aufführen, spielen I
°Act out ... Spiele/Spielt ... vor.
action ['ækʃn] Tat, Handlung; Handeln VI 2 (30/167) • **take action** handeln; etwas unternehmen VI 3 (50)
action film ['ækʃn fɪlm] Actionfilm V
activity [æk'tɪvəti] Aktivität, Tätigkeit I
actor ['æktə] Schauspieler/in II
actually ['æktʃuəli] nebenbei bemerkt; übrigens IV
ad [æd] *(infml)* Anzeige, Inserat; *(im Fernsehen)* Werbespot V
°**adapted** [ə'dæptɪd] adaptiert, bearbeitet
add (to) [æd] hinzufügen, ergänzen, addieren (zu) I
addicted [ə'dɪktɪd]**: be addicted (to sth.)** abhängig (von etwas) sein, süchtig (nach etwas) sein V
address [ə'dres] Adresse, Anschrift II
adult ['ædʌlt] Erwachsene(r) III
advantage [əd'vɑːntɪdʒ] Vorteil IV
adventure [əd'ventʃə] Abenteuer IV
advert ['ædvɜːt] Anzeige, Inserat; *(im Fernsehen)* Werbespot V
advertisement [əd'vɜːtɪsmənt] Anzeige, Inserat; *(im Fernsehen)* Werbespot V
advice *(no pl)* [əd'vaɪs] Rat, Ratschläge III
afraid [ə'freɪd]
1. be afraid (of) Angst haben (vor) I
2. I'm afraid leider II
African American [ˌæfrɪkən‿ə'merɪkən] Afro-Amerikaner/in; afroamerikanisch IV
after ['ɑːftə] nach *(zeitlich)* I
after that danach I
after ['ɑːftə] nachdem II
afternoon [ˌɑːftə'nuːn] Nachmittag I • **in the afternoon** nachmittags, am Nachmittag I • **on Friday afternoon** freitagnachmittags, am Freitagnachmittag I
again [ə'gen] wieder; noch einmal I
against [ə'genst] gegen III
age [eɪdʒ] Alter III
ago [ə'gəʊ]**: a minute ago** vor einer Minute I
agree (on) [ə'griː] sich einigen (auf) I • **agree with sb./sth.** jm./etwas zustimmen; mit jm./etwas übereinstimmen II
aid: first aid [ˌfɜːst‿'eɪd] Erste Hilfe V
air [eə] Luft V
airport ['eəpɔːt] Flughafen III
alarm clock [ə'lɑːm klɒk] Wecker V
set the alarm clock den Wecker stellen V
alcohol ['ælkəhɒl] Alkohol VI 3 (48)
alive [ə'laɪv] am Leben, lebendig IV
all [ɔːl] alle; alles I • **all alone** ganz allein VI 2 (34) • **all day** den ganzen Tag (lang) I • **all over the world** auf der ganzen Welt III
all right gut, in Ordnung II • **all the time** die ganze Zeit I • **all the way** den ganzen Weg IV
from all over the UK/the world/

England aus dem gesamten Vereinigten Königreich/aus der ganzen Welt/aus ganz England III • **not (...) at all** überhaupt nicht, ganz und gar nicht V • **This is all wrong.** Das ist ganz falsch. I
°**allowance** [ə'laʊəns] Freibetrag; erlaubte Menge
allowed [ə'laʊd]**: be allowed to do sth.** etwas tun dürfen III
almost ['ɔːlməʊst] fast, beinahe VI 2 (34)
alone [ə'ləʊn] allein I • **all alone** ganz allein VI 2 (34) • **leave sb. alone** jn. in Ruhe lassen V
along the street [ə'lɒŋ] entlang der Straße / die Straße entlang II
alphabet ['ælfəbet] Alphabet I
°**alphabetical** [ˌælfə'betɪkl] alphabetisch
already [ɔːl'redi] schon, bereits II
also ['ɔːlsəʊ] auch II
although [ɔːl'ðəʊ] obwohl VI 1 (12)
always ['ɔːlweɪz] immer I
am [ˌeɪ_'em]**: 7 am** 7 Uhr morgens/vormittags I
amazing [ə'meɪzɪŋ] erstaunlich, unglaublich II
ambition [æm'bɪʃn] Ehrgeiz V
ambulance ['æmbjələns] Krankenwagen III
American football [əˌmerɪkən 'fʊtbɔːl] Football I
amnesty ['æmnəsti] Amnestie, Straferlass, Begnadigung IV
an [ən] ein, eine I
ancestor ['ænsestə] Vorfahre/Vorfahrin V
and [ənd, ænd] und I
angel ['eɪndʒl] Engel II
angry (about sth./with sb.) ['æŋgri] wütend, böse (über etwas/auf jn.) II
animal ['ænɪml] Tier II
announcement [ə'naʊnsmənt] Durchsage, Ansage; Ankündigung, Bekanntgabe III
annoy sb. [ə'nɔɪ] jn. (ver)ärgern, stören; jm. auf die Nerven gehen VI 1 (10)
annoyed [ə'nɔɪd]**: be annoyed** verärgert sein V • **get annoyed (with sb.; at/about sth.)** sich ärgern (über jn.; über etwas) V
annoying [ə'nɔɪɪŋ] ärgerlich, lästig V • **sb. is annoying** jemand geht auf die Nerven V
anorak ['ænəræk] Anorak, Windjacke III
another [ə'nʌðə] ein(e) andere(r, s); noch ein(e) I • **another 45 p** weitere 45 Pence, noch 45 Pence II
answer ['ɑːnsə] antworten; beantworten I
answer (to) ['ɑːnsə] Antwort (auf) I
anti- ['ænti] anti- V • **anti-social** [ˌænti'səʊʃl] asozial; antisozial VI 3 (49)
any ['eni] irgendein, irgendwelche; jede(r, s) IV • **any ...?** (irgend)welche ...? I • **not (...) any** kein, keine I • **not (...) any more** nicht mehr III
anybody ['enibɒdi] (irgend)jemand II; jede(r) IV • **not (...) anybody** niemand II
anyone ['eniwʌn] jede(r) IV
anything ['eniθɪŋ] (irgend)etwas II; alles IV • **anything else** [els] (irgend)etwas anderes IV • **not (...) anything** nichts II
anyway ['eniweɪ]
1. sowieso I
2. trotzdem II
3. aber egal; wie auch immer; wie dem auch sei IV
anywhere ['eniweə] irgendwo(hin) II • **not (...) anywhere** nirgendwo(hin) II
apartment [ə'pɑːtmənt] *(AE)* Wohnung IV
appearance [ə'pɪərəns] Aussehen, (äußere) Erscheinung VI 1 (10)
appetite ['æpɪtaɪt] Appetit III
apple ['æpl] Apfel I
appliance [ə'plaɪəns] Gerät *(meist elektrisch)* VI 2 (28)
application [ˌæplɪ'keɪʃn]
1. Bewerbung V • **letter of application** Bewerbungsschreiben V
2. *(kurz auch:* **app***)* Anwendung, Anwendungsprogramm, -software; App VI 2 (33)
apply for sth. [ə'plaɪ] sich bewerben um/für etwas; etwas beantragen V
appointment [ə'pɔɪntmənt] Termin, Verabredung I
apprenticeship [ə'prentɪʃɪp] Lehre, Ausbildung V
April ['eɪprəl] April I
are [ɑː] bist; sind; seid I • **How are you?** Wie geht es dir/Ihnen/euch? II • **The pencils are 35 p.** Die Bleistifte kosten 35 Pence. I • **You're joking, aren't you?** Du machst Witze, nicht wahr? / Das ist nicht dein Ernst, oder? II
area ['eəriə] Bereich; Gebiet, Gegend III
argue ['ɑːgjuː] sich streiten, sich zanken I
argument ['ɑːgjumənt]
1. Argument IV
2. Streit IV
arm [ɑːm] Arm I
armchair ['ɑːmtʃeə] Sessel I
army ['ɑːmi] Armee, Heer VI 2 (30)
around [ə'raʊnd] um ... (herum); in ... umher, durch III • **around here** hier in/aus der Gegend VI 1 (11) **around six** um sechs herum, gegen sechs III • **around the lake** um den See herum III • **around the town** in der Stadt umher, durch die Stadt III • **run around** herumrennen III • **jump around** herumspringen III • **walk around** herumgehen, umherspazieren III
arrival (arr) [ə'raɪvl] Ankunft III
arrive [ə'raɪv] ankommen, eintreffen II
arrogant ['ærəgənt] arrogant, überheblich VI 1 (6)
art [ɑːt] Kunst I
article ['ɑːtɪkl] (Zeitungs-)Artikel III
artificial [ˌɑːtɪ'fɪʃl] künstlich, Kunst- III
artist ['ɑːtɪst] Künstler/in; Grafiker/in III
artistic [ɑː'tɪstɪk] künstlerisch V
as *(prep)* [əz, æz] als IV • **as a firefighter** als Feuerwehrmann, -frau IV
as *(conj)* [əz, æz] als, während II
as ... as [əz, æz] so ... wie II • **as old/big as** so alt/groß wie II
as usual [əz 'juːʒuəl] wie immer, wie üblich V
ask [ɑːsk] fragen I • **ask about sth.** nach etwas fragen I • **ask questions** Fragen stellen I • **ask sb. for directions** jn. nach dem Weg fragen; jn. um eine Wegbeschreibung bitten IV • **ask sb. out** sich mit jm. verabreden; jn. einladen, zusammen auszugehen V; VI 1 (7/164) • **ask sb. the way** jn. nach dem Weg fragen II • **ask sb. to do sth.** jn. darum bitten etwas zu tun V
► S.164 Relationships
asleep [ə'sliːp]**: be asleep** schlafen I
°fall asleep einschlafen
°**aspect** ['æspekt] Aspekt
Assembly [ə'sembli] Versammlung *(morgendliche Schulversammlung, oft mit Andacht)* III
assessment [ə'sesmənt] Einschätzung, Beurteilung V
assistant: care assistant ['keər_əˌsɪstənt] Pfleger/in *(in einem Altenheim)* V • **vet's assistant** [ˌvets_ə'sɪstənt] Tierarzthelfer/in V

at [ət, æt]**: at 7 Hamilton Street** in der Hamiltonstraße 7 I • **at 8.45** um 8.45 I • **at break** in der Pause *(zwischen Schulstunden)* II • **at first** zuerst, am Anfang IV • **at home** daheim, zu Hause I • **at last** endlich, schließlich I • **at least** zumindest, wenigstens I
at night nachts, in der Nacht I
at school in der Schule I • **at that table** an dem Tisch (dort) / an den Tisch (dort) I • **at the bottom (of)** unten, am unteren Ende (von) II
at the butcher's / at the chemist's beim Metzger/beim Apotheker III
at the end (of) am Ende (von) I
at the same time gleichzeitig VI 1 (12) • **at the Shaws' house** im Haus der Shaws / bei den Shaws zu Hause I • **at the station** am Bahnhof I • **at the top (of)** oben, am oberen Ende, an der Spitze (von) I • **at the weekend** am Wochenende I • **at work** bei der Arbeit / am Arbeitsplatz I • **not (...) at all** überhaupt nicht, ganz und gar nicht V • **one at a time** einzeln VI 3 (48/171) • **two at a time** zwei auf einmal *(zur selben Zeit)* VI 3 (48)
ate [et, eɪt] *siehe* **eat**
athletics [æθ'letɪks] Leichtathletik III
attack [ə'tæk] angreifen III
attack [ə'tæk] Angriff III
attitude (to/towards) ['ætɪtju:d] Haltung (gegenüber) Einstellung (zu) IV
attractive [ə'træktɪv] attraktiv *(Person)*; reizvoll, verlockend *(Idee, Preis)* VI 1 (9)
audience ['ɔ:dɪəns] Publikum; Zuschauer/innen, Zuhörer/innen II
August ['ɔ:gəst] August I
aunt [ɑ:nt] Tante I • **auntie** ['ɑ:nti] Tante II
autumn ['ɔ:təm] Herbst I
avenue ['ævənju:] Allee IV
average ['ævərɪdʒ] Durchschnitt, durchschnittlich, Durchschnitts- IV • **on average** im Durchschnitt
away [ə'weɪ] weg, fort I • **turn away** sich abwenden, sich wegdrehen IV
awesome ['ɔ:səm] *(AE, infml)* klasse, großartig IV
awful ['ɔ:fl] furchtbar, schrecklich II

B

baby ['beɪbi] Baby I • **have a baby** ein Baby/Kind bekommen II
back [bæk] Rücken V
back (to) [bæk] zurück (nach) I
back door [ˌbæk 'dɔ:] Hintertür II
background ['bækgraʊnd] Hintergrund II • **background file** *etwa:* Hintergrundinformation(en) II
backpack ['bækpæk] Rucksack IV
°**backwards** ['bækwədz] nach hinten
bacon ['beɪkən] Schinkenspeck II
bad [bæd] schlecht, schlimm I
be bad at sth. schlecht in etwas sein; etwas schlecht können IV
badly ['bædli]**: do badly (in)** schlecht abschneiden (in) III • **get on badly (with sb.)** sich schlecht verstehen (mit jm.), schlecht auskommen (mit jm.) V
badminton ['bædmɪntən] Badminton, Federball I • **badminton racket** Badmintonschläger III
bag [bæg] Tasche, Beutel, Tüte I
bagel ['beɪgl] Bagel *(ringförmiges Gebäck)* IV
baggy ['bægi] weit (geschnitten) III
bakery ['beɪkəri] Bäckerei III
ball [bɔ:l]
1. Ball *(Sport)* I
2. Ball *(Tanzveranstaltung)* IV
ban (-nn-) [bæn] verbieten; ein (Aufenthalts-)Verbot erteilen V
banana [bə'nɑ:nə] Banane I
band [bænd] Band, (Musik-)Gruppe I
bank [bæŋk] Bank, Sparkasse I
bank robber Bankräuber/in I
bar [bɑ:] Bar II
barbecue ['bɑ:bɪkju:] Grillfest, Grillparty V
baseball ['beɪsbɔ:l] Baseball I
baseball cap Baseballmütze II
based [beɪst]**: be based on** basieren auf VI 1 (12)
basement ['beɪsmənt] Keller V
basic ['beɪsɪk] grundlegend; Grund-, Haupt- V
basket ['bɑ:skɪt] Korb I • **a basket of apples** ein Korb Äpfel I
basketball ['bɑ:skɪtbɔ:l] Basketball I
bat [bæt]**: table tennis bat** Tischtennisschläger III
bath [bɑ:θ] Bad, Badewanne II
have a bath baden, ein Bad nehmen II
bathroom ['bɑ:θru:m] Badezimmer I
be [bi:]**, was/were, been** sein I
be with sb. mit jemandem zusammen sein IV • **want to be sth.** etwas werden wollen *(beruflich)* V
be a no-no *(infml)* tabu sein, nicht in Frage kommen VI 2 (34)
beach [bi:tʃ] Strand II • **on the beach** am Strand II
bean [bi:n] Bohne IV
bear [beə] Bär II
beard [bɪəd] Bart IV
beat [bi:t]**, beat, beaten** schlagen; besiegen III
beaten ['bi:tn] *siehe* **beat**
beautiful ['bju:tɪfl] schön I
beauty ['bju:ti] Schönheit III
became [bɪ'keɪm] *siehe* **become**
because [bɪ'kɒz] weil I
become [bɪ'kʌm]**, became, become** werden II
bed [bed] Bett I • **Bed and Breakfast (B&B)** [ˌbed_ən 'brekfəst] Frühstückspension *(wörtlich:* Bett und Frühstück) I • **go to bed** ins Bett gehen I
bedroom ['bedru:m] Schlafzimmer I
beef [bi:f] Rindfleisch III
been [bi:n] *siehe* **be**
°**beer** [bɪə] Bier
before [bɪ'fɔ:] vor *(zeitlich)* I
before [bɪ'fɔ:] bevor II
°**before** [bɪ'fɔ:]**: the night/week/... before** in der Nacht/Woche/... davor
beg (for) (-gg-) [beg] betteln (um); eindringlich bitten (um) IV
began [bɪ'gæn] *siehe* **begin**
begin (-nn-) [bɪ'gɪn]**, began, begun** beginnen, anfangen (mit) IV
beginning [bɪ'gɪnɪŋ] Beginn, Anfang; Einleitung II
begun [bɪ'gʌn] *siehe* **begin**
behaviour (towards sb.) [bɪ'heɪvjə] Verhalten, Benehmen (gegenüber jm.) V
behind [bɪ'haɪnd] hinter II
believe (in) [bɪ'li:v] glauben (an) IV
bell [bel] Klingel, Glocke III
The bell rang. Es klingelte. III
below [bɪ'ləʊ] unten; unter, unterhalb (von) IV
°**bend** [bend]**, bent, bent** [bent] (ver)biegen
°**bent** [bent] *siehe* **bend**
best [best] am besten II • **the best ...** der/die/das beste ...; die besten ... I • **like sth. best** etwas am meisten mögen III • **Best wishes** *etwa:* Alles Gute / Mit besten Grüßen *(als Briefschluss)* IV
What was the best thing about ...? Was war das Beste an ...? II
bet (-tt-) [bet]**, bet, bet** wetten III

better ['betə] besser I • **like sth. better** etwas lieber mögen II
between [bɪ'twi:n] zwischen II
°**beverage** ['bevərɪdʒ] Getränk
°**beyond the story** [bɪ'jɒnd] über die Geschichte hinaus
big [bɪg] groß I • **big wheel** [ˌbɪg 'wi:l] Riesenrad III
bike [baɪk] Fahrrad I • **bike ride** (Rad-)Fahrt II • **ride a bike** Rad fahren I
bill [bɪl] Rechnung III
bin [bɪn] Mülltonne II
biology [baɪ'ɒlədʒi] Biologie I
bird [bɜ:d] Vogel I
birdcage ['bɜ:dkeɪdʒ] Vogelkäfig III
birth [bɜ:θ] Geburt V • **date of birth** Geburtsdatum V • **place of birth** Geburtsort V
birthday ['bɜ:θdeɪ] Geburtstag I **Happy birthday.** Herzlichen Glückwunsch zum Geburtstag. I • **My birthday is in May.** Ich habe im Mai Geburtstag. I • **My birthday is on 13th June.** Ich habe am 13. Juni Geburtstag. I • **When's your birthday?** Wann hast du Geburtstag? I
biscuit ['bɪskɪt] Keks, Plätzchen I
bit [bɪt]: **a bit** ein bisschen, etwas II
bit [bɪt] *siehe* **bite**
bite [baɪt], **bit, bitten** beißen V
bite [baɪt] Biss V
bitten ['bɪtn] *siehe* **bite**
black [blæk] schwarz I
blame sb. (for) [bleɪm] jm. die Schuld geben (an); jm. Vorwürfe machen (wegen) III
blanket ['blæŋkɪt] Decke *(zum Zudecken)* V
bled [bled] *siehe* **bleed**
bleed [bli:d], **bled, bled** bluten V
bleep [bli:p] piepsen II
bleep [bli:p] Piepton II
block [blɒk] (Häuser-, Wohn-)Block IV
blog [blɒg] Blog *(Internet-Tagebuch)* IV
blond [blɒnd] blond IV
blood [blʌd] Blut V
bloody ['blʌdi] blutig V
blue [blu:] blau I
board [bɔ:d] (Wand-)Tafel I **notice board** Anschlagtafel, schwarzes Brett I
boat [bəʊt] Boot, Schiff I
body ['bɒdi] Körper I
bone [bəʊn] Knochen VI 2 (35)
book [bʊk] Buch I • °**book review** [rɪ'vju:] Buchkritik, -besprechung
book [bʊk] buchen, reservieren V
booked [bʊkt]: **fully booked** ausgebucht V
boot [bu:t] Stiefel I
border ['bɔ:də] Grenze IV
bored [bɔ:d]: **get bored** sich langweilen V
boring ['bɔ:rɪŋ] langweilig I
born [bɔ:n]: **be born** geboren sein/werden II
borough ['bʌrə, *AE:* 'bɜ:rəʊ] (Stadt-)Bezirk IV
borrow sth. (from) ['bɒrəʊ] (sich) etwas (aus)leihen, borgen (von) VI 2 (34/168)
► S.168 (to) lend – (to) borrow
boss [bɒs] Chef/in, Boss III
bossy ['bɒsi] herrisch VI 1 (6)
both [bəʊθ] beide I
bottle ['bɒtl] Flasche I • **a bottle of milk** eine Flasche Milch I
bottom ['bɒtəm] unteres Ende II **at the bottom (of)** unten, am unteren Ende (von) II
bought [bɔ:t] *siehe* **buy**
bowl [bəʊl] Schüssel I • **a bowl of cornflakes** eine Schale Cornflakes I
box [bɒks] Kasten, Kästchen, Kiste I • **sandwich box** Brotdose I
boy [bɔɪ] Junge I
boyfriend ['bɔɪfrend] (fester) Freund IV
°**bracket** ['brækɪt] Klammer
brainstorm ['breɪnstɔ:m] brainstormen *(so viele Ideen wie möglich sammeln)* III
brave [breɪv] mutig IV
bread *(no pl)* [bred] Brot I
break [breɪk], **broke, broken** brechen; zerbrechen; kaputt gehen VI 3 (48) • **break a journey** eine Reise unterbrechen III
break [breɪk] Pause I • **at break** in der Pause *(zwischen Schulstunden)* II • **take a break** eine Pause machen IV
breakfast ['brekfəst] Frühstück I **have breakfast** frühstücken I
bridge [brɪdʒ] Brücke I
bright [braɪt] hell, leuchtend II
brilliant ['brɪliənt] toll, genial, großartig III
bring [brɪŋ], **brought, brought** (mit-, her)bringen I
British ['brɪtɪʃ] britisch; Brite, Britin II
brochure ['brəʊʃə] Prospekt, Broschüre II
broke [brəʊk] *siehe* **break**
broken ['brəʊkən] *siehe* **break**
broken *(adj)* ['brəʊkən] gebrochen; zerbrochen, kaputt II
brother ['brʌðə] Bruder I
brought [brɔ:t] *siehe* **bring**
brown [braʊn] braun I
budgie ['bʌdʒi] Wellensittich I
build [bɪld], **built, built** bauen II
builder ['bɪldə] Bauarbeiter/in V
building ['bɪldɪŋ] Gebäude II °**building company** Bauunternehmen
built [bɪlt] *siehe* **build**
bulletin board ['bʊlətɪn bɔ:d] *(AE)* schwarzes Brett, Anschlagtafel IV
bully ['bʊli] einschüchtern, tyrannisieren II
bully ['bʊli] (Schul-)Tyrann III
bunk (bed) [bʌŋk] Etagenbett, Koje II
burger ['bɜ:gə] Burger IV
burn [bɜ:n] brennen; verbrennen VI 2 (31)
bus [bʌs] Bus I • **bus stop** Bushaltestelle III
bush [bʊʃ] Busch, Strauch V • **the bush** der Busch *(unkultiviertes, „wildes" Land in Australien, Afrika)* V
business ['bɪznəs] Geschäft; Handel IV • **Mind your own business.** Das geht dich nichts an! / Kümmere dich um deine eigenen Angelegenheiten! II • **start a business** eine Firma gründen V
businesswoman/businessman ['bɪznəswʊmən, -mən] Geschäftsfrau/Geschäftsmann V
busy ['bɪzi] belebt, verkehrsreich; hektisch III
but [bət, bʌt]
1. aber I
2. sondern IV
butcher ['bʊtʃə] Fleischer/in, Metzger/in III • **at the butcher's** beim Metzger III
°**butt** [bʌt] *(infml)* Hintern
butter ['bʌtə] Butter III
button ['bʌtn] Knopf III
buy [baɪ], **bought, bought** kaufen I
by [baɪ]
1. von I
2. an; (nahe) bei II
3. bis spätestens, nicht später als III
by car/train/bike/... mit dem Auto/Zug/Rad/... II • **by ten o'clock** bis (spätestens) zehn Uhr III • **by the way** übrigens II • **one by one** einer nach dem anderen VI 2 (34)
Bye. [baɪ] Tschüs! I

C

cab [kæb] Taxi • **get a cab** ein Taxi nehmen IV
cabin ['kæbɪn] Hütte III
cable ['keɪbl] Kabel; Kabel- IV
café ['kæfeɪ] *(kleines)* Restaurant, Imbissstube, Café II
cafeteria [ˌkæfə'tɪəriə] Cafeteria; *(USA)* Schulmensa IV
cage [keɪdʒ] Käfig I
cake [keɪk] Kuchen, Torte I
°**calculate** ['kælkjuleɪt] berechnen, ermitteln
°**calculator** ['kælkjuleɪtə] Taschenrechner
calendar ['kælɪndə] Kalender I
call [kɔ:l] rufen; anrufen; nennen I
call sb. names jn. mit Schimpfwörtern hänseln, jm. Schimpfwörter nachrufen III
call [kɔ:l] Anruf, Telefongespräch I
wake-up call Weckanruf V
called [kɔ:ld]**: be called** genannt werden, heißen IV
caller ['kɔ:lə] Anrufer/Anruferin V
calm [kɑ:m] ruhig, still V
calm down [ˌkɑ:m 'daʊn] sich beruhigen II
came [keɪm] *siehe* **come**
camel ['kæml] Kamel II
camera ['kæmərə] Kamera, Fotoapparat I
camp [kæmp] zelten III
camp [kæmp] Camp, (Ferien-)Lager IV
campaign [kæm'peɪn] Kampagne, (Werbe-)Feldzug VI 3 (47)
camping ['kæmpɪŋ] Camping, Campen V
can [kən, kæn]
1. können I
2. dürfen I
Can I help you? Kann ich Ihnen helfen?/ Was kann ich für Sie tun? *(im Geschäft)* I
canal [kə'næl] Kanal III
candidate ['kændɪdət] Kandidat/in, Bewerber/in V
canoe [kə'nu:] Kanu III
canoe [kə'nu:] Kanu fahren III
canteen [kæn'ti:n] Kantine, Schulmensa II
canyon ['kænjən] Schlucht, Canyon IV
cap [kæp] Mütze, Kappe II
capital ['kæpɪtl] Hauptstadt III
captain ['kæptɪn] Kapitän/in III
°**caption** ['kæpʃn] Bildunterschrift
car [kɑ:] Auto I • **car park** Parkplatz III
caravan ['kærəvæn] Wohnwagen II
carbon ['kɑ:bən] Kohlenstoff; *(oft auch kurz für:)* Kohlendioxid VI 2 (29/166)
carbon dioxide (CO_2) [ˌkɑ:bən daɪ'ɒksaɪd], [ˌsi:_əʊ 'tu:] Kohlendioxid (CO_2) VI 2 (29)
°**carbon footprint** [ˌkɑ:bən 'fʊtprɪnt] „CO_2-Fußabdruck", CO_2-Bilanz
card [kɑ:d] (Spiel-, Post-)Karte I
care about sth. [keə] etwas wichtig nehmen VI 1 (6); VI 3 (46) • **I don't care.** Es ist mir egal. IV • **Who cares?** Wen interessiert das (schon)? VI 3 (46/170)
► S.170 (to) care
care assistant ['keər_əˌsɪstənt] Pfleger/in *(in Altenheim)* V
career [kə'rɪə] Karriere III
careful ['keəfl]
1. vorsichtig II
2. sorgfältig II
3. aufmerksam V
caretaker ['keəteɪkə] Hausmeister/in II
carrot ['kærət] Möhre, Karotte I
carry ['kæri] tragen V
cartoon [kɑ:'tu:n] Cartoon (Zeichentrickfilm; Bilderwitz) II
case [keɪs] Fall II
cash [kæʃ] Bargeld V • **pay cash** bar bezahlen V
castle ['kɑ:sl] Burg, Schloss II
cat [kæt] Katze I
catch [kætʃ]**, caught, caught** fangen; erwischen II
cathedral [kə'θi:drəl] Kathedrale, Dom III
► S.165 Religions
Catholic ['kæθlɪk] Katholik/in; katholisch VI 1 (13/165)
► S.165 Religions
caught [kɔ:t] *siehe* **catch**
cause sth. [kɔ:z] etwas verursachen V
CD [ˌsi:'di:] CD I • **CD player** CD-Spieler I
ceilidh ['keɪli] *Musik- und Tanzveranstaltung, vor allem in Schottland und Irland* III
cellphone ['selfəʊn] *(AE)* Handy, Mobiltelefon IV
Celsius (C) ['selsiəs] Celsius IV
cent (c) [sent] Cent I
centimetre (cm) ['sentɪmi:tə] Zentimeter III
central ['sentrəl] Zentral-, Mittel- III
centre ['sentə] Zentrum, Mitte I
city centre Stadtzentrum, Innenstadt I • **community centre** Gemeindezentrum V • **sports centre** Sportzentrum I
century ['sentʃəri] Jahrhundert II
cereal ['sɪəriəl] Getreideflocken, Frühstücksflocken IV
°**certainly** ['sɜ:tnli] mit Sicherheit
certificate [sə'tɪfɪkət] Zertifikat, Urkunde, Bescheinigung V
chair [tʃeə] Stuhl I
champion ['tʃæmpiən] Meister/in, Champion I
championship ['tʃæmpiənʃɪp] Meisterschaft III
change [tʃeɪndʒ]
1. (sich) ändern, (sich) verändern IV
2. wechseln IV
3. umsteigen III
4. sich umziehen IV
change channels umschalten *(Fernsehprogramm)* IV
change [tʃeɪndʒ]
1. (Ver-)Änderung; Wechsel IV
2. Wechselgeld I; Kleingeld IV
channel ['tʃænl] (Radio-, Fernseh-) Kanal, (Radio-, Fernseh-)Programm IV • **change channels** umschalten *(Fernsehprogramm)* IV
character ['kærəktə]
1. Charakter, Wesen IV
2. Person, Figur *(in Roman, Film)* VI 3 (53)
chart [tʃɑ:t] Diagramm V
chat (-tt-) [tʃæt] plaudern; chatten II • **chat sb. up** *(infml)* jn. anquatschen, anbaggern VI 1 (7/164)
chat room ['tʃæt ru:m] Chatroom III
chat-up line ['tʃæt_ʌp laɪn] *(infml)* Anmachspruch VI 1 (7)
cheap [tʃi:p] billig I
check [tʃek]
1. (über)prüfen, kontrollieren I
2. check in einchecken *(Hotel, Flughafen)* V • **check out** auschecken *(Hotel)* V
checkpoint ['tʃekpɔɪnt] Kontrollpunkt *(hier auch: zur Selbstüberprüfung)* I
cheer [tʃɪə] jubeln, Beifall klatschen II
cheese [tʃi:z] Käse I
chemist ['kemɪst] Drogerie, Apotheke II • **at the chemist's** beim Apotheker III
cheque (for) [tʃek] Scheck (über) V
cherry ['tʃeri] Kirsche II
chicken ['tʃɪkɪn] Huhn; (Brat-)Hähnchen I
child [tʃaɪld]**,** *pl* **children** ['tʃɪldrən] Kind I • **only child** Einzelkind V
°**childhood love** [ˌtʃaɪldhʊd 'lʌv] Sandkastenliebe
chips *(pl)* [tʃɪps]
1. *(BE)* Pommes frites I
2. *(AE)* Chips IV • **potato chips** *(AE)* Kartoffelchips IV

chocolate ['tʃɒklət] Schokolade I
choice [tʃɔɪs] Wahl, Auswahl VI 2 (30)
choir ['kwaɪə] Chor I
choose [tʃu:z], **chose, chosen** (sich) aussuchen, (aus)wählen I
chorus ['kɔ:rəs] Refrain III
chose [tʃəʊz] *siehe* **choose**
chosen ['tʃəʊzn] *siehe* **choose**
Christian ['krɪstʃən] Christ/in; christlich VI 1 (13/165)
► S.165 Religions
Christmas ['krɪsməs] Weihnachten I
church [tʃɜ:tʃ] Kirche I
► S.165 Religions
cigarette [ˌsɪgə'ret] Zigarette VI 3 (48)
cinema ['sɪnəmə] Kino I • **go to the cinema** ins Kino gehen II
°**circle** ['sɜ:kl]: °**double circle** Doppelkreis, „Kugellager" *(als Kommunikationsform)*
circus ['sɜ:kəs] (runder) Platz III
citizen ['sɪtɪzn] (Staats-)Bürger/in, Staatsangehörige(r) IV; VI 3 (48)
citizenship ['sɪtɪzənʃɪp] Staatsbürgerschaft VI 3 (48/171)
city ['sɪti] (Groß-)Stadt I • **city centre** Stadtzentrum, Innenstadt I
clap (-pp-) [klæp] (Beifall) klatschen IV
class [klɑ:s]
1. (Schul-)Klasse I
2. Unterricht; Kurs IV
class teacher Klassenlehrer/in I
classical ['klæsɪkl] klassisch III
classmate ['klɑ:smeɪt] Klassenkamerad/in, Mitschüler/in I
classroom ['klɑ:sru:m] Klassenzimmer I
clean [kli:n] sauber II
clean [kli:n] sauber machen, putzen I • **I clean my teeth.** Ich putze mir die Zähne. I
cleaner ['kli:nə] Putzfrau, -mann II
clear [klɪə] klar, deutlich I
clever ['klevə] schlau, klug I
click on sth. [klɪk] etwas anklicken II
climate ['klaɪmət] Klima V; VI 2 (29)
climate change ['klaɪmət tʃeɪndʒ] (der) Klimawandel VI 2 (29)
climb [klaɪm] klettern; hinaufklettern (auf) I • **Climb a tree.** Klettere auf einen Baum. I
clinic ['klɪnɪk] Klinik II
clock [klɒk] (Wand-, Stand-, Turm-) Uhr I • **alarm clock** [ə'lɑ:m klɒk] Wecker V
clone [kləʊn] Klon III
close (to) [kləʊs] nahe (bei, an) IV
That was close. Das war knapp. II
close [kləʊz] schließen, zumachen I
closed [kləʊzd] geschlossen II
°**closing phrase** ['kləʊzɪŋ freɪz] Grußformel *(am Briefende)*
clothes *(pl)* [kləʊðz, kləʊz] Kleider, Kleidung(sstücke) II
cloud [klaʊd] Wolke II
cloudless ['klaʊdləs] wolkenlos IV
cloudy ['klaʊdi] bewölkt II
clown [klaʊn] Clown/in II
club [klʌb] Klub; Verein I
clumsy ['klʌmzi] ungeschickt, tollpatschig IV
coach [kəʊtʃ] Trainer/in III; Coach V
coast [kəʊst] Küste III • **on the coast** an der Küste III
coffee ['kɒfi] Kaffee IV • **coffee to go** Kaffee zum Mitnehmen IV
cola ['kəʊlə] Cola I
cold [kəʊld] kalt I • **be cold** frieren I
cold [kəʊld]
1. Kälte IV
2. Erkältung II • **have a cold** erkältet sein, eine Erkältung haben II
collect [kə'lekt] sammeln I
collector [kə'lektə] Sammler/in II
°**college** ['kɒlɪdʒ] Hochschule, Fachhochschule.
colour ['kʌlə] färben III
colour ['kʌlə] Farbe I • **What colour is ...?** Welche Farbe hat ...? I
colourful ['kʌləfl] farbenfroh, farbenprächtig, farbig V
colourless ['kʌlələs] farblos IV
°**combine** [kəm'baɪn] kombinieren, verbinden
come [kʌm], **came, come** kommen I • **come home** nach Hause kommen I • **come in** hereinkommen I • **Come on. 1.** Na los, komm. II; **2.** Ach komm! / Na hör mal! II
come true wahr werden; in Erfüllung gehen IV • **the lights came on** das Licht ging an V
comedy ['kɒmədi] Komödie; Comedy IV
comfortable ['kʌmftəbl] bequem, behaglich, angenehm IV • **Make yourself comfortable.** Machen Sie es sich bequem. / Mach es dir bequem. IV
comic ['kɒmɪk] Comic-Heft I
comment (on, about) ['kɒment] Kommentar (zu, über) IV
°**comment on sth.** ['kɒment] einen Kommentar zu etwas abgeben, sich zu etwas äußern
Commonwealth ['kɒmənwelθ]: **the Commonwealth** *Gemeinschaft der Länder des ehemaligen Britischen Weltreichs* III
communicate [kə'mju:nɪkeɪt] kommunizieren V
communication [kəˌmju:nɪ'keɪʃn] Kommunikation V
community [kə'mju:nəti]: **community centre** Gemeindezentrum V
community hall Gemeinschaftshalle, -saal, Gemeindehalle, -saal III
company ['kʌmpəni] Firma, Gesellschaft IV • °**building company** ['bɪldɪŋ ˌkʌmpəni] Bauunternehmen
compare [kəm'peə] vergleichen V
comparison [kəm'pærɪsn] Steigerung; Vergleich II
competition [ˌkɒmpə'tɪʃn] Wettbewerb, Wettkampf III
complain (to sb. about sth.) [kəm'pleɪn] sich beschweren, sich beklagen (bei jm. über etwas) VI 3 (47)
complete [kəm'pli:t] völlig, vollständig V
complete [kəm'pli:t] ergänzen, vervollständigen V
complicated ['kɒmplɪkeɪtɪd] kompliziert V
compliment ['kɒmplɪmənt] Kompliment VI 2 (33)
computer [kəm'pju:tə] Computer I
concert ['kɒnsət] Konzert III
conclusion [kən'klu:ʒn] Schluss(folgerung) IV • **draw conclusions** Schlüsse ziehen, schlussfolgern IV
conditions *(pl)* [kən'dɪʃnz] Bedingungen, Verhältnisse VI 2 (29)
confident ['kɒnfɪdənt] selbstbewusst, (selbst)sicher V
conflict ['kɒnflɪkt] Konflikt VI 3 (55)
Congratulations. [kənˌgrætʃu'leɪʃnz] Herzlichen Glückwunsch! VI 2 (33)
connect (to/with) [kə'nekt] verbinden (mit) V
connection [kə'nekʃn] Verbindung V
console ['kɒnsəʊl] Konsole, Steuerpult VI 2 (28)
contact ['kɒntækt] Kontakt, Verbindung V • **contacts** *(pl) Liste von Bekannten/Kontakten (im Handy, im Mailprogramm)* V
°**context** ['kɒntekst]: **from the context** aus dem Zusammenhang, aus dem Kontext
continent ['kɒntɪnənt] Kontinent V
contrast ['kɒntrɑ:st] Kontrast, Gegensatz V

control (of/over) [kən'trəʊl] Kontrolle (über) VI 1 (12) • **remote control** [rɪˌməʊt kən'trəʊl] Fernbedienung IV
conversation [ˌkɒnvə'seɪʃn] Unterhaltung, Gespräch V • **have a conversation** ein Gespräch, eine Unterhaltung führen V
cook [kʊk] kochen, zubereiten II
cook [kʊk] Koch/Köchin III
cooker ['kʊkə] Herd I
cookie ['kʊki] Keks IV
cool [ku:l]
1. kühl II
2. cool I
copy ['kɒpi] kopieren; abschreiben II
copy ['kɒpi] Kopie II
corner ['kɔ:nə] Ecke I • **on the corner of Green Street and London Road** Green Street, Ecke London Road II
cornflakes ['kɔ:nfleɪks] Cornflakes I
correct [kə'rekt] berichtigen, korrigieren II
°**correct** [kə'rekt] richtig, korrekt
°**corridor** ['kɒrɪdɔ:] Gang, Korridor
cost [kɒst], **cost, cost** kosten IV
costume ['kɒstju:m] (Bühnen-)Kostüm VI 1 (14)
couch [kaʊtʃ] Couch, Sofa V
couch potato *(infml)* Stubenhocker/in *(jd., der immer nur vor dem Fernseher sitzt)* V
could [kəd, kʊd]
1. **he could ...** er konnte ... II
2. **he could ...** er könnte ... IV
count [kaʊnt] zählen II
countable ['kaʊntəbl] zählbar IV
country ['kʌntri] Land *(auch als Gegensatz zur Stadt)* II • **in the country** auf dem Land II
countryside ['kʌntrisaɪd] Land(schaft), Natur IV
couple ['kʌpl] Paar, Pärchen VI 1 (13)
course [kɔ:s] Kurs, Lehrgang III
course: of course [əv 'kɔ:s] natürlich, selbstverständlich I
court [kɔ:t] Gericht(shof) V
cousin ['kʌzn] Cousin, Cousine I
cover ['kʌvə]
1. (CD-)Hülle I
°2. **front inside cover** [ˌfrʌnt‿ˌɪnsaɪd 'kʌvə] Umschlaginnenseite
cow [kaʊ] Kuh II
crazy ['kreɪzi] verrückt V
cream [kri:m] Sahne; Creme IV; Salbe V • **cream cheese** Frischkäse IV
°**creative** [kri'eɪtɪv] kreativ, schöpferisch

credit card ['kredɪt kɑ:d] Kreditkarte V • **pay by credit card** mit Kreditkarte bezahlen V
°**creeps** [kri:ps]: **it gives me the creeps** *(infml)* es ist mir unheimlich; es ist mir nicht geheuer
cricket ['krɪkɪt] Kricket *(Schlagballspiel)* V
crime [kraɪm] Kriminalität; Verbrechen IV • **crime film** Krimi IV **crime series** Krimiserie IV • **crime story** Krimi IV
crisps *(pl)* [krɪsps] Kartoffelchips I
crocodile ['krɒkədaɪl] Krokodil II
cross [krɒs] überqueren II
cross [krɒs]: **be cross (with)** böse, sauer sein (auf) I
cross [krɒs] Kreuz V
crowd [kraʊd] (Menschen-)Menge, Masse; *(infml auch:)* Clique, Gruppe IV
crowded ['kraʊdɪd] überfüllt, voll V
cry [kraɪ] weinen IV
cultural ['kʌltʃərəl] kulturell V
culture ['kʌltʃə] Kultur IV • **culture shock** Kulturschock V
cup [kʌp]
1. Tasse III • **a cup of tea** eine Tasse Tee III
2. Pokal III
cupboard ['kʌbəd] Schrank I
curriculum vitae [kəˌrɪkjələm 'vi:taɪ] **(CV)** Lebenslauf V
curry ['kʌri] Curry(gericht) III
customer ['kʌstəmə] Kunde, Kundin II
cut (-tt-) [kʌt], **cut, cut** schneiden III • °**cut sth. down** etwas zurückschneiden; *(Baum)* fällen • **cut sth. off** etwas abtrennen, abschneiden III • **cut the grass** Rasen mähen IV
CV [si: 'vi:] **(curriculum vitae** [kəˌrɪkjələm 'vi:taɪ]**)** Lebenslauf V
cycle ['saɪkl] (mit dem) Rad fahren II • **cycle path** Radweg II
cyclist ['saɪklɪst] Radfahrer/in VI 2 (31)

D

dad [dæd] Papa, Vati; Vater I
dance [dɑ:ns] tanzen I
dance [dɑ:ns] Tanz I • **dance floor** Dancefloor, Tanzfläche IV
dancer ['dɑ:nsə] Tänzer/in II
dancing ['dɑ:nsɪŋ] Tanzen I **dancing lessons** Tanzstunden, Tanzunterricht I
danger ['deɪndʒə] Gefahr III
dangerous ['deɪndʒərəs] gefährlich II

dark [dɑ:k] dunkel I
dark [dɑ:k] Dunkelheit VI 2 (34)
darling ['dɑ:lɪŋ] Liebling V
date [deɪt] Datum I • **date of birth** Geburtsdatum V • **to date** bis heute V
daughter ['dɔ:tə] Tochter I
day [deɪ] Tag I • **days of the week** Wochentage I • **day trip** Tagesausflug IV • **one day** eines Tages I • **in the old days** früher; in alten Tagen VI 2 (32) • **one-day ticket** Tageskarte III
dead [ded] tot I
dear [dɪə] Schatz, Liebling I • **Oh dear!** Oje! II
dear [dɪə]: **Dear Jay ...** Lieber Jay, ... I **Dear Sir or Madam** Sehr geehrte Damen und Herren *(Anrede in Briefen)* V
death [deθ] Tod IV
debate [dɪ'beɪt] Debatte, Diskussion VI 3 (52)
debate [dɪ'beɪt] debattieren, erörtern, diskutieren VI 3 (52)
December [dɪ'sembə] Dezember I
decide (on sth.) [dɪ'saɪd] (etwas) beschließen; sich entscheiden (für etwas) V
decision [dɪ'sɪʒn] Entscheidung V **make a decision** eine Entscheidung treffen/fällen VI 3 (49)
deep [di:p] tief V
deer, *pl* **deer** [dɪə] Reh, Hirsch II
degree [dɪ'gri:] Grad II
deli ['deli] *Kombination aus Lebensmittelgeschäft und Fastfoodrestaurant* IV
delicious [dɪ'lɪʃəs] köstlich, lecker II
democracy [dɪ'mɒkrəsi] Demokratie VI 3 (49)
demonstration [ˌdemən'streɪʃn] Demonstration VI 3 (47)
dentist ['dentɪst] Zahnarzt, -ärztin IV
department store [dɪ'pɑ:tmənt stɔ:] Kaufhaus II
departure (dep) [dɪ'pɑ:tʃə] Abfahrt, Abflug; Abreise III
describe sth. (to sb.) [dɪ'skraɪb] (jm.) etwas beschreiben II
description [dɪ'skrɪpʃn] Beschreibung II
desert ['dezət] Wüste V
deserve [dɪ'zɜ:v] verdienen *(zu Recht bekommen)* VI 3 (48)
design [dɪ'zaɪn] entwerfen, gestalten II
design [dɪ'zaɪn] Design; Gestaltung; Entwurf V
desk [desk] Schreibtisch I
detail ['di:teɪl] Detail, Einzelheit II

detective [dɪ'tektɪv] Detektiv/in I
develop (into) [dɪ'veləp] entwickeln; sich entwickeln (zu) VI 2 (30)
device [dɪ'vaɪs] Vorrichtung, Gerät VI 3 (49)
dial (*BE:* **-ll-**) ['daɪəl] *(Telefonnummer)* wählen V
dialogue ['daɪəlɒg] Dialog III
diary ['daɪəri] Tagebuch; Terminkalender I
dice, *pl* **dice** [daɪs] Würfel II
dictionary ['dɪkʃənri] Wörterbuch, *(alphabetisches)* Wörterverzeichnis I
did [dɪd] *siehe* **do** • **Did you go ...?** Bist du ... gegangen? / Seid ihr ... gegangen? I • **we didn't sing** ['dɪdnt] wir sangen nicht / wir haben nicht gesungen I
die (of) *(-ing form:* **dying***)* [daɪ] sterben (an) II
difference ['dɪfrəns] Unterschied IV **make a difference** etwas bewirken, etwas bewegen VI 2 (36)
different (from) ['dɪfrənt] verschieden, unterschiedlich; anders (als) I
difficult ['dɪfɪkəlt] schwierig, schwer I
dining room ['daɪnɪŋ ru:m] Esszimmer I
dinner ['dɪnə] Abendessen, Abendbrot I • **have dinner** Abendbrot essen I
directions *(pl)* [də'rekʃnz] Wegbeschreibung IV • **ask sb. for directions** jn. nach dem Weg fragen; jd. um eine Wegbeschreibung bitten IV
director [də'rektə] Regisseur/in VI 1 (14)
dirty ['dɜ:ti] schmutzig II
disabled [dɪs'eɪbld] (körper)behindert III
disadvantage [ˌdɪsəd'vɑ:ntɪdʒ] Nachteil IV
disagree (with sb.) [ˌdɪsə'gri:] nicht übereinstimmen (mit jm.); anderer Meinung sein (als jd.) VI 1 (13)
disappear [ˌdɪsə'pɪə] verschwinden II
disappointed (about/in) [ˌdɪsə'pɔɪntɪd] enttäuscht (von/über) IV
discipline ['dɪsəplɪn] Disziplin V
disc jockey (DJ) ['dɪsk dʒɒki] Diskjockey III
disco ['dɪskəʊ] Disko I
discover [dɪ'skʌvə] entdecken IV
discriminate against sb. [dɪ'skrɪmɪneɪt] jn. diskriminieren, jn. benachteiligen VI 3 (46/169)
discrimination (against) [dɪˌskrɪmɪ'neɪʃn] Diskriminierung (von), Benachteiligung (von) VI 3 (46)
discuss [dɪ'skʌs] diskutieren, besprechen V
discussion [dɪ'skʌʃn] Diskussion II **written discussion** Erörterung VI 2 (37)
disgusting [dɪs'gʌstɪŋ] widerlich, ekelhaft VI 3 (50)
dish [dɪʃ] Gericht *(Speise)* III
dishwasher ['dɪʃwɒʃə] Geschirrspülmaschine I
°**distance** ['dɪstəns] Entfernung, Distanz
divide sth. (into) [dɪ'vaɪd] etwas (auf)teilen (in) V
divorced [dɪ'vɔ:st] geschieden I **get divorced** sich scheiden lassen VI 3 (48)
DJ ['di: dʒeɪ] (Musik/CDs/Platten) auflegen *(in der Disko)* III
DJ ['di: dʒeɪ] Diskjockey III
do [du:], **did, done** tun, machen I **Do you like ...?** Magst du ...? I • **do a gig** einen Auftritt haben, ein Konzert geben III • **do a good job** gute Arbeit leisten II • **do a project** ein Projekt machen, durchführen II **do an exercise** eine Übung machen II • **do badly/well (in)** schlecht/gut abschneiden (in) III • **do sport** Sport treiben I • **do work experience** ein Praktikum machen V **How are you doing?** Wie geht's? V
doctor ['dɒktə] Doktor; Arzt/Ärztin II • **to the doctor's** zum Arzt III
documentary [ˌdɒkju'mentri] Dokumentation, Dokumentarfilm IV
dog [dɒg] Hund I
dollar ($) ['dɒlə] Dollar IV
done [dʌn] *siehe* **do** • **Well done!** [ˌwel 'dʌn] Gut gemacht. VI 2 (33)
don't [dəʊnt]: **Don't listen to Dan.** Hör/Hört nicht auf Dan. I • **I don't know.** Ich weiß es nicht. I • **I don't like ...** Ich mag ... nicht. / Ich mag kein(e) ... I
door [dɔ:] Tür I
doorbell ['dɔ:bel] Türklingel I
dorm [dɔ:m] *(infml)* Schlafsaal V
dormitory ['dɔ:mətri] Schlafsaal V
dossier ['dɒsieɪ] Mappe, Dossier *(des Sprachenportfolios)* I
double ['dʌbl] zweimal, doppelt, Doppel- I • °**double circle** ['sɜ:kl] Doppelkreis, „Kugellager" *(als Gesprächskreis)* • **double room** Doppelzimmer V
down [daʊn] hinunter, herunter, nach unten I • **down there** dort unten II • **fall down** hinfallen II
download [ˌdaʊn'ləʊd] runterladen, downloaden III
downloadable [ˌdaʊn'ləʊdəbl] herunterladbar, zum Herunterladen IV
downstairs [ˌdaʊn'steəz] unten; nach unten I
downtown [ˌdaʊn'taʊn] (im/in das) Stadtzentrum IV
drama ['drɑ:mə]
1. Schauspiel, darstellende Kunst I
2. Drama VI 1 (6)
3. Spielfilm *(im Fernsehen)* IV
drank [dræŋk] *siehe* **drink**
draw [drɔ:], **drew, drawn**
1. zeichnen III
2. draw conclusions Schlüsse ziehen, schlussfolgern IV
drawing ['drɔ:ɪŋ] Zeichnung III
drawn [drɔ:n] *siehe* **draw**
dream [dri:m] Traum I • **dream house** Traumhaus I
dream (of, about) [dri:m] träumen (von) IV
dreamer ['dri:mə] Träumer/in V
dress [dres] Kleid I
dress [dres] sich kleiden V
dress code ['dres kəʊd] Kleiderordnung, Bekleidungsvorschrift III
dressed [drest]: **get dressed** sich anziehen *(sich ankleiden, Kleidung anziehen)* I
drew [dru:] *siehe* **draw**
drink [drɪŋk] Getränk I
drink [drɪŋk], **drank, drunk** trinken I
drive [draɪv] Fahrt III
drive [draɪv], **drove, driven** *(ein Auto / mit dem Auto)* fahren II
driven ['drɪvn] *siehe* **drive**
driver ['draɪvə] Fahrer/in II
°**driving licence** ['draɪvɪŋ laɪsns] Führerschein
drop (-pp-) [drɒp] fallen lassen I
drove [drəʊv] *siehe* **drive**
drug [drʌg] Droge, Rauschgift; Medikament • **be on drugs** Drogen, Rauschgift / Medikamente nehmen IV
drum [drʌm] Trommel III
drums *(pl)* [drʌmz] Schlagzeug III **play the drums** Schlagzeug spielen III
drunk [drʌŋk] *siehe* **drink**
drunk [drʌŋk] betrunken IV
dry [draɪ] trocken V
dump sb. [dʌmp] *(infml)* mit jm. Schluss machen V
during ['djʊ:rɪŋ] während IV
dustbin ['dʌstbɪn] Mülltonne II
DVD [ˌdi: vi:' di:] DVD I

E

each [iːtʃ] jeder, jede, jedes (einzelne) I
each other [iːtʃ_'ʌðə] einander, sich (gegenseitig) III
°**eagle** ['iːgl] Adler
ear [ɪə] Ohr I
earache ['ɪəreɪk] Ohrenschmerzen II
early ['ɜːli] früh I
earn [ɜːn] verdienen IV
earring ['ɪərɪŋ] Ohrring I
earth [ɜːθ] Erde IV
earthquake ['ɜːθkweɪk] Erdbeben IV
east [iːst] Osten; nach Osten; östlich III
Easter ['iːstə] Ostern IV
easy ['iːzi] leicht, einfach I
easy-going [ˌiːzi'gəʊɪŋ] gelassen, locker V
eat [iːt], **ate, eaten** essen I
eaten ['iːtn] *siehe* **eat**
editor ['edɪtə] Redakteur/in III
°letter to the editor Leserbrief
education [ˌedʒʊ'keɪʃn] (Aus-)Bildung V • **outdoor education** Unterricht im Freien V
effect (on) [ɪ'fekt] (Aus-)Wirkung (auf), Effekt VI 2 (29) • **special effect** Spezialeffekt V
egg [eg] Ei II
elect sb. sth. [ɪ'lekt] jn. zu etwas wählen IV
election [ɪ'lekʃn] Wahl *(von Kandidaten bei einer Abstimmung)* IV
electric [ɪ'lektrɪk] elektrisch, Elektro- III
electricity [ɪˌlek'trɪsəti] Strom, Elektrizität V
electronic [ɪˌlek'trɒnɪk] elektronisch III
elementary school [ˌelɪ'mentri skuːl] *(USA) Grundschule für 6- bis 11-Jährige* IV
elephant ['elɪfənt] Elefant I
elevator ['elɪveɪtə] *(AE)* Fahrstuhl, Aufzug II
else [els]**: anything else** (irgend-) etwas anderes IV • **somebody else** jemand anders IV • **What else?** Was (sonst) noch? IV
e-mail, email ['iːmeɪl] E-Mail I
e-mail, email ['iːmeɪl] mailen VI 3 (47)
embarrassed [ɪm'bærəst]**: I'm embarrassed.** Das ist mir peinlich. IV
embarrassing [ɪm'bærəsɪŋ] peinlich IV
empty ['empti] leer I
enclose sth. [ɪn'kləʊz] etwas *(einem Brief)* beilegen V
end [end] Ende, Schluss I • **at the end (of)** am Ende (von) I • **in the end** schließlich, zum Schluss III
°the top end [ˌtɒp_'end] das obere Ende
end [end] (be)enden, zu Ende gehen IV
ending ['endɪŋ] Ende, (Ab-)Schluss *(einer Geschichte, eines Films usw.)* III
endless ['endləs] endlos IV
enemy ['enəmi] Feind/in II
energetic [ˌenə'dʒetɪk] aktiv, tatkräftig V
energy ['enədʒi] Energie V
engine ['endʒɪn] Motor IV
engineer [ˌendʒɪ'nɪə] Ingenieur/in II
English ['ɪŋglɪʃ] Englisch; englisch I
enjoy [ɪn'dʒɔɪ] genießen II • **Enjoy yourself.** Viel Spaß! / Amüsier dich gut! III
enough [ɪ'nʌf] genug I
enter ['entə]
1. betreten; eintreten (in) III
2. eingeben *(Geheimzahl)* V
environment [ɪn'vaɪrənmənt] Umwelt; Umgebung VI 2 (28)
episode ['epɪsəʊd] Folge *(einer Fernsehserie)* VI 1 (7)
equal ['iːkwəl] gleich *(Rechte, Bezahlung usw.)* VI 3 (48)
equipment *(no pl)* [ɪ'kwɪpmənt] Ausrüstung, Geräte V
eraser [ɪ'reɪsər] *(AE)* Radiergummi IV
escape (from sb./sth.) [ɪ'skeɪp] fliehen (vor jm./aus etwas); entkommen III
especially [ɪ'speʃəli] besonders, vor allem V
essay (about, on) ['eseɪ] Aufsatz (über) I
°**ethnic** ['eθnɪk] ethnisch, Volks-
euro (€) ['jʊərəʊ] Euro I
even ['iːvn] sogar II • **not even** (noch) nicht einmal VI 2 (35)
evening ['iːvnɪŋ] Abend I • **in the evening** abends, am Abend I
on Friday evening freitagabends, am Freitagabend I
event [ɪ'vent] Ereignis; Veranstaltung IV
ever? ['evə] je? / jemals? / schon mal? II
every ['evri] jeder, jede, jedes I
everybody ['evribɒdi] jeder, alle II
everyday *(adj)* ['evrideɪ] Alltags-; alltägliche(r, s) III
everyone ['evrɪwʌn] jeder, alle IV
everything ['evriθɪŋ] alles I
exact [ɪg'zækt] genau, exakt V
exactly [ɪg'zæktli] genau III
example [ɪg'zɑːmpl] Beispiel IV
for example zum Beispiel IV
excellent ['eksələnt] ausgezeichnet, hervorragend IV
exchange: exchange rate [ɪks'tʃeɪndʒ reɪt] Wechselkurs V
exchange student [ɪks'tʃeɪndʒ ˌstjuːdnt] Austauschschüler/in III
excited [ɪk'saɪtɪd] begeistert, aufgeregt III
exciting [ɪk'saɪtɪŋ] aufregend, spannend I
Excuse me, ... [ɪk'skjuːz miː] Entschuldigung, ... / Entschuldigen Sie, ... I
exercise ['eksəsaɪz]
1. Übung, Aufgabe I
2. *(no pl)* (körperliche) Bewegung, Training IV
exercise book ['eksəsaɪz bʊk] Schulheft, Übungsheft I
expect [ɪk'spekt] erwarten III
expensive [ɪk'spensɪv] teuer I
experience [ɪk'spɪəriəns] Erfahrung, Erlebnis V • **work experience** Praktikum; Arbeits-, Praxiserfahrungen V • **do work experience** ein Praktikum machen V
experiment [ɪk'sperɪmənt] Experiment VI 2 (31)
explain sth. to sb. [ɪk'spleɪn] jm. etwas erklären, erläutern II
explanation [ˌeksplə'neɪʃn] Erklärung II
explore [ɪk'splɔː] erkunden, erforschen I
explorer [ɪk'splɔːrə] Entdecker/in, Forscher/in II
explosion [ɪk'spləʊʒn] Explosion IV
extra ['ekstrə] zusätzlich I
extracurricular activities *(kurz:* **extracurriculars***)* [ˌekstrəkə'rɪkjələz] *schulische Angebote außerhalb des regulären Unterrichts, oft als Arbeitsgemeinschaften* IV
eye [aɪ] Auge I

F

face [feɪs] Gesicht I
facilities *(pl)* [fə'sɪlətiz] Einrichtungen, Anlagen VI 3 (46)
fact [fækt] Tatsache, Fakt III • **in fact** tatsächlich; in Wirklichkeit; um genau zu sein VI 3 (49)
factory ['fæktri] Fabrik II
failure *(n)* ['feɪljə] ungenügend *(USA, Schulnote)* IV

fair [feə] fair, gerecht II
faithfully ['feɪθfəli]**: Yours faithfully** mit freundlichen Grüßen *(Briefschluss bei namentlich unbekanntem Empfänger)* V
fall [fɔ:l]**, fell, fallen** fallen, stürzen II • **°fall asleep** einschlafen • **fall down** hinfallen II • **fall in love (with sb.)** sich verlieben (in jn.) IV **fall off** herunterfallen (von) II
fallen ['fɔ:lən] *siehe* **fall**
false [fɔ:ls] falsch IV
family ['fæməli] Familie I • **family name** Nachname, Familienname V • **family tree** (Familien-)Stammbaum I
famous (for) ['feɪməs] berühmt (für, wegen) II
fan [fæn] Fan I
fancy sb. ['fænsi] *(infml)* auf jn. stehen VI 1 (6)
fantastic [fæn'tæstɪk] fantastisch, toll I
fantasy ['fæntəsi] Fantasy V
far [fɑ:] weit (entfernt) II
farm [fɑ:m] Bauernhof, Farm II
farmer ['fɑ:mə] Landwirt/in, Bauer/Bäuerin IV
farmhouse ['fɑ:mhaʊs] Farmhaus, Bauernhaus IV
farming ['fɑ:mɪŋ] Landwirtschaft IV
fashion ['fæʃn] Mode II • **fashion show** ['fæʃn ʃəʊ] Modenschau V
fast [fɑ:st] schnell II • **fast food** [ˌfɑ:st 'fu:d] Fastfood III
fat [fæt] dick; fett IV
fat [fæt] Fett VI 2 (30)
father ['fɑ:ðə] Vater I
fault [fɔ:lt]**: It's not my fault.** Es ist nicht meine Schuld. III
favourite ['feɪvərɪt] Lieblings- I **my favourite colour** meine Lieblingsfarbe I
February ['februəri] Februar I
fed [fed] *siehe* **feed** • **be fed up (with sth.)** [ˌfed‿'ʌp] die Nase voll haben (von etwas) II
feed [fi:d]**, fed, fed** füttern I
feel [fi:l]**, felt, felt** sich fühlen; fühlen; sich anfühlen II • **I feel sick.** Mir ist schlecht. IV
feet [fi:t] *Plural von „foot"* I
fell [fel] *siehe* **fall**
felt [felt] *siehe* **feel**
felt tip ['felt tɪp] Filzstift I
female ['fi:meɪl] weiblich III
fence [fens] Zaun V
ferry ['feri] Fähre III
festival ['festɪvl] Fest, Festival, Festspiele III
few [fju:]**: a few** ein paar, einige II
fiction: science fiction [ˌsaɪəns 'fɪkʃn] Sciencefiction V
fiddle ['fɪdl] *(infml)* Fiedel, Geige III **play the fiddle** Geige, Fiedel spielen III
field [fi:ld] Feld, Acker, Weide II **in the field** auf dem Feld II
fight [faɪt]**, fought, fought** kämpfen III • **fight for** kämpfen (für, um) III
fight [faɪt] Kampf; Schlägerei IV
figure ['fɪgə] Zahl, Ziffer V
figure sth. out ['fɪgə] etwas ausrechnen; etwas herausfinden, herauskriegen VI 3 (52)
file [faɪl]**: background file** *etwa:* Hintergrundinformation(en) II **grammar file** *Grammatikanhang* I • **skills file** *Anhang mit Lern- und Arbeitstechniken* I • **sound file** Tondatei, Soundfile III
fill [fɪl] füllen; sich füllen VI 2 (34) **fill in 1.** ausfüllen; **°2.** einsetzen
film [fɪlm] Film I • **action film** Actionfilm V • **°film review** ['fɪlm rɪˌvju:] Filmkritik, Filmbesprechung • **film star** Filmstar I
film [fɪlm] filmen V
final ['faɪnl] Finale, Endspiel III
final ['faɪnl] letzte(r, s); End- III **final score** Endstand *(beim Sport)* III
finally ['faɪnəli] zuletzt, als letztes V; schließlich, endlich VI 2 (34)
find [faɪnd]**, found, found** finden I **find out (about)** herausfinden (über) I
finder ['faɪndə] Finder I
fine [faɪn]
1. gut, schön; in Ordnung II
2. *(gesundheitlich)* gut II
I'm/He's fine. Es geht mir/ihm gut. II
finger ['fɪŋgə] Finger I
finish ['fɪnɪʃ] beenden, zu Ende machen; enden I
fire ['faɪə] Feuer, Brand II • **fire safety** Verhalten im Brandfall IV **fire station** Feuerwache IV • **put out a fire** ein Feuer löschen IV
firefighter ['faɪəfaɪtə] Feuerwehrfrau, -mann IV
fireman ['faɪəmən] Feuerwehrmann II
firewoman ['faɪəˌwʊmən] Feuerwehrfrau II
first [fɜ:st]
1. erste(r, s) I
2. zuerst, als Erstes I
be first der/die Erste sein I • **first aid** Erste Hilfe V • **first-aid kit** Erste-Hilfe-Kasten, Verbandskasten V • **first name** Vorname V • **the first half** die erste Halbzeit III
fish [fɪʃ] fischen, angeln III
fish, *pl* **fish** [fɪʃ] Fisch I
°fishbowl ['fɪʃbəʊl] Fischglas
fit (-tt-) [fɪt] passen I
fit [fɪt]**: be fit** fit sein III
fitness ['fɪtnəs] Fitness IV • **fitness centre** Fitnesscenter IV
flag [flæg] Flagge, Fahne V
flash [flæʃ] Lichtblitz III
flat [flæt] Wohnung I
flat screen ['flæt skri:n] Flachbildschirm IV
flew [flu:] *siehe* **fly**
flight [flaɪt] Flug II • **a 14-hour flight** ein 14-stündiger Flug, ein 14-Stunden-Flug III
flirt [flɜ:t] flirten VI 1 (9)
floor [flɔ:]
1. Fußboden I
2. Stockwerk IV
°flow chart ['fləʊ tʃɑ:t] Flussdiagramm
flown [fləʊn] *siehe* **fly**
flu [flu:] Grippe V
flute [flu:t] Querflöte III
fly [flaɪ]**, flew, flown** fliegen II
°fly [flaɪ] Fliege
fog [fɒg] Nebel II
foggy ['fɒgi] neblig II
folk music ['fəʊk ˌmju:zɪk] Folk *(englische, schottische, irische oder nordamerikanische Volksmusik des 20. Jahrhunderts)* III
follow ['fɒləʊ] folgen; verfolgen I; befolgen V • **°the following ...** die folgenden ...
food [fu:d]
1. Essen; Lebensmittel I
2. Futter I
foot [fʊt]**,** *pl* **feet** [fi:t]
1. Fuß I
2. Fuß *(Längenmaß: 30,48 cm)* IV
football ['fʊtbɔ:l] Fußball I **football boots** Fußballschuhe I
footprint ['fʊtprɪnt] Fußabdruck VI 2 (29)
for [fə, fɔ:] für I • **for breakfast/lunch/dinner** zum Frühstück/Mittagessen/Abendbrot I • **for example** zum Beispiel IV • **for lots of reasons** aus vielen Gründen I • **for miles** meilenweit II **for the first time** zum ersten Mal VI 2 (30) • **for three days** drei Tage (lang) I • **for 20 minutes** seit 20 Minuten; 20 Minuten lang IV **just for fun** nur zum Spaß I **What for?** Wofür? II • **What's for homework?** Was haben wir als Hausaufgabe auf? I

foreground ['fɔ:graʊnd] Vordergrund II
foreign ['fɒrən] ausländisch, fremd VI 2 (30)
foreigner ['fɒrənə] Ausländer/in VI 3 (52)
forest ['fɒrɪst] Wald II
forever [fər'evə] *(BE auch:* **for ever***)* für immer VI 2 (30)
forgave [fə'geɪv] *siehe* **forgive**
forget (-tt-) [fə'get], **forgot, forgotten** vergessen I
forgive [fə'gɪv], **forgave, forgiven** vergeben, verzeihen IV
forgiven [fə'gɪvn] *siehe* **forgive**
forgot [fə'gɒt] *siehe* **forget**
forgotten [fə'gɒtn] *siehe* **forget**
fork [fɔ:k] Gabel III
forklift ['fɔ:klɪft] Gabelstapler V
form [fɔ:m]
1. (Schul-)Klasse I • **form teacher** Klassenlehrer/in I
2. Formular V
°3. Form
°form [fɔ:m] bilden
°formal letter [ˌfɔ:ml 'letə] formeller Brief, förmlicher Brief
forward ['fɔ:wəd]
1. **look forward to sth.** sich auf etwas freuen V
°2. vorwärts
fought [fɔ:t] *siehe* **fight**
found [faʊnd] *siehe* **find**
found [faʊnd] gründen IV
fox [fɒks] Fuchs II
free [fri:]
1. frei I • **free time** Freizeit, freie Zeit I
2. kostenlos I
freezing ['fri:zɪŋ] eisig; eiskalt VI 2 (35)
French [frentʃ] Französisch I
French fries *(AE)* Pommes Frites IV
fresh [freʃ] frisch VI 2 (32)
Friday ['fraɪdeɪ, 'fraɪdi] Freitag I
fridge [frɪdʒ] Kühlschrank I
friend [frend] Freund/in I • **make friends** Freundschaften schließen, sich anfreunden V
friendly ['frendli] freundlich III
fries [fraɪz]: **French fries** *(AE)* Pommes Frites IV
frog [frɒg] Frosch II
from [frəm, frɒm]
1. aus I
2. von I
from all over the UK/the world/ England aus dem gesamten Vereinigten Königreich / aus der ganzen Welt / aus ganz England III
from Monday to Friday von Montag bis Freitag III • **I'm from ...** Ich komme aus ... / Ich bin aus ... I
Where are you from? Wo kommst du her? I
front [frʌnt]: **in front of** vor *(räumlich)* I • **front door** [ˌfrʌnt 'dɔ:] Wohnungstür, Haustür I • **°front page** [ˌfrʌnt 'peɪdʒ] Titelseite
°front inside cover [ˌfrʌnt‿ˌɪnsaɪd 'kʌvə] vordere Umschlaginnenseite
fruit [fru:t] Obst, Früchte; Frucht I
fruit salad ['fru:t ˌsæləd] Obstsalat I
full [fʊl] voll I • **°full sentence** ganzer Satz
full-time job [ˌfʊl taɪm 'dʒɒb] Ganztagsbeschäftigung VI 3 (49/171)
fully [fʊli]: **fully booked** ausgebucht V
fun [fʌn] Spaß I • **have fun** Spaß haben, sich amüsieren I • **Have fun!** Viel Spaß! I • **just for fun** nur zum Spaß I • **Riding is fun.** Reiten macht Spaß. I
funeral ['fju:nərəl] Trauerfeier, Beerdigung V
funny ['fʌni] witzig, komisch I
future ['fju:tʃə] Zukunft; Zukunfts-, zukünftige(r, s) V

G

°gallery walk ['gæləri wɔ:k] Galerierundgang
game [geɪm] Spiel I • **°game machine** Spielautomat
°gap [gæp] Lücke
garage ['gærɑ:ʒ]
1. Garage II
2. Autowerkstatt V
garbage ['gɑ:rbɪdʒ] *(AE)* Müll, Abfall IV
garden ['gɑ:dn] Garten I
gardener ['gɑ:dnə] Gärtner/in V
gas [gæs] Gas VI 2 (29)
°gasifier ['gæsɪfaɪə] Vergaser
gate [geɪt]
1. Flugsteig III
2. Tor V
gave [geɪv] *siehe* **give**
general ['dʒenrəl] allgemeine(r, s) III • **in general** im allgemeinen IV
generation [ˌdʒenə'reɪʃn] Generation V
geography [dʒi'ɒgrəfi] Geografie, Erdkunde I
German ['dʒɜ:mən] Deutsch; deutsch; Deutsche(r) I
Germany ['dʒɜ:məni] Deutschland I
get (-tt-) [get], **got, got**
1. bekommen, kriegen II
2. holen, besorgen II
3. gelangen, (hin)kommen I
4. **get angry/hot/...** wütend/ heiß/... werden II
get a cab ein Taxi nehmen IV
get bored sich langweilen V
get divorced sich scheiden lassen VI 3 (48) • **get dressed** sich anziehen I • **get involved (in)** sich engagieren (für, bei); sich beteiligen (an) VI 3 (47) • **get married (to sb.)** (jn.) heiraten IV • **get off (the train/bus)** (aus dem Zug/Bus) aussteigen I • **get on (the train/bus)** (in den Zug/Bus) einsteigen I
get on well/badly (with sb.) sich gut/schlecht verstehen (mit jm.), gut/schlecht auskommen (mit jm.) V • **get ready (for)** sich fertig machen (für), sich vorbereiten (auf) I
get things ready Dinge fertig machen, vorbereiten I • **get to know sb.** jn. kennenlernen IV • **get up** aufstehen I
getting by in English [ˌgetɪŋ 'baɪ] *etwa:* auf Englisch zurechtkommen I
ghost [gəʊst] Geist, Gespenst II
gig [gɪg] *(infml)* Gig, Auftritt III
do a gig einen Auftritt haben, ein Konzert geben III
giraffe [dʒə'rɑ:f] Giraffe II
girl [gɜ:l] Mädchen I
girlfriend ['gɜ:lfrend] (feste) Freundin IV
give [gɪv], **gave, given** geben I
give a talk (on sth.) einen Vortrag/ eine Rede halten (über etwas) V
give sth. up auf etwas verzichten V • **give up** aufgeben, resignieren IV • **°it gives me the creeps** *(infml)* es ist mir unheimlich; es ist mir nicht geheuer
given ['gɪvn] *siehe* **give**
glad [glæd] froh, dankbar III
glass [glɑ:s] Glas I • **a glass of water** ein Glas Wasser I
glasses *(pl)* ['glɑ:sɪz] (eine) Brille I
global ['gləʊbl] global, weltweit VI 2 (29/166) • **global warming** Erwärmung der Erdatmosphäre, globaler Temperaturanstieg VI 2 (29)
glue [glu:] (auf-, ein)kleben II
glue [glu:] Klebstoff I • **glue stick** ['glu: stɪk] Klebestift I
go [gəʊ], **went, gone** gehen I; fahren II • **go by car/train/bike/...** mit dem Auto/Zug/Rad/... fahren II • **go for a walk** spazieren gehen, einen Spaziergang machen II • **go home** nach Hause gehen I • **go on** weitermachen I • **°How does**

the story go on? Wie geht die Geschichte weiter? • **go on a trip** einen Ausflug machen II • **go on holiday** in Urlaub fahren II • **go out** ausgehen, weggehen, sich verabreden VI 1 (7/164); miteinander gehen, zusammen sein VI 1 (7/164)
go red rot werden, erröten V
go riding reiten gehen I • **go shopping** einkaufen gehen I • **go surfing** wellenreiten gehen, surfen gehen II • **go swimming** schwimmen gehen I • **go through sth.** etwas durchgehen *(Text, Formular)* VI 2 (34) • **go to bed** ins Bett gehen I • **go to the cinema** ins Kino gehen II • **go together** zusammenpassen, -gehören II • **go well** gut (ver)laufen, gutgehen III • **go with** gehören zu, passen zu III • **coffee to go** Kaffee zum Mitnehmen IV • **Let's go.** Auf geht's! (*wörtlich:* Lass uns gehen.) I
► S.164 Relationships
goal [gəʊl] Tor *(im Sport)* III
goalkeeper ['gəʊlki:pə] Torwart, Torfrau III
God [gɒd] Gott IV
go-kart ['gəʊkɑ:t] Gokart III
gold [gəʊld] Gold IV
golden ['gəʊldən] goldene(r, s) IV
gone [gɒn] *siehe* **go**
good [gʊd]
1. gut I
2. brav II
Good afternoon. Guten Tag. *(nachmittags)* I • **Good luck (with ...)!** Viel Glück (bei/mit ...)! I • **Good morning.** Guten Morgen. I
Good to have you back. Schön, dass du wieder da bist. IV • **be good at sth.** gut in etwas sein; etwas gut können IV
Goodbye. [,gʊd'baɪ] Auf Wiedersehen. I • **say goodbye** sich verabschieden I
good-looking [,gʊd'lʊkɪŋ] gut aussehend VI 1 (6)
got [gɒt] *siehe* **get**
got [gɒt]: **I've got ...** Ich habe ... I
I haven't got a chair. Ich habe keinen Stuhl. I
government ['gʌvənmənt] Regierung V
°**GPS** [,dʒi: pi:‿'es] **(Global Positioning System** [pə'zɪʃnɪŋ]**)** Globales Positionsbestimmungssystem; Satellitennavigationssystem
grab sth. (-bb-) [græb] sich etwas schnappen IV
grade [greɪd]
1. Klasse, Jahrgangsstufe IV
2. (Schul-)Note, Zensur IV
°**graffiti** [grə'fi:ti] Graffiti
grammar ['græmə] Grammatik I
grammar file *Grammatikanhang* I
°**gran** [græn] *(infml)* Oma
grand [grænd] eindrucksvoll, beeindruckend IV
grandchild ['græntʃaɪld], *pl* **grandchildren** Enkel/in I
grandfather ['grænfɑ:ðə] Großvater I
grandma ['grænmɑ:] Oma I
grandmother ['grænmʌðə] Großmutter I
grandpa ['grænpɑ:] Opa I
grandparents ['grænpeərənts] Großeltern I
granny ['græni] Oma II
grape [greɪp] Weintraube IV
grass [grɑ:s] Gras, Rasen IV • **cut the grass** Rasen mähen IV
great [greɪt] großartig, toll I
green [gri:n] grün I • **green energy** grüne Energie; Ökoenergie VI 2 (29)
greenhouse ['gri:nhaʊs] Gewächshaus, Treibhaus VI 2 (29)
grew [gru:] *siehe* **grow**
grey [greɪ] grau II
ground [graʊnd] (Erd-)Boden III
grounded ['graʊndɪd]: **be grounded** Ausgehverbot/Hausarrest haben III
group [gru:p] Gruppe I • **group word** Oberbegriff II
grow [grəʊ], **grew, grown**
1. *(Getreide usw.)* anbauen, anpflanzen II
2. grow up erwachsen werden; aufwachsen III
grown [grəʊn] *siehe* **grow**
grumble ['grʌmbl] murren, nörgeln I
guess [ges] raten, erraten, schätzen III
guest [gest] Gast I
guide [gaɪd] (Fremden-)Führer/in, Reiseleiter/in IV
guidebook ['gaɪdbʊk] Reiseführer IV
guilty ['gɪlti] schuldig IV
guinea pig ['gɪni pɪg] Meerschweinchen I
guitar [gɪ'tɑ:] Gitarre I
gun [gʌn] Gewehr, Schusswaffe IV
guy [gaɪ] *(infml)* Typ, Kerl IV
guys *(pl)* [gaɪz] *(AE, infml)* Leute III
gym [dʒɪm] Sport-, Turnhalle; Fitnessstudio IV

H

had [hæd] *siehe* **have** *und* **have got**
hair *(no pl)* [heə] Haar, Haare I
hairdresser ['heədresə] Friseur/Friseurin IV
hairdryer ['heədraɪə] Föhn, Haartrockner VI 2 (28)
hairless ['heələs] haarlos, kahl, unbehaart IV
half [hɑ:f], *pl* **halves** [hɑ:vz]
1. Hälfte III
2. Halbzeit III
half [hɑ:f]: **half an hour** eine halbe Stunde III • **half past 11** halb zwölf (11.30/23.30) I • **three and a half days** dreieinhalb Tage IV
half-time [,hɑ:f 'taɪm] Halbzeit(pause) III
hall [hɔ:l] Flur, Diele I • **study hall** *(AE) Zeit zum selbstständigen Arbeiten/Lernen in der Schule* IV
halves [hɑ:vz] *Plural von „half"*
hamburger ['hæmbɜ:gə] Hamburger I
hamster ['hæmstə] Hamster I
hand [hænd] Hand I
handball ['hændbɔ:l] Handball III
hang [hæŋ], **hung, hung:**
1. hang out (with friends) *(infml)* rumhängen, abhängen (mit Freunden/Freundinnen) III
2. hang up *(den Telefonhörer)* auflegen V
happen (to) ['hæpən] geschehen, passieren (mit) I
happiness ['hæpinəs] Glück IV
happy ['hæpi] glücklich, froh I
Happy birthday. Herzlichen Glückwunsch zum Geburtstag. I
happy ending Happyend II
harbour ['hɑ:bə] Hafen II
hard [hɑ:d] hart; schwer, schwierig II • **work hard** hart arbeiten II
hard-working [,hɑ:d 'wɜ:kɪn] fleißig, tüchtig V
hat [hæt] Hut II
hate [heɪt] hassen, gar nicht mögen I
have [həv, hæv], **had, had** haben, besitzen II • **have a baby** ein Baby/Kind bekommen II • **have a bath** baden, ein Bad nehmen II
have a cold erkältet sein, eine Erkältung haben II • **have a conversation** ein Gespräch, eine Unterhaltung führen V • **Have a good holiday.** Schöne Ferien! V • **Have a good time.** Viel Spaß! V • **Have a good trip/journey.** Gute Reise! V
Have a good weekend. Schönes Wochenende! V • **have a look**

ansehen, einen Blick werfen auf IV **have a picnic** ein Picknick machen I • **Have a pleasant stay.** Einen angenehmen Aufenthalt. V **have a sauna** in die Sauna gehen II • **have a shower** (sich) duschen I • **have a sore throat** Halsschmerzen haben II • **have a temperature** Fieber haben II • **have breakfast/dinner** frühstücken/Abendbrot essen I • **have ... for breakfast** ... zum Frühstück essen/trinken I • **have fun** Spaß haben, sich amüsieren I • **have sleepovers** Schlafpartys veranstalten III • **have to do** tun müssen I **Have your say!** *etwa:* Übe dein Mitspracherecht aus! / Rede mit! VI 3 (46) • **Can I have a word with you?** Kann ich mal kurz mit dir reden? VI 3 (55) • **Good to have you back.** Schön, dass du wieder da bist. IV • **I'll have** *(bei einer Bestellung)* Ich nehme ... IV

have got: I've got ... [aɪv 'gɒt] Ich habe ... I • **I haven't got a chair.** Ich habe keinen Stuhl. I

he [hiː] er I

head [hed] Kopf I • **head teacher** Schulleiter/in III

headache ['hedeɪk] Kopfschmerzen II

°**heading** ['hedɪŋ] Überschrift, Titel

headline ['hedlaɪn] Schlagzeile IV

headphones *(pl)* ['hedfəʊnz] Kopfhörer V

health [helθ] Gesundheit; Gesundheitslehre IV

healthy ['helθi] gesund II

hear [hɪə], **heard, heard** hören I

heard [hɜːd] *siehe* **hear**

heart [hɑːt] Herz II

heat [hiːt] Hitze, Wärme VI 2 (28/166)

heat [hiːt] heizen, erhitzen VI 2 (28/166)

heating ['hiːtɪŋ] Heizung VI 2 (28)

heaven ['hevn] Himmel IV

heavy ['hevi] schwer *(Gewicht)* V

hedgehog ['hedʒhɒg] Igel II

held [held] *siehe* **hold**

helicopter ['helɪkɒptə] Hubschrauber, Helikopter II

hell [hel] Hölle IV

Hello. [hə'ləʊ] Hallo. / Guten Tag. I

helmet ['helmɪt] Helm III

help [help] helfen I • **Help yourself!** Bedien dich! / Greif zu! III **Can I help you?** Kann ich Ihnen helfen? / Was kann ich für Sie tun? *(im Geschäft)* I

help [help] Hilfe I

helpful ['helpfl] hilfsbereit; hilfreich V

helpless ['helpləs] hilflos V

her [hə, hɜː]
1. ihr, ihre I
2. sie; ihr I

here [hɪə]
1. hier I
2. hierher I
Here you are. Bitte sehr. / Hier bitte. I

hero ['hɪərəʊ], *pl* **heroes** ['hɪərəʊz] Held/in; Idol, Vorbild V

hers [hɜːz] ihrer, ihre, ihrs II

herself [hə'self, hɜː'self] sich (selbst) III

hesitate ['hezɪteɪt] zögern V

Hey. [heɪ] Hallo! III

Hi! [haɪ] Hallo! I • **Say hi to Dilip for me.** Grüß Dilip von mir. I

hid [hɪd] *siehe* **hide**

hidden ['hɪdn] *siehe* **hide**

hide [haɪd], **hid, hidden** sich verstecken; *(etwas)* verstecken I

high [haɪ] hoch III • **high school** *(USA) Schule für 14-18-Jährige* IV

°**highlighted** ['haɪlaɪtɪd] hervorgehoben

hike [haɪk] wandern IV

hike [haɪk] Wanderung IV • **go on a hike** wandern gehen IV

hill [hɪl] Hügel II

hilly ['hɪli] hügelig III

him [hɪm] ihn; ihm I

himself [hɪm'self] sich (selbst) III

Hindu ['hɪnduː] Hindu; hinduistisch, Hindu- VI 1 (13/165)
► S.165 Religions

hip hop ['hɪp hɒp] Hip Hop III

hippo ['hɪpəʊ] Flusspferd II

his [hɪz]
1. sein, seine I
2. seiner, seine, seins II

history ['hɪstri] Geschichte I

hit (-tt-) [hɪt], **hit, hit** schlagen II

hobby ['hɒbi] Hobby I

hockey ['hɒki] Hockey I • **hockey shoes** Hockeyschuhe I

hold [həʊld], **held, held** halten II **Hold the line, please.** Bitte bleiben Sie am Apparat. V • **hold sb. up** jn. aufhalten VI 2 (34)

hole [həʊl] Loch V

holiday ['hɒlədeɪ]
1. Ferien I
2. Feiertag IV
holiday flat Ferienwohnung II
go on holiday in Urlaub fahren II
a two-week holiday ein zweiwöchiger Urlaub III • **Have a good holiday.** Schöne Ferien! V

home [həʊm] Heim, Zuhause I **at home** daheim, zu Hause I **come home** nach Hause kommen I • **get home** nach Hause kommen I • **go home** nach Hause gehen I • **leave home** von zu Hause ausziehen VI 3 (48) • **old people's home** Alten-, Seniorenheim V

homeless ['həʊmləs] obdachlos IV

homesick ['həʊmsɪk]**: be homesick** Heimweh haben IV

hometown ['həʊmtaʊn] Heimatstadt IV

homework *(no pl)* ['həʊmwɜːk] Hausaufgabe(n) I • **do homework** die Hausaufgabe(n) machen I **What's for homework?** Was haben wir als Hausaufgabe auf? I

honest ['ɒnɪst] ehrlich V

Hooray! [hu'reɪ] Hurra! II

hope [həʊp] hoffen II

hope [həʊp] Hoffnung III

horrible ['hɒrəbl] scheußlich, grauenhaft II

horror film ['hɒrə fɪlm] Horrorfilm VI 1 (14)

horse [hɔːs] Pferd I

hospital ['hɒspɪtl] Krankenhaus II

hostel ['hɒstl] Herberge, Wohnheim III • **youth hostel** Jugendherberge III

hot [hɒt] heiß I • **hot chocolate** heiße Schokolade I

hotel [həʊ'tel] Hotel II

hotline ['hɒtlaɪn] Hotline II

hour ['aʊə] Stunde II • **half an hour** [ˌhɑːf‿ən‿'aʊə] eine halbe Stunde III • **a 14-hour flight** ein 14-stündiger Flug, ein 14-Stunden-Flug III • **a 24-hour supermarket** ein Supermarkt, der 24 Stunden geöffnet ist III • **rush hour** Hauptverkehrszeit V

house [haʊs] Haus I • **at the Shaws' house** im Haus der Shaws / bei den Shaws zu Hause I

how [haʊ] wie I • **How about ...?** Wie wär's mit ...? III • **How am I doing?** Wie komme ich voran? *(Wie sind meine Fortschritte?)* III **How are you?** Wie geht es dir/Ihnen/euch? II • **How are you doing?** Wie geht's? V • **How do you know ...?** Woher weißt/kennst du ...? I • **how long?** seit wann? IV • **how many?** wie viele? I **how much?** wie viel? I • **How much is/are ...?** Was kostet/kosten ...? / Wie viel kostet/kosten ...? I • **How old are you?** Wie alt bist du? I • **how to do sth.** wie man

etwas tut / tun kann/ tun soll V
How was ...? Wie war ...? I
huge [hjuːdʒ] riesig, sehr groß III
human ['hjuːmən] Menschen-, menschlich VI 2 (31)
hundred ['hʌndrəd] hundert I
hung [hʌŋ] *siehe* **hang**
hungry ['hʌŋgri] hungrig III • **be hungry** Hunger haben, hungrig sein III
hunt [hʌnt] jagen III
hunt [hʌnt] Jagd III
hurry ['hʌri] eilen; sich beeilen II
hurry up sich beeilen I
hurry ['hʌri]**: be in a hurry** in Eile sein, es eilig haben I
hurt [hɜːt]**, hurt, hurt** wehtun; verletzen I
hurt [hɜːt] verletzt II
husband ['hʌzbənd] Ehemann II
hutch [hʌtʃ] (Kaninchen-)Stall I

I

I [aɪ] ich I • **I'm** [aɪm] ich bin I
I'm from ... Ich komme aus ... / Ich bin aus ... I • **I'm ... years old.** Ich bin ... Jahre alt. I • **I'm sorry.** Entschuldigung. / Tut mir leid. I
ice [aɪs]**: ice cream** (Speise-)Eis I
ice hockey Eishockey • **ice rink** Schlittschuhbahn II
idea [aɪ'dɪə] Idee, Einfall I
ideal [aɪ'diːəl] ideal V
idiot ['ɪdiət] Idiot/in VI 3 (54)
if [ɪf]
1. falls, wenn II
2. ob II
ill [ɪl] krank II
illegal [ɪ'liːgl] illegal, ungesetzlich IV
illness ['ɪlnəs] Krankheit IV
imagine sth. [ɪ'mædʒɪn] sich etwas vorstellen IV
immigrant ['ɪmɪgrənt] Einwanderer/Einwanderin IV
immigration (to) [ˌɪmɪ'greɪʃn] Einwanderung, Immigration (in, nach) VI 3 (52)
impolite [ˌɪmpə'laɪt] unhöflich V
important (to) [ɪm'pɔːtnt] wichtig (für) II
impossible [ɪm'pɒsəbl] unmöglich II
impressed [ɪm'prest] beeindruckt IV
improve [ɪm'pruːv] (sich) verbessern VI 3 (49)
in [ɪn] in I • **in ... Street** in der ...straße I • **in a friendly/strange/ different way** auf freundliche/ seltsame/andere Art und Weise VI 1 (8) • **in English** auf Englisch I
in fact tatsächlich; in Wirklichkeit; um genau zu sein VI 3 (49) • **in front of** vor *(räumlich)* I • **in here** hier drinnen I • **in my opinion** meiner Meinung nach IV • **in the afternoon** nachmittags, am Nachmittag I • **in the country** auf dem Land II • **in the end** schließlich, zum Schluss III • **in the evening** abends, am Abend I • **in the field** auf dem Feld II • **in the morning** am Morgen, morgens I
in the old days früher; in alten Tagen VI 2 (32) • **in the photo** auf dem Foto I • **in the picture** auf dem Bild I • **in the world** auf der Welt VI 2 (30) • **in time** rechtzeitig II • **in 1837** 1837, im Jahre 1837 IV
in the 1970s in den 70er-Jahren *(des 20. Jahrhunderts)* VI 2 (30)
include [ɪn'kluːd] (mit) einschließen, enthalten *(beinhalten)* V
independent [ˌɪndɪ'pendənt] unabhängig V
°**individual** [ˌɪndɪ'vɪdʒuəl] einzelne(r, s), individuelle(r, s)
indoor ['ɪndɔː] *(nur vor Nomen)* Hallen-; im Gebäude V • **indoor market** Markthalle V • **indoor swimming pool** Hallenbad V
indoor toilet Innentoilette V
industrial [ɪn'dʌstriəl] industriell, Industrie IV
industry ['ɪndəstri] Industrie IV
infinitive [ɪn'fɪnətɪv] Infinitiv *(Grundform des Verbs)* I
inform [ɪn'fɔːm] informieren VI 2 (30/167)
information (about/on) *(no pl)* [ˌɪnfə'meɪʃn] Information(en) (über) II
inline skating ['ɪnlaɪn ˌskeɪtɪŋ] Inlineskaten III
inside [ˌɪn'saɪd]
1. innen (drin), drinnen I
2. nach drinnen II
3. inside the car ins Auto (hinein), ins Innere des Autos II
°**front inside cover** [ˌfrʌnt‿ˌɪnsaɪd 'kʌvə] Umschlaginnenseite
install [ɪn'stɔːl] installieren, einrichten II
instant messages *(pl)* [ˌɪnstənt 'mesɪdʒɪz] *Nachrichten, die man im Internet austauscht (in Echtzeit)* III
instructions *(pl)* [ɪn'strʌkʃnz] (Gebrauchs-)Anweisung(en), Anleitung(en) II
instrument ['ɪnstrəmənt] Instrument III
intelligent [ɪn'telɪdʒənt] intelligent, klug VI 1 (13)
interest ['ɪntrəst] Interesse III
interested ['ɪntrəstɪd]**: be interested (in)** interessiert sein (an), sich interessieren (für) III
interesting ['ɪntrəstɪŋ] interessant I
international [ˌɪntə'næʃnəl] international III
internet ['ɪntənet] Internet III
surf the internet im Internet surfen III
interview ['ɪntəvjuː] Interview I
(job) interview Vorstellungsgespräch, Bewerbungsgespräch V
interview ['ɪntəvjuː] interviewen, befragen II
interviewer ['ɪntəvjuːə] Interviewer/in, Befrager/in V
into ['ɪntə, 'ɪntʊ] in ... (hinein) I
introduce sth. [ˌɪntrə'djuːs] etwas einführen *(Thema, Methode, Währung)* V
introduction (to) [ˌɪntrə'dʌkʃn] Einführung (in) III
invent [ɪn'vent] erfinden VI 2 (30/167)
invention [ɪn'venʃn] Erfindung VI 2 (30)
invitation (to) [ˌɪnvɪ'teɪʃn] Einladung (zu) I
invite (to) [ɪn'vaɪt] einladen (zu) I
involved [ɪn'vɒlvd]**: get involved (in)** sich engagieren (für, bei); sich beteiligen (an) VI 3 (47)
°**irregular** [ɪ'regjələ] unregelmäßig
is [ɪz] ist I
island ['aɪlənd] Insel II
issue ['ɪʃuː] Thema, (Streit-)Frage VI 3 (46)
it [ɪt] er/sie/es I • **It's £1.** Er/Sie/Es kostet 1 Pfund. I • **It says here: ...** Hier steht: ... / Es heißt hier: ... II
its [ɪts] sein/seine; ihr/ihre I
itself [ɪt'self] sich (selbst) III

J

jacket ['dʒækɪt] Jacke, Jackett II
jail [dʒeɪl] Gefängnis IV
jam: traffic jam ['træfɪk dʒæm] (Verkehrs-)Stau V
January ['dʒænjuəri] Januar I
jazz [dʒæz] Jazz III
jealous (of) ['dʒeləs] neidisch (auf); eifersüchtig (auf) III
jealousy ['dʒeləsi] Eifersucht IV
jeans *(pl)* [dʒiːnz] Jeans I
Jew [dʒuː] Jude/Jüdin VI 1 (13/165)
► S.165 Religions
jewellery ['dʒuːəlri] Schmuck III

Jewish ['dʒu:ɪʃ] jüdisch VI 1 (13/165)
► S.165 Religions
job [dʒɒb] Aufgabe, Job I • **job interview** Vorstellungsgespräch, Bewerbungsgespräch V
jobless ['dʒɒbləs] ohne Job, arbeitslos V
join sb. [dʒɔɪn] sich jm. anschließen; bei jm. mitmachen II
joke [dʒəʊk] Witz I
joke [dʒəʊk] scherzen, Witze machen II
journey ['dʒɜ:ni] Fahrt, Reise III **Have a good journey.** Gute Reise! V
judge sb. (by) [dʒʌdʒ] jn. beurteilen (nach) IV
judo ['dʒu:dəʊ] Judo I • **do judo** Judo machen I
jug [dʒʌg] Krug I • **a jug of milk** ein Krug Milch I
juice [dʒu:s] Saft I
juicy ['dʒu:si] saftig V
July [dʒu'laɪ] Juli I
jumble sale ['dʒʌmbl seɪl] Wohltätigkeitsbasar I
jump [dʒʌmp] springen II • **jump around** herumspringen III
June [dʒu:n] Juni I
junior ['dʒu:niə] Junioren-, Jugend- I
just [dʒʌst]
1. (einfach) nur, bloß I
2. gerade (eben), soeben II

K

kangaroo [ˌkæŋgə'ru:] Känguru II
keep [ki:p], **kept, kept:**
keep fit fit bleiben • **keep in touch** in Verbindung bleiben, Kontakt halten III • **keep sb. away (from)** jn. fernhalten (von) VI 3 (49)
keep sth. going etwas in Gang halten, etwas aufrechterhalten VI 1 (11) • **keep sth. warm/cool/open** etwas warm/kühl/offen halten II
kept [kept] *siehe* **keep**
kettle ['ketl] (Wasser-)Kessel, Wasserkocher VI 2 (34)
key [ki:] Schlüssel • **key ring** Schlüsselring II • **key word** Stichwort, Schlüsselwort I
keyboard ['ki:bɔ:d] Keyboard *(elektronisches Tasteninstrument)* III
kick [kɪk] treten IV
kid [kɪd] Kind, Jugendliche(r) I
kidney ['kɪdni] Niere III
kill [kɪl] töten I
kilogram (kg) ['kɪləgræm], **kilo** ['ki:ləʊ] Kilogramm, Kilo (kg) III
two kilos of oranges zwei Kilo Orangen III • **a 150-kilogram bear** ein 150 Kilogramm schwerer Bär III
kilometre (km) ['kɪləmi:tə] Kilometer III • **a ten-kilometre walk** eine Zehn-Kilometer-Wanderung III
kind [kaɪnd] freundlich, nett V
kind (of) [kaɪnd] Art III • **What kind of car...?** Was für ein Auto III
kindergarten ['kɪndəgɑ:tn] Kindergarten; *(USA)* Vorschule *(für 5- bis 6-jährige)* IV
king [kɪŋ] König I
kiss [kɪs] küssen IV
kiss [kɪs] Kuss IV
kit [kɪt] Ausrüstung V • **first-aid kit** Erste-Hilfe-Kasten, Verbandskasten V • **repair kit** Flickzeug V **survival kit** Überlebenspäckchen V
kitchen ['kɪtʃɪn] Küche I
kite [kaɪt] Drachen I
kiwi ['ki:wi:] Kiwi II
knee [ni:] Knie I
knew [nju:] *siehe* **know**
knife [naɪf], *pl* **knives** [naɪvz] Messer III
knock [nɒk] Klopfen V
knock (at/on sth.) [nɒk] (an etwas) klopfen V
know [nəʊ], **knew, known**
1. wissen I
2. kennen I
know about sth. von etwas wissen; über etwas Bescheid wissen II
get to know sb. jn. kennenlernen IV • **How do you know ...?** Woher weißt du ...? / Woher kennst du ...? I • **I don't know.** Ich weiß es nicht. I • **..., you know.** ..., wissen Sie. / ..., weißt du. I • **You know what, Sophie?** Weißt du was, Sophie? I
known [nəʊn] *siehe* **know**
koala [kəʊ'ɑ:lə] Koala V

L

label ['leɪbl] Marke, Label VI 3 (47)
°**label** ['leɪbl] beschriften, etikettieren
laid [leɪd] *siehe* **lay**
lake [leɪk] (Binnen-)See II
lamb [læm] Lamm(fleisch) III
lamp [læmp] Lampe I
land [lænd] landen II
land [lænd] Land, Grund und Boden II
lane [leɪn] Gasse, Weg III
language ['læŋgwɪdʒ] Sprache I
laptop ['læptɒp] Laptop VI 2 (35)
large [lɑ:dʒ] groß II
lasagne [lə'zænjə] Lasagne I
last [lɑ:st] letzte(r, s) I • **the last day** der letzte Tag I • **at last** endlich, schließlich I
last [lɑ:st] halten *(fortdauern, von Bestand sein)* VI 1 (9)
late [leɪt] spät; zu spät I • **be late** zu spät sein/kommen I • **Sorry, I'm late.** Entschuldigung, dass ich zu spät bin/komme. I
later ['leɪtə] später I
latest ['leɪtɪst] neueste(r, s) III
laugh [lɑ:f] lachen I • **laugh at sb.** jn. auslachen IV
laughter ['lɑ:ftə] Gelächter II
law [lɔ:]
1. Gesetz IV
°**2.** Jura, Rechtswissenschaften
lay [leɪ], **laid, laid:**
lay the table den Tisch decken I
lazy ['leɪzi] faul V
leader ['li:də] (An-)Führer/in, Leiter/in, III
leaf [li:f], *pl* **leaves** [li:vz] Blatt *(an Pflanzen)* V
learn [lɜ:n] lernen I • **learn sth. about sth.** etwas über etwas erfahren/herausfinden II
least [li:st] am wenigsten IV • **like sth. least** etwas am wenigsten mögen III • **at least** zumindest, wenigstens I
leave [li:v], **left, left**
1. (weg)gehen; abfahren II
2. verlassen II
3. zurücklassen II
leave a message eine Nachricht hinterlassen V • **leave home** von zu Hause ausziehen VI 3 (48)
leave sb. alone jn. in Ruhe lassen V
leaves [li:vz] *Plural von „leaf"* V
left [left] *siehe* **leave**
left [left] linke(r, s) II • **look left** nach links schauen II • **on the left** links, auf der linken Seite II • **turn left** (nach) links abbiegen II
leg [leg] Bein I
legal ['li:gl] legal, gesetzlich IV
leisure centre ['leʒə sentə] Freizeitzentrum, -park II
lemonade [ˌlemə'neɪd] Limonade I
less [les] weniger IV
lesson ['lesn] (Unterrichts-)Stunde I • **lessons** *(pl)* Unterricht I
let [let], **let, let** lassen II • **Let's go.** Auf geht's! *(wörtlich:* Lass uns gehen.) I
letter ['letə]
1. Buchstabe I

2. letter (to) Brief (an) II
letter of application [ˌæplɪˈkeɪʃn] Bewerbungsschreiben V • **°letter to the editor** [ˈedɪtə] Leserbrief
°formal letter [ˈfɔːml] formeller Brief, förmlicher Brief
lend sb. sth. [lend], **lent, lent** jm. etwas leihen, etwas an jn. verleihen VI 2 (34)
► S.168 (to) lend – (to) borrow
lent [lent] *siehe* **lend**
lettuce [ˈletɪs] (Kopf-)Salat II
library [ˈlaɪbrəri] Bibliothek, Bücherei I
license plate [ˈlaɪsns pleɪt] *(AE)* Nummernschild IV
life [laɪf], *pl* **lives** [laɪvz] Leben I
lifeguard [ˈlaɪfgɑːd] Rettungsschwimmer/in V • **lifeguard station** Station der Rettungsschwimmer/innen V
lift [lɪft] Fahrstuhl, Aufzug II
light [laɪt] Licht III
like [laɪk] wie I • **What was the weather like?** Wie war das Wetter? II
like [laɪk] mögen, gernhaben I
like sth. best/least etwas am meisten/wenigsten mögen III
like sth. better etwas lieber mögen II • **I like swimming/dancing.** Ich schwimme/tanze gern. I • **I'd like ... (= I would like ...)** Ich hätte gern ... / Ich möchte gern ... I • **I'd like to talk about ... (= I would like to talk about ...)** Ich möchte/würde gern über ... reden I • **Would you like ...?** Möchtest du ...? / Möchten Sie ...? I • **Would you like some?** Möchtest du etwas/ein paar? / Möchten Sie etwas/ein paar? I
likeable [ˈlaɪkəbl] liebenswert, nett, sympathisch IV
likely [ˈlaɪkli] wahrscheinlich VI 3 (48)
line [laɪn]
1. Zeile II
2. (U-Bahn-)Linie III
3. *(AE)* Schlange, Reihe *(wartender Menschen)* IV
4. Hold the line, please. Bitte bleiben Sie am Apparat. V
link [lɪŋk] verbinden, verknüpfen I
link [lɪŋk] Verbindung, Verknüpfung III
linking word [ˈlɪŋkɪŋ wɜːd] Bindewort II
lion [ˈlaɪən] Löwe II
list [lɪst] Liste I
list [lɪst] auflisten, aufzählen II
listen (to) [ˈlɪsn] zuhören; sich etwas anhören I
listener [ˈlɪsnə] Zuhörer/in II
listing [ˈlɪstɪŋ]: **TV listings** *(pl)* Fernsehprogramm IV
little [ˈlɪtl]
1. klein I
2. wenig IV • **a little** ein wenig/ein bisschen
live [lɪv] leben, wohnen I • **live on sth.** von etwas leben; sich von etwas ernähren V
live music [laɪv] Livemusik II
liver [ˈlɪvə] Leber III
lives [laɪvz] *Plural von „life"* I
living room [ˈlɪvɪŋ ruːm] Wohnzimmer I
local [ˈləʊkl] Orts-, örtlich II; einheimisch V
location [ləʊˈkeɪʃn] Wohn-/Standort, Lage III
lock [lɒk] abschließen; sperren III
long [lɒŋ] lang I
look [lʊk]
1. schauen, gucken I
2. look different/great/old anders/toll/alt aussehen I
look after sth./sb. auf etwas/jn. aufpassen; sich um etwas/jn. kümmern II • **look at** ansehen, anschauen I • **look for** suchen II
look forward to sth. sich auf etwas freuen V • **look left/right** nach links/rechts schauen II
look round sich umsehen I • **look sth. up** etwas nachschlagen III
look up (from) hochsehen, aufschauen (von) II
look [lʊk] Blick • **have a look at sth.** sich etwas ansehen, einen Blick werfen auf etwas IV
lorry [ˈlɒri] Lastwagen III
lose [luːz], **lost, lost** verlieren II
lost [lɒst] *siehe* **lose**
lot [lɒt]: **a lot (of)** eine Menge, viel, viele II • **Thanks a lot!** Vielen Dank! I • **He likes her a lot.** Er mag sie sehr. I • **lots more** viel mehr I • **lots of** eine Menge, viele, viel I
loud [laʊd] laut I
love [lʌv] lieben, sehr mögen II
love [lʌv] Liebe II • **Love ...** Liebe Grüße, ... *(Briefschluss)* I • **love story** Liebesgeschichte IV • **fall in love (with sb.)** sich verlieben (in jn.) IV
low [ləʊ] niedrig VI 2 (36)
luck [lʌk]: **Good luck (with ...)!** Viel Glück (bei/mit ...)! I
luckily [ˈlʌkɪli] zum Glück, glücklicherweise II
lucky [ˈlʌki]: **be lucky (with)** Glück haben (mit) IV
lunch [lʌntʃ] Mittagessen I
lunch break Mittagspause I

M

°Ma'am [mæm] *kurz für* **Madam**
machine [məˈʃiːn]
1. Automat IV
2. Maschine I
mad [mæd] verrückt I • **be mad about sth.** verrückt nach/auf etwas sein III
madam
°1. *Anrede für eine Kundin/eine Vorgesetzte*
2. Dear Sir or Madam Sehr geehrte Damen und Herren *(Anrede in Briefen)* V
made [meɪd] *siehe* **make**
madness [ˈmædnəs] Verrücktheit IV
magazine [ˌmægəˈziːn] Zeitschrift, Magazin I
maid [meɪd] Dienstmädchen IV
mail [meɪl] schicken, senden *(per Post oder E-Mail)* III • **mail sb.** jn. anmailen II
mail [meɪl] Mail III
mailbox [ˈmeɪlbɒks] Mailbox V
main [meɪn] Haupt-; wichtigste(r, s) IV
mainly [ˈmeɪnli] hauptsächlich V
majority [məˈdʒɒrəti] Mehrheit IV
make [meɪk], **made, made** machen; bauen I • **make a decision** eine Entscheidung treffen/fällen VI 3 (49) • **make a difference** etwas bewirken, etwas bewegen VI 2 (36)
make a mess alles durcheinanderbringen, alles in Unordnung bringen I • **make a speech** eine Rede halten IV • **make friends** Freundschaften schließen, sich anfreunden V • **°make sb. do sth.** jn. dazu bringen, etwas zu tun • **make sure that ...** dafür sorgen, dass ... VI 3 (50) • **Make yourself comfortable.** Machen Sie es sich bequem. / Mach es dir bequem. IV
make-up [ˈmeɪkʌp] Make-up II
male [meɪl] männlich III
mall [mɔːl]: **(shopping) mall** Einkaufspassage, überdachtes Einkaufszentrum IV
man [mæn], *pl* **men** [men] Mann I
°manager [ˈmænɪdʒə] Geschäftsführer/in, Leiter/in
many [ˈmeni] viele I • **how many?** wie viele? I
map [mæp] Landkarte, Stadtplan II

March [mɑːtʃ] März I
mark [mɑːk] (Schul-)Note, Zensur IV
mark sth. up [ˌmɑːk_'ʌp] etwas markieren, kennzeichnen II
market ['mɑːkɪt] Markt II
marmalade ['mɑːməleɪd] (Orangen-)Marmelade I
married (to) ['mærɪd] verheiratet (mit) I • **get married (to sb.)** (jn.) heiraten IV
mashed potatoes [ˌmæʃt pə'teɪtəʊz] Kartoffelbrei, Kartoffelpüree III
mass [mæs] Messe *(Gottesdienst)* VI 1 (13/165)
► S.165 Religions
match [mætʃ] Spiel, Wettkampf I
°**match** [mætʃ]
1. passen zu
2. zuordnen
°**Match the letters and numbers.** Ordne die Buchstaben den Zahlen zu.
mate [meɪt] *(infml)* Freund/in, Kumpel III
material [mə'tɪəriəl] Material V
maths [mæθs] Mathematik I
matter ['mætə]: **What's the matter?** Was ist los? / Was ist denn? II
°**no matter what/who/...** ganz gleich, was/wer/...
matter ['mætə]: **It doesn't matter.** Es spielt keine Rolle. / Es macht nichts (aus). VI 3 (48)
May [meɪ] Mai I
may [meɪ] dürfen III
maybe ['meɪbi] vielleicht I
me [miː] mir; mich I • **Me too.** Ich auch. I • **more than me** mehr als ich II • **That's me.** Das bin ich. I **Why me?** Warum ich? I
meal [miːl] Mahlzeit, Essen III
mean [miːn], **meant, meant**
1. bedeuten III • **What does 'forest' mean?** Was bedeutet „forest"? III
2. meinen *(sagen wollen)* II
I didn't mean to ... Ich wollte nicht ...; Es war nicht meine Absicht, zu ... VI 3 (55)
meaning ['miːnɪŋ] Bedeutung III
meant [ment] *siehe* **mean**
meat [miːt] Fleisch I
mechanic [mə'kænɪk] Mechaniker/in V
medal ['medl] Medaille III
media *(pl)* ['miːdiə] Medien III
mediation [ˌmiːdi'eɪʃn] Vermittlung, Sprachmittlung, Mediation II
medicine ['medsn, 'medɪsn] Medizin V
medium ['miːdiəm] mittel(groß) II

meet [miːt], **met, met**
1. treffen; kennenlernen I
2. sich treffen I
Nice to meet you. Nett, dich kennenzulernen. III
meeting ['miːtɪŋ] Versammlung, Besprechung IV
melt [melt] schmelzen VI 2 (35)
member ['membə] Mitglied IV
member of parliament Parlamentsmitglied, Abgeordnete(r) VI 3 (49)
men [men] *Plural von „man"* I
°**mention sth. (to sb.)** ['menʃn] etwas erwähnen (jm. gegenüber)
menu ['menjuː] Speisekarte II
mess [mes]: **be a mess** sehr unordentlich sein; fürchterlich aussehen II • **make a mess** alles durcheinanderbringen, alles in Unordnung bringen I
mess sth. up [ˌmes_'ʌp] *(infml)* etwas vermasseln, versauen VI 2 (34)
message ['mesɪdʒ]
1. Nachricht III
°2. Botschaft
leave a message eine Nachricht hinterlassen V • **take a message** eine Nachricht entgegennehmen V • **Can I take a message for him/her?** Kann ich ihm/ihr etwas ausrichten? V • **text message** SMS III
met [met] *siehe* **meet**
metal ['metl] Metall V
°**methane** ['miːθeɪn] Methan(gas)
°**method** ['meθəd] Methode
metre ['miːtə] Meter II
mice [maɪs] *Plural von „mouse"* I
microphone ['maɪkrəfəʊn] Mikrofon III
microwave ['maɪkrəweɪv] Mikrowelle VI 2 (28)
middle (of) ['mɪdl] Mitte I; Mittelteil II • **middle school** *(USA) Schule für 11- bis 14-Jährige* IV
might [maɪt]: **She might be too busy.** Sie könnte zu beschäftigt sein. / Vielleicht ist sie zu beschäftigt. IV
mild [maɪld] mild III
mile [maɪl] Meile *(= ca. 1,6 km)* II
for miles meilenweit II
milk [mɪlk] Milch I
million ['mɪljən] Million III
°**millionaire** [ˌmɪljə'neə] Millionär/in
mime [maɪm] pantomimisch darstellen, vorspielen II
mind [maɪnd]: **Mind your own business.** Das geht dich nichts an! / Kümmere dich um deine eigenen Angelegenheiten! II • **Never mind.** Macht nichts. V
mind map ['maɪnd mæp] Mindmap („Gedankenkarte", „Wissensnetz") I
mine [maɪn] meiner, meine, meins II
minority [maɪ'nɒrəti] Minderheit IV
mints *(pl)* [mɪnts] Pfefferminzbonbons I
minus ['maɪnəs] minus IV
minute ['mɪnɪt] Minute I • **Wait a minute.** Warte mal! / Moment mal! II
mirror ['mɪrə] Spiegel II
miss [mɪs]
1. vermissen II
2. verpassen V
3. **Miss a turn.** Einmal aussetzen. II
Miss White [mɪs] Frau White *(unverheiratet)* I
missing ['mɪsɪŋ]: **be missing** fehlen II • °**the missing information/words** die fehlenden Informationen/Wörter
mistake [mɪ'steɪk] Fehler I
mix [mɪks] mischen, mixen III
mix [mɪks] Mix, Mischung III
mixture ['mɪkstʃə] Mischung III
mobile (phone) ['məʊbaɪl] Mobiltelefon, Handy I
model ['mɒdl] Modell*(-flugzeug, -schiff usw.)* I; (Foto-)Modell II
°**moderator** ['mɒdəreɪtə] Vermittler/in, Moderator/in
modern ['mɒdən] modern III
mole [məʊl] Maulwurf II
mom [mɒm, *AE* mɑːm] *(AE)* Mama, Mutti; Mutter III
moment ['məʊmənt] Moment III
Monday ['mʌndeɪ, 'mʌndi] Montag I • **Monday morning** Montagmorgen I
money ['mʌni] Geld I • **raise money (for)** Geld sammeln (für) IV
monitor ['mɒnɪtə] Monitor, Bildschirm III
monkey ['mʌŋki] Affe II
monster ['mɒnstə] Ungeheuer, Monster II
month [mʌnθ] Monat I
moon [muːn] Mond II
moped ['məʊped] Moped V
more [mɔː] mehr I • **lots more** viel mehr I • **more than** mehr als II • **more than me** mehr als ich II **more boring (than)** langweiliger (als) II • **no more music** keine Musik mehr I • **not (...) any more** nicht mehr III

morning ['mɔːnɪŋ] Morgen, Vormittag I • **in the morning** morgens, am Morgen I • **Monday morning** Montagmorgen I • **on Friday morning** freitagmorgens, am Freitagmorgen I
mosque [mɒsk] Moschee VI 1 (13/165) ► S.165 Religions
mosquito [mə'skiːtəʊ] Moskito, Stechmücke VI 3 (49)
most [məʊst] (der/die/das) meiste ...; am meisten II • **most people** die meisten Leute I • **(the) most boring** der/die/das langweiligste ...; am langweiligsten II
mostly ['məʊstli] hauptsächlich, überwiegend V
motel [məʊ'tel] Motel IV
mother ['mʌðə] Mutter I
motorbike ['məʊtəbaɪk] Motorrad V
mountain ['maʊntən] Berg II
mouse [maʊs], *pl* **mice** [maɪs] Maus I
mouth [maʊθ] Mund I
move [muːv]
1. bewegen; sich bewegen II
Move back one space. Geh ein Feld zurück. II • **Move on one space.** Geh ein Feld vor. II
2. **move (to)** umziehen (nach, in) II • **move in** einziehen II • **move out** ausziehen II
movement ['muːvmənt] Bewegung II
movie ['muːvi] Film III
MP [ˌem'piː] **(member of parliament)** Parlamentsmitglied, Abgeordnete(r) VI 3 (49)
MP3 player [ˌempiː'θriː ˌpleɪə] MP3-Spieler I
Mr ... ['mɪstə] Herr ... I
Mrs ... ['mɪsɪz] Frau ... I
Ms ... [mɪz, məz] Frau ... II
much [mʌtʃ] viel I • **how much?** wie viel? I • **How much is/are ...?** Was kostet/kosten ...? / Wie viel kostet/kosten ...? I • **like/love sth. very much** etwas sehr mögen/sehr lieben II
mud [mʌd] Schlamm, Matsch V
muddy ['mʌdi] schlammig, matschig, schmutzig V
muesli ['mjuːzli] Müsli IV
multiple choice [ˌmʌltɪpl 'tʃɔɪs] Multiple-Choice II
mum [mʌm] Mama, Mutti; Mutter I
museum [mju'ziːəm] Museum I
mushroom ['mʌʃrʊm] Pilz III
music ['mjuːzɪk] Musik I
musical ['mjuːzɪkl] Musical I
Muslim ['mʊzlɪm] Muslim/Muslima, Muslimin; muslimisch VI 1 (13/165) ► S.165 Religions
must [mʌst] müssen I
must [mʌst]: **a must** ein Muss IV
mustn't do ['mʌsnt] nicht tun dürfen II
my [maɪ] mein/e I
myself [maɪ'self] mir/mich (selbst) III

N

name [neɪm] Name I • **My name is ...** Ich heiße ... / Mein Name ist ... I • **What's your name?** Wie heißt du? I • **family name** Nachname, Familienname V
name [neɪm] nennen; benennen II
narrator [nə'reɪtə] Erzähler/in VI 3 (52)
nation ['neɪʃn] Nation IV
national ['næʃnəl] national III
national park Nationalpark IV
nationality [ˌnæʃə'næləti] Staatsangehörigkeit, Nationalität V
Native American [ˌneɪtɪv‿ə'merɪkən] amerikanische(r) Ureinwohner/in, Indianer/in IV
near [nɪə] in der Nähe von, nahe (bei) I
nearly ['nɪəli] fast, beinahe V
neat [niːt] gepflegt II • **neat and tidy** schön ordentlich II
neck [nek] Hals, Genick V
need [niːd] brauchen, benötigen I
need to do sth. etwas tun müssen; etwas zu tun brauchen V
needn't do ['niːdnt] nicht tun müssen, nicht zu tun brauchen II
negative ['negətɪv] negativ V
neighbour ['neɪbə] Nachbar/in I
nephew ['nefjuː] Neffe IV
nervous ['nɜːvəs] nervös, aufgeregt I
nervousness ['nɜːvəsnəs] Nervosität IV
°**network** ['netwɜːk] (Wörter-)Netz
never ['nevə] nie, niemals I
Never mind. Macht nichts. V
new [njuː] neu I
news *(no pl)* [njuːz] Nachrichten, Neuigkeiten III • **That's good news.** Das sind gute Nachrichten. III
newspaper ['njuːspeɪpə] Zeitung I
next [nekst]: **be next** der/die Nächste sein I • **the next morning/day** am nächsten Morgen/Tag I • **What have we got next?** Was haben wir als Nächstes? I
next to [nekst] neben II
nice [naɪs] schön, nett I • **Nice to meet you.** Nett, dich kennenzulernen. III • **Nice try.** Netter Versuch. V
niece [niːs] Nichte IV
night [naɪt] Nacht, später Abend I
at night nachts, in der Nacht I
on Friday night freitagnachts, Freitagnacht I
nightlife ['naɪtlaɪf] Nachtleben V
nil [nɪl] null III
no [nəʊ] nein I
no [nəʊ] kein, keine I • **no more music** keine Musik mehr I • **no one** ['nəʊ wʌn] niemand IV
No smoking. Rauchen verboten. III • **No way!** Auf keinen Fall! / Kommt nicht in Frage! II • **No worries.** *(infml)* Kein Problem! / Ist schon in Ordnung! VI 3 (55) • °**no matter what/who/...** ganz gleich, was/wer/...
no-no ['nəʊ nəʊ]: **be a no-no** *(infml)* tabu sein, nicht in Frage kommen VI 2 (34)
nobody ['nəʊbədi] niemand II
nod (-dd-) [nɒd] nicken (mit) II
noise [nɔɪz] Geräusch; Lärm I
noisy ['nɔɪzi] laut, lärmend II
normal ['nɔːml] normal, üblich V
north [nɔːθ] Norden; nach Norden; nördlich III
north-east [ˌnɔːθ'iːst] Nordosten; nach Nordosten; nordöstlich III
north-west [ˌnɔːθ'west] Nordwesten; nach Nordwesten; nordwestlich III
nose [nəʊz] Nase I
not [nɒt] nicht I • **not (...) any** kein, keine I • **not (...) any more** nicht mehr III • **not (...) anybody** niemand II • **not (...) anything** nichts II • **not (...) anywhere** nirgendwo(hin) II • **not (...) at all** überhaupt nicht, ganz und gar nicht V • **not even** (noch) nicht einmal VI 2 (35) • **not (...) yet** noch nicht II
note [nəʊt] Mitteilung, Notiz I
°**make notes** sich Notizen machen
take notes sich Notizen machen I
nothing ['nʌθɪŋ] nichts II
notice ['nəʊtɪs] bemerken, merken VI 1 (6)
notice board ['nəʊtɪs bɔːd] Anschlagtafel, schwarzes Brett I
novel ['nɒvl] Roman VI 1 (12)
November [nəʊ'vembə] November I
now [naʊ] nun, jetzt I • °**now and then** gelegentlich, hier und da

number ['nʌmbə] Zahl, Ziffer, Nummer I • **number plate** Nummernschild IV
nut [nʌt] Nuss IV

O

o [əʊ] null I
o'clock [ə'klɒk]**: eleven o'clock** elf Uhr I
October [ɒk'təʊbə] Oktober I
of [əv, ɒv] von I • **two kilos of oranges** zwei Kilo Orangen III
of course [əv 'kɔːs] natürlich, selbstverständlich I
off [ɒf] von ... herunter VI 2 (34) • **a week/day/month off** eine Woche/einen Tag/einen Monat frei IV
cut sth. off etwas abtrennen, abschneiden III • **fall off** herunterfallen (von) II • **get off (the train/bus)** (aus dem Zug/Bus) aussteigen I • **take sth. off** etwas ausziehen *(Kleidung)* II • **take 10 c off** 10 Cent abziehen I • **turn on/off** ein-/ausschalten III
offer ['ɒfə] anbieten IV
offer ['ɒfə] Angebot IV
office ['ɒfɪs] Büro V • **office worker** Büroangestellte(r) V
official [ə'fɪʃl] offiziell, amtlich, Amts- V
often ['ɒfn] oft, häufig I
Oh dear! [əʊ 'dɪə] Oje! II
Oh well ... [əʊ 'wel] Na ja ... / Na gut ... I
oil [ɔɪl] Öl III • **oil rig** ['ɔɪl rɪg] (Öl-)Bohrinsel III
OK [əʊ'keɪ] okay, gut, in Ordnung I
I'll/You'll/She'll/ ... be OK. Mir/Dir/Ihr/...wird nichts passieren. IV
okay [əʊ'keɪ] okay IV
old [əʊld] alt I • **in the old days** früher; in alten Tagen VI 2 (32) • **old people's home** Alten-, Seniorenheim V • **a sixteen-year-old** ein/e Sechzehnjährige/r III • **a sixteen-year-old girl** ein sechzehnjähriges Mädchen III
old-fashioned [ˌəʊld'fæʃnd] altmodisch III
on [ɒn]
1. auf I
2. eingeschaltet sein, an sein *(Radio, Licht usw.)* II
on 13th June am 13. Juni I • **on Friday** am Freitag I • **on Friday afternoon** freitagnachmittags, am Freitagnachmittag I • **on Friday evening** freitagabends, am Freitagabend I • **on Friday morning** freitagmorgens, am Freitagmorgen I • **on Friday night** freitagnachts, Freitagnacht I • **on my shift** in meiner Schicht IV • **on the beach** am Strand II • **on the board** an die Tafel I • **on the bus** im Bus III **on the coast** an der Küste III • **on the corner of Green Street and London Road** Green Street, Ecke London Road II • **on the left** links, auf der linken Seite II • **on the phone** am Telefon I • **on the plane** im Flugzeug II • **on the radio** im Radio I • **on the right** rechts, auf der rechten Seite II **on the train** im Zug I • **on TV** im Fernsehen I • **on my/your/... own** allein, selbstständig *(ohne Hilfe)* VI 3 (48) • **be on** gezeigt werden, laufen *(im Fernsehen/Kino)* IV • **the lights came on** das Licht ging an V • **What page are we on?** Auf welcher Seite sind wir? I • **go on holiday** in Urlaub fahren II • **straight on** geradeaus weiter II
once [wʌns] einmal III • **once a week** einmal pro Woche III
one [wʌn] eins, ein, eine I • **one day** eines Tages I • **one-day ticket** Tageskarte III • **one at a time** einzeln VI 3 (48/171) • **one by one** einer nach dem anderen VI 2 (34) • **a new one** ein neuer / eine neue / ein neues II • **my old ones** meine alten II • **no one** niemand IV
onion ['ʌnjən] Zwiebel III
online [ˌɒn'laɪn] online, Online- III
only ['əʊnli]
1. nur, bloß I
2. the only guest der einzige Gast I • **only child** Einzelkind V
onto ['ɒntə, 'ɒntu] auf (... hinauf) III
open ['əʊpən] öffnen, aufmachen I
open ['əʊpən] offen, geöffnet II
°**opening sentence** [ˌəʊpənɪŋ 'sentəns] Einleitungssatz
opera: soap opera ['səʊp‿ɒprə] Seifenoper IV
operation (on) [ˌɒpə'reɪʃn] Operation (an) III
opinion [ə'pɪnjən] Meinung IV
opposite ['ɒpəzɪt] Gegenteil I
or [ɔː] oder I
orange ['ɒrɪndʒ] orange(farben) I
orange ['ɒrɪndʒ] Orange, Apfelsine I • **orange juice** ['ɒrɪndʒ dʒuːs] Orangensaft I
order ['ɔːdə] bestellen IV
order ['ɔːdə]
1. Befehl, Anweisung, Anordnung V
°**2.** Reihenfolge • **in the right order** in der richtigen Reihenfolge
word order Wortstellung
organization [ˌɔːgənaɪ'zeɪʃn] Organisation V
organize ['ɔːgənaɪz] ordnen, organisieren III
organized ['ɔːgənaɪzd] (gut) organisiert V
orphan ['ɔːfn] Waise, Waisenkind V
other ['ʌðə] andere(r, s) I • **the others** die anderen I • **the other way round** anders herum II
Ouch! [aʊtʃ] Autsch! I
our ['aʊə] unser, unsere I
ours ['aʊəz] unserer, unsere, unseres II
ourselves [aʊə'selvz] uns (selbst) III
out [aʊt] heraus, hinaus; draußen II
out of ... aus ... (heraus/hinaus) I
3 out of 5 3 von 5 VI 1 (13)
outback ['aʊtbæk]**: the outback** *(Australien)* das Hinterland V
outdoor ['aʊtdɔː] *(nur vor Nomen)* Außen-; im Freien, Freiluft- V
outdoor education Unterricht im Freien V • **outdoor swimming pool** Freibad V • **outdoor temperature** Außentemperatur V
outfit ['aʊtfɪt] Outfit *(Kleidung; Ausrüstung)* II
outline ['aʊtlaɪn] Gliederung VI 2 (37)
outside [ˌaʊt'saɪd]
1. draußen I
2. nach draußen II
3. outside his room vor seinem Zimmer; außerhalb seines Zimmers I
over ['əʊvə]
1. über, oberhalb von I
2. be over vorbei/zu Ende sein I
all over the world auf der ganzen Welt III • **from all over the UK/the world/England** aus dem gesamten Vereinigten Königreich / aus der ganzen Welt / aus ganz England III • **over there** da drüben, dort drüben I • **over to ...** hinüber zu/nach ... II
overnight [ˌəʊvə'naɪt] über Nacht VI 3 (47)
own [əʊn]
1. our own pool unser eigenes Schwimmbad II
2. on my/our/... own [əʊn] allein, selbstständig *(ohne Hilfe)* VI 3 (48)
owner ['əʊnə] Besitzer/in VI 3 (49)

P

pack [pæk] packen, einpacken II
packet ['pækɪt] Päckchen, Packung, Schachtel I • **a packet of mints** ein Päckchen/eine Packung Pfefferminzbonbons I
pads *(pl)* [pædz] *(Knie- usw.)*Schützer *(für Inlineskater)*; Schulterpolster *(beim American Football)* III
page [peɪdʒ] (Buch-, Heft-)Seite I **What page are we on?** Auf welcher Seite sind wir? I
paid [peɪd] *siehe* **pay**
pain [peɪn] Schmerz(en) V
paint [peɪnt] (an)malen I
painter ['peɪntə] Maler/in II
pair [peə]: **a pair (of)** ein Paar II
palace ['pæləs] Palast, Schloss III
panic ['pænɪk] Panik V
pants *(pl)* [pænts] *(AE)* Hose IV
paper ['peɪpə]
1. Papier I
2. Zeitung II
paragraph ['pærəgrɑːf] Absatz *(in einem Text)* II
Paralympics [ˌpærə'lɪmpɪks] Paralympische Spiele *(Olympische Spiele für Sportler/innen mit körperlicher Behinderung)* III
paramedic [ˌpærə'medɪk] Sanitäter/in II
paraphrase ['pærəfreɪz] umschreiben, anders ausdrücken III
parcel ['pɑːsl] Paket I
parents ['peərənts] Eltern I
park [pɑːk] Park I • **(park) ranger** *Ranger sind eine Art Aufseher/in in Nationalparks, die auch Führungen machen und als Wald- und Wildhüter/innen arbeiten* IV
parliament ['pɑːləmənt] Parlament III • **member of parliament** Parlamentsmitglied, Abgeordnete(r) VI 3 (49)
parrot ['pærət] Papagei I
part [pɑːt] Teil I • **be part of sth.** Teil von etwas sein V • **take part (in)** teilnehmen (an) VI 2 (31)
part-time job [ˌpɑːt taɪm 'dʒɒb] Teilzeitbeschäftigung VI 3 (49)
partner ['pɑːtnə] Partner/in I
party ['pɑːti]
1. *(politische)* Partei VI 3 (49)
2. Party I
pass [pɑːs] (herüber)reichen, weitergeben I • **pass round** herumgeben I
passport ['pɑːspɔːt] (Reise-)Pass V
past [pɑːst] Vergangenheit I
past [pɑːst] vorbei (an), vorüber (an) II • **half past 11** halb zwölf (11.30/23.30) I • **quarter past 11** Viertel nach elf (11.15/23.15) I
pasta *(no pl)* ['pæstə] Pasta, Nudeln, Teigwaren IV
path [pɑːθ] Pfad, Weg II
pavement ['peɪvmənt] Gehweg, Bürgersteig IV
pay (for) [peɪ], **paid, paid** bezahlen II • **pay by credit card** mit Kreditkarte bezahlen V • **pay cash** bar bezahlen V
pay [peɪ] Bezahlung, Lohn V
PE [ˌpiː‿'iː], **Physical Education** [ˌfɪzɪkəl‿edʒu'keɪʃn] Turnen, Sportunterricht I
pea [piː] Erbse III
peace [piːs] Friede(n) VI 3 (47)
peanut ['piːnʌt] Erdnuss VI 1 (6)
pen [pen] Kugelschreiber, Füller I
pence (p) *(pl)* [pens] Pence *(Plural von „penny")* I
pencil ['pensl] Bleistift I • **pencil case** Federmäppchen I • **pencil sharpener** Bleistiftanspitzer I
penny ['peni] *kleinste britische Münze* I
people ['piːpl] Menschen, Leute I **old people's home** Alten-, Seniorenheim V
pepper ['pepə] Pfeffer V
per [pɜː, pə] pro III
per cent (%) [pə' sent] Prozent III
percentage [pə'sentɪdʒ] Prozentsatz, prozentualer Anteil VI 3 (49)
perfect ['pɜːfɪkt] perfekt; ideal; vollkommen IV
°**perfume** ['pɜːfjuːm] Parfüm
perhaps [pə'hæps] vielleicht V
period ['pɪəriəd] (Unterrichts-/Schul-)Stunde IV
person ['pɜːsn] Person II
personal ['pɜːsənl] persönliche(r, s) III • °**personal stereo** *Überbegriff für tragbare Musikabspielgeräte wie etwa MP3-Spieler*
pet [pet] Haustier I • **pet shop** Tierhandlung I
petition [pə'tɪʃn] Unterschriftensammlung, Petition VI 3 (47)
petrol ['petrəl] Benzin V
phone [fəʊn] Telefon I • **on the phone** am Telefon I • **phone call** Anruf, Telefongespräch I • **phone number** Telefonnummer I
phone [fəʊn] telefonieren, anrufen I
photo ['fəʊtəʊ] Foto I • **in the photo** auf dem Foto I • **take photos** Fotos machen, fotografieren I
photographer [fə'tɒgrəfə] Fotograf/in III
phrase [freɪz] Ausdruck, (Rede-)Wendung V
piano [pi'ænəʊ] Klavier, Piano I **play the piano** Klavier spielen I
pick up [ˌpɪk‿'ʌp]: **pick sb. up** jn. abholen III • **pick sth. up** etwas hochheben, aufheben II
picnic ['pɪknɪk] Picknick I • **have a picnic** ein Picknick machen I
picture ['pɪktʃə] Bild I • **in the picture** auf dem Bild I • **picture story** Bildergeschichte IV
pie [paɪ] Obstkuchen; Pastete II
piece [piːs]: **a piece of** ein Stück I **a piece of paper** ein Stück Papier I
piercing ['pɪəsɪŋ] Piercing III
pig [pɪg] Schwein III
pill [pɪl] Pille, Tablette V
°**pine tree** ['paɪn triː] Kiefer *(Nadelbaum)*
pink [pɪŋk] pink(farben), rosa I
pirate ['paɪrət] Pirat, Piratin I
pitch [pɪtʃ] Fußball-/Hockeyplatz III
pizza ['piːtsə] Pizza I
place [pleɪs] Ort, Platz I • **place of birth** Geburtsort V
°**placemat** ['pleɪsmæt] Set, Platzdeckchen
plan [plæn] Plan I
plan (-nn-) [plæn] planen I
plane [pleɪn] Flugzeug II • **on the plane** im Flugzeug II
planet ['plænɪt] Planet II
plant [plɑːnt] Pflanze V
plant [plɑːnt] pflanzen, einpflanzen V
plastic ['plæstɪk] Plastik VI 2 (35)
plate [pleɪt]
1. Teller I • **a plate of chips** ein Teller Pommes frites I
2. license plate *(AE)* Nummernschild IV • **number plate** *(BE)* Nummernschild IV
platform ['plætfɔːm] Bahnsteig, Gleis IV
play [pleɪ] spielen I • **play football** Fußball spielen I • **play the drums** *(pl)* Schlagzeug spielen III **play the fiddle** Geige, Fiedel spielen III • **play the guitar** Gitarre spielen I • **play the piano** Klavier spielen I
play [pleɪ] Theaterstück I
player ['pleɪə] Spieler/in I
pleasant ['pleznt] angenehm V
please [pliːz] bitte *(in Fragen und Aufforderungen)* I
plot [plɒt] Handlung *(eines Romans, Films)* VI 1 (12)
plug [plʌg] Stecker III
plus [plʌs] plus IV

pm [ˌpiː‿ˈem]: **7 pm** 7 Uhr abends/ 19 Uhr I
pocket [ˈpɒkɪt] Tasche *(an Kleidungsstück)* II • **pocket money** Taschengeld II
poem [ˈpəʊɪm] Gedicht I
point [pɔɪnt] Punkt II • **°point of view** Standpunkt • **10.4 (ten point four)** 10,4 (zehn Komma vier) III
point (at/to sth.) [pɔɪnt] zeigen, deuten (auf etwas) II
poison [ˈpɔɪzn] Gift V
poisonous [ˈpɔɪzənəs] giftig V
police *(pl)* [pəˈliːs] Polizei I • **police station** Polizeiwache, Polizeirevier II
policeman [pəˈliːsmən] Polizist II
policewoman [pəˈliːswʊmən] Polizistin II
°policy [ˈpɒləsi] Politik, Vorgehensweise
polite [pəˈlaɪt] höflich V
political [pəˈlɪtɪkl] politisch VI 3 (47/170)
politician [ˌpɒləˈtɪʃn] Politiker/in VI 3 (47)
politics [ˈpɒlətɪks] Politik VI 3 (47/170)
pollute [pəˈluːt] verschmutzen, verunreinigen VI 2 (30/167)
pollution [pəˈluːʃn] (Umwelt-)Verschmutzung V
poltergeist [ˈpəʊltəgaɪst] Poltergeist I
poor [pɔː, pʊə]
1. arm I • **poor Sophie** (die) arme Sophie I
°2. schlecht, armselig
pop [pɒp] Pop(musik) III
popcorn [ˈpɒpkɔːn] Popcorn II
popular [ˈpɒpjələ] beliebt, populär III
population [ˌpɒpjuˈleɪʃn] Bevölkerung, Einwohner(zahl) IV
pork [pɔːk] Schweinefleisch III
positive [ˈpɒzətɪv] positiv V
possible [ˈpɒsəbl] möglich II
postcard [ˈpəʊstkɑːd] Postkarte II
postcode [ˈpəʊstkəʊd] Postleitzahl V
poster [ˈpəʊstə] Poster I
post office [ˈpəʊst‿ɒfɪs] Postamt II
postscript (PS) [ˈpəʊstskrɪpt] Postskript (PS) *(Nachschrift unter Briefen)* III
potato [pəˈteɪtəʊ], *pl* **potatoes** Kartoffel I • **potato chips** *(AE)* Kartoffelchips IV
poultry [ˈpəʊltri] Geflügel IV
pound (£) [paʊnd] Pfund *(britische Währung)* I
poverty [ˈpɒvəti] Armut VI 3 (46)
power [ˈpaʊə] Kraft, Energie, Strom VI 2 (31)
power cut [ˈpaʊə kʌt] Stromabschaltung, Stromausfall VI 2 (35)
power station [ˈpaʊə steɪʃn] Kraftwerk, Elektrizitätswerk VI 2 (31)
practice [ˈpræktɪs] *hier:* Übungsteil I
practise [ˈpræktɪs] üben; trainieren I
pray [preɪ] beten V
prayer [ˈpreə] Gebet V
pregnant [ˈpregnənt] schwanger VI 1 (12)
prejudice (against) [ˈpredʒudɪs] Voreingenommenheit (gegen), Vorurteil (gegenüber) IV
prepare (for) [prɪˈpeə] vorbereiten; sich vorbereiten (auf) II
prescription [prɪˈskrɪpʃn] Rezept *(für Medikamente)* V
present [ˈpreznt]
1. Gegenwart I
2. Geschenk I
present sth. (to sb.) [prɪˈzent] (jm.) etwas präsentieren, vorstellen V
presentation [ˌpreznˈteɪʃn] Präsentation, Vorstellung I
presenter [prɪˈzentə] Moderator/in II
president [ˈprezɪdənt] Präsident/in IV
press [pres] drücken III
pressure [ˈpreʃə] Druck V
pretty [ˈprɪti] hübsch I
pretty healthy/good/useful ... [ˈprɪti] ziemlich gesund/gut/nützlich ... II
price [praɪs] (Kauf-)Preis I
primary school [ˈpraɪməri skuːl] Grundschule V
°principal [ˈprɪnsəpl] Schulleiter/in
print [prɪnt] drucken V
printer [ˈprɪntə] Drucker V
prison [ˈprɪzn] Gefängnis V
prisoner [ˈprɪznə] Gefangene(r) V
prize [praɪz] Preis, Gewinn I
probably [ˈprɒbəbli] wahrscheinlich II
problem [ˈprɒbləm] Problem II
produce [prəˈdjuːs] produzieren, herstellen III
product [ˈprɒdʌkt] Produkt IV
production [prəˈdʌkʃn] Produktion V
profile [ˈprəʊfaɪl] Porträt, Steckbrief III; Profil V
programme [ˈprəʊgræm]
1. Programm I
2. (Fernseh-)Sendung IV
project (about, on) [ˈprɒdʒekt] Projekt (über, zu) I • **do a project** ein Projekt machen, durchführen II
promise [ˈprɒmɪs] versprechen II
pronounce [prəˈnaʊns] aussprechen VI 2 (30/167)
pronunciation [prəˌnʌnsiˈeɪʃn] Aussprache I
proof *(no pl)* [pruːf] Beweis(e) II
protect [prəˈtekt] schützen IV
Protestant [ˈprɒtɪstənt] Protestant/in; protestantisch VI 1 (13/165)
► S.165 Religions
proud (of sb./sth.) [praʊd] stolz (auf jn./etwas) II
PS [ˌpiː‿ˈes] **(postscript** [ˈpəʊstskrɪpt]**)** PS (Postskript; *Nachschrift unter Briefen*) III
pub [pʌb] Kneipe, Lokal II
public [ˈpʌblɪk] öffentlich; Öffentlichkeit IV • **public transport** *(no pl)* [ˌpʌblɪk ˈtrænspɔːt] öffentliche Verkehrsmittel, öffentlicher Personennahverkehr V
publish [ˈpʌblɪʃ] veröffentlichen III
pull [pʊl] ziehen I
pullover [ˈpʊləʊvə] Pullover II
purple [ˈpɜːpl] violett; lila I
purse [pɜːs] Geldbörse II
push [pʊʃ] drücken, schieben, stoßen I
put (-tt-) [pʊt]**, put, put** legen, stellen, *(etwas wohin)* tun I • **put out a fire** ein Feuer löschen IV • **put sth. on** etwas anziehen *(Kleidung)* II; etwas aufsetzen *(Hut, Kopfhörer)* VI 2 (30) • **put sth. up** etwas aufhängen V • **°Put up your hand.** Heb deine Hand. / Hebt eure Hand.
puzzled [ˈpʌzld] verwirrt II
pyjamas *(pl)* [pəˈdʒɑːməz] Schlafanzug II

Q

qualification [ˌkwɒlɪfɪˈkeɪʃn] Abschluss, Qualifikation V
quality [ˈkwɒləti] Qualität; Eigenschaft V
quarter [ˈkwɔːtə]**: quarter past 11** Viertel nach 11 (11.15/23.15) I
quarter to 12 Viertel vor 12 (11.45/ 23.45) I
quay [kiː] Kai, Kaimauer III
queen [kwiːn] Königin III
question [ˈkwestʃn] Frage I • **ask questions** Fragen stellen I
°question word Fragewort
°questionnaire [ˌkwestʃəˈneə] Fragebogen
queue [kjuː] sich anstellen; anstehen V
queue [kjuː] Schlange, Reihe *(wartender Menschen)* IV

quick [kwɪk] schnell I
quiet ['kwaɪət] leise, still, ruhig I
quite bad/quick/good ... [kwaɪt] ziemlich schlimm/schnell/gut/... II
quiz [kwɪz], *pl* **quizzes** ['kwɪzɪz] Quiz, Ratespiel I

R

rabbit ['ræbɪt] Kaninchen I
rabbit-proof ['ræbɪtpru:f] kaninchen-sicher, kaninchen-fest V
race [reɪs] Rasse V
racism ['reɪsɪzəm] Rassismus VI 1 (12)
racist ['reɪsɪst] rassistisch; Rassist/Rassistin V
racket ['rækɪt]**: badminton racket** Badmintonschläger III • **tennis racket** Tennisschläger VI 3 (48)
radio ['reɪdiəʊ] Radio I • **on the radio** im Radio I
rafting ['rɑ:ftɪŋ] Rafting IV
railway ['reɪlweɪ] Eisenbahn II
rain [reɪn] Regen II
rain [reɪn] regnen II
rainproof ['reɪnpru:f] regendicht *(Kleidung)* V
rainy ['reɪni] regnerisch II
raise money (for) [reɪz] Geld sammeln (für) IV
ran [ræn] *siehe* **run**
rang [ræŋ] *siehe* **ring**
ranger ['reɪndʒə]**: (park) ranger** *Ranger sind eine Art Aufseher/in in Nationalparks, die auch Führungen machen und als Wald- und Wildhüter/innen arbeiten* IV
rap [ræp] Rap *(rhythmischer Sprechgesang)* I
rapper ['ræpə] Rapper/in IV
rate: exchange rate [ɪks'tʃeɪndʒ reɪt] Wechselkurs V
°**ration** ['ræʃn] Ration
°**rationing** ['ræʃənɪŋ] Rationierung
razor ['reɪzə] Rasierapparat, Rasierer VI 2 (28)
RE [,ɑ:r_'i:], **Religious Education** [rɪ,lɪdʒəs_edʒu'keɪʃn] Religion, Religionsunterricht I
react (to) [ri'ækt] reagieren (auf) VI 2 (35/169)
reaction (to) [ri'ækʃn] Reaktion (auf) VI 2 (35)
read [ri:d], **read, read** lesen I
°read out vorlesen • **°Read out loud.** Lies laut vor. • **°Read the poem to a partner.** Lies das Gedicht einem Partner/einer Partnerin vor.
read [red] *siehe* **read**
reader ['ri:də] Leser/in II
ready ['redi] bereit, fertig I • **get ready (for)** sich fertig machen (für), sich vorbereiten (auf) I • **get things ready** Dinge fertig machen, vorbereiten I
real [rɪəl] echt, wirklich I • **real-life** im wirklichen Leben, aus dem wirklichen Leben VI 1 (8)
realistic [,ri:ə'lɪstɪk] realistisch, wirklichkeitsnah III
reality [ri'æləti] Realität, Wirklichkeit IV
°**realize** ['ri:əlaɪz] verwirklichen, realisieren
really ['rɪəli] wirklich I
reason ['ri:zn] Grund, Begründung I • **for lots of reasons** aus vielen Gründen I
receipt [rɪ'si:t] Quittung, Kassenbon V
receive [rɪ'si:v] empfangen IV
°**recently** ['ri:sntli] in letzter Zeit; neulich, vor kurzem
reception [rɪ'sepʃn] Rezeption, Empfang V
°**receptionist** [rɪ'sepʃənɪst] Rezeptionist/in; Empfangsdame
°**recommend sth. (to sb.)** [,rekə'mend] (jm.) etwas empfehlen
record [rɪ'kɔ:d] *(Musik / einen Film)* aufnehmen III
recorder [rɪ'kɔ:də] Blockflöte III
recording [rɪ'kɔ:dɪŋ] Aufnahme, Aufzeichnung III
recycle [,ri:'saɪkl] wiederverwerten, wiederverwenden VI 2 (36)
recycled [,ri:'saɪkld] wiederverwertet, wiederverwendet, recycelt II
recycling [,ri:'saɪklɪŋ] Wiederverwertung, Recycling II
red [red] rot I • **go red** rot werden, erröten V
reduce [rɪ'dju:s] verringern, vermindern, reduzieren VI 2 (29)
reef [ri:f] Riff V
reference ['refrəns] Referenz, Empfehlung V
reggae ['regeɪ] Reggae III
regular ['regjələ] normal *(Größenangabe bei Getränken/Fastfood)* IV
rehearsal [rɪ'hɜ:sl] Probe *(am Theater)* I
rehearse [rɪ'hɜ:s] proben *(am Theater)* I
relations *(pl)* [rɪ'leɪʃnz] Beziehungen IV
relationship [rɪ'leɪʃnʃɪp] Beziehung V
relax [rɪ'læks] (sich) entspannen, sich ausruhen II
relaxed [rɪ'lækst] entspannt, gelassen V
reliable [rɪ'laɪəbl] zuverlässig, verlässlich V
religion [rɪ'lɪdʒn] Religion VI 1 (13)
► S.165 Religions
religious [rɪ'lɪdʒəs] religiös; gläubig VI 1 (13/165)
► S.165 Religions
remember sth. [rɪ'membə]
1. sich erinnern (an etwas) I
2. sich etwas merken I
3. an etwas denken *(nicht vergessen)* VI 2 (28)
remote control [rɪ,məʊt kən'trəʊl] Fernbedienung IV
rent sth. [rent] etwas mieten, etwas leihen V
repair sth. [rɪ'peə] etwas reparieren V • **repair kit** Flickzeug V
°**repeat** [rɪ'pi:t] wiederholen
°**replace** [rɪ'pleɪs] ersetzen
report (on) [rɪ'pɔ:t] Bericht, Reportage (über) I
report (to sb.) [rɪ'pɔ:t] (jm.) berichten II
reporter [rɪ'pɔ:tə] Reporter/in IV
represent [,reprɪ'zent] repräsentieren, vertreten III
rescue helicopter ['reskju: ,helɪkɒptə] Rettungshubschrauber II
research (on) *(no pl)* [rɪ'sɜ:tʃ, 'ri:sɜ:tʃ] Recherche (zu, über); Nachforschungen (zu, über) IV • **do research** recherchieren IV
respect [rɪ'spekt] achten, respektieren V
respect [rɪ'spekt] Achtung, Respekt V
responsible [rɪ'spɒnsəbl] verantwortlich; verantwortungsbewusst VI 2 (34)
rest [rest] Rest II
restaurant ['restrɒnt] Restaurant II
result [rɪ'zʌlt] Ergebnis, Resultat I
return [rɪ'tɜ:n] zurückkehren IV
return ticket Rückfahrkarte II
return [rɪ'tɜ:n] Rückkehr IV
review [rɪ'vju:] *(Buch-, Film-)*Kritik, Besprechung, Rezension VI 1 (12)
reviewer [rɪ'vju:ə] Rezensent/in, Kritiker/in *(von Büchern, Filmen usw.)* VI 1 (12/165)
revise [rɪ'vaɪz]
1. überarbeiten III
2. wiederholen III
revision [rɪ'vɪʒn] Wiederholung *(des Lernstoffs)* I
°**rewrite** [,ri:'raɪt] neu schreiben
rhino ['raɪnəʊ] Nashorn II
rice [raɪs] Reis IV
rich [rɪtʃ] reich II
ridden ['rɪdn] *siehe* **ride**

ride [raɪd], **rode, ridden** reiten I
go riding ['raɪdɪŋ] reiten gehen I
ride a bike Rad fahren I
ride [raɪd] Fahrt VI 2 (34) • **bike ride** Radfahrt II
right [raɪt] Recht IV
right [raɪt] richtig I • **all right** [ɔːl 'raɪt] gut, in Ordnung II • **be right** Recht haben I • **That's right.** Das ist richtig. / Das stimmt. I • **You need a school bag, right?** Du brauchst eine Schultasche, stimmt's? / nicht wahr? I
right [raɪt] rechte(r, s) II • **look right** nach rechts schauen II • **on the right** rechts, auf der rechten Seite II • **turn right** (nach) rechts abbiegen II
right [raɪt]: **right now** jetzt sofort; jetzt gerade I
ring [rɪŋ] Ring II
ring [rɪŋ], **rang, rung** klingeln, läuten II • **The bell rang.** Es klingelte. III
ringtone ['rɪŋtəʊn] Klingelton III
river ['rɪvə] Fluss II
RnB [ˌɑːr‿ən'biː] RnB *(Rhythm and Blues; Form des Blues, in der Rhythmus eine große Rolle spielt)* III
road [rəʊd] Straße I • **Park Road** [ˌpɑːk 'rəʊd] Parkstraße I
rock [rɒk] Fels, Felsen III
rock (music) [rɒk] Rock(musik) III
rode [rəʊd] *siehe* **ride**
role [rəʊl] Rolle III • **role play** Rollenspiel II
roll [rəʊl] Brötchen I
rollerblades ['rəʊləbleɪdz] Rollerblades IV
rollerskating ['rəʊləskeɪtɪŋ] Rollerskaten IV
Roman ['rəʊmən] römisch; Römer, Römerin II
romantic [rəʊ'mæntɪk] romantisch; Liebes- VI 1 (13)
roof [ruːf] Dach V
roofer ['ruːfə] Dachdecker/in V
room [ruːm] Raum, Zimmer I
double room Doppelzimmer V
single room Einzelzimmer V
round [raʊnd] rund II
round [raʊnd] um ... (herum); in ... umher II • **the other way round** anders herum II
route [ruːt] Strecke, Route IV
rubber ['rʌbə] Radiergummi I
rubbish ['rʌbɪʃ] (Haus-)Müll, Abfall II
rucksack ['rʌksæk] Rucksack III
rude [ruːd] unhöflich, unverschämt II
rule [ruːl] Regel, Vorschrift III
ruler ['ruːlə] Lineal I
run [rʌn] (Wett-)Lauf II
run (-nn-) [rʌn], **ran, run**
1. laufen, rennen I • **run around** herumrennen III
2. run sth. etwas leiten, führen V
rung [rʌŋ] *siehe* **ring**
runner ['rʌnə] Läufer/in II
running shoes ['rʌnɪŋ ʃuːz] Laufschuhe III
rush hour ['rʌʃ‿aʊə] Hauptverkehrszeit V

S

sad [sæd] traurig II
saddle ['sædl] Sattel III
safe (from) [seɪf] sicher, in Sicherheit (vor) II
safety ['seɪfti] Sicherheit IV • **fire safety** Verhalten im Brandfall IV
said [sed] *siehe* **say**
sailor ['seɪlə] Seemann, Matrose II
salad ['sæləd] Salat *(als Gericht oder Beilage)* I
sale [seɪl] (Aus-, Schluss-)Verkauf IV • **for sale** *(auf Schild)* zu verkaufen IV
salt [sɔːlt] Salz V
same [seɪm]: **the same ...** der-/die-/dasselbe ...; dieselben ... I • **be/look the same** gleich sein/aussehen I
sandwich ['sænwɪtʃ] Sandwich, *(zusammengeklapptes)* belegtes Brot I • **sandwich box** Brotdose I
sang [sæŋ] *siehe* **sing**
sat [sæt] *siehe* **sit**
satellite ['sætəlaɪt] Satellit IV
Saturday ['sætədeɪ, 'sætədi] Samstag, Sonnabend I
sauna ['sɔːnə] Sauna II • **have a sauna** in die Sauna gehen II
sausage ['sɒsɪdʒ] (Brat-, Bock-) Würstchen, Wurst I
save [seɪv]
1. retten II
2. sparen II
3. (ab)speichern *(Daten, Telefonnummern)* V
saw [sɔː] *siehe* **see**
saxophone ['sæksəfəʊn] Saxophon III
say [seɪ], **said, said** sagen I • **It says here: ...** Hier steht: ... / Es heißt hier: ... II • **say goodbye** sich verabschieden I • **Say hi to Dilip for me.** Grüß Dilip von mir. I **say sorry** sich entschuldigen II
say [seɪ]: **Have your say!** *etwa:* Übe dein Mitspracherecht aus! / Rede mit! VI 3 (46)
scan a text (-nn-) [skæn] einen Text schnell nach bestimmten Wörtern/Informationen absuchen II
scared [skeəd] verängstigt II • **be scared (of)** Angst haben (vor) I
scarf [skɑːf], *pl* **scarves** [skɑːvz] Schal III
scary ['skeəri] unheimlich; gruselig I
scene [siːn] Szene I
schedule ['skedʒuːl] *(AE)*
1. Fahrplan IV
2. Stundenplan IV
school [skuːl] Schule I • **at school** in der Schule I • **school bag** Schultasche I • **school subject** Schulfach I
science ['saɪəns] Naturwissenschaft I • **science fiction** [ˌsaɪəns 'fɪkʃn] Sciencefiction V
scientist ['saɪəntɪst] (Natur-)Wissenschaftler/in VI 2 (30)
score [skɔː] Spielstand; Punktestand III • **final score** Endstand *(beim Sport)* III • **What's the score? – 2–0 (two nil)** Wie steht es? *(beim Sport)* – 2:0. III
score (a goal) [skɔː] ein Tor schießen, einen Treffer erzielen III
scoreless ['skɔːləs] torlos IV
°**scrapbook** ['skræpbʊk] Sammelalbum
scream [skriːm] schreien, kreischen IV
screen [skriːn] Bildschirm IV • **flat screen** Flachbildschirm IV
sea [siː] Meer, *(die)* See I
season ['siːzn] Jahreszeit V
second ['sekənd] zweitens VI 2 (37)
second ['sekənd] zweite(r, s) I
second-hand [ˌsekənd 'hænd] gebraucht; aus zweiter Hand III
secondary school ['sekəndri skuːl] weiterführende Schule V
secret ['siːkrət] Geheimnis V
secret ['siːkrət] geheim V
secretly ['siːkrətli] heimlich V
section ['sekʃn] Abschnitt, Teil, (Themen-)Bereich III
see [siː], **saw, seen**
1. sehen I
2. see sb. jn. besuchen, jn. aufsuchen II
I see. Ich verstehe. / Aha. / Ach so. V • **See?** Siehst du? I • **See you.** Tschüs. / Bis bald. I • **Wait and see!** Wart's ab! III
seem (to be/do) [siːm] (zu sein / zu tun) scheinen IV

seen [siːn] *siehe* **see**
sell [sel], **sold, sold** verkaufen II
semester [sɪ'mestə] Semester *(Schulhalbjahr in den USA)* IV
semi-final [ˌsemi'faɪnl] Halbfinale III
send (to) [send], **sent, sent** schicken, senden (an) II
sent [sent] *siehe* **send**
sentence ['sentəns] Satz I
September [sep'tembə] September I
series, *pl* **series** ['sɪəriːz] (Sende-)Reihe, Serie II
serious ['sɪəriəs] ernst, ernsthaft IV **be serious about sth.** etwas ernst nehmen V • **take sb./sth. seriously** jn./etwas ernst nehmen VI 3 (48)
serve [sɜːv] bedienen *(Kunden)* V
service ['sɜːvɪs] Gottesdienst VI 1 (13/165)
► S.165 Religions
set (-tt-) [set], **set, set:**
1. set the alarm clock den Wecker stellen V
2. the film/novel is set in … der Film/Roman spielt in … VI 1 (12)
setup ['setʌp] Setup II
sex [seks] Geschlecht III
shake [ʃeɪk], **shook, shaken** schütteln; zittern V
shaken ['ʃeɪkn] *siehe* **shake**
shampoo [ʃæm'puː] Shampoo VI 3 (55)
share sth. (with sb.) [ʃeə] sich etwas teilen (mit jm.) I
she [ʃiː] sie I
sheep, *pl* **sheep** [ʃiːp] Schaf II
sheet [ʃiːt] Blatt, Bogen *(Papier)* V
shelf [ʃelf], *pl* **shelves** [ʃelvz] Regal(brett) I
shift [ʃɪft] Schicht IV
shine [ʃaɪn], **shone, shone** scheinen *(Sonne)* II
ship [ʃɪp] Schiff I
shirt [ʃɜːt] Hemd I
shock [ʃɒk] Schock V
shocked [ʃɒkt] schockiert III
shocking ['ʃɒkɪŋ] schockierend V
shoe [ʃuː] Schuh I
shone [ʃɒn] *siehe* **shine**
shook [ʃʊk] *siehe* **shake**
shoot [ʃuːt], **shot, shot** schießen, erschießen III
shop [ʃɒp] Laden, Geschäft I
shop assistant ['ʃɒp‿əˌsɪstənt] Verkäufer/in I • **shop window** Schaufenster II
shop (-pp-) [ʃɒp] einkaufen (gehen) I
shopping ['ʃɒpɪŋ] (das) Einkaufen I
go shopping einkaufen gehen I
shopping mall Einkaufspassage, überdachtes Einkaufszentrum IV
shopping list Einkaufsliste I
short [ʃɔːt]
1. kurz I
2. klein *(Person)* IV
shorts *(pl)* [ʃɔːts] Shorts, kurze Hose I
shot [ʃɒt] *siehe* **shoot**
should [ʃəd, ʃʊd]: **we should …** wir sollten … IV
shoulder ['ʃəʊldə] Schulter I
shout [ʃaʊt] schreien, rufen I
shout at sb. jn. anschreien V
shout [ʃaʊt] Schrei, Ruf V
show [ʃəʊ] Show, Vorstellung I
show [ʃəʊ], **showed, shown** zeigen I
shower ['ʃaʊə] Dusche I • **have a shower** (sich) duschen I
shown [ʃəʊn] *siehe* **show**
shut up [ˌʃʌt‿'ʌp], **shut, shut** den Mund halten II
shy [ʃaɪ] schüchtern, scheu II
sick [sɪk]
1. I feel sick. Mir ist schlecht. IV
2. *(besonders AE)* krank V
side [saɪd] Seite II
sidewalk ['saɪdwɔːk] *(AE)* Gehweg, Bürgersteig IV
sights *(pl)* [saɪts] Sehenswürdigkeiten II
sightseeing trip ['saɪtsiːɪŋ trɪp] Besichtigungstour IV
sign [saɪn] Schild; Zeichen III
sign [saɪn] unterschreiben, unterzeichnen VI 3 (47)
silent letter [ˌsaɪlənt 'letə] „stummer" Buchstabe *(nicht gesprochener Buchstabe)* II
silly ['sɪli] albern, dumm I
SIM card [sɪm] SIM-Karte V
similar (to) ['sɪmələ] ähnlich (wie) V
simple ['sɪmpl] einfach, nicht kompliziert V
since [sɪns]: **since April 4th** seit dem 4. April IV • **since then** seitdem VI 2 (30)
sincerely [sɪn'sɪəli]: **Yours sincerely** mit freundlichen Grüßen *(Briefschluss bei namentlich bekanntem Empfänger)* V
sing [sɪŋ], **sang, sung** singen I
singer ['sɪŋə] Sänger/in II
single ['sɪŋgl]
1. ledig, alleinstehend I
2. single room Einzelzimmer V
single (ticket) ['sɪŋgl] einfache Fahrkarte *(nur Hinfahrt)* III
sink [sɪŋk] Spüle, Spülbecken I
sir [sɜː, sə]
°**1.** *Anrede für einen Kunden/Vorgesetzten*
2. Dear Sir or Madam Sehr geehrte Damen und Herren *(Anrede in Briefen)* V
sister ['sɪstə] Schwester I
sit (-tt-) [sɪt], **sat, sat** sitzen; sich setzen I • **sit down** sich hinsetzen II • **Sit with me.** Setz dich zu mir. / Setzt euch zu mir. I
site [saɪt] (Internet-)Seite VI 2 (30)
situation [ˌsɪtʃu'eɪʃn] Situation, Lage VI 1 (8)
size [saɪz] Größe I
skate ['skeɪt] Inliner fahren I
skateboard ['skeɪtbɔːd] Skateboard I
skates *(pl)* [skeɪts] Inliner I
sketch [sketʃ] Sketch I
ski [skiː] Ski fahren/laufen III
ski [skiː] Ski III
skill [skɪl] Fähigkeit, Fertigkeit V
skills file ['skɪlz faɪl] *Anhang mit Lern- und Arbeitstechniken* I
skim a text (-mm-) [skɪm] einen Text überfliegen *(um den Inhalt grob zu erfassen)* III
skin [skɪn] Haut IV
skinny ['skɪni] mager IV
skirt [skɜːt] Rock II
sky [skaɪ] Himmel II
skyscraper ['skaɪskreɪpə] Wolkenkratzer IV
slave [sleɪv] Sklave, Sklavin II
sledge [sledʒ] Schlitten III
sleep [sliːp], **slept, slept** schlafen I
sleep [sliːp] Schlaf III
sleepless ['sliːpləs] schlaflos IV
sleepover ['sliːpəʊvə] Schlafparty III
slept [slept] *siehe* **sleep**
slide [slaɪd] Folie *(bei einer Computerpräsentation);* Dia V
slow [sləʊ] langsam II
slum [slʌm] Slum, Elendsviertel V
small [smɔːl] klein I
smart [smɑːt] clever, schlau II
smell [smel] riechen II
smell [smel] Geruch II
smile [smaɪl] lächeln I • **smile at sb.** jn. anlächeln II
smile [smaɪl] Lächeln II
smoke [sməʊk] rauchen III • **No smoking.** Rauchen verboten. III
smoke [sməʊk] Rauch III
snack [snæk] Snack, Imbiss II
snake [sneɪk] Schlange I
snow [snəʊ] Schnee II
snowball ['snəʊbɔːl] Schneeball IV
snowshoe ['snəʊʃuː] Schneeschuh III

snowshoeing ['snəʊʃu:ɪŋ] Schneeschuhwandern III
snowstorm ['snəʊstɔ:m] Schneesturm VI 2 (35)
so [səʊ]
1. also; deshalb, daher I • **So?** Und? / Na und? II
2. **so sweet** so süß I
3. **so that** sodass, damit VI 3 (52)
4. **Do you really think so?** Meinst du wirklich? / Glaubst du das wirklich? II
soap [səʊp] Seife I • **soap opera** ['səʊp‿ɒprə] *(kurz:* **soap***)* Seifenoper IV
soccer ['sɒkə] Fußball IV
social ['səʊʃl] sozial, Sozial- IV
°**social networking site** [ˌsəʊʃl 'netwɜ:kɪŋ saɪt] *Website zur Bildung und Unterhaltung sozialer Netzwerke*
sock [sɒk] Socke, Strumpf I
soda ['səʊdə] *(AE)* Limonade IV
soda machine *(AE)* Getränkeautomat IV
sofa ['səʊfə] Sofa I
soft [sɒft] weich IV • **soft drink** alkoholfreies Getränk IV
software ['sɒftweə] Software II
sold [səʊld] *siehe* **sell**
soldier ['səʊldʒə] Soldat/in IV
solve [sɒlv] lösen V
some [səm, sʌm] einige, ein paar I
some cheese/juice etwas Käse/Saft I
somebody ['sʌmbədi] jemand I
Find/Ask somebody who ... Finde/Frage jemanden, der ... II
somebody else jemand anders IV
someone ['sʌmwʌn] jemand IV
something ['sʌmθɪŋ] etwas II
sometimes ['sʌmtaɪmz] manchmal I
somewhere ['sʌmweə] irgendwo(hin) II • **somewhere to stay** ein Platz zum Übernachten V
son [sʌn] Sohn I
song [sɒŋ] Lied, Song I
soon [su:n] bald I
sore [sɔ:]: **have a sore throat** Halsschmerzen haben II
sorry ['sɒri]: **(I'm) sorry.** Entschuldigung. / Tut mir leid. I • **Sorry, I'm late.** Entschuldigung, dass ich zu spät bin/komme. I • **Sorry?** Wie bitte? I • **say sorry** sich entschuldigen II
sort [sɔ:t] Art, Sorte II
sound [saʊnd] klingen, sich *(gut usw.)* anhören I
sound [saʊnd] Laut; Klang I
sound file ['saʊnd faɪl] Tondatei, Soundfile III
soundtrack ['saʊndtræk] Soundtrack, Filmmusik V
soup [su:p] Suppe II
source [sɔ:s] Quelle *(von Informationen, Energie usw.)* VI 3 (47)
south [saʊθ] Süden; nach Süden; südlich III
south-east [ˌsaʊθ'i:st] Südosten; nach Südosten, südöstlich III
south-west [ˌsaʊθ'west] Südwesten; nach Südwesten; südwestlich III
souvenir [ˌsu:və'nɪə] Souvenir, Mitbringsel IV
space [speɪs]: **Move back one space.** Geh ein Feld zurück. II • **Move on one space.** Geh ein Feld vor. II
spaghetti [spə'geti] Spaghetti II
speak (to) [spi:k], **spoke, spoken** sprechen (mit), reden (mit) II
speak out seine Meinung (offen) sagen VI 3 (47)
special ['speʃl] besondere(r, s) I • **a special day** ein besonderer Tag I
special effect Spezialeffekt V
What's special about ...? Was ist das Besondere an ...? VI 1 (14)
speech [spi:tʃ] Rede IV • **make a speech** eine Rede halten IV
°**speech bubble** Sprechblase
spell [spel] buchstabieren I
spelling ['spelɪŋ] (Recht-)Schreibung, Schreibweise III
spend [spend], **spent, spent: spend money (on)** Geld ausgeben (für) II • **spend time (on)** Zeit verbringen (mit) II
spent [spent] *siehe* **spend**
spicy ['spaɪsi] würzig, scharf gewürzt III
spider ['spaɪdə] Spinne V
spoke [spəʊk] *siehe* **speak**
spoken ['spəʊkən] *siehe* **speak**
spoon [spu:n] Löffel III
sport [spɔ:t] Sport; Sportart I
do sport *(BE)* Sport treiben I
sports centre Sportzentrum I
sportsman ['spɔ:tsmən] Sportler IV
sportswoman ['spɔ:tswʊmən] Sportlerin IV
sporty ['spɔ:ti] sportlich III
spotlight ['spɒtlaɪt] Spotlight IV
spring [sprɪŋ] Frühling I
spy [spaɪ] Spion/in I
square [skweə] Platz III
squirrel ['skwɪrəl] Eichhörnchen II
stadium ['steɪdiəm] Stadion III
stage [steɪdʒ] Bühne III
stairs *(pl)* [steəz] Treppe; Treppenstufen I
stamp [stæmp] Briefmarke I
stand [stænd], **stood, stood** stehen; sich (hin)stellen II
standby ['stændbaɪ]: **on standby** *(Elektrogeräte)* im Standby-Betrieb VI 2 (30)
star [stɑ:]
1. Stern II
2. (Film-, Pop-)Star I
star [stɑ:]: **the film stars ...** der Film hat ... in der Hauptrolle / in den Hauptrollen VI 1 (12)
stare (at sb.) [steə] (jn. an)starren VI 3 (53)
start [stɑ:t] starten, anfangen, beginnen (mit) I • **start a business** eine Firma gründen V
start [stɑ:t]: **at the start** zu Beginn, am Anfang VI 3 (53)
state [steɪt] Staat III
statement ['steɪtmənt] Aussage, Feststellung III
station ['steɪʃn] Bahnhof I • **at the station** am Bahnhof I
statue ['stætʃu:] Statue II
stay [steɪ]
1. bleiben I
2. wohnen, übernachten II
somewhere to stay ein Platz zum Übernachten V
stay [steɪ] Aufenthalt V • **Have a pleasant stay.** Einen angenehmen Aufenthalt. V
steak [steɪk] Steak III
steal [sti:l], **stole, stolen** stehlen II
steel [sti:l] Stahl III • **steel drum** [ˌsti:l 'drʌm] Steeldrum III
step [step] Schritt I
stereo ['steriəʊ] Stereoanlage I
°**stick** [stɪk] Stock
still [stɪl] (immer) noch I
°**still** [stɪl] Standfoto
stole [stəʊl] *siehe* **steal**
stolen ['stəʊlən] *siehe* **steal**
stomach ['stʌmək]
1. Magen II
2. Bauch III
stomach ache Magenschmerzen, Bauchweh II
stone [stəʊn] Stein II
stood [stʊd] *siehe* **stand**
stop [stɒp] Halt IV
stop (-pp-) [stɒp]
1. aufhören I
2. anhalten I
Stop that! Hör auf damit! / Lass das! I
storm [stɔ:m] Sturm; Gewitter II
stormy ['stɔ:mi] stürmisch II
story ['stɔ:ri] Geschichte, Erzählung I

straight on [streɪt_'ɒn] geradeaus weiter II
strange [streɪndʒ] seltsam, sonderbar; fremd IV
strawberry ['strɔ:bəri] Erdbeere II
street [stri:t] Straße I • **at 7 Hamilton Street** in der Hamiltonstraße 7 I
strength [streŋθ] Stärke, Kraft V
stress [stres] Betonung III
strict [strɪkt] streng III
strike [straɪk] Streik III • **be on strike** streiken, sich im Streik befinden III • **go on strike** streiken, in den Streik treten III
strong [strɒŋ] stark II
structure ['strʌktʃə] strukturieren, aufbauen II
student ['stju:dənt] Schüler/in; Student/in I
study ['stʌdɪ] studieren; sorgfältig durchlesen; lernen IV • **study hall** *Zeit zum selbstständigen Arbeiten/Lernen in der Schule* IV • **study skills** *(pl)* Lern- und Arbeitstechniken I
stuff [stʌf] Zeug, Kram II
stupid ['stju:pɪd] blöd, dämlich II
subject ['sʌbdʒɪkt]
1. Schulfach I
°2. *Betreff in einer E-Mail*
suburb ['sʌbɜ:b] Vorort V
subway ['sʌbweɪ]: **the subway** *(AE)* die U-Bahn II
successful [sək'sesfl] erfolgreich IV
suddenly ['sʌdnli] plötzlich, auf einmal I
sugar ['ʃʊgə] Zucker II
suit [su:t] (Damen-)Kostüm VI 1 (14/166)
suitable ['su:təbl] geeignet, passend V
suitcase ['su:tkeɪs] Koffer II
sum sth. up (-mm-) [ˌsʌm_'ʌp] etwas zusammenfassen V
summarize sth. ['sʌməraɪz] etwas zusammenfassen IV
summary ['sʌməri] Zusammenfassung IV
summer ['sʌmə] Sommer I
sun [sʌn] Sonne II
Sunday ['sʌndeɪ, 'sʌndi] Sonntag I
sung [sʌŋ] *siehe* **sing**
sunglasses *(pl)* ['sʌnglɑ:sɪz] (eine) Sonnenbrille I
sunny ['sʌni] sonnig II
sunrise ['sʌnraɪz] Sonnenaufgang V
sunscreen ['sʌnskri:n] Sonnenschutzmittel V
sunset ['sʌnset] Sonnenuntergang V
super ['su:pə] super IV
supermarket ['su:pəmɑ:kɪt] Supermarkt II • **a 24-hour supermarket** ein Supermarkt, der 24 Stunden geöffnet ist III
°**support** [sə'pɔ:t] unterstützen, untermauern
°**supporter** [sə'pɔ:tə] Befürworter/in, Unterstützer/in
sure [ʃʊə, ʃɔ:] sicher, klar • **be sure** sicher sein II • **make sure that ...** dafür sorgen, dass ... VI 3 (50)
surf the internet [sɜ:f] im Internet surfen III
surfboard ['sɜ:fbɔ:d] Surfbrett II
surfing ['sɜ:fɪŋ]: **go surfing** wellenreiten gehen, surfen gehen II
surname ['sɜ:neɪm] Nachname V
surprise [sə'praɪz] Überraschung III
surprised (at sth.) [sə'praɪzd] überrascht (über etwas) IV
surprising [sə'praɪzɪŋ] überraschend, erstaunlich IV
survey (on) ['sɜ:veɪ] Umfrage, Untersuchung (über) II
survival [sə'vaɪvl] Überleben V
survival kit Überlebenspäckchen V
survive [sə'vaɪv] überleben II
swam [swæm] *siehe* **swim**
swap sth. (for sth.) (-pp-) [swɒp] etwas (ein)tauschen (für etwas/gegen etwas) IV
sweatshirt ['swetʃɜ:t] Sweatshirt I
sweet [swi:t] süß I
sweetheart ['swi:thɑ:t] Liebling, Schatz II
sweets *(pl)* [swi:ts] Süßigkeiten I
swim (-mm-) [swɪm], **swam, swum** schwimmen I • **go swimming** schwimmen gehen I
swimmer ['swɪmə] Schwimmer/in II
swimming ['swɪmɪŋ]: **swimming pool** Schwimmbad, Schwimmbecken I • **swimming trunks** *(pl)* ['swɪmɪŋ trʌŋks] Badehose III
swimsuit ['swɪmsu:t] Badeanzug III
°**swipe a card** [swaɪp] eine Karte durchziehen
swum [swʌm] *siehe* **swim**
syllable ['sɪləbl] Silbe I
synagogue ['sɪnəgɒg] Synagoge VI 1 (13/165)
► S.165 Religions
system ['sɪstəm] System IV

T

table ['teɪbl] Tisch I
table tennis ['teɪbl tenɪs] Tischtennis I • **table tennis bat** Tischtennisschläger III
take [teɪk], **took, taken**
1. nehmen I
2. (weg-, hin)bringen I
3. dauern, *(Zeit)* brauchen III
take a break eine Pause machen IV • **take action** handeln; etwas unternehmen VI 3 (50) • **take a message** eine Nachricht entgegennehmen V • **Can I take a message for him/her?** Kann ich ihm/ihr etwas ausrichten? V • **take notes** sich Notizen machen I
take off *(infml)* sich davonmachen, sich aus dem Staub machen IV • **take out** herausnehmen I
°**take over a plane** die Kontrolle über ein Flugzeug übernehmen
take part (in) teilnehmen (an) VI 2 (31) • **take photos** Fotos machen, fotografieren I • **take place** stattfinden IV • **take sth. off** etwas ausziehen *(Kleidung)* II
take 10 c off 10 Cent abziehen I
take sb./sth. seriously jn./etwas ernst nehmen VI 3 (48) • °**Take turns.** Wechselt euch ab. • **We'll take them.** *(beim Einkaufen)* Wir nehmen sie. I
taken ['teɪkən] *siehe* **take**
talk (to sb. about sth.) [tɔ:k] (mit jm. über etwas) reden, sich (mit jm. über etwas) unterhalten I
talk [tɔ:k] Vortrag, Rede V • **give a talk (on sth.)** einen Vortrag/eine Rede halten (über etwas) V
tall [tɔ:l] hoch *(Bäume, Türme usw.)*; groß *(Person)* IV
target ['tɑ:gɪt] Ziel; Zielscheibe VI 2 (29)
°**task** [tɑ:sk] Aufgabe
tattoo [tə'tu:] Tattoo, Tätowierung VI 1 (11)
taught [tɔ:t] *siehe* **teach**
tax [tæks] *(die)* Steuer VI 3 (52)
taxi ['tæksi] Taxi III
tea [ti:] Tee; *(auch:) leichte Nachmittags- oder Abendmahlzeit* I
teach [ti:tʃ], **taught, taught** unterrichten, lehren I
teacher ['ti:tʃə] Lehrer/in I • **head teacher** Schulleiter/in III
team [ti:m] Team, Mannschaft I
tear [tɪə] Träne VI 2 (34)
teaspoon ['ti:spu:n] Teelöffel III
technology [tek'nɒlədʒi] Technologie V
teddy ['tedi] Teddy III
teen [ti:n] Teenager-, Jugend- III
teenager ['ti:neɪdʒə] Teenager, Jugendliche(r) II
teeth [ti:θ] *Plural von „tooth“* I

telephone ['telɪfəʊn] Telefon I
telephone number Telefonnummer I • **What's your telephone number?** Was ist deine Telefonnummer? I
television (TV) ['telɪvɪʒn] Fernsehen I
tell (about) [tel]**, told, told** erzählen (von), berichten (über) I • **Tell me your names.** Sagt mir eure Namen. I • **tell sb. the way** jm. den Weg beschreiben II • **tell sb. to do sth.** jm. sagen, dass er/sie etwas tun soll V
temperature ['temprətʃə] Temperatur II • **have a temperature** Fieber haben II
temple ['templ] Tempel VI 1 (13/165)
► S.165 Religions
tennis ['tenɪs] Tennis I
tennis racket ['tenɪs rækɪt] Tennisschläger VI 3 (48)
tent [tent] Zelt IV
term [tɜ:m] Trimester II
terrible ['terəbl] schrecklich, furchtbar I
test [test] Test, Prüfung II
text [tekst] Text I
text sb. [tekst] jm. eine SMS schicken III
text message ['tekst ˌmesɪdʒ] SMS III
than [ðæn, ðən] als II • **more than** mehr als II • **more than me** mehr als ich II
thank [θæŋk]**: Thank you.** Danke (schön). I • **Thanks.** Danke. I
Thanks a lot! Vielen Dank! I
Thanks very much! Danke sehr! / Vielen Dank! II
that [ðət, ðæt]
1. das (dort) I
2. jene(r, s) I
That's me. Das bin ich. I • **That's right.** Das ist richtig. / Das stimmt. I • **That's up to you.** Das liegt bei dir. / Das kannst/musst du (selbst) entscheiden. III • **that's why** deshalb, darum V • **That was close.** Das war knapp. II
that [ðət, ðæt] der, die, das; die *(Relativpronomen)* III
that [ðət, ðæt] dass I • **so that** sodass; damit VI 3 (52)
that far/good/bad/... [ðæt] so weit/gut/schlecht/... III
the [ðə, ði] der, die, das; die I
theatre ['θɪətə] Theater II
°**theft** [θeft] Diebstahl
their [ðeə] ihr, ihre *(Plural)* I
theirs [ðeəz] ihrer, ihre, ihrs II
them [ðəm, ðem] sie; ihnen I
themselves [ðəm'selvz] sich (selbst) III
then [ðen] dann, danach I • °**now and then** gelegentlich, hier und da
since then seitdem VI 2 (30)
there [ðeə]
1. da, dort I
2. dahin, dorthin I
down there dort unten II • **over there** da drüben, dort drüben I
there are es sind (vorhanden); es gibt I • **there's** es ist (vorhanden); es gibt I • **there isn't a ...** es ist kein/e ...; es gibt kein/e ... I
thermometer [θə'mɒmɪtə] Thermometer II
these [ði:z] diese, die (hier) I
they [ðeɪ] sie *(Plural)* I
thick [θɪk] dick VI 1 (7/164)
thief [θi:f]**,** *pl* **thieves** [θi:vz] Dieb/in II
thin [θɪn] dünn VI 1 (7)
thing [θɪŋ] Ding, Sache I • **What was the best thing about ...?** Was war das Beste an ...? II
think [θɪŋk]**, thought, thought** glauben, meinen, denken I
think about 1. nachdenken über II; 2. denken über, halten von II
think of 1. denken über, halten von II; 2. denken an; sich ausdenken II
third [θɜ:d] dritte(r, s) I
third [θɜ:d]**: a third** ein Drittel V
this [ðɪs]
1. dies (hier) I
2. diese(r, s) I
This is Isabel. Hier spricht Isabel. / Hier ist Isabel. *(am Telefon)* II
this morning/afternoon/evening heute Morgen/Nachmittag/Abend I • **this way** 1. hier entlang, in diese Richtung II; 2. so, auf diese Weise VI 3 (47)
those [ðəʊz] die (da), jene (dort) I
thought [θɔ:t] *siehe* **think**
thought [θɔ:t] Gedanke III
thousand ['θaʊznd] tausend I
threw [θru:] *siehe* **throw**
thriller ['θrɪlə] Thriller VI 1 (12)
throat [θrəʊt] Hals, Kehle II
through [θru:] durch II • **go through sth.** etwas durchgehen *(Text, Formular)* VI 2 (34)
throw [θrəʊ]**, threw, thrown** werfen I
thrown [θrəʊn] *siehe* **throw**
°**thump** [θʌmp] pochen
Thursday ['θɜ:zdeɪ, 'θɜ:zdi] Donnerstag I
°**tick** [tɪk] Häkchen
°**tick** [tɪk] ankreuzen, ein Häkchen machen
ticket ['tɪkɪt]
1. Eintrittskarte I
2. Fahrkarte II • **return ticket** Rückfahrkarte II • **single ticket** einfache Fahrkarte *(nur Hinfahrt)* III
tidy ['taɪdi] aufräumen I
tidy ['taɪdi] ordentlich, aufgeräumt II
tie [taɪ] Krawatte V
tie *(-ing form:* **tying***)* [taɪ] binden V
tiger ['taɪgə] Tiger II
tight [taɪt] eng III
till [tɪl] bis *(zeitlich)* I
time [taɪm]
1. Zeit; Uhrzeit I
2. **time(s)** Mal(e); -mal II
at the same time gleichzeitig VI 1 (12) • **for the first time** zum ersten Mal VI 2 (30) • **Have a good time.** Viel Spaß! V • **in time** rechtzeitig III • **one at a time** einzeln VI 3 (48/171) • **two at a time** zwei auf einmal *(zur selben Zeit)* VI 3 (48) • **three times** dreimal III
What's the time? Wie spät ist es? I
°**timeline** ['taɪmlaɪn] Zeitleiste
timetable ['taɪmteɪbl]
1. Stundenplan I
2. Fahrplan II
timing ['taɪmɪŋ] Timing IV
tip [tɪp] Tipp II
tired ['taɪəd] müde I • **be tired of sth.** genug von etwas haben, etwas satt haben IV
title ['taɪtl] Titel, Überschrift I
to [tə, tu]
1. zu, nach I • **to Jenny's** zu Jenny I • **to the doctor's** zum Arzt III
°**to the front** nach vorn
2. **an e-mail to** eine E-Mail an I
write to schreiben an I
3. **quarter to 12** Viertel vor 12 (11.45/23.45) I • **from Monday to Friday** von Montag bis Freitag III
4. **try to help/to play/...** versuchen, zu helfen/zu spielen/... I
5. um zu II
toast [təʊst] Toast(brot) I
toaster ['təʊstə] Toaster VI 2 (34)
tobacco [tə'bækəʊ] Tabak II
today [tə'deɪ] heute I
toe [təʊ] Zeh I
together [tə'geðə] zusammen I
toilet ['tɔɪlət] Toilette I
told [təʊld] *siehe* **tell**
tomato [tə'mɑ:təʊ]**,** *pl* **tomatoes** Tomate II
tomorrow [tə'mɒrəʊ] morgen I
tomorrow's weather das Wetter von morgen II

tongue [tʌŋ] Zunge VI 1 (10)
tonight [tə'naɪt] heute Nacht, heute Abend I • **tonight's programme** das Programm von heute Abend; das heutige Abendprogramm II
tonne [tʌn] Tonne *(Gewichtseinheit)* VI 2 (29)
too [tuː]: **from Bristol too** auch aus Bristol I • **Me too.** Ich auch. I
too much/big/... [tuː] zu viel/groß/... I
took [tʊk] *siehe* **take**
tooth [tuːθ], *pl* **teeth** [tiːθ] Zahn I
toothache ['tuːθeɪk] Zahnschmerzen II
toothbrush ['tuːθbrʌʃ] Zahnbürste VI 2 (28)
top [tɒp]
1. Spitze, oberes Ende I • **at the top (of)** oben, am oberen Ende, an der Spitze (von) I • **on top of sth.** oben, oben drauf (auf etwas) V • **°top end** [ˌtɒp‿'end] oberes Ende
2. Top, Oberteil I
topic ['tɒpɪk] Thema, Themenbereich I • **topic sentence** *Satz, der in das Thema eines Absatzes einführt* II
tornado [tɔː'neɪdəʊ] Tornado, Wirbelsturm II
tortoise ['tɔːtəs] Schildkröte I
touch [tʌtʃ] berühren, anfassen II
keep in touch in Verbindung bleiben, Kontakt halten III
tough [tʌf] knallhart, streng V
tour (of the house) [tʊə] Rundgang, Tour (durch das Haus) I
°tourism ['tʊərɪzəm] Tourismus
tourist ['tʊərɪst] Tourist/in II
tourist information Fremdenverkehrsamt II
towards sb./sth. [tə'wɔːdz] auf jn./etwas zu II
tower ['taʊə] Turm I
town [taʊn] (Klein-)Stadt I
town councillor ['kaʊnsələ] Stadtrat/Stadträtin VI 3 (49)
town hall [ˌtaʊn 'hɔːl] Rathaus VI 3 (47)
trade [treɪd] Handel VI 3 (47)
tradition [trə'dɪʃn] Tradition IV
traditional [trə'dɪʃənl] traditionell V
traffic ['træfɪk] Verkehr II • **traffic jam** ['træfɪk dʒæm] (Verkehrs-)Stau V
train [treɪn] Zug I • **on the train** im Zug I
train [treɪn] trainieren III
trainers *(pl)* ['treɪnəz] Turnschuhe II
training ['treɪnɪŋ]
1. (berufliche) Ausbildung V
2. training session ['seʃn] Trainingsstunde, -einheit III
tram [træm] Straßenbahn III
translate (from ... into) [træns'leɪt] übersetzen (aus ... ins) III
translation [træns'leɪʃn] Übersetzung III
°transparency [træns'pærənsi] Folie *(für Overheadprojektoren)*
transport ['trænspɔːt] Beförderung, Transport III • **public transport** *(no pl)* [ˌpʌblɪk 'trænspɔːt] öffentliche Verkehrsmittel, öffentlicher Personennahverkehr V
travel (-ll-) ['trævl] reisen II
travel ['trævl] *(das)* Reisen VI 2 (34)
Travelcard ['trævlkɑːd] Tagesfahrkarte *(der Londoner Verkehrsbetriebe)* III
tree [triː] Baum I
trendy ['trendi] modisch, schick III
trick [trɪk]
1. (Zauber-)Kunststück, Trick I
do tricks (Zauber-)Kunststücke machen I
2. Streich II
trip [trɪp] Reise; Ausflug I • **day trip** Tagesausflug IV • **go on a trip** einen Ausflug machen II
Have a good trip. Gute Reise! V
tropical ['trɒpɪkl] tropisch, Tropen- V
trouble ['trʌbl] Schwierigkeiten, Ärger II • **be in trouble** in Schwierigkeiten sein; Ärger kriegen II
troublemaker ['trʌblmeɪkə] Randalierer/in, Unruhestifter/in V
trousers *(pl)* ['traʊzəz] Hose II
truck [trʌk] LKW, Lastkraftwagen V
true [truː] wahr II • **come true** wahr werden; in Erfüllung gehen IV
trumpet ['trʌmpɪt] Trompete III
try [traɪ]
1. versuchen I
2. probieren, kosten I
try and do sth. / try to do sth. versuchen, etwas zu tun I • **try on** anprobieren *(Kleidung)* I
try [traɪ] Versuch V • **Nice try.** Netter Versuch. V
T-shirt ['tiːʃɜːt] T-Shirt I
tsunami [tsuː'nɑːmi] Tsunami IV
tube [tjuːb]: **the Tube** *(no pl)* die Londoner U-Bahn III
Tuesday ['tjuːzdeɪ, 'tjuːzdi] Dienstag I
tunnel ['tʌnl] Tunnel II
turkey ['tɜːki] Truthahn III
turn [tɜːn]
1. sich umdrehen II • **turn away** sich abwenden, sich wegdrehen IV
turn left/right (nach) links/rechts abbiegen II • **turn to sb.** sich jm. zuwenden; sich an jn. wenden II
2. turn on/off ein-/ausschalten III
3. turn sth. down/up etwas leiser/lauter stellen IV; etwas höher/niedriger stellen VI 2 (28)
turn [tɜːn]: **It's your turn.** Du bist dran / an der Reihe. I • **Miss a turn.** Einmal aussetzen. II • **°Take turns.** Wechselt euch ab. • **Whose turn is it?** Wer ist dran / an der Reihe? II
TV [ˌtiː'viː] Fernsehen I; Fernsehgerät IV • **on TV** im Fernsehen I • **watch TV** fernsehen I • **TV listings** *(pl)* Fernsehprogramm IV
°TV dinner [ˌtiːviː 'dɪnə] *(infml)* Fertiggericht
twenty-four seven (24/7) rund um die Uhr, sieben Tage die Woche VI 2 (35)
twice [twaɪs] zweimal III • **twice a week** zweimal pro Woche III
°twilight ['twaɪlaɪt] Dämmerung, Zwielicht
twin [twɪn]: **twin brother** Zwillingsbruder I • **twins** *(pl)* Zwillinge I
type [taɪp] *(infml)* Typ III
typical (of) ['tɪpɪkl] typisch (für) V

U

unattractive [ˌʌnə'træktɪv] unattraktiv; wenig verlockend VI 1 (9/164)
unbelievable [ˌʌnbɪ'liːvəbl] unglaublich IV
unbreakable [ʌn'breɪkəbl] unzerbrechlich IV
uncle ['ʌŋkl] Onkel I
uncomfortable [ʌn'kʌmftəbl] unbequem, unbehaglich, unangenehm IV
uncool [ˌʌn'kuːl] *(infml)* uncool III
uncountable [ʌn'kaʊntəbl] unzählbar IV
under ['ʌndə] unter I
underground ['ʌndəgraʊnd]: **the underground** die U-Bahn II
°underline [ˌʌndə'laɪn] unterstreichen
understand [ˌʌndə'stænd], **understood, understood** verstehen, begreifen I
understood [ˌʌndə'stʊd] *siehe* **understand**
underwear ['ʌndəweə] Unterwäsche III

unemployment [ˌʌnɪm'plɔɪmənt] Arbeitslosigkeit V
unfair [ˌʌn'feə] unfair III
unforgettable [ˌʌnfə'getəbl] unvergesslich V
unforgivable [ˌʌnfə'gɪvəbl] unverzeihlich V
unfriendly [ʌn'frendli] unfreundlich III
unhappy [ʌn'hæpi] unglücklich III
unhealthy [ʌn'helθi] ungesund III
uniform ['juːnɪfɔːm] Uniform I
unit ['juːnɪt] Lektion, Kapitel I
united: the United Kingdom (UK) [juˌnaɪtɪd 'kɪŋdəm], [ˌjuː 'keɪ] das Vereinigte Königreich *(Großbritannien und Nordirland)* III • **United States (US)** [juˌnaɪtɪd 'steɪts], [ˌjuː‿'es] die Vereinigten Staaten *(von Amerika)* III
unkind [ˌʌn'kaɪnd] unfreundlich V
unless [ən'les] es sei denn; wenn ... nicht VI 3 (48)
unlock [ˌʌn'lɒk] aufschließen; entsperren III
unreadable [ʌn'riːdəbl] unleserlich IV
unrealistic [ˌʌnrɪə'lɪstɪk] unrealistisch IV
unsafe [ʌn'seɪf] nicht sicher, gefährlich III
untidy [ʌn'taɪdi] unordentlich III
until [ən'tɪl] bis III
up [ʌp] hinauf, herauf, nach oben I
up the hill den Hügel hinauf II
That's up to you. Das liegt bei dir./ Das kannst/musst du (selbst) entscheiden. III
upset [ˌʌp'set] aufgebracht, gekränkt, mitgenommen III
upset sb. (-tt-) [ʌp'set], **upset, upset** jn. ärgern, kränken, aus der Fassung bringen III
upstairs [ˌʌp'steəz] oben; nach oben I
us [əs, ʌs] uns I
use [juːz] benutzen, verwenden I; verbrauchen *(Energie)* VI 2 (28)
useful ['juːsfəl] nützlich IV
useless ['juːsləs] nutzlos IV
usual ['juːʒuəl]: **as usual** wie immer, wie üblich V
usually ['juːʒuəli] meistens, gewöhnlich, normalerweise I

V

vacation [və'keɪʃn, *AE:* veɪ'keɪʃn] *(AE)* Urlaub, Ferien III
valley ['væli] Tal II
°**vampire** ['væmpaɪə] Vampir/in
°**vandalism** ['vændəlɪzəm] Vandalismus, Zerstörungswut
vandalize ['vændəlaɪz] mutwillig beschädigen, mutwillig zerstören V
vegetable ['vedʒtəbl] *(ein)* Gemüse III
vegetarian [ˌvedʒə'teəriən] vegetarisch IV; Vegetarier/in IV
°**version** ['vɜːʃn, 'vɜːʒn] Version
very ['veri] sehr I • **like/love sth. very much** etwas sehr mögen/ sehr lieben II • **Thanks very much!** Danke sehr! / Vielen Dank! II
vet [vet] Tierarzt/-ärztin V • **vet's assistant** [ˌvets‿ə'sɪstənt] Tierarzthelfer/in V
victim ['vɪktɪm] Opfer III
video ['vɪdiəʊ] Video III
view [vjuː]
1. Aussicht, Blick II
°2. **point of view** Standpunkt
°**view** [vjuː] betrachten; *(im Fernsehen/Kino)* anschauen
viewer ['vjuːə] Zuschauer/in IV
village ['vɪlɪdʒ] Dorf I
violin [ˌvaɪə'lɪn] Violine, Geige III
virus ['vaɪrəs], *pl* **viruses** ['vaɪrəsəs] Virus V
visit ['vɪzɪt] besuchen II
visit ['vɪzɪt] Besuch II
visitor ['vɪzɪtə] Besucher/in, Gast I
visual ['vɪʒuəl] visuell; optisch V
vitae: curriculum vitae [kəˌrɪkjələm 'viːtaɪ] **(CV)** Lebenslauf V
vocabulary [və'kæbjələri] Vokabelverzeichnis, Wörterverzeichnis I
voice [vɔɪs] Stimme V
voicemail ['vɔɪsmeɪl] Voicemail III
volleyball ['vɒlibɔːl] Volleyball I
volume ['vɒljuːm] Lautstärke IV
volunteer [ˌvɒlən'tɪə] Freiwillige(r) IV • **volunteer work** Arbeit als Freiwillige(r) IV
°**volunteer** [ˌvɒlən'tɪə] sich freiwillig melden, sich bereit erklären
vote [vəʊt]
1. wählen *(zur Wahl gehen)* VI 3 (46)
2. abstimmen VI 3 (46)
vote for/against sb./sth. für/gegen jn./etwas stimmen VI 3 (46/169)

W

wait (for) [weɪt] warten (auf) I
Wait a minute. Warte mal! / Moment mal! II • **Wait and see!** Wart's ab! III • **I can't wait to see ...** ich kann es kaum erwarten, ... zu sehen I
waiter ['weɪtə] Kellner II
waiting room ['weɪtɪn ruːm] Wartezimmer IV
waitress ['weɪtrəs] Kellnerin II
wake [weɪk], **woke, woken:**
1. wake sb. (up) jn. (auf)wecken IV
2. wake up aufwachen IV
wake-up call ['weɪk‿ʌp ˌkɔːl] Weckanruf V
walk [wɔːk] (zu Fuß) gehen I
walk around herumlaufen, umherspazieren III • **walk around the town** in der Stadt umhergehen, durch die Stadt gehen III
walk [wɔːk] Spaziergang II • **go for a walk** spazieren gehen, einen Spaziergang machen II • **a ten-kilometre walk** eine Zehn-Kilometer-Wanderung III
wall [wɔːl] Wand; Mauer II
want [wɒnt] (haben) wollen I
want to do sth. etwas tun wollen I • **want sb. to do sth.** möchten/ wollen, dass jemand etwas tut V
want to be sth. etwas werden wollen *(beruflich)* V
war [wɔː] Krieg VI 3 (47/170)
wardrobe ['wɔːdrəʊb] Kleiderschrank I
warm [wɔːm] warm II
was [wəz, wɒz]: **(I/he/she/it) was** *siehe* **be**
wash [wɒʃ] waschen I; sich waschen VI 1 (10) • **I wash my face.** Ich wasche mir das Gesicht. I
washing machine ['wɒʃɪŋ məˌʃiːn] Waschmaschine I
waste sth. (on) [weɪst] etwas verschwenden, etwas vergeuden (für) VI 3 (47)
watch [wɒtʃ] beobachten, sich etwas ansehen; zusehen I
watch TV fernsehen I
watch [wɒtʃ] Armbanduhr I
water ['wɔːtə] Wasser I; Mineralwasser IV
waterproof ['wɔːtəpruːf] wasserdicht *(Uhr, Kleidung)* V
wave [weɪv] winken II
way [weɪ]
1. Weg II • **all the way** den ganzen Weg IV • **ask sb. the way** jn. nach dem Weg fragen II • **on the way (to)** auf dem Weg (zu/nach) II • **tell sb. the way** jm. den Weg beschreiben II
2. Richtung II • **the other way round** anders herum II • **the wrong way** in die falsche Richtung II • **this way** hier entlang, in diese Richtung II • **which way?** in welche Richtung? / wohin? II

3. Art und Weise V • **in a friendly/strange/different way** auf freundliche/seltsame/andere Art und Weise VI 1 (8) • **this way** so, auf diese Weise VI 3 (47)
4. **by the way** übrigens II
5. **No way!** Auf keinen Fall! / Kommt nicht in Frage! II

we [wi:] wir I
weak [wi:k] schwach II
weakness ['wi:knəs] Schwäche IV
wear [weə], **wore, worn** tragen, anhaben *(Kleidung)* I
weather ['weðə] Wetter II
weatherproof ['weðəpru:f] wetterfest *(Kleidung)* V
webcam ['webkæm] Webcam, Internetkamera III
website ['websaɪt] Website II
wedding ['wedɪŋ] Hochzeit, Trauung V
Wednesday ['wenzdeɪ, 'wenzdi] Mittwoch I
week [wi:k] Woche I • **days of the week** Wochentage I • **a two-week holiday** ein zweiwöchiger Urlaub III
weekend [ˌwi:k'end] Wochenende I **at the weekend** am Wochenende I • **Have a good weekend.** Schönes Wochenende! V
welcome ['welkəm]
1. **Welcome (to Bristol).** Willkommen (in Bristol). I
2. **You're welcome.** Gern geschehen. / Nichts zu danken. I

welcome sb. (to) ['welkəm] jn. begrüßen, willkommen heißen (in) I **They welcome you to ...** Sie heißen dich in ... willkommen I
well [wel]
1. gut II • **get on well (with sb.)** sich gut verstehen (mit jm.), gut auskommen (mit jm.) V • **go well** gut (ver)laufen, gutgehen III • **do well (in)** gut abschneiden (in) III **You did well.** Das hast du gut gemacht. II • **Oh well ...** Na ja ... / Na gut ... I • **Well, ...** Nun, ... / Also, ... I • **Well done!** [ˌwel 'dʌn] Gut gemacht. VI 2 (33)
2. *(gesundheitlich)* gut; gesund, wohlauf II

Welsh [welʃ] walisisch; Walisisch II
went [went] *siehe* **go**
were [wə, wɜ:]: **(we/you/they) were** *siehe* **be**
west [west] Westen; nach Westen; westlich III
western ['westən] westlich, West- III
wet [wet] feucht, nass III
what [wɒt]
1. was I
2. welche(r, s) I
What about ...? 1. Was ist mit ...? / Und ...? I; 2. Wie wär's mit ...? I **What are you talking about?** Wovon redest du? I • **What a great idea.** Was für eine tolle Idee! VI 2 (33) • **What colour is ...?** Welche Farbe hat ...? I • **What for?** Wofür? II • **What have we got next?** Was haben wir als Nächstes? I • **What kind of car ...?** Was für ein Auto...? III • **What page are we on?** Auf welcher Seite sind wir? I • **What's for homework?** Was haben wir als Hausaufgabe auf? I • **What's special about ...?** Was ist das Besondere an ...? VI 1 (14) • **What's the matter?** Was ist los? / Was ist denn? II • **What's the time?** Wie spät ist es? I **What's your name?** Wie heißt du? I • **What's your telephone number?** Was ist deine Telefonnummer? I • **What was the weather like?** Wie war das Wetter? II • **I don't know what to do** Ich weiß nicht, was ich machen soll. V

°**whatever** [wɒt'evə] was (auch) immer
wheel [wi:l] Rad III • **big wheel** Riesenrad III
wheelchair ['wi:ltʃeə] Rollstuhl I
when [wen] wann I • **When's your birthday?** Wann hast du Geburtstag? I
when [wen]
1. wenn I
2. als I

where [weə]
1. wo I
2. wohin I
Where are you from? Wo kommst du her? I • **He had no idea where to go.** Er hatte keine Ahnung, wohin er gehen sollte. V

which [wɪtʃ]: **Which picture ...?** Welches Bild ...? I • **which way?** in welche Richtung? / wohin? II
which [wɪtʃ] der, die, das; die *(Relativpronomen)* III
while [waɪl] während III
whisky ['wɪski] Whisky II
whisper ['wɪspə] flüstern I
whistle ['wɪsl] pfeifen II
white [waɪt] weiß I
who [hu:]
1. wer I
2. wen / wem II
Who else? Wen (sonst) noch? IV **He had no idea who to ask.** Er hatte keine Ahnung, wen er fragen könnte. V

who [hu:] der, die, das; die *(Relativpronomen)* III • **Find/Ask somebody who ...** Finde/Frage jemanden, der ... II
whole [həʊl] ganze(r, s), gesamte(r, s) IV
whole-grain ['həʊlgreɪn] Vollkorn- IV
whose? [hu:z] wessen? II • **Whose are these?** Wem gehören diese? II **Whose turn is it?** Wer ist dran / an der Reihe? II
why [waɪ] warum I • **Why me?** Warum ich? I • **that's why** deshalb, darum V
wife [waɪf], *pl* **wives** [waɪvz] Ehefrau II
wild [waɪld] wild II
will [wɪl]: **you'll be cold (= you will be cold)** du wirst frieren II • **you won't be cold** [wəʊnt] **(= you will not be cold)** du wirst nicht frieren II
win (-nn-) [wɪn], **won, won** gewinnen I
wind [wɪnd] Wind I
window ['wɪndəʊ] Fenster I
windproof ['wɪndpru:f] winddicht V
windsurfing ['wɪndsɜ:fɪŋ] Windsurfen III
windy ['wɪndi] windig I
wine [waɪn] Wein IV
wing [wɪŋ] Flügel IV
winner ['wɪnə] Gewinner/in, Sieger/in II
winter ['wɪntə] Winter I
wish [wɪʃ] Wunsch VI 3 (47) • **Best wishes** *etwa:* Alles Gute / Mit besten Grüßen *(als Briefschluss)* IV
with [wɪð]
1. mit I
2. bei I
be with sb. mit jemandem zusammen sein IV • **go with** gehören zu, passen zu III • **Sit with me.** Setz dich zu mir. / Setzt euch zu mir. I

without [wɪ'ðaʊt] ohne I
witness ['wɪtnəs] Zeuge/Zeugin V
wives [waɪvz] *Plural von „wife"* II
woke [wəʊk] *siehe* **wake**
woken [wəʊkən] *siehe* **wake**
wolf [wʊlf], *pl* **wolves** [wʊlvz] Wolf II
woman ['wʊmən], *pl* **women** ['wɪmɪn] Frau I
won [wʌn] *siehe* **win**
wonder ['wʌndə] sich fragen, gern wissen wollen II

won't [wəʊnt]: **you won't be cold (= you will not be cold)** du wirst nicht frieren; ihr werdet nicht frieren II
wood [wʊd] Holz V
woodpecker ['wʊdpekə] Specht II
word [wɜːd] Wort I • **Can I have a word with you?** Kann ich mal kurz mit dir reden? VI 3 (55) • **word building** Wortbildung II
°**word order** Wortstellung
wore [wɔː] *siehe* **wear**
work [wɜːk]
1. arbeiten I
2. funktionieren V
work hard hart arbeiten II
work on sth. an etwas arbeiten I
work sth. out etwas herausarbeiten, herausfinden IV
work [wɜːk] Arbeit I • **at work** bei der Arbeit/am Arbeitsplatz I
work experience Praktikum; Arbeits-, Praxiserfahrungen V • **do work experience** ein Praktikum machen V
worker ['wɜːkə] Arbeiter/in II
office worker ['ɒfɪs wɜːkə] Büroangestellte(r) V
worksheet ['wɜːkʃiːt] Arbeitsblatt I
workshop ['wɜːkʃɒp] Workshop, Lehrgang III
world [wɜːld] Welt I • **all over the world** auf der ganzen Welt III • **from all over the UK/the world/England** aus dem gesamten Vereinigten Königreich / aus der ganzen Welt / aus ganz England II • **in the world** auf der Welt VI 2 (30)
worn [wɔːn] *siehe* **wear**
worried ['wʌrid] besorgt, beunruhigt (wegen, um) IV
worry ['wʌri] Sorge, Kummer II
No worries. *(infml)* Kein Problem!/ Ist schon in Ordnung! VI 3 (55)
worry (about) ['wʌri] sich Sorgen machen (wegen, um) I • **Don't worry.** Mach dir keine Sorgen. I
worse [wɜːs] schlechter, schlimmer II
worst [wɜːst]: **(the) worst** am schlechtesten, schlimmsten; der/die/das schlechteste, schlimmste ... II
would [wəd, wʊd]: **I/you/... would ...** ich würde/du würdest ... III • **I'd like ... (= I would like ...)** Ich hätte/möchte gern ... I • **Would you like ...?** Möchtest du ...? /Möchten Sie ...? I • **Would you like some?** Möchtest du etwas/ein paar? / Möchten Sie etwas/ein paar? I
I'd like to talk about ... (= I would like to talk about ...) Ich möchte über ... reden / Ich würde gern über ... reden I
write [raɪt], **wrote, written** schreiben I • **write down** aufschreiben I • **write to** schreiben an I
writer ['raɪtə] Schreiber/in; Schriftsteller/in II
written ['rɪtn] *siehe* **write**
written discussion [ˌrɪtn dɪ'skʌʃn] Erörterung VI 2 (37)
wrong [rɒŋ] falsch, verkehrt I
be wrong 1. falsch sein I; 2. sich irren, Unrecht haben II • **the wrong way** in die falsche Richtung II
wrote [rəʊt] *siehe* **write**

X

°**xenophobic** [ˌzenə'fəʊbɪk] fremdenfeindlich

Y

yard [jɑːd] Hof II • **in the yard** auf dem Hof II
yawn [jɔːn] gähnen II
year [jɪə]
1. Jahr I
2. Jahrgangsstufe I
a sixteen-year-old ein/e Sechzehnjährige/r III • **a sixteen-year-old girl** ein sechzehnjähriges Mädchen III
yellow ['jeləʊ] gelb I
yes [jes] ja I
yesterday ['jestədeɪ, 'jestədi] gestern I • **yesterday morning/afternoon/evening** gestern Morgen/Nachmittag/Abend I • **yesterday's homework** die Hausaufgaben von gestern II
yet [jet]: **not (...) yet** noch nicht II
yet? schon? II
yoga ['jəʊgə] Yoga I
you [juː]
1. du; Sie I
2. ihr I • **you two** ihr zwei I
3. dir; dich; euch I
young [jʌŋ] jung I
your [jɔː]
1. dein/e I
2. Ihr I
3. euer/eure I
yours [jɔːz]
1. deiner, deine, deins II
2. Ihrer, Ihre, Ihrs II
3. eurer, eure, eures II
yourself [jɔː'self] dir/dich (selbst) III
yourselves [jɔː'selvz] euch (selbst) III
youth [juːθ] Jugend, Jugend- III
youth club Jugendclub III • **youth group** Jugendgruppe IV • **youth hostel** Jugendherberge III
yuck [jʌk] igitt III

Z

zebra ['zebrə] Zebra II
zone [zəʊn] Zone, Gebiet IV
zoo [zuː] Zoo IV

First names
(Vornamen)

Abraham ['eɪbrəhæm]
Adisa [ə'di:sə]
Adrian ['eɪdriən]
Afra ['æfrə]
Ali ['æli]
Ally ['æli]
Andrew ['ændru:]
Arnie ['ɑ:ni]
Arnold ['ɑ:nəld]
Ashton ['æʃtən]
Barack [bə'rɑ:k]
Barry ['bæri]
Baz, Bazza [bæz], ['bæzə]
Becky ['beki]
Belinda [bə'lɪndə]
Bella ['belə]
Bex [beks]
Cameron ['kæmrən]
Celia ['si:liə]
Chris [krɪs]
Dani ['dæni]
Daniel ['dænjəl]
David ['deɪvɪd]
Davina [də'vi:nə]
Dayamayee [ˌdaɪəmaɪ'i:]
Denny ['deni]
Dev [dev]
Diana [daɪ'ænə]
Dustin ['dʌstɪn]
Earl [ɜ:l]
Edward ['edwəd]
Ella ['elə]
Elly ['eli]
Fay [feɪ]
Felice [fə'li:s]
Freida ['fri:də]
Gary ['gæri]
Hanif ['hænɪf]
Harita [hə'ri:tə]
Helen ['helən]
Holly ['hɒli]
Jack [dʒæk]
Jake [dʒeɪk]
Jamal [dʒə'mɑ:l]
James [dʒeɪmz]
Jane [dʒeɪn]
Janet ['dʒænɪt]
Jérôme [dʒə'rəʊm]
Jess [dʒes]
Jill [dʒɪl]
Joe [dʒəʊ]
John [dʒɒn]
Josh [dʒɒʃ]
Joy [dʒɔɪ]
Julian ['dʒu:liən]
Julie ['dʒu:li]
Juno ['dʒu:nəʊ]
Kate [keɪt]
Katy ['keɪti]
Kristen ['krɪstən]
Latika ['lætɪkə]
Laura ['lɔ:rə]
Laurie ['lɒri]
Layla ['leɪlə]
Leo ['li:əʊ]
Lucy ['lu:si]
Maria [mə'ri:ə]
Mark [mɑ:k]
Martin ['mɑ:tɪn]
Mel [mel]
Melinda [mə'lɪndə]
Mia ['mi:ə]
Michael ['maɪkəl]
Mike [maɪk]
Minty ['mɪnti]
Morpheus ['mɔ:fiəs]
Murat [mu:'rɑ:t]
Nadia ['nɑ:diə]
Nat [næt]
Neil [ni:l]
Neo ['ni:əʊ]
Nikki ['nɪki]
Oliver ['ɒlɪvə]
Parminder [pɑ:'mɪndə]
Patricia [pə'trɪʃə]
Paul [pɔ:l]
Paulie ['pɔ:li]
Penelope [pə'neləpi]
Petra ['petrə]
Philip ['fɪlɪp]
Rebecca [ri'bekə]
Reg [redʒ]
Robert ['rɒbət]
Roger ['rɒdʒə]
Rose [rəʊz]
Saci ['sæʃi]
Sarah ['seərə]
Sean [ʃɔ:n]
Seb [seb]
Sharon ['ʃærən]
Sherman ['ʃɜ:mən]
Stephenie ['stefəni]
Sue [su:]
Tasha ['tæʃə]
Tina ['ti:nə]
Toby ['təʊbi]
Vanessa [və'nesə]
Vikas ['vi:kəs]

Family names
(Familiennamen)

Alexie [ə'leksi]
Beckham ['bekəm]
Blanchett ['blɑ:ntʃɪt]
Bleaker ['bli:kə]
Boateng ['bwɑ:teŋ]
Boyle [bɔɪl]
Broun [braʊn]
Dee [di:]
Diaz ['di:æs]
Ford [fɔ:d]
Halse Anderson [ˌhæls‿'ændəsən]
Kennedy ['kenədi]
Kutcher ['kʊtʃə]
Lincoln ['lɪŋkən]
Lloyd [lɔɪd]
Martin ['mɑ:tɪn]
McBeath [mək'bi:θ]
McCormick [mə'kɔ:mɪk]
Meyer ['maɪə]
Minton ['mɪntən]
Mitchell ['mɪtʃəl]
Munslow ['mʌnsləʊ]
Nagra ['nɑ:grə]
Neck [nek]
Nutt [nʌt]
Obama [əʊ'bɑ:mə]
Parks [pɑ:ks]
Patel [pə'tel]
Pattinson ['pætɪnsən]
Petrakis [pə'trɑ:kɪs]
Pierson ['pɪəsn]
Pinto ['pɪntəʊ]
Presley ['presli], ['prezli]
Pym [pɪm]
Sandburg ['sændbɜ:g]
Shrimpton ['ʃrɪmptən]
Smith [smɪθ]
Stewart ['stju:ət]
Swarup ['swɑ:rəp]
Thompson ['tɒmpsən]
Wilde [waɪld]
Wood [wʊd]

Place names
(Ortsnamen)

Banff [bænf]
Bavaria [bə'veəriə] *Bayern*
Birmingham ['bɜ:mɪŋəm]
Brighton ['braɪtn]
Bristol ['brɪstl]
Broughton ['brɔ:tn]
Cambridge ['keɪmbrɪdʒ]
Cape Breton [ˌkeɪp 'bretɒn]
Cardiff ['kɑ:dɪf]
Cashel ['kæʃl]
Chicago [ʃɪ'kɑ:gəʊ]
Colorado [ˌkɒlə'rɑ:dəʊ]
Delhi ['deli]
Eastville Park [ˌi:stvɪl 'pɑ:k]
Edinburgh ['edɪnbərə]
Fort William [ˌfɔ:t 'wɪljəm]
Getafe [he'tɑ:feɪ]
Glasgow ['glɑ:zgəʊ]
Hallow Road [ˌhæləʊ 'rəʊd]
Hamilton ['hæmltən]
Hexham ['heksəm]
Hobart ['həʊbɑ:t]
Holborn ['həʊbən]
Hollywood ['hɒliwʊd]
Hove [həʊv]
Iveragh Peninsula [ˌaɪvrə pə'nɪnsjʊlə]
Las Vegas [læs 'veɪgəs]
Launceston ['lɒnsəstən]
Liverpool ['lɪvəpu:l]
London ['lʌndən]
Malaga ['mæləgə]
Manchester ['mæntʃɪstə]
Marineland [mə'ri:nlənd]
Marseille [mɑ:'seɪ]
Melbourne ['melbən]
Michigan ['mɪʃɪgən]
Mt. Cameron [ˌmaʊnt 'kæmrən]
Mumbai [ˌmʊm'baɪ]
Niagara Falls [naɪˌægərə 'fɔ:lz]
Norfolk ['nɔ:fək]
Norwich ['nɒrɪdʒ]
Nova Scotia [ˌnəʊvə 'skəʊʃə]
Ontario [ɒn'teəriəʊ]
Ottawa ['ɒtəwə]
Oxford ['ɒksfəd]
Park Grove [ˌpɑ:k 'grəʊv]
Peterborough ['pi:təbərə]
Rearden ['rɪədn]
Spokane [spəʊ'kæn]
St Pauls [sənt 'pɔ:lz]
Stranraer [stræn'rɑ:]
Sydney ['sɪdni]
Tianjin [tiˌæn'dʒɪn]
Toronto [tə'rɒntəʊ]
Toulouse [tu:'lu:z]
Washington ['wɒʃɪŋtən]
Wellington ['welɪŋtən]
Wellpinit ['welpɪnɪt]

Other names
(Andere Namen)

Air Force One [ˌeə fɔ:s 'wʌn]
Arsenal ['ɑ:snəl]
Aviator ['eɪvieɪtə]
Beluga [bə'lu:gə]
Boeing ['bəʊɪŋ]
Celtic Tiger [ˌkeltɪk 'taɪgə]
Galadriel [gə'lɑ:driəl]
the **Gallup Organization** ['gæləp‿ɔ:gənaɪˌzeɪʃn]
Matrix ['meɪtrɪks]
Meatrix ['mi:trɪks]
Moopheus ['mu:fiəs]
Titanic [taɪ'tænɪk]
Vatican ['vætɪkən]
Volpi Cup ['vɒlpi kʌp]

Country/Continent	Adjective	Person	People
Africa ['æfrɪkə] *Afrika*	African ['æfrɪkən]	an African	the Africans
America [ə'merɪkə] *Amerika*	American [ə'merɪkən]	an American	the Americans
Asia ['eɪʃə, 'eɪʒə] *Asien*	Asian ['eɪʃn, 'eɪʒn]	an Asian	the Asians
Australia [ɒ'streɪliə] *Australien*	Australian [ɒ'streɪliən]	an Australian	the Australians
Austria ['ɒstriə] *Österreich*	Austrian ['ɒstriən]	an Austrian	the Austrians
Belgium ['beldʒəm] *Belgien*	Belgian ['beldʒən]	a Belgian	the Belgians
Canada ['kænədə] *Kanada*	Canadian [kə'neɪdiən]	a Canadian	the Canadians
China ['tʃaɪnə] *China*	Chinese [ˌtʃaɪ'ni:z]	a Chinese	the Chinese
Croatia [krəʊ'eɪʃə] *Kroatien*	Croatian [krəʊ'eɪʃn]	a Croatian	the Croatians
the Czech Republic [ˌtʃek rɪ'pʌblɪk] *Tschechien, die Tschechische Republik*	Czech [tʃek]	a Czech	the Czechs
Denmark ['denmɑ:k] *Dänemark*	Danish ['deɪnɪʃ]	a Dane [deɪn]	the Danes
Egypt ['i:dʒɪpt] *Ägypten*	Egyptian [i'dʒɪpʃn]	an Egyptian	the Egyptians
England ['ɪŋglənd] *England*	English ['ɪŋglɪʃ]	an Englishman/-woman	the English
Europe ['jʊərəp] *Europa*	European [ˌjʊərə'pi:ən]	a European	the Europeans
Finland ['fɪnlənd] *Finnland*	Finnish ['fɪnɪʃ]	a Finn [fɪn]	the Finns
France [frɑ:ns] *Frankreich*	French [frentʃ]	a Frenchman/-woman	the French
Germany ['dʒɜ:məni] *Deutschland*	German ['dʒɜ:mən]	a German	the Germans
(Great) Britain ['brɪtn] *Großbritannien*	British ['brɪtɪʃ]	a Briton ['brɪtn]	the British
Greece [gri:s] *Griechenland*	Greek [gri:k]	a Greek	the Greeks
Holland ['hɒlənd] *Holland, die Niederlande*	Dutch [dʌtʃ]	a Dutchman/-woman	the Dutch
Hungary ['hʌŋgəri] *Ungarn*	Hungarian [hʌŋ'geəriən]	a Hungarian	the Hungarians
India ['ɪndiə] *Indien*	Indian ['ɪndiən]	an Indian	the Indians
Ireland ['aɪələnd] *Irland*	Irish ['aɪrɪʃ]	an Irishman/-woman	the Irish
Italy ['ɪtəli] *Italien*	Italian [ɪ'tæliən]	an Italian	the Italians
Japan [dʒə'pæn] *Japan*	Japanese [ˌdʒæpə'ni:z]	a Japanese	the Japanese
Malaysia [mə'leɪʒə, mə'leɪziə] *Malaysia*	Malaysian [mə'leɪʒn, mə'leɪziən]	a Malaysian	the Malaysians
the Netherlands ['neðələndz] *die Niederlande, Holland*	Dutch [dʌtʃ]	a Dutchman/-woman	the Dutch
New Zealand [ˌnju: 'zi:lənd] *Neuseeland*	New Zealand [ˌnju: 'zi:lənd]	a New Zealander	the New Zealanders
Nigeria [naɪ'dʒɪəriə] *Nigeria*	Nigerian [naɪ'dʒɪəriən]	a Nigerian	the Nigerians
Norway ['nɔ:weɪ] *Norwegen*	Norwegian [nɔ:'wi:dʒən]	a Norwegian	the Norwegians
Pakistan [ˌpækɪ'stæn, ˌpɑ:kɪ'stɑ:n] *Pakistan*	Pakistani [ˌpækɪ'stæni, ˌpɑ:kɪ'stɑ:ni]	a Pakistani	the Pakistanis
the Philippines ['fɪlɪpi:nz] *die Philippinen*	Philippine ['fɪlɪpi:n]	a Filipino [ˌfɪlɪ'pi:nəʊ]/ Filipina [ˌfɪlɪ'pi:nə]	the Filipinos/ Filipinas
Poland ['pəʊlənd] *Polen*	Polish ['pəʊlɪʃ]	a Pole [pəʊl]	the Poles
Portugal ['pɔ:tʃʊgl] *Portugal*	Portuguese [ˌpɔ:tʃu'gi:z]	a Portuguese	the Portuguese
Russia ['rʌʃə] *Russland*	Russian ['rʌʃn]	a Russian	the Russians
Scotland ['skɒtlənd] *Schottland*	Scottish ['skɒtɪʃ]	a Scotsman/-woman, a Scot [skɒt]	the Scots, the Scottish
Slovakia [sləʊ'vɑ:kiə, sləʊ'vækiə] *die Slowakei*	Slovak ['sləʊvæk]	a Slovak	the Slovaks
Slovenia [sləʊ'vi:niə] *Slowenien*	Slovenian [sləʊ'vi:niən], Slovene ['sləʊvi:n]	a Slovene, a Slovenian	the Slovenes, the Slovenians
Spain [speɪn] *Spanien*	Spanish ['spænɪʃ]	a Spaniard ['spænɪəd]	the Spaniards
Sweden ['swi:dn] *Schweden*	Swedish ['swi:dɪʃ]	a Swede [swi:d]	the Swedes
Switzerland ['swɪtsələnd] *die Schweiz*	Swiss [swɪs]	a Swiss	the Swiss
Tanzania [ˌtænzə'ni:ə] *Tansania*	Tanzanian [ˌtænzə'ni:ən]	a Tanzanian	the Tanzanians
Turkey ['tɜ:ki] *die Türkei*	Turkish ['tɜ:kɪʃ]	a Turk [tɜ:k]	the Turks
the United Kingdom (the UK) [juˌnaɪtɪd 'kɪŋdəm, ju:'keɪ] *das Vereinigte Königreich (Großbritannien und Nordirland)*	British ['brɪtɪʃ]	a Briton ['brɪtn]	the British
the United States of America (the USA) [juˌnaɪtɪd ˌsteɪts‿əv‿ə'merɪkə, ju:‿es‿'eɪ] *die Vereinigten Staaten von Amerika*	American [ə'merɪkən]	an American	the Americans
Wales [weɪlz] *Wales*	Welsh [welʃ]	a Welshman/-woman	the Welsh

Getting ready for a test 1 Revision ► pp. 20–23

1 A holiday by the sea is more exciting ► p. 20

1. I think that ... is more / less exciting than ...
2. In my opinion ... is / isn't / is not as comfortable as ...
3. ... is cooler than ...
4. ... are more / less crowded than ...
5. ... is more / less expensive than ...
6. ... is more / less interesting than ...
7. ... is / is not / isn't as exciting as ...

2 SPEAKING Making holiday plans ► p. 20

a)

1	B	4	C	7	G
2	E	5	F	8	I
3	D	6	H	9	A

b) (individual conversations)

3 SPEAKING Likes and dislikes ► p. 20

(model answers)

I like: I quite like swimming. I like Jazz better than Hip Hop. Dancing is pretty/quite good. I'm looking forward to our camping trip to Italy.

I love: I like Italian sunsets a lot/very much. I like karaoke the best/most. Cooking is great/fantastic. I can't wait to go to the cinema.

I hate: I can't stand watching TV. I like soccer the least. Techno music is terrible/awful.

I don't mind: Going for walks is OK/all right. I don't like skiing very much. I'm not very interested in soaps.

4 WORDS A teenage magazine ► p. 21

(model answers)

a) cinema & TV: cable, channel, episode, presenter, plot, cartoon, prime time, repeat (n.), suggest, scene, *soap opera, series, news*

sport: athletics, competition, exercise, pitch, train, *soccer, ballet, match, team, coach*

health: fruit, healthy food, vegetables, menu, whole-grain, *organic food, low-fat products*

music: concert, sound file, label, release, playlist, *CD, MP3 player, tune, instruments, melody, lyrics*

books: comic, novel, plot, release, cartoon, writer, suggest, *cover, pages*

computer: menu, link, cable, install, save, surf the internet, *download, screen, keyboard*

b)

1	exercise	4	install
2	energetic	5	episode
3	thriller	6	concert

5 WORDS Talking about religions ► p. 21

a)		b)	
1	English	1	Muslim
2	cathedral	2	Protestant
3	palace	3	synagogue
4	bell	4	bell
5	believe	5	believe

6 WORDS The world of soap opera ► p. 22

a)		b)	
1	father	1	divorced
2	uncle	2	love
3	granddaughter	3	relationship
4	wife	4	baby
5	lover	5	father
6	ex-husband	6	single

7 Are you fit and healthy? ► p. 22

a)
1. Do you live a healthy life?
2. Do you play any sport in your free time?
3. How often do you train every week?
4. Do you go to school by bike?
5. How many meals do you have every day?
6. What do you usually have for breakfast?
7. How often do you eat fruit and vegetables?
8. Do you get enough sleep every night?
9. What else do you do to stay fit and healthy?

b) (individual answers)

c) (individual answers)

d) (model answers)

If you can choose, do you use the stairs or the elevator?
Do you cycle or take the bus to go shopping?
How often do you and your friends do sport together?
What do you usually have for lunch/dinner?

8 Being a teenage mum is not easy ▸ p. 23

b) 1 False. Rebecca got pregnant because she sometimes forgot to take the pill.
2 False. When she told her parents that she was pregnant they were really upset.
3 False. Rebecca lives alone with her son because her boyfriend left them to live his own life.
4 True.
5 True.
6 False. Rebecca wants help from her parents because she wants to go back and finish school.
7 True.

9 SPEAKING Giving your opinion ▸ p. 23

a) (individual dialogues)

b) (individual answers)

Getting ready for a test 1 Practice test ▸ pp. 24–26

1 LISTENING What can we do this weekend? ▸ p. 24

a) B

b) Helen's ideas:
- go to the theatre
- play new computer game
- each stay at home and listen to music
- listen to music and watch TV together
- watch 'Strictly Come Dancing'
- watch 'The Thirty-Nine Steps'

2 SPEAKING Holidays plans ▸ p. 24

(model answer)

b) Partner A: ... a youth hostel near the sea. It costs 15 Euros a night, so it's pretty cheap. You can also do lots of different sports, for example swimming, surfing and beach volleyball.
Partner B: Well, that sounds great, but listen to my idea: I'd like to go camping with a group in the mountains. It's a bit more expensive; it will be 35 Euros a night. But there are lots of activities: you can go hiking, mountain biking or swimming in lakes.
Partner A: That's a great idea too – but I like the sea better than the mountains.
Partner B: Well, let me think ... What about this: we could spend the first half of our holidays near the sea and then we could travel to the mountains to spend the rest of the time there!
Partner A: Brilliant, that's it! Let's book right now!

3 LISTENING Living together ▸ p. 25

1 D 3 D 5 D
2 C 4 A 6 C

4 LISTENING Radio adverts ▸ p. 25

a) 1: true 2: false

b) 3: false 4: true

c) 5: true 6: true

5 SPEAKING Too young to be a mum? ▸ p. 26

(model answers)
I can see two teenage girls. The girl in the first picture is pregnant and she is on her own. She is looking quite serious. In the second picture there is a young girl with a baby on her knees. She is looking down at her child but she isn't smiling.
I don't think the girls in the photos are very happy. They aren't smiling and might be thinking about the problems they have as a teenage mum. Maybe they had to leave school or their boyfriends broke up with them. They are probably worrying about their future (getting a job, finding sb. to care for their children, ...).
It must have been a shock when their friends and families heard the news. Nobody expects teenagers to become pregnant; especially when they haven't finished school yet.

Teenagers usually don't have to worry about anyone except themselves, but teenage parents have to look after a baby too. They cannot go out and meet friends. Teenage mothers especially may not be able to go to school and get an education just as easily as their friends can because they first have to find someone who looks after their baby when they're at school. The baby's father should do just as much as the mother, for example look after the child and try to help with money for the baby's food, clothes, etc.
I think there is no "best" age to have a baby, but maybe one should have finished school first and at least one of the parents should have a job.

6 PRESENTATION My lifestyle ► p. 26
(individual answers)

Getting ready for a test 2 Revision ► pp. 38–41

1 WORDS Travel ► p. 38

a) air: airport, flight, plane, gate, (to) land, *wing*
railway: platform, train, the Tube, underground, *rail, station*
road: cab, (to) cycle, (to) drive, motorway, petrol station, traffic jam, truck, *wheel, taxi, bus, rush hour*
sea: ferry, boat, harbour, ship, *lifeguard*

b)
1 went
2 picked
3 travel
4 closed
5 drive
6 ask

2 London's underground ► p. 38
1 opened
2 was
3 travelled
4 has become
5 have been
6 has been

3 Transport in London ► p. 38
1 I always try to sit at the top so I can enjoy the view.
2 I was in a terrible traffic jam yesterday. I don't think that I'll go into London by car again.
3 I wanted to reduce my carbon footprint, so I sold my car a long time ago.
4 Will bus drivers give me information about travel times if I ask them?
5 When I got to the stop, the last bus had left early.
6 I always take the Tube on Saturdays when I go shopping.

4 WORDS After the accident ► p. 39
1 accident
2 operations
3 drunk
4 healthy
5 hurts
6 headache
7 weak
8 sick
9 ambulance
10 first aid

5 STUDY SKILLS Writing ► p. 39

a) 1f, 2d, 3a, 4b, 5c, 6f

b) What? one of the worst accidents
When? in the late afternoon rush hour
Where? St Pauls and Eastville Park
Why? he was driving at over 80 miles per hour
How? when broken glass flew into it

6 WORDS For a greener world ► p. 40

a)
1 sun
2 oil
3 pollute
4 green energy
5 trees

b) 1b, 2a, 3d, 4f, 5c, 6e

7 Our green holiday ► p. 40
So did you enjoy your holiday? Where did you stay? How did you find out about it? What was special about the hotel? And was it organic food? What did you do? How far was it from the hotel? Did you have nice weather?

8 Ben's blog ► p. 41
1 did not / didn't take the bus because it uses too much energy.
2 Asked for recycled paper but they did not / didn't have any.
3 The big red apples from Italy looked nice, but I did not / didn't choose them.

4 I did not / didn't buy organic ones, but they came from a local farm, so I think that was OK.
5 I wanted to go to the second-hand shops, but I did not / didn't know they are closed on Sundays.
6 I just did not / didn't see any that were made in this country.

9 WRITING An essay ► p. 41

B D A C

Getting ready for a test 2 Practice test ► pp. 42–44

1 LANGUAGE Congestion charge ► p. 42

1 became	5 traffic
2 work	6 department stores
3 pay	7 have had
4 has gone down	8 drive

2 WRITING A visit to the doctor's ► p. 42
(model answers)
1 I fell off my bike yesterday evening.
2 Yes, I do. My left arm hurts really badly.
3 Yes, I've got a terrible headache, and I've also got stomach ache.
4 Well, I felt very weak and sick. And I was shaking all the time because I felt really, really cold.
5 So, what do you think: Is my arm broken?
6 School tomorrow – are you sure? OK. Bye. And thank you.

3 WRITING A report ► p. 43
(model answers)
a) At about 7.40 am I was walking to school. I was on the pavement just before the corner of Herzogstraße and Königstraße and there was a cycle path on my left. There were some big trucks standing on the other side of the cycle path. A girl of about 15 cycled past and a moment later I heard a loud cry. A bus had turned right and run into the girl, who had fallen to the ground. The bus driver hadn't seen her. Somebody called an ambulance and the girl was taken to hospital. Luckily she wasn't badly hurt.

b) Last summer my parents decided to do something different for our holiday, so we went on a camping trip instead of our usual beach holiday in Spain. We drove to a beautiful place in the country, about 85 miles away. We parked our car in a big field close to a forest. Then we put up our tent and went to sleep. The next morning, we woke up very early, because we heard some strange noises. When we looked out of our tent, we saw lots of sheep that were running around in the field. They had come through a broken fence. We told the farmer and he caught the sheep and repaired the fence.

4 WRITING A shopping survey ► p. 43
(individual answers)

5 WRITING A letter to a newspaper ► p. 44
(model answer)
Dear Sir or Madam
I would like to comment on the article "Child slaves work for western fashion companies". I have to say that I was shocked when I read it. It makes me sad when I think about children who have to work under these conditions – instead of going to school or having free time! Here in the western world all that children have to do is go to school. I think working is really bad for children and that children in developing countries often don't get a good education. Children should not have to work anywhere in the world. To help them, we should boycott products from companies that use children for the production of their clothes.
Yours faithfully (student's name)

6 WRITING Opinions ▸ p. 44

(model answers)

a) City centres are often so full of traffic that it isn't nice or to walk around or go shopping in polluted air. Some people would like to ban cars from city centres so they could enjoy their cities more. I think this is a good idea because it would make city life easier and maybe less dangerous. There would be fewer accidents and less traffic jams and the air would be cleaner. But how would people get into the city centres to go shopping? I think that if we want to have fewer cars in the city centres, we will need a really good public transport system.

b) Food is important to most people. Some people think the most important thing about food is the price and that only cheap food is good food. But low prices sometimes mean that the food is of worse quality or that it has been imported from countries that are far away but where production costs are lower. Also, 'ready' meals and fast food are often cheap. But they are often unhealthy, too, because there's too much fat and sugar in them. In my opinion people should buy more fresh food and cook it at home because that is healthier than eating cheap 'ready' meals or fast food.

c) You often hear people say that they can't worry about what clothes workers in developing countries earn, because they don't have enough money themselves. I can understand what they mean because I usually try to go shopping in places that sell cheap clothes, too. It is good to save money so you can spend it on other things. I know that cheap clothes probably mean that the workers who produced them worked under very bad conditions. But what should I do? I don't have a lot of money myself.

Getting ready for a test 3 Revision ▸ pp. 56–58

1 WORDS Getting involved ▸ p. 56

1 decided	5 raise
2 speech	6 organize
3 opened	7 demonstration
4 have	8 vote

2 Are you going to work in the holidays? ▸ p. 56

b) (individual dialogues)

3 EVERYDAY ENGLISH What are we going to do tomorrow? ▸ p. 56

D Let's go to the park and play football.
C Oh yes. Let's do that. But which film are we going to watch?
A Good idea ... Do you know what time it starts?
B That's a bit early for me. Is 3.15 OK?

4 READING Which event? ▸ p. 57

a) Event 2 (RSPCA Volunteer Information Day) is suitable for Lily because she wants to get involved in helping animals. Looking after animals as a volunteer will be the right thing to do for her because she has very little money. Event 1 (RSPCA Christmas Event) is not suitable for Lily because the decorations aren't cheap and she can't spend too much money to help animals in trouble.

b) Ella should choose event 2 (Queen's Park project week) because there she can practise her garden skills and also get a few tips from the experts. Adam is interested in global warming so event 1 (Film and discussion) is the most suitable for him because the documentary deals with the possible consequences of climate change.

5 WORDS Paraphrasing ▸ p. 58

a) 1 B (driving licence), 2 C (chat-show host) 3 A (citizens advice bureau)

b) 1b *(goal)*, 2d *(cartoon character)*, 3c *(subtitles)*, 4a *(MP)*

6 READING What does it mean? ▸ p. 58

a) (model answer)
1: opposition, region
2: popularity, collection
3: sit

Getting ready for a test 3 Practice test ▸ pp. 59–62

1 READING Events ▸ p. 59

Jill C, Ben A, Megan B

2 MEDIATION An advertisement ▸ p. 60

(model answers)

- Hauptaufgabe: Aktivitäten für Jugendliche aus aller Welt organisieren
- Voraussetzungen: zwischen 17 und 20 Jahre alt; kann gut mit 11- bis 15-Jährigen umgehen; tatkräftig
- Wohnen: kostenloses Zimmer im internationalen Dorf des Camps
- Verdienst: 25 Pfund Taschengeld pro Woche

3 MEDIATION Helping a visitor to Germany ▸ p. 60

(model answer)

Hi Maggie, I've found an event at the youth club in Böllstraße that you might be interested in. You can watch a DVD about German politics, which explains the ideas/goals of the most important German parties. The film is illustrated by cartoons and funny drawings, and has English subtitles. It will start at 7.30 pm and it'll take about 45 minutes. Afterwards, there is going to be a discussion and then some live music by the band Poll Position.

4 READING Notices, short ads and signs ▸ p. 61

1 false; 2 true; 3 false; 4 false; 5 false; 6 true; 7 true; 8 false

5 READING A news report ▸ p. 62

1 a) false; b) false; c) true; d) not in the text
2 A
3 C
4 B
5 B

Unit 2 Part A

1 Inventions that changed the world ▸ Unit 2, Part A (p. 30)

One of these inventions is a joke! Can you guess which one it is? Here is the answer:

The last invention is a joke. (Did you notice that the date on the article was 1st April?) The Language Mediator hasn't been invented yet – so your language teacher's job is safe for now! But scientists in America are trying to develop one.

Unit 3 Lead-in

1 What's the right age? ▸ Unit 3, Part A (p. 48)

Ages for Germany:	
get married:	18
drive a car (on your own):	18
vote in an election:	18 (bei Kommunalwahlen in vielen Bundesländern: 16)
buy cigarettes	18
buy alcohol	16 (Bier, Wein) bzw. 18 (Schnaps, Liköre, Alkopops)
leave home	18

Unit 3 Lead-in

4 How much do you care?

▸ Unit 3, Lead-in (p. 47)

QUIZ

a) Calculate your score.

1:	A = 2	B = 3	C = 1
2:	A = 1	B = 3	C = 2
3:	A = 2	B = 1	C = 3
4:	A = 1	B = 2	C = 3
5:	A = 2	B = 3	C = 1
6:	A = 2	B = 1	C = 3
7:	A = 3	B = 2	C = 1

b) Read your result.

17–21 points

Wow! No one cares more than you, right? A fair world, human rights, peace – all these things are really important to you. If you think something is unfair, you speak out and you work hard to change things. We're impressed! You have your own opinions and you want everyone to agree with you. Hmm, just a minute! We're not saying you're bossy, but ... Our advice to you: It's great that you care so much, but remember that it's important to listen to other people too. If you want to change someone's opinion, you can't just shout: 'How stupid. You can't possibly believe that!' You might be more successful if you say in a calm way: 'That's an interesting argument. I see what you mean, but ...' Try it!

12–16 points

You care a lot and you try to do as much as you can to make the world a better place. Like most people, you know that you probably could do more. But sometimes you think: 'The problems in the world are just too big and I'm too small. I can't change the world.' Our advice to you: If you don't like something, it is important to speak out. You can make a difference!

7–11 points

You probably think you already know what your result says. You've heard it a million times: Young people are lazy ... they only think about themselves ... they're not interested ... they just don't care. Is it true? We don't think so. You're just a normal teenager! You care about lots of things: sport, fashion, friends, family, music, going out, having fun. Of course you want the world to be a better place, but you think no one listens to your generation. Our advice to you: Remember it's your world too. When things happen that you don't like, it's important to speak out and get involved.

Illustrationen

Silke Bachmann, Hamburg (S. 52; 53; 111 TF 4 (u. 118)); **Roland Beier**, Berlin (32; 36 oben re.; 54; 80; 82; 106; 124; 125; 127; 129; 130; 132; 133 oben; 134; 136; 138–172); **Carlos Borrell**, Berlin (Umschlaginnenseite 2); **Karin Mall**, Berlin (S. 72 (u. 131)); **Dylan Gibson**, Pitlochry (S. 15 unten (u. 104); 33 Mitte; 55 (u. 110)); **Alfred Schüssler**, Frankfurt/Main (48; 49; 51 unten; 74)

Bildquellen

action press, Hamburg (S. 114 unten re.: REX FEATURES LTD.); **Alamy**, Abingdon (Inhaltsverz. (u. 28) mobile charger (M): Chas Spradbery (RF), Inhaltsverz. Juno film still re.: PHOTOS 12, Inhaltsverz. (u. 46 Bild D): David Levenson; S. 7 oben lesbian couple: Image Source Pink (RF); S. 13 Bild A, B, D: Moviestore collection Ltd, Bild C: PHOTOS 12; S. 25 oben 2. v. li.: Wedding Day; S. 26 oben re.: Catchlight Visual Services, unten: Image Source; S. 30 Bild 5: shinypix; S. 41 unten: British Retail Photography; S. 43 oben re.: Peter Horree; S. 46 Bild F (u. 126 oben): Beyond Fotomedia GmbH; S. 51 Mitte: DBURKE, oben (u. 109): Blend Images; S. 58 li.: Alex Segre; S. 83: National Geographic Image Collection; S. 89 Bild G: Somos Images (RF); S. 99 unten re.: Boel Ferm); **Associated Press**, New York (S. 62: PA Wire); **www.carbonfootprint.com** (S. 29 unten (u. Hintergrund 28/29)); **CBC** (S. 50: stills from news report "The mosquito". Copyright © CBC Vancouver); **Cinetext**, Frankfurt/Main (Inhaltsverz. Juno poster: 20th Century Fox; S. 15 oben; S. 123 unten li., re.: Cinetext Bildarchive); **Corbis**, Düsseldorf (Inhaltsverz. (u. 6 Ed): moodboard (RF); S. 10 unten (u. 103): cultura (RF); S. 20 oben: Biscuit Eight LLC (RF); S. 79 oben: Monalyn Gracia (RF); S. 85: Matilda Hartman; S. 87 unten: Asia Images/Alex Mares-Manton; S. 88 unten: Image Source (RF); S. 91: Blend Images/Jose Luis Pelaez, Inc. (RF); S. 122 unten re.: Reuters/Darren Staples); **Corel Library** (S. 137); **Cornelsen Verlag**, Berlin (Inhaltsverz. film still from DVD Juno review; S. 114 unten li.); **Philip Devlin**, Berlin (S. 88 oben); **Financial Times**, London (S. 126 unten); **Fotex**, Hamburg (S. 8 unten: Susa); **Ellen Forney** (S. 16–18: From THE ABSOLUTELY TRUE DIARY OF A PART-TIME INDIAN by Sherman Alexie. Copyright © 2007 by Sherman Alexie. Illustrations copyright 2007 by Ellen Forney. By permission of LITTLE, BROWN & COMPANY); **Fotolia**, New York (S. 36 oben li.: Dustin Lyson; S. 99: Phototom); **Getty Images**, München (Inhaltsverz. (u. 6 Toby): A J James (RF), Inhaltsverz. (u. 6 Minty): Thinkstock (RF); S. 21: Zador; S. 75: Fuse (RF); S. 86 oben: Winston Davidian (RF); S. 94 unten: Pieter Folkens, S. 111 TF 5 li. (u. 123 oben): AFP, TF 1 (u. 112); S. 122 oben re.; S. 125 unten: Ghislain & Marie David de Lossy); **GRACE** (S. 111 TF 3 (u. 117 unten): Produced by Free Range Studios, www.freerangestudios.com, in conjunction with GRACE/Sustainable Table, www.sustainabletable.org. Copyright © 2003 GRACE. Reproduced and distributed with the permission of GRACE); **Hachette**, London (S. 34: from "The Carbon Diaries" by Saci Lloyd, first published in the UK by Hodder Children's, an imprint of Hachette Children's Books, 338 Euston Road, London NW1 3BH); **iStockphoto**, Calgary (Inhaltsverz. Cartoon factory (u. 29 oben li.: michael harvey, Inhaltsverz. (u. 7 Peanut): Don Bayley, Inhaltsverz. (u. 28) toothbrush (M): alejandro Soto, mobile (M): Amanda Rhode, airplane (M): Björn Kindler, fridge (M): pixel107, washing machine (M): Oman Mirzaie, controller (M): Michal Rozanski, MP3 (M): yuriyza, laptop (M): Rafal Zdeb, DVD player (M): Uyen Le, flats (M): Chris Schmidt, houses (M): Matthew Dixon, hair dryer (M): Don Nichols; S. 6 oben gay couple: Libby Chapman, oben Hintergrund blond girl: mammamaart, oben Hintergrund group of friends: mandygodbehear, oben girl with headphones: Skip ODonnell; S. 7 oben Hintergrund group: Don Bayley, oben Hintergrund re. friends: Chris Schmidt; S. 9 oben: asiseeit; S. 10 oben: Lukasz Kulicki; S. 20 unten: Linda Bucklin; S. 24 unten: mbbirdy; S. 25 oben li.: Adam James; S. 26 oben li.: Lone Elisa Plougmann; S. 28 unten: johanna goodyear; S. 29 Mitte: bill whitney, re.: Heather McGrath; S. 30 Bild 2: Niels Laan, Bild 3: Paula Connelly, Bild 6: subjug; S. 36 unten re.: ranplett; S. 40 oben: Robert Byron; S. 41 oben: Borut Trdina; S. 58 re.: David Spieth; S. 59 oben li.: Wilson Valentin, oben re.: Ana Abejon, Mitte li.: ericsphotography, unten li.: Rhienna Cutler, unten re.: Lynn Seeden; S. 61 unten: DHuss; S. 99 oben re.: Dan Moore; S. 115: Shelly Perry; S. 116 unten li.: poco_bw, unten 2. v. re.: 4FR); **ITN Source** (S. 31: still from "Bang goes the theory – The Human Power Station". Courtesy of ITN Source); **Brent Martin**, Cambridge, NZ (S. 33 oben); **Photofusion**, London (Inhaltsverz. (u. 46 Bild B): Janine Wiedel; S. 46 Bild A: Joanne OBrien); **Photolibrary**, London (Inhaltsverz. b/w girls (u. 46 Bild C): INC SUPERSTOCK, Inhaltsverz. (u. 6 Bex): Design Pics Inc (RF); S. 87 oben: age fotostock/Saxpixcom Saxpixcom); **Picture-Alliance**, Frankfurt/Main (S. 11: chromorange; S. 33 unten map (M): dieKLEINERT.de;

S. 90: dpa; S. 111 TF 5 re.: dpa; S. 114 oben: dpa; S. 122 oben li.: abaca, unten li.: dpa); **Picture-Desk**, London (S. 12 unten: THE KOBAL COLLECTION/FILM COUNCIL/BEND IT FILMS, oben: THE KOBAL COLLECTION/MAVERICK FILMS; S. 98: THE KOBAL COLLECTION/CELADOR FILMS/PATHE INTERNATIONAL/FILM 4; S. 117 oben: THE KOBAL COLLECTION/WARNER BROS; S. 123 Mitte 2. v. li.: THE KOBAL COLLECTION/Columbia Tri Star; © 2007 **Bill Porter** (S. 79 Mitte); **Rex Features**, London (S. 123 unten: SNAP); **Marion Schönenberger**, Berlin (S. 64–73 li.); **Shutterstock**, New York (Inhaltsverz. (u. 8 oben) Jake (M): Yuri Arcurs, Inhaltsverz. oben Hintergrund (u. 8 oben Hintergrund): Binkski, Inhaltsverz. oben li. monster (u. 8/9 oben u. Hintergrund): Elise Gravel, Inhaltverz. (u. 28) underground (M): Michal Rosak, car (M): efiplus, jumping woman (M): Sergey Rusakov, dancing boy (M): AYAKOVLEV.COM, bus (M): James Steidl, dishwasher (M): akva, razor (M): Carla Donofrio; S. 6 oben Asian boy: Apollofoto; S. 7 oben re. boy and girl: Tracy Whiteside; S. 9 unten mobile phone (M): Jaroslaw Grudzinski; S. 22 oben: Deklofenak, unten: Denis Vrublevski; S. 23 oben: Tomasz Trojanowski, unten li.: Sergey Peterman, unten re.: ARENA Creative; S. 24 oben li.: blueking, oben re.: PSD photography; S. 25 oben re.: Elzbieta Sekowska, oben 2. v. re.: AZPworldwide, unten: Planner; S. 30 Bild 1: jeff Metzger, Bild 4: cybrain; S. 33 unten smartphones (M): Danylchenko Iaroslav, icons: Maisei Raman (1), Hudyma Natallia (4), jamaican (1), magicinfoto (6); S. 36 unten li.: Gualberto Becerra; S. 38 oben: Lance Bellers, unten: Chris Jenner; S. 39: Orientaly; S. 40 unten: Inc; S. 42 oben: Stephen Finn, unten: Monkey Business Images; S. 43 oben li.: Michael Rosa, unten li.: NatUlrich, unten guy (M): Andresr, unten girl (M): Gelpi; S. 44: paul prescott; S. 46 Bild E: Lisa F. Young; S. 46/47 (Hintergrund): Chen Ping Hung; S. 56 oben (M): stephenkirsh, unten: Rick Becker-Leckrone; S. 57: Galina Barskaya; S. 58 2. v. li., 3. v. li.: TrAj43; S. 61 oben: wavebreakmedia ltd; S. 64 2. v. oben re. Hintergrund (u. 71 unten): Nick Lamb; S. 73 oben re.: Maceofoto; S. 79 unten re.: Galyna Andrushko, unten li.: AVAVA; S. 86 unten: Marijus Seskauskas; S. 89 oben: Klaus-Peter Adler, Bild A: Alexander Raths, Bild B: Monkey Business Images, Bild C: Andresr, Bild D: Titov Andriy, Bild E: Andrey Arkusha, Bild F: empipe, Bild H: Yuri Arcurs, Bild I: Dmitriy Shironosov, Bild J: Vibrant Image Studio, Bild K: Patrizia Tilly, Bild L: Piotr Marcinski; S. 93: Algecireño; S. 94 oben re.: VanHart, Mitte 2. v. li.: Carlos E. Santa Maria, Mitte 2. v. re., Mitte re. (M): Anton Novik; S. 96: Alexey Stiop; S. 99 unten li. printer (M): Natalia Siverina, recycle sign (M): aispl; S. 101 li.: Kuzma, re.: Fedorov Oleksiy; S. 102: Elise Gravel; S. 111 TF 2 (u. 116 oben): RS; S. 112 Hintergrund: Mitar Vidakovic; S. 116 unten 2. v. li.: vgstudio, unten re.: Alen; S. 133 unten: Holger Mette); **Andy Singer**, Saint Paul, MN (Inhaltsverz. Cartoon (u. 36)); **Thomas Thesen**, Seoul (S. 136 unten); **ullstein bild**, Berlin (S. 114 Mitte re.: Rauhe)

Titelbild

Corbis, Düsseldorf (cyclist (M): Patrik Giardino); **Getty Images**, München (high-rise building (M): Bryan Mullennix)

Liedquellen

S. 112: *BYE BYE LOVE.* Text: Bordleaux Bryant, Felice Bryant © Acuff Rose Music. Alle Rechte für Deutschland, Österreich, Schweiz bei Sony/ATV Music Publishing (Germany) GmbH, *LOVE IS ALL AROUND* Musik & Text: Reg Presley © Dick James Music Ltd./Universal Music Publishing GmbH.

Textquellen

S. 16–18: *The Absolutely True Diary of a Part-time Indian.* Extracts from THE ABSOLUTELY TRUE DIARY OF A PART-TIME INDIAN by Sherman Alexie. Copyright © 2007 by Sherman Alexie. Illustrations copyright by Ellen Forney. By permission of LITTLE, BROWN & COMPANY; **S. 34–35:** *The Carbon Diaries 2015* adapted and abridged from "The Carbon Diaries" by Saci Lloyd, first published in the UK by Hodder Children's, an imprint of Hachette Children's Books, 338 Euston Road, London NW1 3BH; **S. 52–53:** *A class debate.* Adapted from SPEAK by Laurie Halse Anderson. Copyright © 1999 by Laurie Halse Anderson. Reprinted by permission of Farrar, Straus and Giroux, LLC.; **S. 118–120:** *If only Papa hadn't danced.* Copyright © 2009 by Patricia McCormick. Veröffentlichung mit Genehmigung Nr. 68568 der Paul & Peter Fritz AG in Zürich; **S. 128:** Auszug v. S. 516 aus „English G 2000 Wörterbuch – Das Wörterbuch zum Lehrwerk". Herausgegeben von der Langenscheidt-Redaktion Wörterbücher und der Cornelsen-Redaktion Englisch. © 2007 Cornelsen Verlag GmbH & Co. OHG, Berlin und Langenscheidt KG, Berlin und München.

Infinitive	Simple past form	Past participle	
(to) **be**	**was/were**	**been**	sein
(to) **beat**	**beat**	**beaten**	schlagen; besiegen
(to) **become**	**became**	**become**	werden
(to) **begin**	**began**	**begun**	beginnen, anfangen (mit)
(to) **bet**	**bet**	**bet**	wetten
(to) **bite** [aɪ]	**bit** [ɪ]	**bitten** [ɪ]	beißen
(to) **bleed** [iː]	**bled** [e]	**bled** [e]	bluten
(to) **break**	**broke**	**broken**	(zer)brechen; kaputt gehen
(to) **bring**	**brought**	**brought**	(mit-, her)bringen
(to) **build**	**built**	**built**	bauen
(to) **buy**	**bought**	**bought**	kaufen
(to) **catch**	**caught**	**caught**	fangen; erwischen
(to) **choose** [uː]	**chose** [əʊ]	**chosen** [əʊ]	(aus)wählen; (sich) aussuchen
(to) **come**	**came**	**come**	kommen
(to) **cost**	**cost**	**cost**	kosten
(to) **cut**	**cut**	**cut**	schneiden
(to) **do**	**did**	**done** [ʌ]	tun, machen
(to) **draw**	**drew**	**drawn**	zeichnen
(to) **drink**	**drank**	**drunk**	trinken
(to) **drive** [aɪ]	**drove**	**driven** [ɪ]	*(ein Auto)* fahren
(to) **eat**	**ate** [et, eɪt]	**eaten**	essen
(to) **fall**	**fell**	**fallen**	(hin)fallen, stürzen
(to) **feed**	**fed**	**fed**	füttern
(to) **feel**	**felt**	**felt**	(sich) fühlen; sich anfühlen
(to) **fight**	**fought**	**fought**	kämpfen
(to) **find**	**found**	**found**	finden
(to) **fly**	**flew**	**flown**	fliegen
(to) **forget**	**forgot**	**forgotten**	vergessen
(to) **forgive**	**forgave**	**forgiven**	vergeben, verzeihen
(to) **get**	**got**	**got**	bekommen; holen; werden; (hin)kommen
(to) **give**	**gave**	**given**	geben
(to) **go**	**went**	**gone** [ɒ]	gehen, fahren
(to) **grow**	**grew**	**grown**	wachsen; anbauen, anpflanzen
(to) **hang**	**hung**	**hung**	hängen
(to) **have (have got)**	**had**	**had**	haben, besitzen
(to) **hear** [ɪə]	**heard** [ɜː]	**heard** [ɜː]	hören
(to) **hide** [aɪ]	**hid** [ɪ]	**hidden** [ɪ]	(sich) verstecken
(to) **hit**	**hit**	**hit**	schlagen
(to) **hold**	**held**	**held**	halten
(to) **hurt**	**hurt**	**hurt**	wehtun; verletzen
(to) **keep**	**kept**	**kept**	(be)halten
(to) **know** [nəʊ]	**knew** [njuː]	**known** [nəʊn]	wissen; kennen
(to) **lay** the table	**laid**	**laid**	den Tisch decken

Infinitive	Simple past form	Past participle	
(to) **leave**	**left**	**left**	(weg)gehen; abfahren; verlassen; zurücklassen
(to) **lend**	**lent**	**lent**	verleihen
(to) **let**	**let**	**let**	lassen
(to) **lose** [uː]	**lost** [ɒ]	**lost** [ɒ]	verlieren
(to) **make**	**made**	**made**	machen; bauen; bilden
(to) **mean** [iː]	**meant** [e]	**meant** [e]	bedeuten; meinen
(to) **meet**	**met**	**met**	(sich) treffen
(to) **pay**	**paid**	**paid**	bezahlen
(to) **put**	**put**	**put**	legen, stellen, *(wohin)* tun
(to) **read** [iː]	**read** [e]	**read** [e]	lesen
(to) **ride** [aɪ]	**rode**	**ridden** [ɪ]	reiten; *(Rad)* fahren
(to) **ring**	**rang**	**rung**	klingeln, läuten
(to) **run**	**ran**	**run**	rennen, laufen
(to) **say** [eɪ]	**said** [e]	**said** [e]	sagen
(to) **see**	**saw**	**seen**	sehen; besuchen, aufsuchen
(to) **sell**	**sold**	**sold**	verkaufen
(to) **send**	**sent**	**sent**	schicken, senden
(to) **set** the alarm clock	**set**	**set**	den Wecker stellen
(to) **shake**	**shook**	**shaken**	schütteln; zittern
(to) **shine**	**shone** [ɒ]	**shone** [ɒ]	scheinen *(Sonne)*
(to) **shoot** [uː]	**shot** [ɒ]	**shot** [ɒ]	schießen, erschießen
(to) **show**	**showed**	**shown**	zeigen
(to) **shut up**	**shut**	**shut**	den Mund halten
(to) **sing**	**sang**	**sung**	singen
(to) **sit**	**sat**	**sat**	sitzen; sich setzen
(to) **sleep**	**slept**	**slept**	schlafen
(to) **speak**	**spoke**	**spoken**	sprechen
(to) **spend**	**spent**	**spent**	*(Zeit)* verbringen; *(Geld)* ausgeben
(to) **stand**	**stood**	**stood**	stehen; sich (hin)stellen
(to) **steal**	**stole**	**stolen**	stehlen
(to) **swim**	**swam**	**swum**	schwimmen
(to) **take**	**took**	**taken**	nehmen; (weg-, hin)bringen; dauern, *(Zeit)* brauchen
(to) **teach**	**taught**	**taught**	unterrichten, lehren
(to) **tell**	**told**	**told**	erzählen, berichten
(to) **think**	**thought**	**thought**	denken, glauben, meinen
(to) **throw**	**threw**	**thrown**	werfen
(to) **understand**	**understood**	**understood**	verstehen
(to) **upset**	**upset**	**upset**	ärgern, kränken, aus der Fassung bringen
(to) **wake** up	**woke**	**woken**	aufwachen; wecken
(to) **wear** [eə]	**wore** [ɔː]	**worn** [ɔː]	tragen *(Kleidung)*
(to) **win**	**won** [ʌ]	**won** [ʌ]	gewinnen
(to) **write**	**wrote**	**written**	schreiben